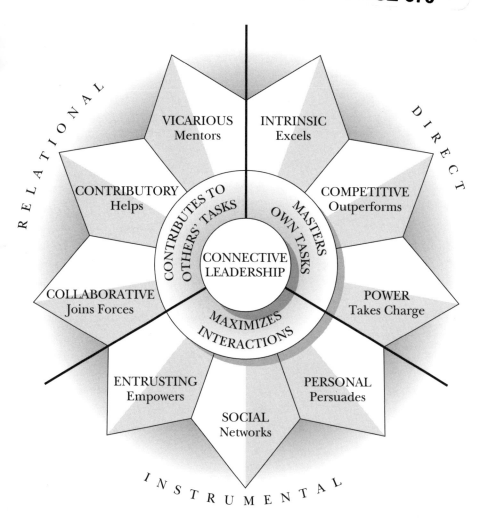

The
CONNECTIVE
EDGE

The CONNECTIVE EDGE

Leading in an Interdependent World

Jean Lipman-Blumen

Jossey-Bass Publishers • San Francisco

Substantial discounts on bulk quantities of Jossey-Bass books are available to corporations, professional associations, and other organizations. For details and discount information, contact the special sales department at Jossey-Bass Inc., Publishers (415) 433–1740; Fax (800) 605–2665.

For sales outside the United States, please contact your local Simon & Schuster International Office.

 Manufactured in the United States of America on Lyons Falls Pathfinder Tradebook. This paper is acid-free and 100 percent totally chlorine-free.

Library of Congress Cataloging-in-Publication Data

Lipman-Blumen, Jean.
    The connective edge : leading in an interdependent world / Jean
Lipman-Blumen. — 1st ed.
      p.   cm.—(The Jossey-Bass business & management series)
    Includes bibliographical references and index.
    ISBN 0-7879-0243-8
    1. Leadership.   2. Interpersonal communication.
3. Interorganizational relations.   I. Title. II. Series: Jossey-
Bass business and management series.
HD57.7.L57   1996
303.3′4—dc20   96–12800

Credits are on pp. 402–403.

FIRST EDITION
HB Printing 10 9 8 7 6 5 4 3 2 1

The Jossey-Bass
Business & Management Series

Consulting Editors
Organizations and Management

WARREN BENNIS
University of Southern California

RICHARD O. MASON
Southern Methodist University

IAN I. MITROFF
University of Southern California

To Harold Leavitt

Contents

Part Three: Bridging to the Stage 3 World

Preface

Another Book About Leadership? Yes, but this one is quite different. Most leadership books have gone off in three directions:

- The old, power-driven, General Patton direction
- The manipulative, Machiavellian direction
- More recently, the collaborative, empowering, good-guy direction

Yet even current arguments for sharing power and collaborating with competitors miss a critical point about the contemporary world:

> Around the globe, two antithetical forces—interdependence and diversity—are generating tensions that will fundamentally change the conditions under which leaders must lead. To succeed in this dramatically altered environment, where inclusion is critical and connection is inevitable—that is, in the *Connective Era*—we need a new kind of leadership.

As the tensions between interdependence and diversity escalate, the individualistic, competitive, charismatic leadership strategies, whelped on the American frontier, will no longer work. The ego-driven, manipulative, Machiavellian leadership style (never particularly appealing to Americans) won't suffice either. Even the more recently celebrated collaborative management, by itself, can't do the trick. We have little choice but to develop new models of leadership, leadership more appropriate for coping with these contradictory forces.

The Connective Edge describes a different approach to leadership: one that is more politically savvy and instrumental, yet more ethical, authentic, accountable, and, particularly, more ennobling. This new approach, which I call *connective leadership,* can potentially transform the destructive tensions of diversity and interdependence into constructive leadership action. This book looks at numerous individuals, in many economic and political sectors and from several nations, who exemplify an emerging alternative to Patton, Machiavelli, and the good-guy team leaders.

Even as the Connective Era begins, many traditional leaders persist in their old ways. Here and there, however, new leaders are appearing. Many of us, though, don't know quite what to make of these newcomers, and because we don't, these leaders are often forced to retreat into more familiar, but increasingly archaic, strategies.

This book is intended to hearten those leaders and constituents ready to embark on a journey into this new era. Depending on how we lead, these escalating forces of diversity and interdependence will either tear us apart or offer us the possibility of greater and greater wholeness.

The Book's Audience

This book is written largely for a business audience, but it speaks to leaders in the political and volunteer arenas, as well. It proposes new strategies sorely needed in business and political institutions, large and small, public and private, for-profit and not-for-profit. The book is for leaders who are interested in understanding what leadership is *always* all about, well beyond management for short-term profit. It is also for leaders who care about being better leaders *now*, in today's rapidly changing world.

Since none of us escapes the direct impact of organizations, the book is also intended for everyone who must interact day in and day out with the leadership in complex organizations—and who must face the consequences of those interactions. It is meant for everyone who wishes there were better ways to make things happen in organizations, better ways to make his or her own work and life more meaningful.

Constituents, too, face important choices in the Connective Era. They must choose between traditional, passive followership and active responsibility. This book is written for those who yearn to do something more than simply follow, who are willing to take risks to transcend the ordinariness of their organizational lives.

Overview of the Contents

The Connective Edge has three major sections:

- Part One, which looks at the origins and evolution of the human need for leadership,
- Part Two, which presents the Connective Leadership Model in detail, and
- Part Three, which explores the empirical organizational results and the philosophical implications of the Connective Leadership Model.

Within Part One, Chapter One examines the forces that are changing the conditions for leadership. It introduces the Connective Leadership Model and key ideas for rethinking leadership. Chapter Two probes the psychological and existential factors that drive our human yearning for powerful leaders. Chapter Three shifts the focus to an historical view of the American scene. It describes how the troika of individualism, cooperation, and authoritarianism has prevented connective leadership from emerging before now in the corporate environment. Chapter Four explores six worldwide forces catapulting us into the Connective Era. It presents examples of several early connective leaders and considers how both leaders and followers need to change.

As the opening chapter of Part Two, Chapter Five develops the concept of connective leadership and describes the repertoire of nine leadership strategies. Chapters Six through Eight examine the nine styles in three related sets: direct, relational, and instrumental, respectively. Chapter Nine offers a more complete picture of connective leaders acting in this new world.

Chapter Ten, the opening chapter in Part Three, analyzes survey data on more than five thousand executives and managers at middle and senior levels in corporate America. It interprets how leadership styles work or don't work for organizational leaders, entrepreneurs, and intrapreneurs. Chapter Eleven examines the issue of female leadership in the Connective Era, questions whether women in corporate and political roles lead differently than their male counterparts, and reviews leadership styles of some female leaders. Chapter Twelve demonstrates how connective leadership empowers us personally to wrestle with the core of human existence: life, death, and the search for meaning.

The Research Behind This Book

Three kinds of research inform this book. The first is qualitative research, consisting mostly of interviews with leaders from many different arenas. In this book, the reader will meet leaders from the for-profit, the not-for-profit, and the political worlds. In a few cases, to maintain confidentiality, I have used pseudonyms. In other cases, inasmuch as some of our most visible leaders work in the public arena, the glare of media attention makes well-known leaders easily accessible examples. Not all the leaders who appear in these pages are well known, nor are they necessarily perfect. Few are full-blown connective leaders; yet each exemplifies certain aspects of connective leadership.

The second type of research uses historical, biographical, and autobiographical sources. These materials have been mined to allow us to understand important historical figures, like Mohandas Gandhi and Martin Luther King, Jr., as well as more contemporary leaders like Irish president Mary Robinson.

The third type of research is much more quantitative, based on two survey instruments, the individual *L-BL Achieving Styles Inventory* (ASI) and the *L-BL Organizational Achieving Styles Inventory* (OASI). Between 1973 and 1982, my colleague, Harold J. Leavitt, of the Stanford Graduate School of Business, and I developed the Achieving Styles Model, comprising nine styles that individuals characteristically use to accomplish their goals and that organizations reward. Taken together, the nine achieving styles represent the repertoire of the connective leader. For simplicity's sake, in this book I refer to the model as the Connective Leadership Model.

During that time, we also developed the two instruments previously mentioned: the ASI, for measuring an individual's achieving styles; and the OASI, for measuring the behavioral styles that organizations reward.[1] Later, my students and I developed the *Achieving Styles Situational Assessment Inventory* (ASSAI) for assessing the achieving styles required by each unique situation.

Over the past two decades, we have collected ASI data from nearly thirty-nine thousand people, mostly managers and leaders.

To ensure that our findings are both timely and substantial, I use only the most recent ASI data in this book—more than five thousand cases collected and analyzed since 1984. During much of this same period, we have also collected organizational data, using the OASI. While we have gathered data from managers and leaders in fourteen other nations in Europe, Latin America, and Asia, the major focus of the book remains here in the United States. Where it seems relevant, however, I compare our American subjects with their counterparts abroad.

Since 1982, I have continued to elaborate the Connective Leadership Model, applying it first to individuals and later to organizations (Leavitt contributed significantly to the original Achieving Styles Model before moving on in the early 1980s to other research interests). Using both the ASI and the OASI, I have focused on the fit between the individual's profile and the ideal profile supported by the organization and reflected in its culture. I have been concerned with the relevance of that fit for individual performance and job satisfaction, as well as for organizational effectiveness. I have also been intrigued by the importance of matching individuals', often team members', achieving styles to the demands of any given situation. The ASSAI, used in conjunction with the ASI and the OASI, has been extremely useful for this purpose.

In the mid 1980s, working primarily with students at The Claremont Graduate School in the Peter F. Drucker Graduate Management Center and the organizational division of the psychology program, I became increasingly interested in the link between achieving styles and leadership. This interest grew as I observed the difficulties traditional leaders were encountering everywhere in the world. The leap from achieving styles to the concept of connective leadership came later as I noticed that leaders who used rather unorthodox behavior seemed to open new opportunities for their constituents. That unusual behavior combined very political or instrumental, but also ethical and often altruistic, action. It was also marked by a constant awareness of the connections among people, ideas, and processes. The link between connective leadership and achieving styles has been strengthened by results from ongoing research on achieving styles conducted not only by me and my students at Claremont but by students and colleagues from Finland to South Africa.

Despite its research foundations, this book is not intended as a research report. Although research provides its conceptual basis, the book also draws on a wide range of consulting experience with companies, nonprofit organizations, and governments. That combination has led me to write this book primarily for a nonacademic audience. Readers interested in finding out more about the methodology and other research findings supporting this book may write to me c/o The Business & Management Series at Jossey-Bass Publishers.

This book offers a different and intentionally positive perspective on leadership. It describes leadership behavior that is both provocative and savvy, yet pragmatic and honorable. In the Connective Era, traditional approaches to leadership cannot address the complexities created by increasing diversity and interdependence. I believe that connective leadership offers new possibilities for learning effectively in these turbulent times.

Pasadena, California JEAN LIPMAN-BLUMEN
February 1996

Acknowledgments

Like leadership, writing a book requires many contributions from individuals who fall below the casual observer's angle of vision. During the overly long journey that this book has become, I have had help, comfort, and chastisement (to get on with it) from my family as well as from many colleagues, students, and friends.

First, Hal Leavitt, my primary intellectual colleague, has listened patiently, critiqued honestly, and even edited mercilessly when necessary. From the very outset, my beloved colleague Jessie Bernard goaded me to do two things: write faster and emphasize the critical importance of women leaders. I am particularly indebted to Warren Bennis, who barely knew me at the time, for his generous encouragement after reading an earlier draft of the book. It was Sol Levine's probing questions about the connective leader's special capacity to handle serious societal issues that prompted me to address those questions in a way that I believe moves the discourse of the book to a different level in the final chapter. Maura Harrington, my major research assistant on the Achieving Styles Project, ran the achieving styles data with expertise and good humor. Another valued research assistant, Mike Henderson, tracked down many elusive references. Greig Stewart has been a dear friend, an intellectual gadfly, a clipping service *par excellence,* as well as a one-person rooting section for almost two decades. Connie Martinson, my friend since adolescence, was an endless source of support and wise logistical advice, including suggestions for titles. Denise Marcil offered great savvy and sympathy about the content and the publication of the book.

The editorial work that such an undertaking inevitably demands is daunting. Everyone at Jossey-Bass with whom I worked was endlessly enthusiastic and supportive. I was extremely fortunate to have as my initial editor at Jossey-Bass Bill Hicks, who had a great feel for the ideas in this book. It was into his very large shoes that Cedric Crocker ably stepped when Bill undertook a new assignment. John Bergez's suggestions about the structure of the manuscript were absolutely crucial. Thomas Finnegan was wonderfully helpful in the final stages of preparing the manuscript for publication. Lasell Whipple's intelligence, patience, and tact eased the difficult process of putting the book to bed. Terri Welch and Lisa Shannon guided the marketing plan and cover design.

Yolanda Soto and Donna El Hayek typed numerous versions of each chapter. Yolanda kept track of the hundreds of articles and books that I constantly needed and continually misplaced. Both Yolanda and Donna also meticulously checked the endnotes and references. In the final stages of the book, I was fortunate to have the estimable help of Dona Bailey, Sharon Sand, Susan Cole, and Ellen Reinstein. I am particularly grateful to all the other colleagues and students at The Claremont Graduate School and other institutions who have sensitized me both to theoretical issues and to specific materials that have become part of this book.

Most of all, I am indebted to the leaders who allowed me to interview them and glean new insights not only from their thoughtful responses but also from their leadership examples. On a very personal level, my husband and family have been enormously understanding and patient. So have my friends.

For all this incredible help, I am beholden beyond measure.

Jean Lipman-Blumen

The Author

Jean Lipman-Blumen is the Thornton F. Bradshaw Professor of Public Policy and professor of organizational behavior at the Peter F. Drucker Graduate Management Center in Claremont, California. She is also cofounder and codirector of the Drucker Center's Institute for Advanced Studies in Leadership. Her research interests include organizational and managerial behavior, leadership and power, crisis management, strategic planning, public policy, and gender roles. Her major public policy areas include the management of science, particularly agricultural research policy, as well as international development, education, and women's issues.

Prior to moving to California, Lipman-Blumen served as president of LBS International, Ltd., a Washington, D.C., policy analysis and management consulting firm. She served as a special consultant to the White House Domestic Policy Staff under President Jimmy Carter and has consulted to various departments and agencies of the U.S. government, such as the Executive Office of the President (the White House), the Department of State, and the National Institutes of Health. She has also consulted to numerous private sector organizations, such as the Ford Foundation and Bell Laboratories, as well as to many foreign governments, including Bulgaria, Egypt, Norway, Sweden, Thailand, and the USSR.

Lipman-Blumen has published numerous book chapters and contributed articles to journals such as *Scientific American, Harvard Business Review, Harvard Educational Review, Journal of Marriage and the Family, Liberal Education,* and *Stanford Magazine.* She is the author of *Gender Roles and Power* (1984) and *Sex Roles and Social Policy* (1978, with J. Bernard).

Lipman-Blumen received her A.B. degree in English literature and her A.M. degree in sociology from Wellesley College. She received her Ph.D. degree in sociology from the Harvard Graduate School of Arts and Sciences and did her postdoctoral work in mathematics, statistics, and computer science at Carnegie Mellon and Stanford Universities. She is listed in *Who's Who in the World, Who's Who in Social Science, Who's Who in Science and Engineering, Who's Who in American Men and Women in Science, The World's Who's Who of Women,* and *Women's Organizations and Leaders.*

The
CONNECTIVE
EDGE

Part One

The Changing Dynamics of Leadership

Chapter One

New World, New Leadership
A Fundamental Shift

> *Something is on the way out and something else is*
> *painfully being born. It is as if something were crumbling,*
> *decaying and exhausting itself, while something else, still*
> *indistinct, were arising from the rubble. . . . We are in a*
> *phase when one age is succeeding another, when*
> *everything is possible.*
> VÁCLAV HAVEL[1]

A new wind is blowing, a wind that is changing the leadership climate around the world. The time-worn foundations of authoritarian, competitive, and ruggedly individualistic leadership are eroding. Even the more current leadership architecture, desperately seeking to fuse competition and collaboration, seems destined to topple before the gusts of change.

Even before the dust settles, the outlines of a new era are emerging. It is a time marked by two contradictory forces, *interdependence* and *diversity,* pulling in opposite directions. The tensions from these twin forces are rapidly rendering traditional leadership behaviors obsolete.

In this new era, which I call the Connective Era, a more complex, but attainable, leadership repertoire offers challenge and promise. This repertoire of related behaviors I label *connective leadership*. It allows leaders to draw upon a broader spectrum of behaviors than they may be accustomed to, most importantly a set of political or "instrumental" styles that use the self and others as

3

instruments for accomplishing goals. Because connective leaders use these instrumental styles ethically and altruistically, they can integrate the otherwise centrifugal forces of diversity and interdependence.

The model of connective leadership put forward in this book is specific, detailed, and supported by empirical research as well as historical and biographical examples. In later chapters, we shall see how the model casts new light on familiar issues, giving us quite a different view of such topics as the role of leaders in organizations and women as leaders. Most consequentially, however, we shall see how the model is responsive both to the leadership crisis of our own times and to profound and enduring human needs.

To set the stage for what follows, this first chapter surveys how the changing landscape at the close of the twentieth century is outmoding the way we currently think about leadership. We then take a preliminary look at what connective leaders are like and why they will probably succeed in the new environment, while old-style authoritarian and even newer collaborative leaders are doomed to failure. We also present a brief overview of the nine-faceted behavioral model that underlies connective leadership. This model not only describes connective leadership, but it also provides a conceptual tool and a vocabulary that cast a different light on our traditional ideas about leaders.

A World Torn by Interdependence and Diversity[2]

All signs indicate that global *interdependence* is accelerating at a furious pace. Politically, economically, and environmentally, we are living in a world where leadership decisions anywhere now affect everything and everyone everywhere. Autonomous decisions have become a thing of the past. The newest technological revolution—wireless and digital—will exponentially complicate these connections across the globe. (A revealing illustration of this interconnectedness came with the 1995 edict by Germany that CompuServe make pornographic material unavailable to users of the online service within that nation. In complying, CompuServe discovered that its technology initially left the company no choice but to block access *worldwide*.)

At the same time, wildfires of *diversity* are breaking out everywhere. Wherever we look, globally and locally, we see assertions of distinctive identities and individualism:

In the new pluralism and simmering nationalism of emerging and fragmenting nations, from Quebec to the Czech Republic

In redrawn or disintegrating geopolitical alliances, from NATO to the Warsaw Pact

In the endless restructuring of established organizations and the appearance of new ones, with different shapes and life spans, from short-term alliances, to sprawling and amorphous networks, to partnerships and joint ventures

In increasing ethnic and racial pride among blacks, Latinos, Asians, and others

In heightened consciousness among women

In racially and gender-mixed workforces

In shifting demographics that redraw the age and economic profiles of developed and developing nations

In the proliferation of narrowly defined, often single-issue political constituencies

In the growing diversification within major religions, notably Christianity and Islam, where mainstream beliefs now sit cheek by jowl with radical fundamentalism

In the uniqueness of each individual's gifts and limitations

This escalating differentiation—whether of nations, organizations, or individuals—demands recognition of separate entities with distinctive and valued identities. The cumulative effect creates a thrust toward diversity on a previously unknown scale.

The clashing fronts of diversity and interdependence generate paradoxical effects. For one, the enormous changes wrought by interdependence make us seek the shelter of familiar, distinctive identities. As Václav Havel suggests, we "stand helpless" before the global challenges the world faces "because our civilization has essentially globalized only the surface of our lives."[3] Our changing world adds new existential questions for which science can offer no answers. In Havel's view, this drives people to "cling to the ancient certainties of their tribe," leading to increasingly dangerous cultural conflicts.[4] At the same time, diversity promotes new forms of individualism that sociologists suggest "leave [us] suspended in glorious, but terrifying, isolation."[5]

As a result, even as diversity evokes independence, separatism, tribalism, and individual identities, interdependence pulls in a different direction, promoting alliances, collaboration, mutuality, and universalism. In these radically altered circumstances, competitive and authoritarian leaders are destined to fail. To be sure, simply seasoning authoritarianism with collaboration (presumably based on more and better "teams") will not provide a sufficiently potent remedy for what ails leadership.

New Challenges for Leaders

Ambiguities and discontinuities shroud the present[6] and becloud the future, greatly complicating the leader's task. In an era bristling with unprecedented problems, solutions to earlier dilemmas are essentially irrelevant.[7] Like early morning fog, the changing demands upon leaders seep through every cranny of society: families, schools, churches, grassroots political movements, corporations, and governments.

The Connective Era is marked by constant jostling and movement in the connections among people, organizations, and ideas. In this intricately connected yet diversifying world, traffic is always heavy and getting heavier.

These multiple changes, amplified by rapid technological advances, have altered the ways in which leaders can and must make decisions. Some of the challenges are immediately apparent:

- Leaders are confronted with shorter and shorter time frames. Speed and agility are essential.[8]
- Leaders get few second chances. They have to get it right the first time.
- Leaders need new ways of diagnosing and solving labyrinthine problems.
- Leaders have to forge innovative solutions since disconnects with the past have obviated the old ones.
- Leaders need to envision and achieve goals stretching beyond the initial problem, in fact far beyond their organizational walls and national borders.
- Leaders have to think for the long term, despite pressures to succeed in the short term and uncertainties about the future.

In the Connective Era, the tensions between diversity and interdependence will create the backdrop for virtually all decision making. In a world where France's 1995 decision to test nuclear weapons in the South Pacific provoked a worldwide protest,

- Leaders find it ever more difficult to make those heroic, autonomous decisions[9] that many traditional followers have come to expect. Conflicts percolating among diverse groups, all wanting to pursue their own ends, place serious obstacles in the leader's path.
- Like it or not, commands are out; negotiations are in. Each leader must negotiate continually with a wide assortment of other leaders and unfamiliar groups.
- Leaders face unparalleled ethical dilemmas, generated by the mix of hitherto unimagined circumstances, relationships, and technological opportunities. From Wall Street to the White House, constituents have begun to demand new ethical standards.

In this new connected world, leaders whose repertoires are limited to the more traditional behaviors of dominating, competing, or collaborating will be left far behind. Connective leadership offers leaders an extensive set of strategies for moving flexibly and confidently. These strategies also distribute the leadership burdens and bring other leaders as well as followers into the process.

Getting to the Connective Era: Three Stages in the Evolution of Leadership

To put this new era into perspective, let's take a quick look backward. Over the course of human history, at least two previous shifts in the conditions of leadership have occurred. Right now, we are sensing the first tremors of a third.

Each of these three broad historical eras can be thought of as representing a distinctive stage in the conditions of leadership. There are no sharp cut-off points between these major historical periods; instead, one stage recedes while another emerges. The inevitable result is a mismatch between historical conditions and the leadership models carried over from an earlier era.

Stage 1: The Physical Era

The Physical Era began long before recorded history. In this era, *physical boundaries*—forests, mountains, and oceans—formed nearly impenetrable barriers, both protective and obstructive. Leaders needed independence and strength to defend the primitive sovereignty of a well-defined group of followers against occasional marauders and the ravages of nature. The Physical Era demanded intrepid leaders who could take their followers through imposing physical barriers to colonize every habitable spot on the planet.

Stage 2: The Geopolitical Era

In the Geopolitical Era, when geopolitical boundaries and ideologies still defined the important differences among us, they shaped long-term political *alliances,* like NATO and the Warsaw Pact, for defending their members against enduring enemies. Clearly marked borders and ideologies allowed organizations and institutions that jealously guarded their sovereignty to live in relative isolation. Although geopolitical leaders needed to cooperate with their allies, pragmatically, the member with the greatest economic and military power usually dominated the alliance. In this competitive environment, authoritarian leaders, even those with great charm, counted on having or creating fearful, passive, and obedient followers.

Long-lived, these geopolitical alliances moved from one problem to the next, sometimes with a knee-jerk response, at other times reluctantly, but mostly in unison. Change in alignments was glacial. When it did come, change usually stemmed from military defeat or the fall of power-addicted leaders.

Stage 3: The Connective Era

We are just now crossing the threshold into the Connective Era. As the old geopolitical alliances are dissolving, the *connections* between concepts, people, and the environment are tightening. Technology makes these linkages ever tighter. It is an era of interpenetration, where physical and political boundaries no longer shield us against outsiders or prevent us from moving freely into others' space. In the Connective Era, a new form of sovereignty—environmental sovereignty—has emerged. It expands the domain of our conventional sovereignty to include "the air [we] breathe, the water off [our] shore and the whole extended food chain upon which [we] rely."[10] Even as technology and new understanding bind us closer, new groups with new identities, not yet comfortable with interdependence, increase overall diversity.

As ideological differences dissolve and geopolitical boundaries shift,

- Fledgling nations struggle to shape their own identities. As they do, *new leaders step forward.*
- The profusion of emerging nations and leaders generates *contradictory effects,* such as teeming opportunities for political and economic *alliances* coupled with an increasing sense of differences that create a *thirst for independence.*
- *Cross-national industrial alliances* are spreading.
- The precedent of these international partnerships has encouraged *domestic industrial collaboration* between former arch rivals such as East Coast IBM and California-based Apple.
- Major *ideologies,* along with their priority-setting function, have collapsed. The result: we look more to leaders than to ideologies to set our new course.
- Crises and transition points, such as the end of historical eras (the forty-year Cold War), wars, famines, and depressions, bring *realignments of priorities* around new issues defining the next stage. Inevitably, reordered priorities also open the door to new and radically different categories of leaders.[11] New leaders, in turn, introduce still other priorities.

The identifying marks of the Connective Era can be seen at all levels of organizations and in all spheres of human activity: politics and government, business and industry, education and religion. Wherever we look, we see loosely structured global networks of organizations and nations tied to multiple subnetworks, living in a clumsy, federated world (and sharing space in the archetype of interdependence, the natural environment).[12] These networks link all kinds of groups, with long chains of leaders and supporters who communicate, debate, negotiate, and collaborate to accomplish their objectives.

Technological advances, particularly in communication and transportation, are accelerating these trends. In this new transphysical world, physical boundaries are easily penetrated. Even as the paper slides through the sender's fax machine, its message is flickering to a destination oceans away. Yet a new technological revolution in the making promises a quantum change to a *wireless, digital* world studded with possibilities most of us cannot yet imagine.[13] Microsoft Corp.'s Bill Gates predicts that a constellation of 840 refrigerator-size satellites will soon link every point on the globe in an explosion of interconnections.

Despite our past failures at forecasting the effects of innovations,[14] several predictions seem feasible:

First, *short-term* coalitions, changing kaleidoscopically, will replace long-term political and business alliances. Like children's Lego toys, which are easily assembled, pulled apart, and then reassembled into different structures, temporary networks will form, disband, and reform with pragmatic ease. All kinds of temporary groups (task forces, commissions, and production teams are familiar examples[15]) have already sprouted between and within the more stable, long-lived structures we have all come to think of as "real" organizations.[16]

Once they achieve their objectives, these groups will dissolve until the next wave of problems generates other short-lived alliances with different casts of partners. Even in the waning days of the Geopolitical Era, we have seen temporary alliances, such as the Alaskan pipeline consortium and Operation Desert Storm, work very well. These new structures will change the architecture of megaorganizations by forcing them to accommodate the comings and goings of these more temporary units.

Second, *flexible, fast-moving* organizations, extremely sensitive to any change in their environments, will become the mode. In the ever more volatile world ahead, long-range forecasting is not likely to improve greatly. The sensible alternative is to develop effective early warning sensors and a capacity for rapid, adaptive response based on a broad range of leadership strategies.

Third, *connections* among organizations and networks will take on new importance as major discontinuities sever the links to our own traditions. Ironically, the disconnection from our separate histories is forcing us to come together to deal with our shared, uncertain future. Thus global political networks—perhaps a revitalized United Nations or its successor, as well as a transfigured NATO—will need to join forces to tackle supranational problems. Their movements will be ungainly at first. We can also expect complications to arise from swings toward nationalistic isolation,[17] as some nations, like certain members of the former Soviet Union, shake off involuntary incorporation into larger states and move toward independence. Yet increasing interdependence among nations old and new is inevitable. Ultimately, even newborn countries must be drawn into the global network.

A Fundamental Shift in Leadership

Everywhere the search is on for new leaders, different categories of leaders, and more relevant forms of leadership. These seismic changes in leadership also create new and reordered priorities.

The Search for New Leaders

In these chaotic times, traditional leaders are finding it increasingly difficult to remain credible, much less in office. In the United States, corporate chieftains who recently sat atop some of our most powerful companies have been swept out, among them Westinghouse's John Marous, General Motors' Robert Stempel, Time Warner's Nicholas Nicholas, Jr., Goodyear's Tom Barrett, IBM's John Akers, Apple's Michael Spindler, Digital Equipment's founder and CEO Kenneth Olsen, Tenneco's James Ketelsen, and Borden's Anthony D'Amato. New CEOs are in, many with considerably diminished clout.[18] Boards of directors and shareholders have stepped closer to center stage, with greatly expanded roles in the evolving organizational drama.

In the political arena, as well, waves of popular protest toppled more heads of government from 1987 to 1992 than in the entire previous quarter century.[19] Within a two-year span, not only was Soviet president Mikhail Gorbachev, *Time* magazine's erstwhile "Man of the Decade," ousted by Boris Yeltsin, but Yeltsin himself had already stumbled into political hot water.

In place of the "great leaders" of previous eras, we are now witnessing a search for new leaders who can deal with the highly charged tensions of diversity and interdependence. The search is especially visible as newly independent nations rise from the ashes of the Soviet Union. The elections of Czech playwright Václav Havel, Bulgarian philosopher Zhelyu Zhelev, Hungarian writer Arpad Goncz, and Lithuanian musicologist Vytautas Landsbergis— all definitely political outsiders—suggest that the quest is not merely for new leaders but for a new *kind* of leadership.

In the United States too, we are caught up in that search, from the corporate boardroom to Congress and the presidency, from religious pulpits to university campuses. On the political scene, the appearance of Ross Perot as a significant independent candidate for president in 1992 may be read as a symptom of that quest. The 1994 congressional midterm elections signaled an unequivocal demand for new leaders.

The leadership transformation we are witnessing is not just a matter of personalities or even generations of leaders. Nor is it merely a case of throwing out the bunglers and bad guys. New historical conditions have created a growing call for changes in leadership that penetrates to the *basic forms,* indeed, to the very core of leadership. The John Wayne–Fidel Castro leadership tide is finally turning.

Entrenched leadership elites are finding that not just they themselves but the very *leadership concepts* they exemplify are being challenged by candidates from previously excluded minorities. As groups with different backgrounds and values enter the fray, leaders' approaches to diversity must transcend the Geopolitical Era's commitment to the melting-pot model.[20] Leaders in the Connective Era have to emphasize both *mutuality* (a focus on common interests and values) and *inclusiveness* (the willingness to include even those very different from the rest, without requiring their homogenization). Leaders who grasp this more complex meaning of diversity are more likely to create a multihued mosaic of constituents instead of the customary monochromatic herd of faithful followers.

Even many small firms recognize that a culturally diverse workforce can enhance their competitive position. They make cultural diversity a priority, rather than a problem. For example, at its Cambridge, Massachusetts, headquarters, Voice Processing Corp., developers of speech-recognition software, employs forty staff members representing eleven nationalities and speaking thirty languages, from Mandarin Chinese to Serbo-Croatian.[21] David Shipman, vice president for technology, attributes the young company's ability to move easily into world markets to its employees' "global orientation and understanding of different cultures." For example, senior software engineer Tonytip Ketudat is developing a strategy for penetrating the market in his Thai homeland.

Larger companies as well, such as Kaiser Permanente Healthcare in Burbank, California, place support programs for culturally diverse workers high on their priority list. With the HMO's blessings, numerous support groups have sprung up to deal with the inevitable complexities confronted by employees from diverse backgrounds.

In the move toward constructive engagement with diversity, the very categories of potential leaders have broadened to include groups deliberately excluded before now: women, blacks, Latinos, Asians, Native Americans, lesbians and gays, religious fundamentalists, and others. Poets, playwrights, artists, and humanists, all previously overlooked, are now increasingly perceived as potential political and industrial leaders. John D. Steinbrunner, program director of Foreign Policy Studies at The Brookings Institution, describes this shift as a "radical devolution of power."[22]

In recent years, business schools have begun to search for a more diverse population of MBA candidates. Rather than continuing to limit the pool to economics, math, and engineering majors, admissions officers are recruiting humanists, artists, historians, anthropologists, and psychologists. Some business schools have designed special courses, such as "Quantitative Methods for Poets," to accommodate these new future leaders.

Women too have made significant leadership headway. For example, in 1991, only eight years after its founding, the Women's Alliance captured 8 percent of the parliamentary seats in the world's oldest ongoing parliamentary body, Iceland's Althing. At that time, nine countries had female presidents or prime ministers, and Canada, Turkey, and Pakistan soon joined the list. (Turnover in leadership, however, is brisk. Notably, Canada's Kim Campbell, the Philippines' Corazon Aquino, and France's Edith Cresson have already stepped down or been turned out of office.)

Beyond the political realm, women have made significant inroads into organizational leadership. In fact, since 1983 the largest increases in U.S. female employment have come in managerial and professional occupations, involving 4.7 million women.[23] From 1983 to 1993, in the United States alone, the percentage of executive positions held by women rose from 33 to 42 percent.[24] The search for new leaders and new forms of leadership to address Stage 3 conditions is gradually producing results.

New Centers of Power, New Priorities

The appearance of fresh leaders representing new centers of power brings different issues to the table. In corporations, governments, and foundations, Stage 3 leaders, despite belt-tightening and downsizing, are identifying new priorities well beyond profit management, including:

- A growing emphasis upon employees that rivals the traditional focus on shareholders and customers, plus a broader orientation that includes responsibility for employees' intellectual and spiritual growth
- An interest in environmental protection, developing nations, and consumer protection, with accountability to the larger community beyond narrow organizational walls
- Renewed ethnic pride
- Equitable treatment for women and other minority groups
- Concern with the problems of hunger, health care, and homelessness

Activist businesswoman Anita Roddick, CEO of The Body Shop, is a prime example of a Stage 3 corporate leader whose nonestablishment values—concern for the environment, trade with developing nations rather than aid, education for rather than pressure on customers, promotion of social causes and volunteerism, emphasis on employees as well as customers—drive her very successful natural cosmetics company. Not too long ago, Roddick found herself questioned very intently by skeptical Stanford MBA students who doubted that The Body Shop could continue to "do well while doing good." (In Chapter Eleven, we view this maverick entrepreneur through a different lens, that of connective leadership.)

Independent TV producer Lillian Gallo, president of Los Angeles-based Gallo Entertainment, Inc., often addresses serious societal issues far ahead of their time. For example, Gallo's celebrated film *Fun and Games,* starring Valerie Harper, examined sexual harassment in the workplace half a decade before the Clarence Thomas U.S. Supreme Court nomination hearings ignited a firestorm of public concern.

Billy Shore, president of Share Our Strength (S.O.S.), a Washington, D.C., not-for-profit organization, raises both money and public consciousness in his innovative efforts to end worldwide hunger. Shore brings chefs, restaurateurs, poets, physicists, and other professionals together to fashion new solutions to the problems of hunger.

These new priorities are beginning to rub off even on mature, mainstream organizations such as Levi Strauss. Chairman and CEO Robert Haas, great-great-grandnephew of the founder, has moved his company from preaching the right words to practicing the right behavior. He champions "*responsible* commercial success." Haas's vision embraces diversity, management openness, recognition for innovative individuals and teams, self-conscious ethical management practices, and employee empowerment. Unfortunately, the business media, still caught up in bottom line myopia, raise a skeptical eyebrow.[25]

Two more corporate leaders introduce fresh priorities that focus on the intellectual and spiritual development of employees. Morton Meyerson, CEO and chairman of Perot Systems (and a computer professional by training), seeks fresh initiatives for engaging his employees in "authentic experiences."[26] Convinced that corporate emphasis on physical fitness isn't enough, Meyerson has created an Intellectual Fitness Center at the Dallas corporate headquarters (more on this in Chapter Nine). There, under the full-time guidance of a retired history professor, employees and their spouses can engage in a variety of new experiences. From language courses to weekend retreats, they explore other cultures as well as their own spiritual and artistic potential.

The furniture design company Herman Miller, Inc., of Zeeland, Michigan, points proudly to its own cutting-edge tradition.[27] During his three-year term, former president, CEO, and chairman Kermit Campbell (a self-described "chemical engineer by training, but a right-brain thinker"[28]) was not content to rest on the company's acknowledged laurels. Instead, Campbell energetically charted a new course designed to "liberate the human spirit" of employees and customers alike, before coming to a parting of the ways with the company over downsizing and other issues.

Many Stage 3 leaders use nontraditional strategies to address these new priorities. They recognize that conflicting agendas of their diverse constituencies demand innovation so broadly defined that it reaches into the very core of leadership. That kind of innovation calls for a much greater spectrum of leadership behaviors than traditional leaders have drawn upon in the past. A principal aim of this book is to describe an expanded palette of leadership styles to implement these new priorities.

The Connective Era poses challenges not only to leaders but to followers as well: to transform themselves into active and responsible constituents who can endorse, and more importantly engage in, a radically different leadership dynamic. Their priorities too must shift. Forget about waiting for the leader to point the way. Forget about spectatorship. Constituents must abandon old passive ways and energetically and consistently endorse new leadership strategies. They must learn to deal with ambiguity and resist the temptation to insist upon a new leadership orthodoxy. Otherwise we face the prospect of reverting to the hobbling authoritarianism of the Geopolitical Era.

Connective Leaders for a Stage 3 World: A First Look

Connective leaders discern that no easy mix of authoritarianism, competition, and collaboration can meet the serious challenges posed by Stage 3. We see their special approach to interdependence and diversity described in the following six areas.

Beyond Manipulative Machiavellianism to "Denatured Machiavellianism"

First, connective leaders use various types of political but ethical action to navigate difficult organizational currents; to negotiate conflicts for the community's benefit; to exploit people and processes not to increase the leader's power but to solve group problems; to engage constituents through dramatic, unexpected symbols and gestures; and to expand supporters' abilities and loyalty by entrusting them with challenging tasks. In so doing, these new leaders deliberately redirect the otherwise centrifugal forces of diversity and interdependence.

Traditionally, we have rejected instrumentalism (using the self and others as instruments for accomplishing goals) as unethical manipulation, tainted by its association with Machiavelli's advice to the prince.[29] Nonetheless, *used ethically for the good of the whole community,* instrumental strategies can be extremely effective— particularly in dealing with the political realities that lace an interdependent world. Thus we might think of "denatured Machiavellianism" as a term for principled instrumental action, action that uses the self and others ethically as the means to an end. Drained of self-aggrandizing toxins, this type of political behavior is particularly relevant to a complex, interdependent world. It is a key facet of the connective leader's repertoire.

Connective leaders know how to use these political strategies and skills. They intuit and exploit the interconnections among people, institutions, and processes everywhere. Connective leaders depart from the Machiavellianism of *The Prince* not only by operating from a consistently ethical base but in other significant ways as well:

- By joining their vision to the dreams of others; by connecting and combining, rather than dividing and conquering
- By striving to overcome mutual problems instead of common enemies exaggerated to corral frightened followers behind their leader
- By creating a sense of community, where many diverse groups can hold valued membership
- By bringing together committed leaders and constituents for common purposes
- By encouraging active constituents to assume responsibilities at every level, rather than manipulating passive followers[30]
- By joining with other leaders, even former adversaries, as colleagues, not as competitors

- By nurturing potential leaders, including possible successors
- By renewing and building broad-based democratic institutions instead of creating dynasties and oligarchies
- By demonstrating authenticity through consistent dedication to supra-egoistic goals
- By demanding serious sacrifice first from themselves and only then from others

Connective leaders, like servant leaders,[31] serve their societies, not themselves. Using ethical instrumentality, however, connective leaders act with greater personal agency than servant leaders usually do. They concentrate less self-righteously on their stewardship and obligations to the organization. They focus more pragmatically on their instrumental skills to turn the connections among people, organizations, and dreams to the advantage of the larger community.

In their pursuit of solutions to Stage 3 problems, connective leaders use themselves and everyone around them as instruments to their goals. In their hands, instrumentalism takes on a fresh, unsullied meaning.

Authenticity and Accountability: Stage 3 Imperatives

Second, connective leaders fortify their denatured Machiavellianism with a strong dose of authenticity and accountability. They recognize that a leader's complex behaviors can confuse supporters. Because their own actions are often more complicated than their Stage 2 predecessors', connective leaders appreciate the special significance that authenticity and accountability hold for them.

Like obscenity, authenticity is that ineffable quality we can instantly detect but rarely define.[32] Emanating from an ethical core,[33] authenticity sustains supporters' faith in the *person* of the leader, even when the leader's *behavior* seems confusing or contradictory. It stems the corrosion of cynicism. It helps us determine whether the leader's policy change is the result of new information or a failure of will.

Authenticity is palpable when leaders harness their egos to the chariot of the greater cause. Constituents intuitively sense authenticity when their leaders consistently place organizational or societal goals above their personal glory, if necessary even above their lives.

Accountability, authenticity's twin imperative, means accepting the obligation to explain, the willingness to be held responsible to a widening jury of stakeholders. Accountability means the leader knows beforehand that every choice will be seriously scrutinized. Accountability, coupled with authenticity, blocks unethical, irresponsible, or simply thoughtless action. In a post-Watergate world, abetted by the watchful eye of the TV camera and an aggressive media corps, constituents expect full disclosure.

If this makes connective leaders sound like saints, they're not. Like the rest of us, they are imperfect humans. As we shall see, connective leaders often can be as stubborn and ornery as the next guy. They can get angry. They can be totally exasperating. Sometimes connective leaders so infuriate people that their constituents drive them out. But generally, they more than make up for all that by their capacity to lead in exciting, effective ways.

Building Community: The Politics of Commonalities

Third, connective leaders prefer a politics of commonalities to the politics of differences favored by traditional, divisive leaders. They build community where the most diverse groups can enjoy a sense of belonging. In a world connected by technology but fragmented by diversity, leaders need to build community, where everyone wins something at least some of the time. For the moment, let's define community simply as an environment in which individuals and groups, representing a broad band of ideas and values, can all hold rewarding membership. As impersonal technology increasingly drives interdependence, community becomes even more essential to fill the human yearning for belonging.

Building community means taking the very widest view of what is needed and who needs what. It means foregoing competitive, zero-sum games, particularly with other leaders, where some must lose so others can win. Community must include even those passionately committed groups bound together by the most narrowly defined ideology, like the Trotskyites of an earlier epoch.

In organizations, this means leaders have to foster a broadly inclusive, "total system" view. This perspective ensures that everyone's needs are reasonably met, if not simultaneously, then at least sequentially. To achieve this, Stage 3 leaders have to create a politics of commonalities that emphasizes similarities, rather than a politics of differences.

The complex issues generated by diverse groups, particularly those newly formed, frequently tear the fabric of organizations and societies. Only leaders who can assemble multiple changing coalitions, rather than enduring elites, will find the common ground within divisive issues. They are the ones who can best reweave the social fabric and build genuine community.

Leaders who can work effectively with other leaders—that is, multiple networks of leaders—know the algorithm for developing community. Achieving community goals requires leaders who can avoid tripping over their egos, who can resist the urge to become *the* leader of all leaders. An interdependent environment calls for leaders who can relate as peers to other leaders in other institutions worldwide. In the Connective Era, leaders cannot just issue orders; instead, they have to join forces, persuade, and negotiate to resolve conflicts.

One particularly intriguing aspect of connective leadership involves unexpected rapprochements with former adversaries as well as with other nontraditional constituents. Stage 3 leaders do so to expand the touching points of their different agendas. Soviet president Mikhail Gorbachev, Egyptian leader Anwar Sadat, and Israeli prime minister Yitzhak Rabin stunned the world and confused their own constituents by stepping across the inherited divide between themselves and their countries' sworn enemies. (In so doing, Gorbachev risked his political career, while Sadat and Rabin ultimately sacrificed their lives.) In dramatic initiatives, each of these nascent connective leaders unexpectedly joined forces with former opponents to advance their intersecting agendas.

Forging community is not easy. It demands altruism on the part of leaders themselves. Allowing room for the needs of others, sharing scarce resources, protecting alternatives for generations yet unborn, accepting critical challenges that may threaten the leader's place in history: all these require large quantities of character, not ego. To paraphrase Abraham Lincoln, connective leaders represent our "last great hope" for building community.

Adopting a Long-Term Perspective

Fourth, despite the turbulent immediacy of the Connective Era, creating community also means taking a very long-term perspective. A long-range view is needed to ensure that whatever choices we make today do not bar future actions required by unanticipated events. Here we confront the rub of balance. Connective leaders need to commit themselves steadfastly to the long term, even when the envisioned future unsettles the short-term arrangements of particular community members.[34]

Long-term vision also requires moving past one's own ego to allow an organization to prosper after the current leader steps aside. In John Gardner's view, responsibility for growing new leaders at all levels must fall to existing leaders.[35] Yet our current traditional leaders may be the *least* able to develop the necessary means: broad-based selection criteria and a strong succession mechanism. They are too prone to choose successors who are clones of themselves. They are also quite likely to scuttle any succession planning. Connective leaders do not fear their young; they nourish and groom them for leadership.

Leadership Through Expectation: Entrusting, Enabling, and Ennobling

Fifth, connective leaders encourage the widest set of participants to join in the leadership process. They spread the burden of leadership and entrust responsibility to others, rather than commandeering the troops. They even entrust their visions to others who, they sense, can grow in response to the challenge.

The connective leader's gift of trust, wrapped in the compliment of confidence, usually is reciprocated by the recipient's outstanding performance.[36] By these more subtle acts, connective leaders exercise leadership through expectation.

Leadership through expectation involves reasonable risks. Connective leaders are not blind to the rigors of learning and the time demands for growth. They know that new missions sometimes fail, so they allow a reasonable margin for failure. Connective leaders value the good near miss. They provide the constant support that those entrusted with new challenges need if they are to hit the target on the next project.

Leaders who create conditions that allow others to ennoble themselves will find eager recruits and loyal supporters. The opportunity for self-transcendence is, for many, the greatest gift of all. It permits the largest expression of individualism in the Connective Era, an individualism that builds, rather than fragments, community.

These connective strategies, so clearly founded in ethical instrumental action, increase leadership strength at every level. They also build leadership for the future.

Leaders and the Search for Life's Meaning: Their Personal Odyssey

Sixth, most connective leaders are embarked upon a personal odyssey. They are committed to an ongoing search for deeper understanding of themselves, their constituents, and the organizations they lead. They dedicate themselves to larger purposes through which they can transcend their finite limitations and set extraordinary examples for others. The result: the enterprises they lead give supporters many opportunities to ennoble their spirits.

Throughout human history, we have sought leaders. That endless quest is part of our larger search for the meaning of life and where we fit into the picture. Living life in the shadow of inevitable death colors everything we do. It drives us to seek security through gods, ideologies, and mortal leaders. It compels us to search for life's central meaning, for an increasingly complex understanding of our lives. To obscure our fear of death, we undertake life-expanding enterprises. As we mature, an awareness of our mortality stimulates a commitment to altruistic goals through which we may symbolically transcend physical death. We turn to leaders to guide us through these complicated, lifelong tasks.

Just as the Connective Era is driven by the fluctuations of diversity and interdependence, so individual development represents an oscillating focus on the self and the Other. Only by integrating these parallel forces can we finally come to terms with our fear of death. Leaders help us to do so by drawing our attention to worldly problems: economic cycles, the production of goods and services, national conflicts, environmental degradation, disease, homelessness, and hunger. These problems serve as metaphors for our own personal issues. By struggling with society's problems, we symbolically deal with our own unconscious anxieties, particularly our central terror of death.

By committing ourselves to enterprises that benefit the community, be it our work group or the international community, we reach beyond ourselves and our narrow, personal interests. In the process, we reconcile diversity and interdependence, self and Other. By responding heroically to the leader's call to action and sometimes to sacrifice, we symbolically stare down death. Paradoxically, immersed in causes far greater than ourselves, we ultimately emerge as our most unique selves. We shall return to these all-important dilemmas in the concluding chapter.

Why Isn't Collaboration Enough? Is Individualism Dead?

In describing connective leaders' propensity to move beyond individualism, let's not overstate the case. Individualism is hardly dead, nor is it time to kill it. On the contrary, diversity is promoting new and interesting forms of individualism. But old, ego-ensnarled individualism cannot address the new leadership conditions we confront.

Connective leaders are not naive dreamers. They know that individualism often drives us to reach deep within our souls to create powerful visions and strive for their fulfillment. They appreciate that top-down power methods can be both useful and necessary, particularly during crises.

Connective leaders also value the synergy that can flow from collaboration, particularly from "hot groups,"[37] whose participants are charged up by an enormously challenging task. But where collaborative types often overvalue consensus, connective leaders understand the limits of consensual decision making. While collaborative leaders build enduring teams, connective leaders serve as the threaded needle stitching together multiple shorter-term alliances.

Connective leaders understand something else as well: old-style collaboration, played out as participative management, often harbors covert authoritarianism (as we shall see). While participative management appreciates the diverse gifts individuals bring to organizations, connective leadership comprehends the complexity of integrating diversity and interdependence in a global context.

Although connective leaders favor innovative actions, they do not discard the strengths of traditional leadership. To engage in a politics of commonalities, to build community, to think long-term, and to enable others, connective leaders combine traditional leadership behaviors with several Stage 3 strategies. They blend the ethical exploitation of self and others with more familiar behaviors based on self-reliance, power, delegation, collaboration, and assistance. In the process, they revitalize traditional leadership behavior.

The Connective Leadership Model: Nine Behavioral Facets

The idea of ennobling ourselves and confronting our existential demons may sound abstract and philosophical, yet the behaviors that connective leaders use are drawn from the same reservoir of everyday behaviors that we all utilize.

Early in childhood, we begin to learn different behaviors for getting what we want. These behaviors become "personal technologies" for accomplishing our tasks or achieving our goals, be they studying or designing rockets. These behaviors I call "achieving styles."

The limited set of achieving styles that most of us use seems adequate for our tasks until leadership roles prompt us to expand our repertoire. Connective leaders keep expanding their behavioral options, while most of us (Stage 2 leaders included) restrict ourselves to a much narrower slice of the behavioral pie.

As described in detail in Part Two, the Connective Leadership Model consists of three major sets of behavioral styles: direct, relational, and instrumental. Turning the microscope down another level reveals three styles nested within each set, producing nine achieving styles.

People who prefer the direct set like to confront their own tasks individually and directly (hence the "direct" label), emphasizing mastery, competition, and power. They prefer their own tasks.

These are the styles most closely linked to diversity and its various expressions of individualism. People who prefer to work on group tasks or help others to attain their goals emphasize the relational set. The relational styles speak to the issues inherent in the many forms of interdependence. Finally, individuals who use themselves and others as instruments toward community goals prefer the instrumental set. These "political" styles are particularly useful in harnessing the forces of diversity and interdependence.

The quality that most clearly differentiates connective leaders is their instrumental virtuosity. Connective leaders use these more complex strategies to integrate their own (often contradictory) direct and relational actions. In addition, they draw upon their instrumental strengths to reduce the dissonance that diversity and interdependence create in the Stage 3 environment.

Leadership studies spanning more than half a century have demonstrated that leadership is not reducible to a set of inborn traits.[38] Despite the fact that some people may have greater natural talent than others, leadership can be learned. While there may be only a few pianists with Vladimir Horowitz's virtuosity, many others, with some coaching and practice, can learn to play respectably. Similarly, even some leaders we all acknowledge as giants have had to undergo painful learning and growth. Given the increasing demand for leaders, those of us who expect to try our hand at leadership will benefit from practice and a study of its dynamics.

The Connective Leadership Model, with its underlying roster of achieving styles, provides such a window on the dynamics of leadership. It does so not only by delineating connective leadership but by offering concepts and nomenclature for reevaluating our traditional understanding of leaders. It helps us diagnose leadership situations. And beyond that, the model gives leaders the tools to take three kinds of action:

1. To identify the most effective leadership strategies that they personally might apply to each unique situation
2. To evaluate the leadership potential of *others* and match those leadership behaviors to the demands of complex Stage 3 situations
3. To design new types of structures whose shapes and purposes fit not just the task but also the behavioral preferences of participants

In a world where diversity and interdependence pose serious threats for leaders, the Connective Leadership Model offers serious behavioral ammunition.

Leadership Examples in Unexpected Places

Where can we find leaders who are actually and successfully practicing connective leadership? Where are the people who can even manage to play across the octaves of achieving styles, let alone tackle the virtuosity of connective leadership? To find them, we would do well to search in unexpected places. We are most likely to find them

- In voluntary organizations, where leaders must attract dedicated workers without the crutches of financial incentives or formal authority. The most effective nonprofit leaders provide opportunities for ennobling action. They rely heavily on leadership through expectation.
- Among entrepreneurs, who frequently display the whole spectrum of connective leadership behaviors. As jacks-and-jills-of-all-trades, many of these agile movers and shakers can comfortably use a wide range of leadership strategies. Yet paradoxically, only a few entrepreneurs ever actually become connective leaders.
- Among the latest cadre of female leaders, who stimulate supporters' talents and loyalty. These new leaders fuse familiar female styles of collaboration, nurturance, and altruism with power and instrumental action.[39]
- Among leaders in certain industries, such as entertainment, who periodically must assemble new creative teams from large professional networks for each project they undertake.
- Among a new breed of political leaders, who recognize that enduring coalitions, like the New Deal in American politics, are things of the past. In their place, these connective leaders rally multiple short-term, sometimes overlapping, coalitions to address diverse problems.
- Among some dedicated activists who sacrifice careers, wealth, comfort, and sometimes their very lives to do for the community what it can't do for itself.

The winds of global change are radically transforming the historical climate. Beset by a rising storm, leaders everywhere face a critical challenge. Two new and contradictory forces, interdependence
and diversity, are changing the very conditions for leadership. They
pose new requirements that can only be met by a complex, but
realizable, set of leadership behaviors.

Connective leadership, based on a nine-style Connective Leadership Model, brings an "ethical instrumentalism" to bear on the
politics of human interaction. But it does not throw away everything
else. It revitalizes traditional leadership behaviors by harnessing
individualism and teamwork through the principled deployment of
political strategies.

For leaders, the greatest danger is to keep drawing upon behaviors linked to bygone eras. To do so risks missing the enormous
strategic opportunities that the Connective Era offers. Of course,
risk always keeps company with opportunity. To brave the storm of
change, leaders must be bold enough to redefine the very terms
of leadership.

Chapter Two

Why Are We So Hooked on Leaders Anyway?

The Psychological and Existential Foundations of Leadership

> *One thing is certain, that the problem of anxiety is a nodal point, linking up all kinds of most important questions: a riddle, of which the solution must cast a flood of light upon our whole mental life.*
> SIGMUND FREUD[1]

Although connective leadership still lacks a significant legion of constituents, other forms of leadership have had a strong hold on us for centuries. In particular, what I characterized in the first chapter as Stage 2 leaders describes what many people define as leadership. Before we can fully appreciate the new possibilities offered by connective leadership, we need to probe our images of leaders: where these images come from, why we have them, and in what ways they may be constraining our vision of what leaders can be.

This chapter invites us to ponder leadership itself. Why have leaders appeared in virtually all societies through all recorded history? Do certain individuals have special qualities that make us acknowledge them as leaders? Or are there deep human needs that drive us to search for, and sometimes even to create, leaders? Why do leaders take the job and usually stick it out, despite the enormous burdens of leadership?

This chapter considers some of the profound existential forces and psychological impulses that push followers to seek leaders and, just as frequently, drive leaders to seek supporters. Only if we confront these deep currents can we begin to understand and perhaps revise our traditional images of leadership. That process will help us to embrace a new vision of leadership more suitable to our changed circumstances.

Why Do We Seek Leaders—and Why Do We Fear Them?

Leaders seem to arise in almost all societies and organizations, large and small, simple and complex, in every historical period, and in every part of the world.[2] Of course, there is some variation in the specific leadership characteristics that are valued from one society to the next, but the concept of leaders seems nearly universal. Occasionally, in the throes of a revolution designed to depose an unusually oppressive or corrupt leader, theoreticians call for a leaderless society. Such utopias, however, quickly evaporate amid the rigors and realities of social reconstruction, and distinct leaders emerge.

Wherever leaders appear, in or out of bureaucracies, they are set apart from the crowd and treated as different from, usually superior to, ordinary people. Something pushes us to find and follow leaders. Something makes us treat leaders as special.

Is it something about them?

Or is it something about us?

Is It the Leader's Traits?

Some observers claim that leaders exhibit special traits that compel us to accept their authority. Despite decades of research on long lists of leadership traits, the results remain inconclusive.[3] Leaders, it turns out, come in all shapes and sizes. Bennis and Nanus concluded that the thousands of leadership studies conducted just in the last seventy-five years have failed to provide any "clear and unequivocal understanding . . . as to what distinguishes leaders from non-leaders, and . . . what distinguishes *effective* leaders from *ineffective* leaders."[4]

The Lure of Charisma

Despite researchers' failure to isolate specific personality traits linked to leadership, our common experience suggests there is one leadership characteristic for which followers relentlessly yearn. That lodestone is charisma, the special magnetic quality that fills followers with awe and adoration. The German sociologist Max Weber[5] thought charismatic authority stemmed from the leader's "mana," or divine gift of grace, which compelled the followers' awe. Only when they can no longer demonstrate the divine gifts that set them above their disciples, Weber argued, do charismatics lose their authority.[6]

Charismatic leaders have a way of appearing in times of great distress. They usually espouse a decidedly radical vision that promises to resolve the crisis. Crisis, by definition, is a period of great threat and uncertainty, a time when the existing leadership seems to falter. It is also a period in which the society's ordinary coping mechanisms are out of kilter. It is not, then, all that surprising that a charismatic leader offering a solution, however radical, is particularly welcome in difficult times.

Of course, one might even argue that, in the turmoil and anxiety that keep company with crisis, anyone who confidently proposes a solution is likely to be looked upon as charismatic.[7] Weber, for example, described the followers' response to charismatics as a devotion born of distress.[8]

More recently, Avolio and Bass along with Conger and Kanungo introduced a new twist to the emergence of charismatic leaders in times of trouble.[9] They argue that by their appealing vision of an alternative future, charismatic leaders can actually induce dissatisfaction among followers. By generating a sense of distress among followers, charismatic leaders often create the conditions necessary for their ascension to power.

Bailey proposes that only the masses expect the leader to display charisma.[10] The leader's entourage does not. He reasons that it is the entourage's responsibility, through "humbuggery and manipulation," to project the leader's charisma to the devoted masses. (The leader's inner circle, who understand that the leader's charisma arises largely from smoke and mirrors, must be kept in line by different methods: terror and uncertainty.)

Part of the charisma argument still looks right. The attraction of charisma continues to prove irresistible to followers. Even when they renounce the impressive trappings of formal office, as many wisely do, charismatic leaders still attract disciples who revere them as teachers and protectors. Confined to a prison cell for twenty-seven years, African National Congress leader Nelson Mandela inspired followers worldwide, many of whom had never even seen him.

The pages of history and scripture depict figures radiating undeniable charisma. Jesus Christ, Joan of Arc, Florence Nightingale, Mahatma Gandhi, Martin Luther King, Jr., Adolph Hitler, Franklin D. Roosevelt, Eleanor Roosevelt, Juan Peron, Eva Peron, Winston Churchill, John F. Kennedy, Jim Jones, David Koresh, Ronald Reagan, Margaret Thatcher, Jessie Jackson, Mikhail Gorbachev, Boris Yeltsin, Bill Clinton, Ross Perot, Newt Gingrich . . . all project their special brand of charisma. As this list immediately suggests, charismatic leaders come in many guises: good and bad, saintly and evil, modest and egomaniacal.

Over time, charisma has lost its Weberian meaning and come to signify something akin to attractiveness, sexiness, or media "sizzle." But whether we insist on the classical Weberian definition or settle for the contemporary vernacular, we all readily recognize people who have a certain magnetism that draws followers like iron filings.

Still, charisma per se can hardly be the *total* explanation for the near universality of leaders, since we all can point to political and corporate leaders who *don't* seem the least bit charismatic. For every Ronald Reagan there is a George Bush, for every Henry Ford, Sr., there is an Alfred P. Sloan. Some presidential campaigns and corporate talent searches fail to produce any candidates who generate that special attraction. Although charisma may help to explain the appeal of some leaders, clearly it is neither necessary nor sufficient to create leadership.

Transformational, Transactional, and Servant Leaders

Many leadership scholars have tried to disentangle charisma from other aspects of leadership.[11] Disenchanted by the ambiguity and misuse of the term *charisma*, Pulitzer prize–winning historian-cum-political scientist James MacGregor Burns suggested that we focus instead on the distinction between *transactional* and *transformational* leaders.[12] To oversimplify Burns's argument, transactional leaders take the structure as given and work within it. They strike deals and agree to trade-offs that meet both the followers' and the organization's needs. Building on Weber's notion of charisma, Burns suggests that "transformational leadership" radically transforms and renews the followers, the leader, and the organization.

Not altogether satisfied with this transactional/transformational distinction, Burns adds a further leadership requirement for transformational leaders: intellectual stimulation of the followers.[13] This kind of leadership provides motivation that exceeds organizational incentives and controls. Robert K. Greenleaf, long-time director of management research at AT&T, described "servant-leaders," who use their gifts to serve others. According to Greenleaf, followers are served if they "grow as persons . . . become healthier, wiser, freer, more autonomous, more likely themselves to become servants."[14]

These distinctions add to our ways of thinking about the kinds of leaders we have known. They don't explain, however, why leaders continue to emerge, that is, the ubiquity and attraction of leaders.

Or Is It the Followers' Needs?

If we cannot explain our quest for leaders completely in terms of the leader's qualities, perhaps we should look for clues in the followers' or supporters' camp. Leadership theorists, from Weber and Simmel to Barnard, as well as more recent writers including John Gardner, remind us that leadership is conferred by the followers.[15] Without the supporters' consent, the aspiring leader cannot lead.

Some leadership experts suggest that those individuals who can meet potential followers' needs become leaders. In general, this seems perfectly reasonable. The real issue, however, is: *which* critical needs do followers yearn to have leaders satisfy?

The Need for Effective Group Action

Some argue that leaders meet the need for coordinating group action in the most efficient and effective manner. In this view, leaders, supported by bureaucratic organizations, offer us an efficient and economical way to make decisions and take action.[16]

Corporate and political leaders sit atop the organizational charts in all large bureaucracies. When they appear in our midst, we may not sing "Hail to the Chief," but often our hearts beat a little faster, and a shiver tingles our spine. Frequently, we tell tales about their prodigious feats. (Some tell their own stories in best-selling autobiographies.) Even to the most casual observer, their "chiefdom" is evident from the layers of "subordinates" who report to them.

From the outset, bureaucratic hierarchies have had a dynamic of their own, which always includes a chief. Rudyard Kipling, in "Her Majesty's Servants," painted a vivid picture of how the system works:

> Then I heard an old grizzled long-haired Central Asian chief, who had come down with the Amir, asking questions of a native officer.
>
> "Now," he said, "In what manner was this wonderful thing done?"
>
> And the officer answered, "There was an order and they obeyed."
>
> "But are the beasts as wise as the men?" asked the chief.
>
> "They obey, as the men do. Mule, horse, elephant, or bullock, he obeys his driver, and the driver his sergeant, and the sergeant his lieutenant, and the lieutenant his captain, and the captain his major, and the major his colonel, and the colonel his brigadier commanding three regiments, and the brigadier his general, who obeys the Viceroy, who is the servant of the Empress. Thus it is done."
>
> "Would it were so in Afghanistan," said the chief. "For there we obey only our own wills."
>
> "And for that reason," said the native officer, twirling his mustache, "Your Amir, whom you do not obey, must come here and take orders from our Viceroy."[17]

But does the efficiency explanation really reflect reality? Most of our encounters with bureaucracies suggest they obstruct efficiency more often than they promote it. In fact, virtually everywhere in the contemporary world, "bureaucratic efficiency" has become an oxymoron. The bureaucratic dynamic, closely linked to pyramidal organizations, may require a chief at the top. Yet the presence of a chief is no guarantee of effective or efficient action. Indeed, bureaucracies are notorious for frustrating unpopular chiefs.[18] Presidents of countries and CEOs in private and Third Sector, or non-profit, organizations have often found themselves undermined and ultimately defeated by the Lilliputians of bureaucracy.

So if the need for efficiency does not explain the pervasive presence of leaders, we must look elsewhere. What other forces persistently push us to seek powerful leaders, setting them above ourselves, at the heads of the organizations and institutions that control so much of our lives?

The Need for a Responsible Parent, a Magical Monarch, or a Deity

A more psychoanalytic explanation for our tendency to seek out strong leaders revolves around our longing for a responsible parent. As children, we felt secure when our parents were available to make wise decisions for us and protect us from harm. (Admittedly, we objected when their decisions prevented us from doing what we wanted.) In adolescence, the struggle to become adults some-times swung our behavioral pendulum wildly between dependency and defiance. Yet the parental relationship leaves its mark, rendering us vulnerable to a longing for the comfort and safety that the protective parent provided, particularly when the going gets rough. So we are often relieved when leaders step into that role, and we respond to them with the submissive responses we learned in childhood.

Responsibility goes hand in hand with blame and guilt. Some-times a group member is injured inadvertently by a decision intended to benefit the group. When that happens, the injured party is likely to blame the decision maker. Since the anguish of guilt is a burden many prefer to avoid, the leader-as-decision-maker becomes the perfect mechanism for absorbing that guilt and absolving the followers.

In many cultures, the leader is a parental figure, one who makes decisions for others and shoulders the blame if things go wrong. In a televised interview conducted by Barbara Walters, former Prime Minister Margaret Thatcher insisted, "I've never had difficulty making hard decisions." British voters responded to Thatcher's parental scoldings and homilies by reelecting her to the longest tenure of any British prime minister in the twentieth century.

Throughout history, long before today's sprawling bureaucracies, people have sought out leaders who seemed stronger, better, and wiser than themselves. Followers often endow leaders with royal, magical, and even superhuman traits (even when the leaders themselves reject the role of monarch or god). George Washington denied his followers' ardent desire to crown him king, insisting instead on the more limited role of president. John F. Kennedy's followers responded to the image he projected, viewing him as a charmed royal warrior, surrounded by his knights and lady, a modern day Arthur establishing a magical Camelot. Until Japan's defeat in World War II demythologized Emperor Hirohito, the Japanese revered him as a deity.

From the perspective of childhood, our parents seemed both omnipotent and omniscient. It is hardly surprising then that we search for leaders who project strength and wisdom, even if the reality doesn't always match the image. Research from two decades ago concluded that people who "look the part"—tall, handsome, and masculine—were more likely to command higher salaries and top corporate positions.[19] Recent research suggests that more attractive, taller men earned larger starting salaries and continued this pattern throughout their careers.[20]

Other researchers report that for women, physical attractiveness did not affect starting salaries, but it did make a difference in their later careers.[21] Canadian sociologists also found that physical attractiveness did little to boost annual salaries for women, younger people, and individuals employed in occupations usually designated as "women's roles."[22] This begins to sound like central casting, where those who look like traditional leaders—particularly people we literally can look up to—are likely to win the part. Individuals who project a strong leadership image provide the reassuring illusion that we can depend on them, if not always on ourselves.

The Need for Leaders as Ego Ideals

Our need for leaders has other psychological tributaries, as well. Leaders serve as our ego ideals, offering a model of what we all yearn to be, even if we never really expect to achieve it. These larger-than-life figures nourish our secret hope that, *just possibly,* we—or maybe our children—can become like them. Then, of course, we could be secure without these strong figures.

For this reason, we don't set very severe limits on leaders. As they stride across the political or corporate stage, we allow them excesses, up to some ill-defined point. The British royal family's domestic escapades entrance tabloid readers, who glimpse a sense of human kinship. Eager for the details of their exotic lives, we idolize celebrities as lifestyle leaders. We even admire their excesses, which permit us the fantasy that "there, maybe, someday go I."

When the late magazine publisher Malcolm Forbes flew hundreds of guests to his lavish Arabian Nights birthday celebration in Morocco, readers snapped up every last copy of *People* magazine, relishing each delectable tidbit of gossip. The public follows Donald Trump's corporate and marital exploits with equal fascination. We ordinary folks may grumble a lot, but most of us don't take any concrete action to prevent the Trumps of the world from making outlandish financial deals unavailable to the rest of us. We are secretly awed by such derring-do and fantasize about having millions to use as *we* desire. Of course, we are certain *our* sprees would be in better taste. And if, in the end, we find we really can't emulate these larger-than-life figures, at least they can act as our surrogates.

The Most Compelling Need: Fighting off Existential Uncertainty and Anxiety

Psychological factors undoubtedly contribute some pieces to the puzzle, but a less obvious yet very compelling piece is still missing. At the very core of our human condition lies the immutable reality that we can neither predict nor totally control our destiny. This reality, which I call "existential uncertainty," is the first of a pair of such demons that we fend off with all our might.[23]

The realization of how little we can do to reduce the uncertainty associated with human life provokes the appearance of that demon's mate: a pervasive, deep-seated dread that I'll call "existential anxiety."[24] Always hovering just below our consciousness, existential anxiety silently colors every aspect of our lives, troubling our working hours and haunting our dreams as we sleep.[25]

These two existential demons—uncertainty and the anxiety it generates—perturb our sense of mastery and efficacy. They illuminate the limits of our autonomy and remind us that life itself is only minimally within our control. In truth, accident or death may be waiting just around the corner.

Psychoanalyst Gregory Zilboorg[26] saw the fear of death as necessary both to our normal functioning and our constant alert to self-preservation.[27] Becker viewed humans' terror of death as "one of the great rediscoveries of modern thought," agreeing with Shaler[28] that our search for heroism, both within ourselves and in others, was a "reflex" of that terror.

The world is continually threatening to spin out of control, as we are reminded on the nightly newscasts.[29] The 6:00 P.M. report announces that a plane has crashed, strewing bodies over a corn field in Iowa, while in New York the stock market has taken a 60-point free fall. By 11:00 P.M., these stories take a back seat to the subway stabbing of a visitor to New York, a drive-by shooting on an East Los Angeles freeway, a car bomb explosion on the West Bank of Israel, and a drug-related shoot-out in a Nicaraguan newspaper office. Even through our horror and grief, we know these are just the *ordinary* fare of daily existence, dreaded events careening without warning through human lives, sowing devastation in their wake.

Then there are those *extraordinary*, cataclysmic near misses, like the Three Mile Island nuclear accident, that make us catch our collective breath in terror. Even worse, we humans, deliberately or inadvertently, unleash megacatastrophes—Hiroshima, Bhopal, and Chernobyl—by the technologies we have developed and the hostilities we have initiated.[30] From The Bomb, AIDS, crime, and drugs to terrorism, acid rain, and the deteriorating ozone layer, our safe and orderly world seems in constant danger of falling apart. As if our own mistakes were not terrifying enough, Nature itself steps in, uncorking unpredictable and uncontrollable killers: earthquakes, tornadoes, floods, hurricanes, and droughts.

These hard-to-forecast, uncontrollable events shake us to our psychic foundations. They remind us of the fragility and impermanence of life, and they underscore how little we can do about it.

If we insist upon constantly confronting the existential uncertainty that beclouds our human condition, we'll soon refuse to fly on a plane, ride the subway, drive the freeways, or even walk to the corner market. To go on with our lives, we must quell these less-than-conscious fears, lest they overwhelm and paralyze us in the web of our existential anxiety.

We seek different ways to defend ourselves against these deeply troubling demons. Many of us determinedly drive them from consciousness through action. Others use meditation, positive thinking, or biofeedback. Some practice denial or develop rituals whose exacting performance magically promises to protect them from their existential uncertainty and anxiety.[31]

Still others turn to astrologers and fortune tellers to warn them about dangerous days and courses of action (as former first lady Nancy Reagan did in the wake of the assassination attempt on her husband). In these and countless other ways, we try to insulate ourselves from that terrifying, fundamental, and immutable aspect of our human condition: the knowledge that we do not control our daily existence.[32]

Perhaps the most common method for dealing with existential dread is to seek protectors outside ourselves.[33] That is where gods and heroes—and godlike, heroic leaders—enter the picture. Both divine and human guardians help us maintain the illusion that something or someone more powerful than ourselves knows what is happening and can shield us from the malevolent whims of fate.

Just as we pray to unseen gods to defend and guide our lives, so too we seek human leaders whom we endow with godlike qualities. Strong, authoritarian, controlling leaders evoke our admiration and loyalty because we believe we can count on them to protect us. Particularly in times of crisis, we seek powerful leaders who promise to take charge and set things right.

We trust our leaders to keep the world on an even keel, even if we ourselves cannot. We attribute events, both good and bad, to leaders' intervention or control. Mounting evidence suggests that even sophisticated observers tend to attribute positive organizational outcomes to leaders, rather than to other equally plausible factors.[34] The reassuring conviction that the leader is "on top of things" permits us to set aside our deep anxiety and go about our daily lives.

Therein lies the major attraction of leaders, despite their admitted drawbacks. When we anoint leaders, we generate the illusion that our destiny is in good hands. Becker provides some insight into the attraction and comfort of accepting someone else's leadership:

> What is more natural to banish one's fears than to live on delegated powers? And what does the whole growing-up period signify, if not the giving over of one's life-project? . . . man cuts out for himself a manageable world: he throws himself into action uncritically, unthinkingly. He accepts the cultural programming that turns his nose where he is supposed to look; . . . he learns not to expose himself, not to stand out; he learns to embed himself in other-power, both of concrete persons and of things and cultural commands; the result is that he comes to exist in the imagined infallibility of the world around him.[35]

A Devil's Bargain?

There is more to the story, however. The multiple institutions and interactions, rules and relationships that constitute our world create "truths" that give meaning and legitimacy to our desire to accept leaders.[36] The enormously complicated social context infuses those "truths" with a moral force that increases the likelihood of their acceptance as "natural." We learn to feel comfortable with the idea of leadership and look to leaders to reassure us that the world is not out of hand. Yet this devil's bargain we strike comes at a price. It leads to the profound ambivalence many of us feel about our leaders—and about leadership itself.

The Costs: The Double Price of Protection

The protection and sense of security that strong, mythical leaders provide carry a pair of hefty price tags.

First, the pact we make with such guardians, human or divine, demands our subservience. In return for the safekeeping leaders promise, we have to play by *their* rules. We agree to assume the role of follower with good grace. We recapitulate our roles as children, comforted by the reliability of strong parents, but chafing under the obedience that parental leaders demand.

The role of follower is further burdened with both frustration and boredom. In hierarchical groups, subordinates know their bosses expect them to follow orders unquestioningly. They commonly receive little information or explanation about the demands made upon them. Subordinates frequently see their suggestions rejected by leaders who have already worked out reasonably acceptable solutions. As a result, followers commonly lose interest and tune out. Their dissatisfaction shows itself in behavior that others diagnose as poor performance. Bosses interpret subordinates' boredom, apathy, and laziness as embedded personal characteristics, when in fact these qualities are actually generated by the subordinate role per se.[37]

There is a second bill we have to pay for the security that leaders provide. We agree to overlook all but the most egregious excesses that germinate in the fertile leadership medium of strength, egotism, and self-confidence. This second bargain with leaders who may step beyond the bounds of cultural norms is also uneasy.[38] As Adolph Hitler demonstrated, leaders that strong can easily stir up and sustain contradictory emotions, from awe and love to disgust and terror.

To convince ourselves that our leaders indeed have the magical qualities we so desperately need, we exaggerate their every word and action, until their feats loom as monumental. The leader's exploits grow with each retelling, finally blossoming into cultural myths. Some leaders assiduously cultivate their own legends (as did Alexander the Great, with his brother's help).[39] The Alexander myth grew with such intensity that less than a century after his death it was unclear to chroniclers of the time whether he had ever been a mortal.

Myths surrounding indomitable and indestructible leaders, past and present, buoy their supporters. Myths simultaneously comfort each group and intimidate potential foes. In preliterate societies, these myths play a central role in the group's rich, oral tradition.[40] In literate societies, history books codify these exaggerated tales of power and victory to indoctrinate both the young and other new members.

Heroic myths wrap leaders in a cocoon of their followers' faith that is destroyed only by the leader's misstep or failure. Although we record the ignominious acts of our enemies' leaders, we usually pass quite swiftly over our own heroes' faults—at least up to a point. Despite the many rumors that were swirling around John F.

Kennedy's personal life, the Camelot myth lulled the media into silence.

In the United States, it took two defining moments—Vietnam and Watergate—to goad investigative reporters into scrutinizing our political leaders. Richard Nixon, clearly far from the ideal of a beloved leader, nonetheless maintained a strong grip on the presidency until he overstepped that invisible line; only then did the Nixon presidency begin to disintegrate. Given the followers' needs, the bias toward maintaining the leader's preeminence is no accident.

The Benefits: An Algorithm for Success

As we have seen, reliance on leaders fulfills certain psychological needs and shields us from existential anxiety. Yet our deference to the power and superiority of the leader has some less obvious benefits as well. The demands of the leader usually create a framework that indicates how we must demonstrate our compliance. Meeting these requirements, be they the catechism of the Catholic Church or latrine duty at Gandhi's ashram, may be simultaneously painful and reassuring. The pain lies in our recognition that we are indeed the less powerful partner and therefore must subordinate our own will to the leader's. The reassurance stems from knowing that the leader has provided an algorithm, a "recipe," if not an iron-clad guarantee, for predictability and security.

The belief that following the leader will result in automatic success occasionally reveals itself as little more than magical thinking. Despite the most rigorous conformity to the leader's dictates, the results are not always what we expect. Unwilling to acknowledge that we set ourselves up by expecting too much—if not the impossible—from the leader, we commonly drive out that leader. Then we begin anew the search for a leader who can quiet our existential anxiety.

The Bargain from the Leader's Perspective

All the evidence suggests that, from the leader's perspective, the benefits usually outweigh the costs, despite the renowned "loneliness at the top." Most research on leadership indicates that the higher the individual's rank within an organization, the greater the individual's satisfaction.

In the early 1950s, research on networks at the Massachusetts Institute of Technology offered some clear insight into the differential satisfaction of leaders and followers.[41] Leaders sitting at the apex of an organizational network experienced far greater levels of satisfaction than did those at the bottom. This same research, substantiated by later studies, also suggested that the leadership position, itself, is more likely to make the incumbent look better than the people lower down on the totem pole. The very language of organizations—"subordinates" and "superiors"—conveys an inherent bias.

Yet leaders, no less than followers, need to protect themselves from recognizing their existential fears. Like their followers, leaders have several choices. First, they can entrust themselves to others (divine or human) whom they perceive as even stronger than they are. Second, like their followers, they can consign their fate to a powerful, controlling institution, like the government, the military, General Motors, or the church. Some depend on an ideology to guide their actions and promise results.

And of course leaders, like anyone else, can interpret their leadership position as evidence that they really *are* in control of their own destiny, as well as everyone else's. Leaders are in fact more likely than ordinary folks to fall through the looking glass of megalomania. They succumb to a belief in their own omnipotence. It is a curious, almost predictable process, since to persuade followers that they are truly worth supporting, leaders first must convince themselves.

The leader's belief in his or her own strengths thus can become a self-fulfilling process. This confidence in one's own powers is enhanced in turn by the response that leaders evoke from their followers, who want so much to believe in their leader's ability to protect them.

Yet leaders also feel the need to place their own faith in a benevolent power greater than themselves. How and whom or what they choose to calm their own existential anxiety—be it a divinity, metascience, ideology, religion, or cult—has important consequences for their constituents.

The Danger We Sense, the Ambivalence We Feel

At bottom, our relationship to leaders is profoundly ambivalent. True, powerful leadership lulls our existential anxiety, and we delight in the fantasy that we too might become larger-than-life figures. Yet we also sense the dangers such strong leaders pose. Intuitively, we know that an appetite for power, laced with enormous self-confidence (and eagerly reinforced by awestricken followers), can drift all too easily into corruption and tyranny. An arbitrary and unpredictable leader can intensify, not relieve, our existential anxiety. So to calm our own fear of the human leaders we have created, we paradoxically search out the flaws that make them seem more vulnerable . . . yes, more like us.

Oddly enough, knowing our leaders' faults reassures us in several ways. First, their imperfections ironically allow us to draw a little closer to our ego ideals, to feel that we too, despite our flaws, can aspire to such strength and leadership. Second, and perhaps more importantly, leaders' vulnerabilities offer us an important safety valve. We know these powerful, often arrogant, leaders can be brought down, if necessary. Although we expect our leaders to be strong enough to control our world, we still want to retain the power to topple them if they overstep their bounds.

So we search out their vulnerability, just in case. Henry Kissinger insists that no Soviet leader has escaped vilification, either during his lifetime or posthumously.[42] Removing their statues and rewriting history after their demise became familiar Soviet *rites de passage.*

After Mikhail Gorbachev's ouster as president of the former Soviet Union, Boris Yeltsin, his successor, arranged a series of indignities to strip the fallen leader of his status and prestige. In 1992 alone, Gorbachev was forced to turn in his passport, limit his foreign travel, repeatedly move both his residence and offices to increasingly smaller quarters, and give up his chauffeured limousine. Heaping insult on injury, the Yeltsin government later accused Gorbachev of aiding terrorists.[43]

Defrocking a predecessor, particularly one who is revered, helps the new leader diminish an otherwise overshadowing presence. And of course we can always count on a brash new candidate waiting in the wings to unseat the old leader through a coup d'état, or an election, depending on the time and place.

Increasingly, death offers meager protection. Eager (sometimes mercenary) biographers craft scholarly and not-so-scholarly tomes that exhume the leader's human foibles. Dissecting their romantic peccadilloes or secret eccentricities reduces our heroes and heroines to our own dimensions—all in the name of truth and history. Recent biographies of Franklin and Eleanor Roosevelt,[44] Jack and Jackie Kennedy,[45] and Martin Luther King, Jr.,[46] are studded with innuendo, as well as historical facts.

Our yearning for powerful human leaders, seasoned with our fear of their excesses, stirs within us an abiding ambivalence. We express this ambivalence in myriad ways. A president falls before an assassin's bullet, and citizens who voted against him weep disconsolately. We drive a mendacious president from office. Yet when he resigns, the nation suffers despair and anomie, and in some quarters he remains a political guru. His death becomes an elegiac event.

Most often, the yang is stronger than the yin. Our fear of life's uncertainties overwhelms our fear of the leader's power turned against us. We go right on being drawn to leaders whose strength and self-confidence provide a measure of reassurance against the dreaded inevitabilities that are inherent in the human condition. At the same time, we secretly pray these leaders will never direct their immense powers against us. And just in case they do, we keep a chain of their vulnerability looped around the leadership pedestal, ready to yank them down at a moment's notice.

Leaders appear and recede, rise and fall. At different moments, we are enthralled or intimidated by, even contemptuous of, particular leaders, but we remain hooked on the idea of leadership. Moreover, we do not fathom why we have all these feelings about them. We tend to focus much of our attention on leaders, but we must also explore our stake as followers in the leadership dynamic.

Nonetheless, our ambivalent need for leaders endures, embedded in our psychology and in the inescapable uncertainty and anxiety of human life. Much of the hold that Stage 2 leadership has on us, particularly its authoritarianism, can be explained by these deep-rooted aspects of the human condition and our tendency to entrust our destiny to protector figures, whom we make larger than life. Yet as the forces of diversity and interdependence transform the world, Stage 2 leaders can no longer satisfy our leadership needs. We must learn to relinquish our reliance on them, while we encourage and support the emergence of connective leaders. Chapter Twelve considers how connective leadership responds to these psychological and existential conditions of human life. But first, in Chapter Three we turn to our peculiarly American vision of leadership to gain a deeper grasp of the challenges we face as we enter a Stage 3 world.

Chapter Three

American Leadership

Understanding Our National Addiction to Individualism, Cooperation, and Authoritarianism

> *There are many ways in which the United States has changed only slightly in over 150 years, and one of the stable elements is the continued pursuit of individualism by virtually all sectors of the population.*
> HERBERT J. GANS[1]

American culture reveres leaders with a penchant for individualism, particularly when it's laced with cooperation and discreet authoritarianism. In contrast to the overt authoritarianism of old Europe, our special brand demands a democratic context. Other societies, particularly in Asia and Latin America, gravitate toward leaders who prefer to work through family, friendships, and favors. Yet if the psychological and existential foundations of leadership that we explored in Chapter Two are really valid, shouldn't people in *all* cultures seek the same kinds of leaders?

The answer, as you may suspect, is "yes and no." True, the underlying psychological and existential foundations for the acceptance of leaders exist in all societies. But each culture evolves within its own unique historical, social, political, and geographical conditions. Those special circumstances can either exaggerate or minimize the centrality of different leadership styles. Within each culture, succeeding generations then learn, usually imperfectly, from parents, teachers, media, and individual experience, both to admire and acquire the particular leadership characteristics their society values.

In this chapter, we look backward at the development of our own national psyche. Unless we understand the roots of our addiction to the curious American ménage à trois of individualism, cooperation, and authoritarianism, it is unlikely that we shall ever escape its stranglehold sufficiently to embrace connective leadership.

The Three Roots of the American Leadership Model

American culture perpetuates an uneasy balance among individualism, cooperation, and authoritarianism. From early childhood, we receive very complex messages about this trio of values. Our parents teach us to respect their authority; that's what "being good" is all about. By kindergarten, the message begins to be somewhat more garbled. "Being good" still means obeying authority, only this time it's the teacher's directions.

Curiously enough, being good is often called "being cooperative." Yet, as we progress through school, we discover that our individual performance is what really matters. We are told to be ourselves, to follow our internal lights, to be strong and self-reliant. Moreover, we are evaluated largely for our individual accomplishments . . . tempered of course by obedience and authority.

Yet, democratic values of cooperation do enter in as well. Our teachers urge us to cooperate, to be team players—except on exams. Mary Jane's grades and her test scores reflect her individual performance, not her group's success. Mary Jane soon discerns that cooperation within the group is a desirable "social skill"—but clearly a secondary one. There are limits to the value of cooperation, even if they are exceedingly murky, just as there are limits to individualism when it runs up against authority.

The calibration of individualism versus teamwork, authoritarianism versus participation, competition versus cooperation, leadership versus constituency is very demanding. Is it any wonder that we often give up on this enormous task and come to adulthood still struggling with these issues, still unclear about where to draw the logical and ethical lines? Is it any wonder that we pass on our confusion to our children? The tangled roots of our conflicting attitudes toward leadership can be traced to the formative experiences of American culture in the eighteenth and nineteenth centuries.

Taming the Frontier: Heroic Individualism

Individualism ticks at the heart of the American model of leadership. Early American heroes—George Washington and Thomas Jefferson, Davy Crockett and Daniel Boone—inspired future generations with their intrepid exploits. In the arduous period of industrial growth, only the most independent and competitive sons of immigrants, notably Henry Ford, Andrew Carnegie, Cornelius Vanderbilt, John D. Rockefeller, Andrew Mellon, J. P. Morgan, Thomas Alva Edison, and Alexander Graham Bell, could aspire to stamp their visions on a nation.

Self-reliant, take-charge, competitive leadership styles are deeply embedded in our cultural myths of rugged individuals who overcame poverty and other hardships through sheer grit and ingenuity. Like so many aspects of American life, these myths were profoundly influenced by the frontier experience.

Individualism and the Frontier Experience

In American culture, the early frontier experience provided the first condition for the cultivation of individualistic leaders. Initially isolated both geographically and socially by the frontier, our heroes relied upon their own special talents—ingenuity, self-reliance, and a take-charge attitude—to confront a vast, often formidable, terrain. They shaped their strategies to fit the inimical territory, resolutely seeking the splendor and enduring the anguish of frontier isolation. The rugged individualist, jutting his craggy chin into a hostile wind, became the ultimate symbol of American leadership—a symbol more recognizable than and more personally identified with the bald eagle.

American heroes and leaders set visionary goals and measured their attainments against rigorous standards of excellence. They demanded exacting performance and counted only on themselves to deliver it. Taking control, competing against all contenders, overcoming enormous hardships, and winning against monumental odds, demanding the most of themselves: these are the traditional hallmarks of self-reliant American leaders.

Because the strategies they chose suited their situations, many of these hardy individualists succeeded. Even when they failed, they went down to *glorious* defeat. The cry "Remember the Alamo" is a hymn to individualism, for the heroes it celebrates were brave but solitary men. Thus germinated the seeds that later generations of Americans would nurture into full-grown leadership myths.

The frontier experience profoundly predisposed Americans to a leadership model with a core of individualistic, power-oriented, competitive styles. That basic model survives to this day, even though the conditions that prompted it have long since faded away. As we enter Stage 3, many of our industrial leaders are still stamped from this mold. From the beginning of the twentieth century, corporate America has formed its own Hall of Leadership Fame: Ford Motor Company's Henry Ford, ITT's Harold Geneen, General Motors' Alfred P. Sloan, Polaroid's Edwin H. Land, IBM's Thomas A. Watson, CBS's William S. Paley, Chrysler's Lee Iacocca, *Forbes's* Malcolm Forbes, GE's Jack Welch, EDS's and later Perot Systems' H. Ross Perot,[2] Metromedia's John Kluge, Disney's Michael Eisner, Microsoft's Bill Gates, and Intel's Andy Grove. Every one of these corporate titans projects independence, self-reliance, power, and competitiveness, even to the point of eccentricity. We admire them nonetheless. Many Americans still feel most comfortable with take-charge leaders, counting on them to come to the rescue when the going gets rough.

The American Farmer: Inventor and Entrepreneur by Necessity

The classic American farmer and his oft-ignored wife distilled the frontier mentality into independent individualism. These farm families pitted themselves against nature, clearing the land, tilling the soil, raising poultry and cattle, even making their own home-spun clothes. Resolute individualists, they faced their tasks head on, neither expecting nor welcoming help from anyone but a few close kin.

American farm families knew what had to be done and did it, simply and directly. They lived independently according to their own standards of excellence and focused solidly on their self-defined tasks.[3] The exception to this individualistic isolation, of course, was the sporadic group response to crisis, as in a communal barn raising after a fire.

Farmers also developed and played several archetypically American roles which have influenced our view of leadership. Responding to necessity, they became innovators and inventors, fashioning tools and methods to help them subdue the land. Initially fostered by the isolation of the frontier, independent creativity remains an indelible birthmark of American industry. This heritage often manifests itself in a bedrock belief in ingenuity as an individual talent, rather than a group outcome. The result: we tend to mythologize creative geniuses as brilliant loners, marching to their own internal drum beat.

The farmer and his wife performed still another archetypal role, that of the autonomous entrepreneur. This early role had a special twist: these entrepreneurs both produced and consumed their own products in a way of life that ensured the farm family's independence and self-sufficiency.[4]

In time, the farming culture generated small shopkeepers and artisans, a slightly different and more familiar version of the entrepreneur. In addition, farm families, who originally raised crops and domestic animals for their own personal needs, eventually brought their surplus to market. It was then that entrepreneurs, who created a product to sell to others, began to emerge.

As the European Industrial Revolution spread to American shores, it opened new urban opportunities for the farmer's independent children (particularly for second- and later-born sons, whom primogeniture barred from inheriting the family farm). The bustling urbanization of America was beginning. In this hectic environment, independence, determination, and a competitive spirit would be the sine qua non for all who hoped to succeed.

The early American frontier has given way to urban skyscrapers, freeways, and suburbs. Yet rugged individualism remains our touchstone of creativity, self-reliance, and determination. We continue to bank on the innovative entrepreneur for economic renewal. We disdain large bureaucracies and conformist bureaucrats. Faced with tasks that tap our deepest reservoirs of creativity and resolve, even now we psych ourselves for such challenges by evoking frontier imagery. We seek to tap our earlier creativity as we attempt to conquer "new frontiers" in space, medicine, biology, and technology.

Individualism Tempered by Cooperation: The Democratic Tradition

The American democratic political system created the second condition for our unique leadership model. Individualism, entwined with meritocracy, infuses democracy. The value of individual merit and effort is well suited to the democratic tradition of individual rights and property. It fits hand in glove with our belief in the individual's significance and sovereignty.

Our political forefathers wrote not one but three unique documents to safeguard the individual: the Declaration of Independence, the Constitution, and the Bill of Rights.[5] Democracy acknowledges the importance of the individual, symbolized by each person's right to vote and the underlying belief that each individual's vote counts as much as any other's.

At the same time, the founders enshrined the principle that the majority rules. So it is not surprising that our cultural heroes tip their hats to the group even as they strive to fulfill their individualistic dreams.

The Declaration of Independence bears witness to the tensions between individualism and cooperation that continue, even today, to bedevil the American psyche. Its familiar opening paragraphs insist upon individuals' equality and their "unalienable rights," including "life, liberty, and the pursuit of happiness." Yet in a commonly overlooked pledge, the signers of the Declaration of Independence sought to uphold individual rights through their own cooperation and communal action:

> And for the support of this Declaration . . . we mutually pledge to each other our lives, our fortunes, and our sacred honor.

In this way, the Declaration of Independence directly links individualism and cooperation. Still, the accent is on the individual. Cooperation and teamwork provide the instruments for ensuring individualism.

Our political tradition also contains an antidote to hyperindividualism in its commitment to the democracy of the group or the team. A nation of rugged individualists, we have learned to bow, if only perfunctorily, before the icons of cooperation and collaboration. Yet we rarely glorify those who succeed with the help of others. We admire—but seldom fully comprehend—the pioneering efforts of those, like Martin Luther King, Jr., who try to bring others into the leadership circle.

Leaders who enjoy working with and through others puzzle us. We question whether people who achieve by contributing to another's task, or simply by encouraging others whom they love or admire, could really do it themselves. We publicly congratulate their altruistic contributions, but we privately suspect that these supportive players behave that way more out of weakness than will. Women who contribute to the group, routinely sacrificing themselves for children, spouses, bosses, and co-workers, are admired but only infrequently offered high leadership positions. We regard men who behave this way as too "womanly" or too lacking in their own creative vision to warrant serious leadership roles.

Individualism, we believe, requires stubbornly pursuing our own vision. Those who, like President Bill Clinton, broaden their ideas through consulting with many stakeholders, as well as through negotiating with the opposition, are denigrated by Stage 2 critics as untrustworthy and spineless. We can't imagine how leaders can integrate their own vision with others' dreams, without losing their purpose and integrity.

Until recently, we placed negotiators somewhere between snake-oil hucksters and sellouts, individuals willing to compromise their ideals for pragmatic agreement and action. We strongly suspect that those with the genius or guts to achieve goals single-handedly would prefer that glorious way of doing things. We assume they would choose it over connective leadership, which marries individualistic vision, competition, and power to group-oriented behaviors: contributing, collaborating, networking, negotiating, expecting, entrusting, and mentoring.

Immigration and Industrialization: Enter Authoritarianism

The frontier, as we have seen, ignited our infatuation with individualism. Democracy wedded individualism to a respect for the group and cooperative action. Eventually, the immigrant experience and nineteenth-century industrialization complicated matters by introducing authoritarianism.

Seeking escape from the brutality of the Industrial Revolution and the declining fortunes of agrarianism, waves of hopeful men and women eagerly pursued a better life in the proverbial "land of opportunity." Arrivals from Europe, and later Asia, brought with them their own traditions of independence and entrepreneurship that helped them adapt to the American context. Only those endowed with sufficient self-reliance and stamina were likely to venture into this strange new world and prosper in it.

Later immigrants needed similar qualities to help them compete for jobs against the earlier arrivals, who had by then learned the ropes and could speak the language more fluently. Determination and competitiveness were essential if the newcomers were to overcome the towering obstacles, including language barriers, prejudice, and the resentment of ensconced immigrants, that they encountered in their adopted land. Once again, tough, self-reliant newcomers held an edge.

The American Factory Scene

This immigrant version of rugged individualism ran smack into the developing authoritarianism of the Industrial Revolution. In the early days of industrialization, American factory owners, like their European counterparts, ruled their organizations as fiefdoms.[6] On the factory floor, the foreman held undisputed authority. By the turn of the century, foremen had become expert in using the "'driving method,' an approach to supervision that combined authoritarian combativeness with physical intimidation in order to extract the maximum effort from the worker."[7]

There was nothing covert about the American industrialists' use of authoritarianism. Nor were these bosses any more benevolent than those in Europe. Obsessed with productivity, and morally supported by the Protestant work ethic, bosses decreed hard labor and long work shifts. They showed little concern about the hazards and discomfort their workers endured. For their part, many workers often didn't show up at all. When they did, workers commonly engaged in deliberate slowdown tactics to protect themselves against the exhausting physical conditions that were shortening their lives. Industrial turnover rates were high, sometimes 100 percent per year.[8]

The dynamics of the boss-worker relationship produced an ever-downward spiral. Intent upon curbing what they interpreted as lazy self-indulgences of the workforce, employers devised all sorts of techniques for controlling and squeezing greater productivity from their employees. Authoritarian bosses imposed fines and fired workers for even trivial transgressions, like talking to co-workers or leaving their work stations.[9]

The introduction of steam engines and other costly machines only increased the employers' readiness to fine or dismiss workers who did not exert enough effort to make the industrialists' investments pay off. Still, machines did not eliminate altogether the need for hand work or universally reduce the physical efforts required by the workers.[10] What they did do was introduce a different pace of work, one driven by the automated quality of the equipment rather than by the physical and social responses of the workers.

These new machines also gave rise to new work roles, like the puddler,[11] requiring even more brutal physical labor.[12] In retaliation, workers developed elaborate ruses for slowing production and alleviating their physical hardships, including hiding tools they had invented to ease their work.

Women and Children Taste Authority at Work

Early Stage 2 authoritarianism also affected women and children in the workforce. Although many accounts of American labor history pay them scant attention, substantial numbers of children and young women worked in factories and mills under similarly difficult circumstances. Even before the Industrial Revolution, children had worked in the domestic economic unit of the farm family. For many textile manufacturers who used the "Rhode Island system," based on the English industrial practice of employing the whole family, it was simply a matter of moving children, along with their parents, into factory life.[13]

In the 1830s, New England textile mills recruited female workers, many no more than fifteen years old. In fact, 40 percent of the female workers in Rhode Island had not yet reached their twelfth birthdays.[14] Francis Cabot Lowell, a textile mill owner in Waltham, Massachusetts, established strictly supervised company boarding houses as inducements for Yankee farm families to send their daughters to work as factory hands. The "Waltham plan," as Lowell's practice was known, rarely succeeded in retaining these young women more than a year; however, employers easily replaced them with females from the new waves of immigrants eager for work.[15]

In Lowell, Massachusetts, too, female factory hands labored under extremely autocratic bosses. Eventually, they found themselves swept up in the political protest against exploitative mill owners. As one sociologist has written:

> They were in the eye of an industrial storm. They were not protected from the conflicts of early industrialization. In time the owners no longer had to win the approval of the agricultural community; they could lower wages—and did; they could increase productivity by requiring longer hours—and did; they could worsen working conditions—and did. Many of the original "Lowell girls" participated in "turnouts" or strikes in 1834 and 1836. But there were other young women living at home, not subject to the influence of the boarding-house solidarity, able and willing to take the places of the original "Lowell girls," and they did.[16]

The authoritarian factory conditions that working-class females endured were only slightly more onerous than those their middle-class sisters faced in company offices. Immigrant daughters, unaccustomed to the mores of their adopted land, were among the most hard-pressed of American workers.

Despite oppressive conditions, young women continued to enter the American workforce in large numbers. In fact, at the turn of the century, one-third of all females ages sixteen to twenty were in the paid labor market.[17] By 1920, 24 percent of females over age sixteen were in the paid labor force. Most were presumably working only until marriage "released" them from the heavy discipline of autocratic bosses.[18]

The Workers Rebel

By the middle of the nineteenth century and on into the early decades of the twentieth century, iron-fisted American entrepreneurs, infected by the virus of authoritarianism, held sway. Themselves the sons of immigrants, these tough, autocratic industrialists exploited wave after wave of immigrant workers. Meager education, limited English skills, and economic desperation rendered the new arrivals intensely vulnerable.

From the outset, brutalization of these newcomers also sowed the seeds of their resistance. Open authoritarianism drove workers to develop informal strategies for offsetting their oppressors. Slowdowns, sabotaged machinery, and intimidation of naive rate busters were simply the most obvious informal methods that workers devised for limiting their output and protecting themselves against exploitation on the factory floor.[19]

Trade unions struggled to control workers' hours and wages, as well as to protect their jobs.[20] They translated the workers' informal strategies for self-protection into the language of union contracts.[21] Ironically, the trade unions' efforts to protect workers in various jobs required viewing different kinds of workers not as individuals with unique talents and needs, but as faceless workers. Workers were lumped together first by the American Federation of Labor (AF of L) into job categories and later by the Congress of Industrial Organizations (CIO) into industry-based groups.

Union clout with employers depended upon a large disciplined membership, which union bosses could control. Under Samuel Gompers, the AF of L bargained with employers not on the basis of craft workers' productivity, but of union power.[22] Workers soon realized that the unions too imposed their own brand of authoritarianism on rank and file members.

Early Twentieth-Century Authoritarianism: Scientific Management and the Assembly Line

By the turn of the twentieth century, the three roots of American leadership—individualism, authoritarianism, and cooperation— were firmly embedded in the nation's culture. Despite apparent changes in ideas about management, it was authoritarianism, coupled with the old ideal of top-down, individualistic leadership, that continued to hold sway in the United States, particularly in business and industry. Its effects in economic terms were salutary: "By the turn of the [twentieth] century the United States had pushed past all other nations in industrial production. By 1910 it had outstripped its nearest rival, Germany, by nearly two to one."[23]

The authoritarianism of American industry in the first half of the twentieth century was perhaps best exemplified by two major figures: Frederick Winslow Taylor, a mechanical engineer, and

Henry Ford, the entrepreneurial car maker. Volumes have been devoted to the contributions of both men.[24] Here we recount only a few relevant highlights of their impact, which not only transformed the face of American industrial production but also intensified authoritarianism in the workplace.

Frederick Winslow Taylor

Taylor is best known as the developer of "scientific management," based on a method he called "time study," for "rationalizing" and streamlining every aspect of work.[25] Taylor's was a simple technology, drawn from detailed observations of steel workers, particularly pig-iron handlers, first at Midvale Steel in Philadelphia and later at the Bethlehem Steel Company in Lehigh, Pennsylvania.

Infused by his Quaker-Puritan upbringing with a zeal for efficiency and an abhorrence of waste, Taylor wanted to find the "one best way" that a "first class man" (one who was both able and willing to work) could perform his assigned tasks.[26] In Taylor's view, to determine the one best way—both for the worker and the company—to do any job required decomposing each task into a carefully timed set of exact movements for the worker to follow precisely.[27] With no time or motion wasted, a laborer would work faster and better, avoid fatigue, and receive a higher wage rate to boot.

Taylor contended that everyone would benefit from this highly rational system: the employer from increased profits, the worker from less tiring work and more pay, the consumer from lower prices, and the rapidly developing nation from increased efficient productivity. Taylor's differential piece-rate system allowed employers and workers to share the rewards of boosted production. This mutual benefit, Taylor optimistically argued, would surely lead to a partnership between employer and worker.[28]

Taylor was enthralled by this system not only because it was rational and efficient, but also because it was fair. Faster workers would receive more pay than lazier ones; workers whose physical or mental limitations made them unfit for such difficult, but higher-paying, tasks would be given suitable jobs that matched their abilities. In this rational and just system, they, too, could perform as "first class men."

Ironically, Taylor's standardization of work enabled a very diverse workforce of immigrants to work together effectively, despite limited education and no common language. Taylor's method fit with the prevailing approach to cultural diversity: Americanization through homogenization of Scots, Germans, Hungarians, Irish, and many others seeking new lives in their adopted land.[29]

Taylor's obsession with efficiency blinded him to the dehumanizing results that could flow from authoritarianism, now legitimated by scientific management. Nor did the zealous industrial engineer foresee the firestorm of protest that his work, often misinterpreted, would ignite among workers, unionists, and outraged social reformers.[30]

Taylor coolly (and, of course, rationally) defended his work with pig-iron handlers at Bethlehem Steel:

> First: . . . the pig-iron handler is not an extraordinary man difficult to find; he is merely a man more or less of the type of the ox, heavy both mentally and physically. Second: the work which this man does tires him no more than any healthy normal laborer is tired by a proper day's work. (If this man is overtired by his work, then the task has been wrongly set, and this is as far as possible from the object of Scientific Management.) . . . [E]xperiments . . . [and] . . . observation . . . [have] demonstrated the fact that when workmen of the caliber of the pig-iron handler are given a carefully measured task, which calls for a big day's work on their part, and that when in return for this extra effort they are paid wages up to 60 per cent beyond the wages usually paid, that this increase in wages tends to make them not only more thrifty but better men in every way; that they live rather better, begin to save money, become more sober, and work more steadily. When . . . they receive much more, . . . many . . . will work irregularly and tend to become more or less shiftless, extravagant and dissipated. . . . [F]or their own best interest it does not do for most men to get rich too fast.[31]

Nor did Taylor recognize other dangers that lurked within his systematic approach to work. At the same time that workers became the mechanism for unprecedented productivity, they also became easily interchangeable with other workers. Seen simply as "factors of production," employees were *not* expected to have opinions about how to do things, much less how to do things better.

Nor could these human "factors of production" be expected to have legitimate needs. Instead, many employers insisted that their demands for unquestioning obedience actually benefited, rather than brutalized, these "undisciplined" and faceless laborers.

Widespread criticism of Taylor's methods, union agitation, and a strike by workers at the Watertown, Massachusetts, Army arsenal, where Taylorism had been initiated, sparked a congressional inquiry in October 1911. After five months of acrimonious and widely publicized hearings, the congressional committee determined that no mistreatment of workers had been demonstrated. The committee made no recommendations for remedial legislation.

Nonetheless, pro-union congressmen introduced riders on Navy, Army, and Post Office appropriations bills that prevented the use of these federal operating funds on any site where "Taylorism" was practiced.[32] Such legislation nipped in the bud all efforts to introduce the efficiency of scientific management to government. Still, the obvious increase in productivity and the low cost of implementing the basic ideas of scientific management made them attractive to private employers for decades to come.

Henry Ford

Henry Ford became the best-known apostle of scientific management, carrying it one step further with the highly efficient mass production assembly line.[33] In 1908, spurred by enormous demand for his Model T automobile, the millionaire entrepreneur promised Walter Flanders, an industrial efficiency expert, a twenty-thousand dollar bonus if Flanders could make his plant produce ten thousand cars that year. Flanders reorganized the Ford plant along Tayloristic lines and won the bonus with two days to spare.

Ford eventually became more intrigued by the process than the product. Using new automatic and semiautomatic machines, Ford refined Taylor's methods and ingeniously wed them to the assembly line. The result was nothing short of revolutionary. Before the assembly line, it had taken a worker 728 hours to assemble a car. With the material conveyor belt, the traveling platform, and overhead rails, Ford reduced the time to a breathtaking 93 minutes.

When employees failed to apply themselves in this highly mechanized environment, the Ford Motor Company hired strong-armed guards to enforce company orders. At Ford, "If a worker seemed to be loitering, a foreman simply knocked him down. The rules against talking to each other on the job were strict. Making a worker insecure was of the essence. 'A great business is really too big to be human,' Ford himself once told the historian Allan Nevins."[34]

As employers substituted machines (or capital) for labor, they gained even greater control over the labor process.[35] With reduced call for their craftsmanship, workers found that opportunities to learn new skills dwindled, along with leverage for pressing their demands. As the development of skill became less critical to production jobs, possibilities for advancement to supervisory roles through these positions decreased.

The breakwater of worker's skill and knowledge gave way before the tidal wave of management's autocratic expectations. Ford once allegedly boasted to a reporter that he could guarantee any number of employees would show up at the plant's front gate at 4:00 A.M. simply by issuing the order. Besides, those were the kind of workers he wanted.[36] The gap between labor and management was growing ever wider.

The Rise of Bureaucratic Authority

In the first decades of the twentieth century, management's bare-knuckles authoritarianism was quite unambiguous vis-à-vis both blue- and white-collar workers. Authoritarianism achieved its clarity through hierarchical organizational structures with clearly defined levels of authority linked to specific tasks. Bureaucracy was the perfect organizational form for implementing authoritarian management.

Industrial authoritarianism drew legitimacy from a curious source: a growing interest in authority and organizations among academicians. German sociologist Max Weber's 1925 treatise on the "three pure types of legitimate domination" inadvertently provided major support for the legal authority that bureaucracies claimed.[37] Weber viewed the traditional rule of kings and the charismatic authority of heroic, revolutionary leaders as capricious, irrational, and unjust. He viewed the legal authority accorded to bureaucrats as both even-handed and grounded in rationality: "[Bureaucratic authority] rest[s] on a belief in the legality of enacted rules and the right of those elevated to authority under such rules to issue commands (legal authority). . . . [O]bedience is owed to . . . the persons exercising the authority of office . . . [but] only within the scope of authority of the office.[38]

Reassured by his faith in this impersonal and limited nature of bureaucratic authority, Weber drew a picture of bureaucracy as the ideal organizational structure for accomplishing complex rational tasks. Unlike the pervasive demands of traditional and charismatic forms of authority, bureaucratic order protected workers' independence beyond the factory gate.

Weber tied these more rational and limited conditions for obedience to an expectation that workers were indeed willing and able to perform their bureaucratic roles. Weber also wrote prolifically about workers' independence. Ironically, however, it was his work on bureaucratic authority that organizational scholars used to defend the legitimacy of unquestioning obedience by employees.

Weber depicted the most efficient (that is, bureaucratic) organizational structure for performing complex tasks as a multilevel hierarchy composed of nested "reporting levels" (which industry labeled "divisions" and "departments"). Translated into the industrial context, "superiors" (persons entitled to exercise authority) gave orders to and expected obedience from "subordinates" (people under their direction). The very vocabulary of management bespoke authoritarianism, control, and inequality.

Eventually, the self-defeating effects of naked authoritarianism became evident in sagging morale, skyrocketing turnover, worker sabotage, costly strikes, and low-quality products. Added to this, the increasing magnitude of industrial projects, the specialized skills required for such complex tasks, and the introduction of the assembly line together generated a pragmatic cooperation or teamwork, at least among workers if not between workers and managers.

The reign of such traditional, blatant authoritarianism embedded in bureaucratic structures eventually responded to mounting attacks by workers and managers alike. Not only did worker slowdowns frustrate the time and motion engineers; they generated massive managerial frustration.

The more enlightened managers recognized that treating workers as mechanical cogs in the industrial wheel only provoked hostility and reduced productivity. They understood that Taylorism and

authoritarian management inadvertently gave new impetus to the
modern American labor movement's efforts to preserve workers'
power. Not too surprisingly, these managers were in the minority.

Emerging Quandaries: Individualism
Meets Participative Management

Managers' voices were not the only new ones heard. Even as authoritarian, bureaucratized, and Taylorized organizations flour-
ished, the tensions they generated were precipitating a search for
new solutions. Earlier, in the 1920s, the Frenchman Henri Fayol
and the American Mary Parker Follet were proposing quite different, more humanistic views of the appropriate nature of work.[39]
Gradually through the 1930s, more voices agreed, and additional
evidence accumulated. The whole discourse eventually became
defined enough to merit a label: the human relations movement.

Post-Taylorism: The Human Relations Movement

The human relations movement, offering a people-oriented perspective, was probably articulated earliest and best by Prof. Elton Mayo of
the Harvard Graduate School of Business.[40] Interest in the human relations approach swelled when Fritz J. Roethlisberger (Mayo's young
colleague) and W. J. Dickson published *Management and the Worker,*
documenting years of experiments at the Western Electric Hawthorne
Works.[41] The seminal Western Electric studies generated debate and
research for several decades, well into the postwar period of the 1950s.

Two central notions, simple and clear, provided the framework
for the human relations movement: the importance of small groups
and worker participation. First, researchers noted, groups emerged
naturally in all work situations. It soon became apparent that the
small group—not just managerial authority—was an important
source of workers' commitment and discipline. Group members
kept one another in line—a "new" method for generating "cooperation." While the human relations movement of the fifties and sixties was less concerned with the individual per se than with the
small group, individualism nonetheless sat quietly in the back row.

The second crucial idea of the human relations movement
involved worker participation. The doctrine was simple (and
largely correct): when people participate in the decision making

process, they tend to become more committed to the decision and therefore more likely willing to implement it.

Initially, a few innovative managers applied these two concepts to blue-collar production workers.[42] After World War II, senior managers carried the concept up to the swelling ranks of middle managers. Traditional authoritarianism turned out to be even less effective with middle managers, whose tasks were more mental than physical. "Participative management" provided a way out. Gradually the practice of participative management moved upwards to mid-level management, leaving blue-collar workers largely at the mercy of Taylorists.

Ever since its inception, participative management has waxed and waned. Sometimes encoded as "teamwork" or "cooperation" and more recently as "empowerment," this "people view" has joined authoritarianism and individualism in an uneasy troika.

Self-Actualizers Versus the Organization Man

In the early 1940s, psychologist Abraham Maslow had outlined his now famous five-level hierarchy of human needs, starting with basic physical needs and culminating in needs for "self-actualization."[43] After reaching some level of satisfaction of the most physical needs, as well as those for safety, love, and esteem, Maslow's "self-actualizer" searched for personal growth and self-fulfillment. For Maslow, "what a man can be he must be." The model of the self-actualizer became a sentimental favorite for generations of managers. Not surprisingly, the notion of self-actualization connected readily to the ideas of participative management. Participation, it was argued, provided people with a mechanism for moving up the hierarchy of needs toward self-actualization.

In the ferment of the 1950s, however, when many conflicting ideas about work were being hotly debated, the "man in the gray flannel suit" and "the organization man"[44] encountered growing criticism and disdain. These "modern" middle managers, presumably working in newly "participative" environments, began to be seen as rather sad and unfulfilled figures, marching in conformist ranks to the company tune, obeying the company dress code, and minding their company manners. Camouflaged as teamwork, this version of participation looked more like authoritarianism run amok, transforming its victims, many thought, into new-style organizational robots.

Enter the Computer

In the same decade that the human relations movement with its ideas about participation moved to center stage, information technology also introduced an entirely different set of new ideas. It was in those same years, the 1950s, that the computer entered the workplace, promising enormous increases in productivity and, perhaps more importantly, also offering much tighter methods of control over workers. For hourly workers, the fledgling information technology superseded Taylor's stopwatch, threatening not only narrower tasks but also, under the label *automation,* wholesale replacement of human workers. Most unions understandably initially resisted this new force, fearing further "dehumanization" of their members.

The advent of information technology in the 1950s complicated managerial life even as it simplified it. Not only were information technology and participation odd bedfellows; so were computers and the long-standing concept of decentralization. It was back in the 1920s that General Motors' Alfred P. Sloan, Jr., had introduced the idea of decentralization, giving local managers great control over their own units.[45] But with the advent of the computer, some could argue that decentralization was now over the hill, that we had only decentralized large organizations because we did not have the wherewithal to centralize them. The computer offered headquarters just the control mechanisms it needed and much better methods for tracking—in real time—the operations of even small and distant units. Later generations of computers would add unimaginable power to this thrust. A new form of top-down control began to emerge. In the United States, participative ideas receded somewhat. Authoritarianism took a deep, invigorated breath. But these tightening controls over workers only pushed the pendulum into another swing.

The Revolt Against Hierarchy: Civil Rights, the Vietnam War, the Women's Movement, and the Student Revolution

The turbulent 1960s brought a full-blown reaction against establishment control, establishment values, and establishment institutions. The man in the gray flannel suit was out; long-haired anti–Vietnam War protesters were in. The tsunami of the civil rights movement and an unpopular war seriously undermined American assumptions about equality and justice. Many members of the sixties generation confronted the crucible of young adulthood by "turning on and tuning out," vowing to "do their own thing," to respect each other's individuality, and to work together in nonhierarchical, "nonelitist" organizations.[46]

Feminist theorists in particular dissected the flaws of patriarchy, most clearly expressed in hierarchical organizations with their implied inequalities among people at different levels. In the 1960s and 1970s, the women's movement argued for flatter groups, where consensus among equals would replace commands from higher-ups.[47]

Unfortunately, this revolt against hierarchy had little structural impact on traditional corporate and government hierarchies. Its failure to change mainstream bureaucracies stemmed largely from the radicals' refusal to enter traditional institutions, which they diagnosed as hopelessly "elitist" and "patriarchal." Instead, the rebels of the sixties created their own "consensus" organizations, rejecting corporate and governmental conformity in favor of autonomy and nonconformity.

In a sense, the sixties counterculture represented a temporary triumph for the democratic root of American leadership. In that heady era, "leadership" became the forbidden *L*-word. Many groups deliberately prohibited official leaders; others featured rotating leadership. Paradoxically, the revolt against hierarchy and elite leadership structures led to what one political scientist labeled the "tyranny of structurelessness."[48]

Ultimately, the structurelessness that enthralled the generation of the sixties would prove to be a fatal organizational weakness. Eventually, the structural vacuum simply bred exasperation, without building new and enduring organizations or spawning the next generation of leaders. Indeed, many of these formless groups fragmented beyond repair.

In the late 1960s, the worldwide student revolution demanded greater participation in academic decision making. While mainstream societies despaired at the destruction and chaos fostered by spectacular student uprisings, they also learned a powerful lesson: participation in organizational decisions (cooperation's kin), whether in universities or businesses, was probably now necessary, in form if not in substance.

The first cadre of student revolutionaries finally graduated. Lacking a second generation of leaders to institutionalize its gains, the student revolt settled back into conformity engendered by a constricting job market. Still, the wake-up call for participation had spread beyond the university to the boardrooms of world industry and many governments, and it would not go away.

The Schizophrenia of Participative Management

For decades, management experts had been urging greater participation and communication, particularly among white-collar staff. Sensing there really was something to this call for more cooperation, more participation, and more communication (aside from sugarcoating compliance), a new generation of management gurus set to work. They troweled the mortar of organizational teamwork over the old, flawed, authoritarian foundation. On the organizational front line, however, the lesson took only superficially, sometimes resulting in a dangerous case of organizational schizophrenia.

Psychiatrists often identify mixed messages as a key ingredient in the recipe for schizophrenia. In the organizational setting, the dissonance between ideology and experience communicated just such mixed messages. While middle-level managers were being fed an intellectual diet of participative management, their on-the-job experience still tasted suspiciously like authoritarianism.

Seriously believing (and acting as though) one's opinion should count in organizational decisions often proved hazardous to anyone below top management. Back in the 1950s, Neil Waud, a manufacturing executive at Ford Motor Company, learned that lesson the hard way. As David Halberstam tells it, Waud openly contradicted Chief Financial Officer Robert McNamara's solution for cutting production time:

> The plant men wanted newer and better factories. McNamara wanted greater speed from the existing plants. The bottleneck . . . was the paint ovens . . . old, technologically outdated, and too small for contemporary cars. A manufacturing man, Neil Waud, told McNamara at one meeting of senior officials that there was no way

that the painting could be expedited. Waud was stunned when McNamara then suggested that the chassis be built in two main parts, painted, and then welded together into one piece. Waud quickly explained why it was impractical. . . . But McNamara was insistent. . . . The more insistent he was, the blunter Waud became. "The problem with you," Waud shouted, "is you don't know a goddamn thing about how our cars are actually made." After the meeting broke up, McNamara turned to Sanford Kaplan, one of Waud's superiors, and said, "I don't want that man at any more meetings."[49]

The schizophrenia of so-called participative management continued to take its toll on American industry in the sixties and seventies.

By the early 1980s, it was plain to anyone who cared to notice that American industry was in serious trouble. Domestic labor costs were high, productivity and quality were down, and low-cost foreign competition was moving in fast. Americans were buying less-expensive, high-quality foreign cars and TVs. The burgeoning consumer movement signaled serious concern about product safety and quality issues. These startling events provoked a widespread reevaluation of American management practices.

The Japanese experience in particular prompted American managers to reexamine their Asian counterparts' more participative style, which fostered consensus and commitment to excellence.[50] Spurred by the Japanese example, American industry once more began to sing the praises of participative management.

Many management pundits, even now, continue to endorse one offshoot or another of participative management as the antitoxin for most organizational ills. In theory at least, participative management calls for managers and workers to communicate and collaborate. Nonetheless, while "participation" and "teamwork" have become shibboleths of American business and business education, they still encase a subtle, underlying imperative to follow orders.

In practice, participative management American style continues to mean something different and more complex than true participation. It encourages workers to express their ideas, but once management decides on a particular course of action, workers are expected to get behind it—without complaints. In fact, for a person to earn the cherished accolade of "team player," uncomplaining acquiescence is absolutely essential.

Contrary to what most American business schools teach, then, participative management still does *not* allow workers, or even middle managers, to share in top management decisions—not unless the decision is trivial and there is plenty of time to decide.[51] Despite all the discussion of "Japanese style" management, the consensus-driven Japanese workplace remains an anomaly to many Americans. Japanese cooperation, quality circles, and dedication to company and country seem unreal, bordering on the ludicrous and oppressive. The subtle distinctions among consensus, cooperation, conformity, and compliance, so important to the Japanese, remain beyond our ken.

Until recently, Americans believed that such consensus and cooperation spelled death to creativity and permitted only copycat production. The emergence of original Japanese technology, underscored by the recent spike in Japanese applications at the U.S. Patent Office, is forcing Americans to revise their thinking about consensus and creativity. It also prompts us to reconsider the definitions of cooperation and participation.

Most sophisticated observers concede that wholesale grafting of the Japanese management approach onto American organizations provides no easy panacea either. In San Diego, the experience of Kyocera, manufacturers of ceramics for electronics, suggests that such adaptations call for a delicate touch. There, ethnic workers and Japanese-style managers struggled to replicate Japanese management practices. Originally hailed as a resounding success, the Kyocera experiment ultimately led to the disillusionment of the non-Japanese workers, who found themselves unceremoniously ousted from the organizational "family" when economic hard times hit. In the American context, forcing unfamiliar leadership styles doesn't seem to work very well.

Today, most Americans still work in hierarchical organizations. True, their organizations have been considerably flattened by downsizings born of recent economic belt-tightening. The new structures are rationalized by the notions of re-engineering and participative management. Yet the increased gap between first-line supervisors and top management has further dimmed the prospects for shared decision making, despite much rhetoric to the contrary. Organizational charts still illustrate "reporting" relationships: who answers to whom. These hierarchical designs, with their chains of command, readily lend themselves to giving and following orders, the familiar territory of power and control. Participative management remains largely a schizophrenic contradiction of ideology and reality.

Individualism Reconsidered: Visible Rewards, Invisible Costs

Despite all the swings of the pendulum in management theory, the American ego ideal of the rugged individualist is alive and well. We teach it to our kids, and popular culture glorifies it. As noted in Chapter Two, our adulation of individualistic leaders nourishes the belief that we too can succeed.

The American media have played a central role in celebrating individualism. Their obsession with individualistic heroes—as well as antiheroes—is evident in the endless interviews of newsmakers on TV and in magazines, tabloids, and newspapers. In fact, interviewing individuals, a journalistic form that first appeared in the mid-nineteenth century, was a "distinctively American invention," according to British journalist William Stead.[52]

The rewards these individualistic leaders enjoy are enticingly visible: fortunes earned, industries founded, companies snatched from the jaws of bankruptcy, battles won, even nations saved and resurrected. Less visible are the profound costs—personal, institutional, societal, even global—that these heroic efforts entail. The net price reveals a disheartening disparity between the apparent glory of our individualist ego ideal and the painful actuality it obscures.

Each year, individual performance reviews, universally abhorred by managers and workers, routinely spread misery and rivalry in organizations. First introduced in 1914 by Lord & Taylor, the New York retailers, these individual assessments are now considered a "necessary evil" by many managers.[53] Despite famed management professor Douglas McGregor's prescient pessimism about performance appraisals way back in the 1950s, 70 million Americans now receive the good, bad, or so-so news each year.[54] Only a few rare organizations, like Ceridian Corp. and Wisconsin Power & Light Co., have decided to forego this individualistic evaluation, except ironically in the cases that will hurt the most: the underperformers.[55]

At the personal level, a widely read study entitled *Habits of the Heart* (1985) suggests that "American cultural traditions define personality, achievement, and the purpose of human life in ways that leave the individual suspended in glorious, but terrifying, isolation."[56] This personal isolation leads to loneliness, alienation, and terror from which many have sought relief through food, drugs, sex, even suicide. The endless need to assert one's independence and individualism cuts the bonds that bind us, first to the group and then to a morally coherent pursuit of life. It leaves us confused and searching.

Corporations, even family businesses, are torn apart by the individualistic hero's impulse to rise above everyone, as well as by the founder's inability to share, much less surrender, power. Not too long ago, the Maryland-based Dart Group's founder and chairman, seventy-two-year-old Herbert Haft, ousted both his wife and forty-year-old son Robert (founder of Crown Books) from the family business. The rupture was allegedly provoked by an earlier interview in which son Robert intimated to the *Wall Street Journal* that *he* was charting the course of the huge real estate and retail enterprise. Several directors who sided with the scion's desire to lead the company were shown the door at the same time.[57]

This example, and many others like it, expose the dark side of individualism. Too often the determination of individualistic leaders to achieve their vision is tied to a troubling authoritarianism. Individualistic leaders simply *expect* others to follow unquestioningly both their dreams and their dictates. The *New York Times* obituary described William S. Paley, architect of the CBS communications empire, as a "brilliant executive who could also be an unforgiving tyrant."[58] According to opinion polls, many voters felt that Ross Perot's folksy independence only thinly disguised his appetite for power.

Microsoft's Bill Gates provides another example. With self-deprecating humor, Gates told a Stanford University business school audience that his leadership style offers employees great latitude: they can choose whichever twenty-four hours of the day they would like to work.[59] With or without the softening effect of humor, this link between individualism and authoritarianism is a dangerous flaw that undercuts the kind of leadership sorely needed in a Stage 3 world.

Two Painful Contradictions

By a circuitous route, our history has taken us to a crisis point in leadership. In particular, the American obsession with individualism entraps us in two painful contradictions as we face the challenge of adapting to Stage 3.

The First Contradiction: Individualists and Team Players

We have already described the first contradiction, endemic to a democratic way of life: *we preach teamwork, but we idolize individualism.* As we have seen, individualism is our primary secular religion, part of the democratic creed: each individual's vote is sacred, and each can define happiness to suit himself or herself. Autonomous accomplishments constitute the key rituals of the creed.

Somewhat confused, we also genuflect before the altars of cooperation, teamwork, and the rule of majority. In reality, cooperation and teamwork serve mostly as the *backdrop* for individual performance. More often than not, we recognize American heroes so clearly above the crowd because they are standing on the shoulders of family and supporters, who have often sacrificed themselves for these rugged individuals' dreams. The contributors to the cause are below our angle of vision, so we fail to notice the contradiction between our ego ideal and the reality of the hero's life. We adore the illusion of the hero's "single-handed" competitive victory.

Quite fittingly, baseball, our national game, is also our national metaphor. It allows us the best of all worlds: simultaneous adoration of the individual and avowed support for the team, with just a hint of ambivalence toward authority. As the late baseball commissioner A. Bartlett Giamatti wrote, "Baseball fits America so well because it embodies the interplay of individual and group that we so love, and because it expresses our longing for the rule of law while licensing our resentment of law givers. . . . What each individual must do [is] obvious to all, and each player's initiative, poise, and skill are highlighted."[60]

Baseball permits us the illusion of promoting teamwork, while simultaneously creating stars. The star's scorecard is tallied without acknowledging the teammates' participation in that performance. We revere the individual heroic act. The spotlight we focus on the Ron Mattinglys and the Oral Herscheisers obscures their teammates' vital contributions. The pitcher or the late-inning home run hitter becomes the hero of every World Series. In the postgame celebration, the vital contributions of their teammates are virtually ignored.

Periodically, of course, the "communal choreography" of the team takes over, fusing the individual players into a cohesive group, muting the loneliness, terror, and ecstasy of stardom. And once again we bow reverentially at the altar of cooperation and team-work, before returning to our celebration of individualistic heroes.[61]

The Second Contradiction: Individualists and the Ethos of the Organization

Despite their allure, our individualistic stars engender suspicion. They often stumble when success enlarges the task beyond the lim-its of one larger-than-life hero. This leads to the second painful contradiction: *our individualistic ego ideal is often incompatible with the human institutions in which we inevitably live.*

The institutions we have created—schools, work groups, fami-lies, churches, political parties, even baseball teams—are beset by this contradiction. We teach our children to be individuals, to face their own problems, to set their own goals, and faithfully devote themselves to these isolating tasks until they have painstakingly met their own exacting standards. At the same time, we expect them to join groups that call for collaboration, cooperation, *inter*depen-dency, negotiation, and persuasion.

Organizations ask us to share goals, to collaborate and con-tribute to other people's tasks, "network" with peers, "mentor" our protégés, and even groom our eventual successors. This results in a mélange of confusion, frustration, and anger, all salted with self-doubt. The individualistic, often visionary, star has trouble when the time comes for collaborating, for entrusting the challenge to peers, for making others feel the task is as much theirs as the star's, for contributing to others' success, and for grooming protégés. Often the hero leaves or is driven out, sometimes to start all over again—as the lone hero.

Across the American landscape, the lone ranger rides again. Or maybe now it's the lonely ranger. Rather predictably, Steve Jobs and his original partner, Steve Wozniack, parted company not very long after they initially streaked across the sky with their Apple computer-for-everyone. Subsequently, Jobs recruited John Sculley to head operations. Predictably, after a brief honeymoon Jobs and Sculley locked horns. Eventually, Sculley and the Apple board ousted the charismatic founding entrepreneur. The sequels were equally to be expected. Jobs launched a new, independent venture that he confidently christened NeXT Computer Inc. At Apple, Sculley too eventually found himself replaced by a tough, independent Michael Spindler, who, in turn, was also ousted.

This familiar scenario raises a serious question about ingenious, often charismatic entrepreneurs: can they go beyond jump-starting brilliant new ventures? Can they sustain the enterprise once it takes off, breaking through the familial bonds of the exuberant start-up group and demanding coordinated efforts from a much larger number of people? When they do, we often question their authoritarian tactics, while applauding their spectacular results. Let's not forget that supersuccessful CEO Perot's allegedly authoritarian tactics did become the Texas entrepreneur's Achilles heel in his 1992 presidential bid.

To address the organization's need for teamwork, American managers struggle mightily to implement this hybrid form of cooperation. They rarely succeed, yet they have difficulty forsaking the cooperative ideal. At the same time, their longing for authoritarianism dies hard. Real-life managers still yearn for people who will do what they are told and do it well.

A proud follower of orders, Col. Oliver North U.S.M.C. catapulted into the American consciousness through the televised Iran-Contra hearings. A *Wall Street Journal* poll taken in the heat of those hearings asked a sample of American top executives, "Suppose Oliver North walked into your office looking for a job. Would you hire him?" George S. Kariotis, chairman and CEO of Alpha Industries, Inc., a Woburn, Massachusetts, defense electronics company, echoed the sentiments of many CEOs: "Absolutely, unequivocally yes. I'd love to have him work for me. North's the kind of guy that executives look for, the employee of their dreams."[62] A majority of executives agreed that North would be the ideal employee.

In a *WSJ* poll of the general public, 56 percent of the respondents said that if they ran a business, they would want to hire North as an executive. Interestingly enough, women were somewhat less comfortable with this possibility, giving a positive response only 49 percent of the time, compared to 64 percent for male respondents. (Differences between men's and women's leadership values is a topic we return to later. For now, let's simply suggest that males still seem relatively more comfortable in situations where orders are given and discharged unquestioningly.)

The American hero, raised to value individualism above all, has a hard time succeeding in organizations that require genuine cooperation. Not surprisingly, Ollie North became an American folk hero in a single week of media exposure. When "cooperation" is simply a cover for obedience, the dilemma compounds interest.

The Legacy of Our Contradictions: Increased Ambivalence Toward Leadership

The legacy of these twin contradictions puts a peculiarly American spin on the ambivalence toward leadership discussed in Chapter Two. Our existential anxiety leads us to admire, covet, and distrust leaders, all at the same time. This ambivalence toward leadership finds additional support in our democratic tradition. In the American psyche, perpetual war rages between the heroic ego ideal and the democratic ethos that makes us resist domination by anyone.

Given this tradition, Americans find it unsettling to grapple with "cooperation" that cloaks an underlying demand for obedience. The mixture of cooperation and authority implies that directions are given by more highly valued individuals and carried out by less worthy others. This special brand of cooperation clearly violates our democratic creed, which insists that all individuals are equally valuable.

Can We Reconcile the Contradictions?

These ambiguous, often contradictory messages trouble us individualistic Americans. How are we supposed to flourish in organizations that officially call for collaboration and democratic participation but label as good citizens and team players those who simply obey unquestioningly? How are we to dedicate ourselves selflessly to teams, when promotions and other organizational rewards go to competitive, individualistic go-getters?

How do we Americans deal with the unique individualism that forms the cornerstone of our self-worth? And as a democratic society, how do we create organizations that integrate individualism and ingenuity with cooperation and conformity?

We try to reconcile these contradictory beliefs through a very convoluted logic. First, we reason, individual accomplishment is the true path to glory. Second, we insist, learning to respect authority indirectly teaches us how to *exercise* authority. Third, we agree that large enterprises that sustain our society require teamwork. Fourth, we believe cooperation feels warm and cozy, and we just love people who cooperate. But we don't choose them as leaders.

For leaders, we prefer tough, controlling people, sure of their unique charismatic vision even when the vision turns out to be flawed. We also love TV's neighborly, self-effacing Mr. Rogers, who urges us to help one another. He remains, however, simply a comfortable childhood figure, not someone we would recruit for any serious leadership position.

For many of us, the reconciliation among individualism, cooperation, and authoritarianism is far from complete. How do we grow authentic leaders who can collaborate with other leaders and constituents, entrust their goals to associates, act as mentors to younger leaders, and still maintain the integrity and coherence of their vision? And will our highly individualistic vision of leadership undermine our response to the challenges of an increasingly interdependent world? Or do we need a new image of leadership, one that frees us at last from the contradictory legacy of our history?

The combination of America's early frontier, democratic tradition, and immigrant experiences led to complex expectations of leadership. The result was an uneasy troika of individualism, authoritarianism, and cooperation. American organizations have long sought to reconcile these contradictions, but confusion and frustration, along with ambivalence toward leaders, remain.

Resolving these contradictions will help us to generate and sustain effective organizations in an increasingly globalized Stage 3 environment. To overcome the centrifugal forces of interdependence and diversity, we cannot simply go back to what we have always done best. Individualism, by itself, won't cut it. Neither will the simple choices of competition or collaboration be enough to settle these wrenching contradictions. In the next chapter, we examine major wellsprings of social change that have fueled the need for new leaders. We also consider the experience of several leaders who tried to lead in new ways before the time was ripe.

Chapter Four

A New Era
Intimations of New Leadership

The history of technology is that of human history in all its diversity.
FERNAND BRAUDEL[1]

The universal psychological and existential foundations of leadership, combined with our unique American experience, predispose us to a distinctive image of leaders. In this chapter, we turn to the global forces that are creating a new era in which we need to re-evaluate those old leadership concepts.

Since midcentury, many complex forces have fueled the engines of broad social change. They have radically altered organizations and the politics of human interaction. In the process, these forces of change have eroded the relevance of traditional Stage 2 leadership strategies.

There is no guarantee that new, more appropriate, and desperately needed forms of leadership will automatically emerge or that new types of leaders—particularly connective leaders—will be welcomed. The old addiction to authoritarian leadership, which demands little from us but slavish followership, is hard to shake. Indeed, the difficulties encountered by those who, to date, tried to act connectively before the time was right provide telling evidence of the harsh realities of such groundbreaking efforts. Yet despite frequent failures, nascent connective leaders offer intimations of a new paradigm of leadership.

This chapter surveys the conditions that have jolted us out of Stage 2 into a new era, and it begins to trace the outlines of Stage 3 leadership. After considering the precipitating conditions, we sketch brief portraits of four early connective leaders whose examples point the way to a new model of leadership. Finally, we begin to reflect on the ways in which leaders and followers alike need to rethink their roles in order to meet the challenges of the Connective Era.

Fueling the Engines of Change: Six Major Sources

Many dramatic changes herald the dawn of the Connective Era. Some have increased our global *inter*dependence; others have moved us in the opposite direction, fostering more *in*dependence, greater diversity, and clear-cut identities; still others have done both simultaneously. To illustrate, let's briefly review the six sources of social, political, and economic change that I believe have had the greatest impact and the widest reach.

Science and Technology: Revealing Connections

In every field of science and technology, significant breakthroughs have created a growing awareness of connectedness at all levels. Nuclear energy, computers, satellite TV, lasers and biotechnology, organ transplants, space exploration, and the emerging information superhighway: all these and more have forced us to recognize the reality of interlocking human and technological systems. We have finally come to see the world as a single, albeit complicated, system, one immense set of interrelated pieces.

In this global community, leaders frequently must weigh the potential effects of their decisions on unseen stakeholders at the farthest reaches of the global metropolis. With millions of smaller interconnected communities, even minor actions ripple across the whole system, affecting distant and seemingly unrelated parts. (Chaos scientists have labeled this phenomenon "the butterfly effect.")[2] In this new Connective Era, our old commitment to stubborn individualism is approaching its Waterloo. Autonomy as we have known it is virtually archaic. Increasingly, nations, institutions, and individuals live in a postautonomous world.

The Bomb: Shared Vulnerability

Half a century ago, the atomic bomb created a watershed whose full implications, particularly for global interdependence, would emerge only over many decades. Initially, the bomb snapped open a Pandora's box of military might, offering us previously unimagined control over others. By confirming our military preeminence and supplying limitless nuclear power, it would increase enormously our independence—or so we thought.

Only very gradually did we grasp a profoundly disturbing truth: nuclear weapons connected us at the spine to the very enemies we would destroy. The same nuclear power that would annihilate our adversaries simultaneously would poison our environment and us along with it.

Even nuclear energy for peaceful purposes would not protect our independence. Instead, it connected us all by a shared vulnerability to the nuclear fallout from increasingly "normal accidents"[3] anywhere in the world. Eventually, we had to recognize another inextricable connection: the linkages among our military posture, energy appetites, and ecological condition.

The complex interlacing of so many diverse aspects of life generated conditions we had never before encountered. With them came new choices and dilemmas that individualistic, controlling leaders found themselves ill-equipped to resolve. Paradoxically, it was just here that a new era of "connectedness" was born, quietly and unnoticed.

New Vistas Through Communication and Transportation Technology

In recent decades, communication technology has obliterated the national boundaries so jealously protected by powerful, individualistic leaders. Advances in communications have compacted the world into one vast metropolis that shares a single, complex, geopolitical-economic system. In the somber winter of 1990, East German television viewers first caught unbelievable images of economic prosperity in West Germany and freedom rallies in Gdansk. The yearnings to taste what technology had permitted them to glimpse ultimately drove East Germans to topple the Berlin Wall. A symbol of controlling leadership for twenty-eight years, the wall tumbled in less than twenty-eight hours. Through technology again, the rest of us witnessed that riveting moment of change in real time.

The disintegrating Berlin Wall rumbled along the Communist fault line in Eastern Europe, cracking the foundations of these old-style dictatorships. The aftershocks awakened Eastern European citizens long since numbed into submission. One after another, Eastern European leaders lost their positions and privileges. Some, like Rumanian dictator Nicolae Ceauşescu, also lost their lives.

Technology has pierced another significant boundary, the one between earth and outer space. Only two generations ago, space was a totally foreign frontier. Now we take the exploration of space so much for granted that few viewers bother to set their alarm clocks for an early morning shuttle launch. Moreover, by giving us a view of our home planet as a fragile blue and white ball, astronauts have at last made the image of a simple, boundaryless world a literal reality instead of a visionary metaphor.

Back on earth, information technology has opened new markets and spawned far-flung communication networks. In fact, our burgeoning interdependence is powerfully illustrated by the computer networks that span the globe, operating with casual disregard for political and physical boundaries. No passports needed here.

With the help of computers, a new global economic system has taken shape. Computers create a daisy chain of world financial markets, whose minutest movements flash instantaneously from New York to Tokyo, Hong Kong, Sydney, London, and back again to New York. Computers and markets interact with unforeseen, at times ferocious, results. In minutes, financial markets respond to events thousands of miles away. A drought in Brazil suddenly doubles the price of coffee in Los Angeles.

Transportation technology similarly pries off our cultural blinders. The incredible ease of travel lets us experience different worlds firsthand. We discover foreign cuisines, new clothing styles, unfamiliar music, and ancient as well as avant-garde art. Through travel, we establish human relationships that weaken old cultural stereotypes. By eliminating our blinders, these new encounters force us to recognize the legitimacy of others' goals and teach us new ways to achieve our own objectives.

All these technologies also drive alliances. As my colleague Peter Drucker suggests,[4] technologies overlap, producing a torrent of advances and connections. Technologies from one discipline influence other disciplines. The cloning techniques developed for biotechnology open new possibilities for agriculture and medicine.

After developing new products or processes, organizations usually discover that they need both additional technology and expanded markets to distribute their innovations. Increasingly, they are also finding that they can't do all those things alone. More and more, companies are seeking networks and alliances. Drucker argues that "Not even a big company can any longer get from its own research laboratories all, or even most, of the technology it needs. Conversely, a good lab now produces results in many more areas than can interest even a large and diversified company. So pharmaceutical companies have to ally themselves with geneticists; commercial bankers with underwriters; hardware-makers like IBM with software boutiques."[5]

American biotechnology companies, rather than expanding as they might have a decade ago, now seek alliances for marketing their breakthrough discoveries:

> Despite rapidly growing sales and breathtaking new discoveries in their laboratories, U.S. biotechnology companies are scaling back their ambitions. . . . Rather than attempting to grow to giant size like Merck & Co., or Eli Lilly, biotechnology companies are focusing on developing products that the larger drug companies can sell. . . . The need to form such "strategic alliances" is now the most pressing concern of biotech executives. . . . [S]ixty-one percent of biotech companies want to develop drugs that would be marketed by a corporate partner. Forty percent of chief executives acknowledge that their goal is to "attract an acquisition."[6]

New Dilemmas and Second-Order Problems

Yet technology is not an unmixed blessing. Along with new solutions, it spawns new dependencies, new problems, and new ethical dilemmas. From surrogate motherhood to kidney dialysis, medicine (and biotechnology in particular) symbolically intertwines progress and problems, raising heart-wrenching choices for which we have no ready calculus. We now must decide whose life should be saved: a minister's or a miner's, a child's or a mother's. In fact, the ethical complexities that flow from biotechnological and medical advances have given rise to an entirely new field, bioethics.

In the Connective Era, we find ourselves seeking ever newer technologies to address the second-order problems generated by earlier technological breakthroughs. Advances in transportation have led to gridlocked freeways and polluted skies, so we seek solutions through still other technologies, such as computer-based systems for controlling traffic. These new "solutions" in turn usually lead to still other problems, and so on. Almost always, we fail to predict the second- and third-order effects of our inventions and interventions.

While technology offers innovative ways to master our environment, it also tethers and even addicts us to these magical methods. The pain of our dependency is just a computer breakdown away, as any travel agent can attest when the airline reservation system crashes just before a holiday weekend. Perhaps the greatest technological challenge for current leaders involves harnessing technology without becoming its slave.

Technology has played a key role in dissolving both the simplicity of our existence and the narrow leadership molds that our simpler life supported. Even as technology expands our possibilities for growth, it also requires leaders who can deal with the inevitable consequences: complexity, ambiguity, discontinuity, and tough ethical dilemmas.

Increasing Internationalism: The Shift from Tight Alliances to Loose Global Networks

Internationalism is on the march, stemming largely from economic and industrial globalization. Networks of organizations blanket the global marketplace. With kaleidoscopic movement, many industrial organizations busily restructure themselves, through mergers and acquisitions: Time Warner and Turner Broadcasting, Westinghouse and CBS, and Warner-Lambert and Glaxo Wellcome. Some seek alliances with former competitors. Toyota and General Motors work diligently to make the NUMMI plant hum. IBM, Apple, Microsoft, and Motorola, previously fierce competitors for market share, join forces selectively on rapidly shifting fronts. The first offspring of this previously unimaginable union was the Power PC, an enormously powerful, multiple-platform computer, combining advantages of both DOS and Macintosh operating systems.

Fresh collaborative ventures sprout like weeds across national boundaries. Many of the earliest cross-national efforts, like those between Finnish and Russian supermarket entrepreneurs, foundered on the shoals of inadequate capitalization, cross-cultural ignorance, and fragmented infrastructure. Nonetheless, the greatest barrier to these cross-national ventures is probably the stubbornly independent Stage 2 leader who can't mesh the gears of these new partnerships.

Internationalism has also received a substantial boost from the dissolution of entrenched Cold War geopolitical alliances, the emergence of ethnically based nations, and a loosely coupled global network of nations. Think for a moment of all the social and political changes that have reshaped our world over just the last few decades. First, it was Third World nations breaking away from colonial control. Then, Eastern Europe began to erupt. Next, the two Germanys became one. Eventually, the Soviet-American rapprochement removed the linchpins from entrenched Stage 2 alliances. Indeed, the disintegration of the Soviet Union intoned a solemn requiem for the old geopolitical balance of power. With the disintegration of the Warsaw Pact and the reconfiguration of the NATO alliance, a new global orchestration is in the works. It is conducted simultaneously by many new leaders, with one or two, such as President Václav Havel of the Czech Republic and South African president Nelson Mandela, sounding connective leadership themes. Operation Desert Storm, the U.S.-led initiative against Saddam Hussein in Kuwait and Iraq, produced an unlikely but effective short-term coalition of countries that may be the model of the loose global alliances that will distinguish the Connective Era.

In Western Europe, leaders of twelve independent nations have doggedly struggled to build one interdependent economic community. Jean Monnet, father of the European Community, envisioned a new Europe, linked by shared goals and a common currency.[7] Despite Monnet's connective vision, the long-passed 1992 launch date for the Maastricht agreement is quiet testimony to the inability of Stage 2 leaders to deal with these Connective Era challenges. Still, even these attempts at a new connective arrangement were well beyond imagining only a short time ago.

In Southeast Asia, seven traditionally competing nations now comprise ASEAN,[8] the Association of Southeast Asian Nations, with Laos, Cambodia, and Myanmar vying to join. Stimulated before the

Connective Era by Japan's economic muscle, ASEAN has stepped up its plans for a regional free-trade zone by the year 2000. The ASEAN members are currently considering "European-style economic integration by harmonizing external tariffs, standards for goods and services, and infrastructure for transport and communication by the year 2010."[9] Thailand's foreign minister explained the speedup in the following way: "in the era of global economic liberalization, economic harmonization among our countries is no longer a question of choice but one of necessity."[10] ASEAN continues to search for a larger context within which all members can reach beyond their individual needs and customs to an encompassing, prosperous community. In the background, the enormous and fast-growing shadow of the new China adds urgency, danger, and opportunity to ASEAN's efforts.

Understandably, the United States broods over its shifting international alliances in this rapidly moving world. Changes brew in long-standing relationships with old European friends, whose Maastricht plan essentially excludes the United States. The Bosnian crisis in the former Yugoslavia focused painful light on the festering discord among the World War II allies. Meanwhile, American relations with Japan and China sail on troubled waters, even as U.S. leaders struggle to adapt to the continuing change in the former Soviet Union.

The restructuring of international alliances forces the United States to reconsider its own leadership posture. We labor to transform our role from global policeman to global partner. It remains to be seen whether the (temporarily) last remaining "superpower" can learn to share leadership and responsibility, as well as resources and goals, with the global community of nations. Inevitably, these changes drive us to think much more interdependently, to move more and more toward short-term alliances, kaleidoscopic interconnections, and temporary organizational forms.

The Many Faces of Diversity

Despite spreading interdependence, an opposing force—diversity, both global and local—draws strength from many sources. Fledgling nations and restructured organizations act as powerful seedbeds of diversity, nourishing new identities and new needs. Social movements too have fed diversity within all institutions.

In the United States, both the civil rights and the women's movements spawned an era after which the nation could no longer consider itself complacently white, male, and middle class. The civil rights movement of the late 1960s and 1970s rejected the earlier melting-pot mentality of white ethnic groups and asserted the distinctiveness of black identity.[11] Taking their cue from the civil rights movement, American women began to reassess *their* position in society. Under the scrutiny of the women's movement, many previously accepted leadership practices identified as patriarchal and oppressive began to lose support, even legitimacy.

Yet despite the desperate need for leadership, Stage 2 leaders have consistently failed to deliver on the American Dream to nonwhite, nonmale, non-middle-class constituents. In their quest for recognition, women, blacks, Latinos, Asians, gays and lesbians, the physically and mentally challenged, the aging, and the homeless, all began to call not simply for new leaders but more importantly for new *forms* of leadership. They rebuked leaders for homogenizing constituents to fit into the Hollywood scenario of mainstream USA (itself the wish fulfillment of earlier immigrants-turned-movie moguls). Instead, these groups talked of coalitions, interdependence, and shared, sometimes rotated, leadership. They focused on the unique contribution of each member. They called for a reassessment of the "rules" that disproportionately benefited members of the homogeneous old-boy network but totally ignored those outside its charmed circle.

Other economic and demographic changes multiply these centrifugal forces. Starting in the seventies, women, blacks, Latinos, Asians, and other minorities entered the labor force in the greatest numbers since World War II, nourishing high but decidedly diverse expectations for expanded opportunities.[12] The 1980s and 1990s have brought new arrivals from Asia, Africa, Latin America, Eastern Europe, and the Middle East, with exotic customs and unusual lifestyles. Unlike earlier generations of immigrants, however, these newcomers did not seek to be "Americanized." Proud of their diversity, these recent arrivals preserved their own cultures, even introducing novel ideas and adding complexities to their adopted neighborhoods and workplaces.

Changing mores about dating, marriage, sexuality, sexual preference, abortion, child rearing, and child abuse generate additional diversity in the American way of life. Many dissimilar constituencies, from unmarried domestic partners to advocates for children, the unborn, and the homeless, insist upon the right to be different but accepted nonetheless.

How can leaders fulfill the expectations of such diverse groups, particularly in a period of shrinking resources? Where are equity and opportunity to be found? It will not be easy for leaders to move the dialogue along, particularly on hot issues that raise intense intergroup hackles. Can new leaders create a unifying vision for these very different groups, a vision that will offer hope and community as the American Dream once did to new arrivals to our shores? Theirs is the task of drawing coherence from the turmoil of divergent values and priorities. These are just some of the spectacular challenges that leaders in this new era will be forced to address.

Lost Faith in Ideologies, Institutions, and Leaders

As the Connective Era comes into view, we are witnessing the collapse of political ideologies, compounded by a loss of faith in governmental, corporate, and not-for-profit institutions and leaders. Even religious and educational leaders, usually revered, are tumbling from their pedestals.

This loss of faith in traditional ideologies stimulates a widespread search for meaning and direction, which often gravitates to fundamentalist political and religious belief systems.[13] Ideologies serve many purposes, from explaining reality to providing guidelines for action. When ideologies no longer command our belief, they wither, and their adherents are forced to look elsewhere for direction. When that occurs, the role of the leader assumes even greater importance.

Institutions provide the structures within which much of our human action occurs. They provide the stage on which we act out our ideological assumptions. We look to institutions to meet many human needs, from safety and support to nourishment and challenge. Yet right now, traditional institutions are in serious trouble. As Alvin Toffler has noted, most of these institutions, from governments to churches, were shaped to meet the needs of the Age of Industrialization.[14] In the transition from the industrial era to the information age, these institutions gasp and groan, burdened by their inability to handle society's new needs. The result: we are witnessing a profound shift in attitudes toward the institutions that up to now have molded our lives.

The Crisis of Faith in Political and Economic Institutions

In the United States, attitudes toward traditional institutions have undergone a sea change since the 1960s. The Vietnam War shattered our political innocence. Watergate, reaching deep within the office of the president, left a legacy of enduring mistrust of political leaders and government. Love Canal, Three Mile Island, and the Challenger accident have further eroded the public's belief in governmental vigilance, competence, and integrity. The Iran-Contra hearings, the congressional bank overdrafts, the savings and loan debacle, Wall Street's insider trading, and the Whitewater scandal have heightened cynicism about political and financial institutions. Meanwhile, millions of constituents have come to feel disenfranchised by the tight circle of politicians and their wealthy individual and organizational backers. The political temblor that shook the U.S. Congress in the 1994 midterm election clearly signaled voters' anger, frustration, and disaffection.

Private-sector institutions have not escaped this wave of disillusionment. Opinion polls indicate serious public disappointment with leaders in business and industry, including mounting disapproval of seven-figure salaries for CEOs who head faltering corporations. In addition, industrial accidents and toxic products have severely shaken consumers' faith. Exxon's Valdez oil spill, Union Carbide's toxic explosion in Bhopal, Nestlés Third World tainted baby formula, Gerber's baby food impurities, and General Motors' vulnerable saddle-bag gasoline tanks (compounded by NBC's doctored demonstration of the danger) are simply a few of the most publicized events that have stirred a public outcry against corporate irresponsibility.

Occasionally, however, a little sunshine breaks through the clouds. A few organizations that exhibit exemplary corporate responsibility (like Johnson & Johnson in the 1982 Tylenol poisoning crisis) continue to win the public's respect. With increasing globalization, more corporate leaders will have to take responsibility for distant stakeholders. In the Connective Era, political leaders too will be expected to protect the long-term welfare of groups well beyond their immediate constituencies.

The Fall of Religious Leaders and the
Paradoxical Rise of Fundamentalist Religion

Even American religious institutions have lost considerable luster. At the *fin de siècle* of industrialism, mainstream religious institutions are unprepared to deal with the transition to the Connective Era. Here too, technology gave the world ringside seats, this time at the financial and sexual circuses of idolized TV religionists. Television brought incredulous parishioners unforgettable images of evangelists Jim Bakker in handcuffs and Jimmy Swaggart in tears.

Nor is it simply the TV merchants of religion whose problematic behavior has shaken our belief in religious leaders and the organizations they create. Within mainstream religious institutions, leaders stand accused of violating their own vows of integrity and chastity. During the last decade alone, according to sociologist Andrew Greeley, the Roman Catholic Church has paid out $500 million to settle parishioners' sexual abuse suits in the United States. A maelstrom of public outrage swirls around the reluctance of church leaders to address the sexual abuse of churchgoers, particularly children, by trusted parish priests. Nor is the problem confined within U.S. borders. The *International Herald Tribune* reports that approximately thirty-five thousand Austrians left the church in a single year. Many attributed their defection to the church's handling of a former schoolboy's accusation that an Austrian cardinal had molested him twenty years before.[15]

American disillusionment runs deep. Opinion polls show that a substantial segment of the U.S. public thinks their religious leaders have engaged in behavior unbefitting their roles. Since 1980, when the Gallup Poll first began measuring public opinion about TV ministers, the then-positive views that most Americans held have drastically deteriorated. Moreover, from 1981 to 1986, even *before* the TV ministries' scandals shocked viewers, the public's confidence in organized religion dropped from 64 percent to 57 percent.[16] By 1991, it had slipped to 33 percent.[17]

As faith in mainstream religion has waned, disillusioned believers have begun to look elsewhere. In contrast to the waning membership of traditional Catholic and Protestant churches,

Pentecostalism, the experiential segment of the Christian faith, is growing at an unprecedented rate. The surge in Pentecostalism within the last two decades has swelled its ranks to more than 410 million adherents worldwide, threatening to surpass Catholicism by the year 2000.[18] Young people in particular have joined fundamentalist groups, seeking direction and meaning from stricter religious institutions and leaders.[19] In some cultures, rejection of their parents' values and lifestyles has pushed young adults to accept the comforting purity offered by religious cults. Many social scientists interpret these trends as evidence that established religious institutions have failed.

Have Our Educational Leaders Flunked the Course?

American education is suffering from a similar crisis of faith. From elementary to postgraduate schools, educational leadership is faltering, with vision and responsibility in short supply. One commission report after another demonstrates that schools are not educating the two major sources of our future strength: the young and the immigrant. Each year, U.S. students' test scores fall farther and farther behind those of their international peers despite much hand wringing and excuses by our educational leaders.

Meanwhile, school administrators stand accused of financial mismanagement. Preschools are beset by charges of staff sexually abusing their young students.[20] Some inkling of parents' disappointment in the schools can be gleaned from the precipitous drop in participation in Parent-Teacher Associations.

Many educators have had it too. In school districts across the country, teachers have fled the profession. Those who remain have taken to the sidewalks, striking and refusing to work for substandard wages in classrooms where drugs, knives, and guns endanger their lives. College presidents, under attack by disenchanted trustees, faculty, and students, are leaving their posts at an alarming rate.[21] Unlike the university leaders of midcentury who spoke out on the key issues of the day, those who stay frequently avoid controversial issues for fear of losing the favor of potential donors.

Even the leadership of professional schools is under attack. Educators and practitioners are busy reevaluating the curricula of medical, business, and law schools, in part to modify their Stage 2 traditions to meet Connective Era realities. Critics complain that most medical schools, for example, still teach physicians to play the authoritarian healer role, omnipotently and jealously guarding medical knowledge. They castigate medical schools for underemphasizing preventive medicine and nutrition, and in other ways excluding patients from knowledgeable partnership in their own health care.

To stem the tide of graduates narrowly focused on greed and gain, business school critics[22] are advocating innovative courses in leadership, management, globalization, and business ethics. Law schools too are coming under fire for the adversarial posture they routinely teach. University of Connecticut Law School professor Philip N. Meyer[23] faults traditional law schools for making litigation the norm and focus of professional practice, instead of emphasizing negotiation, mediation, and a host of other more connective techniques.[24]

The manifold crises that beset our institutions are a sign that Stage 2 leadership simply doesn't work in a world entering the Connective Era. Nor is it sufficient to inject a megadose of vision, of which we have deservedly heard a great deal in recent years.[25] Only a totally fresh approach to leadership has any hope of restoring our faith in the institutions that form the infrastructure of our society.

Changes in Organizational Structure and Design

Concurrently with widespread cultural and societal changes, the 1980s and 1990s have witnessed the painful restructuring of organizations: a massive movement from conglomerates and multinationals to leaner structures; from vertically integrated hierarchies to flatter, downsized organizations; from powerful labor unions to unions lacking presence or potency, particularly in the United States; from antagonistic to tentative alliances between management and labor; from mergers and acquisitions to joint ventures and partnerships, and onward to organizational networks.

A Feeding Frenzy of Acquisitions and Mergers

The eighties produced a feeding frenzy of acquisitions and mergers in the corporate world. Behemoth companies clumsily thrashed about to evade the jaws of agile sharks. New financial arrangements saw unfamiliar players staking out leadership claims. Here too, technology played a critical part, linking financial players in a gigantic, often instantaneous, network. Investment bankers and traders, who traditionally inhabited entirely separate worlds, unexpectedly found themselves uneasy partners in historic financial megadeals.[26] Stage 2 financial wizards, seeking tight control over world financial markets, led many of these restructurings, with widespread and long-term disastrous results.

U.S. Trade Unions in Decline

The dynamics of a new organizational era are changing the face of American labor. In the frantic contemporary battle for organizational survival, trade unions have lost much of their membership and clout, as low-cost, high-quality foreign competition has gained ground. From 1955 to 1994, U.S. union membership as a percentage of the labor force dropped from 33.2 percent to 15.5 percent.[27] Mergers and acquisitions have trimmed the number of unions, with the latest blockbuster merger proposal by the United Auto Workers, United Steelworkers of America, and International Association of Machinists to take effect in the year 2000.

Meanwhile, the Chrysler Corp.'s near-death experience was a wake-up call for labor and management alike. In a desperate effort to save the company, Chrysler CEO Lee Iacocca courted unheard-of collaboration with unions. In an action symbolizing a revolutionary new partnership, Iacocca offered United Auto Workers leader Douglas Fraser a seat on Chrysler's board. By early 1994, Chrysler had posted the highest profits in its history, but the new rapprochement between labor and management still threatens to unravel in the struggle over dividing the recouped gains.

Nonetheless, something important emerged from the Chrysler crisis: American management and labor began to learn—albeit painfully—about the necessity and the difficulties of *inter*dependence. Despite their long-term ideological and pragmatic battles with management, unions gradually encouraged those workers still employed to make serious concessions or face permanently closed plants. Only by working together could labor and management hope to save their industries and themselves.

Alliances between these two "natural" enemies have been evolving over many years in some parts of the world. In countries where a more positive union management relationship has long prevailed, the environment is more congenial to new forms of organizational leadership. Particularly in Europe and Asia, managers' limited power to hire and fire has led managers and unionists to greater recognition of their mutual dependence.

Still, most of us remain puzzled by European and Asian patterns of interdependence among business, government, and unions. Ambivalence colors our view of Japan's Ministry of International Trade and Industry (MITI), which supports and guides business initiatives.[28] While American industries welcome some forms of government support, their traditional ideological resistance to government "interference" hampers collaboration with government. Here again, it will take savvy connective leaders to bridge the gulf.

Lost Community, Lost Commitment

The narrowly focused, autonomous organizations that dotted the Stage 2 landscape infected their workers with serious, lasting maladies. The illnesses ranged from deep cynicism about management's humane concern for employees, to pessimism about corporate leaders' competence and integrity, to anomie from which many sought escape in drugs and violence-riddled entertainment. Many others found their expectations for career trajectories like their fathers' splintered into shards of broken promises. Downsizing that disregarded workers' long-term devoted service redefined "loyalty" to the organization, bosses, and co-workers. Safe and harassment-free work environments remained elusive goals. Unanticipated career upheavals turned workers back into themselves and their inner personal resources. Such turbulence frequently set disenfranchised workers on a search for purpose and meaning beyond organizational life.

Intraorganizational competition, downsizing, and continual reshufflings have torn the connective tissue among co-workers, leaving exhaustion and alienation in their wake.[29] The delicate veins of community—among workers, their organizations, and environments—have been ruptured.

Many serious questions remain. How can we stimulate productivity when our sense of community is tattered, when the fear of diminishing resources pits would-be survivors against one another? As the old, embedded, authoritarian hierarchies decline, can new organizations, operating in the emerging milieu of changing partnerships and networks, regenerate community and cooperation?

Stage 2 American business leaders continue to recast the missions[30] and structures of their organizations. Still, severe doubts linger that the twin goals of enhancing the bottom line and satisfying the customer can keep their shareholders, customers, and particularly their employees content for very long. Much more will be needed to achieve those goals, probably far more than Stage 2 leaders have to offer.

New Plagues: AIDS, Drugs, Crime, Urban and Environmental Decay

No one concerned with contemporary forces of change can ignore the rise of AIDS, drugs, and crime, along with urban and environmental decay.[31] All these social ills and more threaten our daily existence and provoke profound concern about the deteriorating quality of life. They compel us to work together to protect our families and our personal health, as well as to take back our neighborhoods, cities, and oceans. Simultaneously, they push us apart through fear, suspicion, and negative stereotypes. Limited resources and haphazard policies compound the problems, and forecasters predict things are likely to get worse before they get better.

These are quintessential contemporary problems that create major stumbling blocks for corporate and political leaders. While the causes are global, the fallout is devastatingly local. Solutions to such problems require both global and local alliances among governments, organizations, professions, and communities. The interdependence generated by a global environment ought to force leaders to think twice, even thrice, before trying to implement autonomous decisions. No longer can they simply do whatever serves their own group's narrow interests. Nor can they act without regard for long-term consequences.

Solutions to intertwined social problems have yet to be devised, but it seems clear that the answers require integrating the most sophisticated knowledge from *all* branches of science, technology, law, and the humanities. In short, intellectual alliances need to be formed across often isolated "disciplines."[32] This is a large order, and leaders in this new era need enormous conceptual breadth to guide such efforts.

The Combined Fallout from These Six Trends

Taken separately, any one of the six wide-ranging trends we have reviewed would cause serious societal waves. Combined, they have undermined our basic assumptions about our world, our organizations, our relationships, and ourselves. Along the way, they have drastically changed the rules of the leadership game.

To attack these concatenated forces of change, particularly in faltering economies, leaders must create innovative, mutually acceptable solutions. They must understand how to integrate the contradictory needs of diverse groups. Among other things, they must have the political savvy to bring opponents to the negotiating table. It is not clear whether our leaders will rise to the challenge. Certainly, the connective leaders who do emerge can expect to meet resistance from old-style leaders and their followers, who remain locked behind the mental bars of individualistic, competitive leadership paradigms.

Fortunately, intimations of a new paradigm can be found in the examples of several leaders who tried to break the bonds of Stage 2 thinking. Although their stories are in many ways familiar, they take on new meaning when viewed in the context of the transition to the Connective Era.

Nascent Connective Leaders in a Pre-Connective World: Intimations of New Ways to Lead

From time to time, nascent connective leaders have appeared on the scene. Although new leaders tend to surface during periods of intense social change or crisis,[33] the paradigmatic shift that could have facilitated these figures' connective leadership was yet to come. Thus the full impact of these new leadership efforts was often blunted. As a result, the vision and leadership styles of these emergent connective leaders both attracted and puzzled their followers. Ironically, leaders who acted connectively before historical conditions were auspicious oftentimes suffered at the hands of their intended constituents as well as those of their enemies. From a short-term perspective, it seems none was completely successful. In some cases, only after they had met a martyr's death did the world acknowledge them as very special trail blazers, if still not completely understood.

Yet something about both their message and their method makes us remember these early connective leaders. Mahatma Gandhi, living in a Stage 2 world, changed the course of British and Indian history. Inspired in part by Gandhi, Martin Luther King, Jr. stamped our national consciousness with images of freedom marches headed by rows of leaders linking arms—not just one solitary leader out in front.

Since we are just entering the Connective Era, few full-blown connective leaders have yet appeared on the scene. Still, one or two nascent connective leaders have stepped to center stage and jolted our traditional ideas about leadership: Gandhi and King, as we have noted, plus Mikhail Gorbachev, President Oscar Arias of Costa Rica, Havel, Mandela, and Brazilian Rubber Tappers' Union leader Chico Mendes. Despite vociferous objections from puzzled Stage 2 followers, the complex achievements of King, Arias, Gorbachev, and Mandela earned them Nobel Peace Prizes. Perhaps this provides some evidence of our budding, if still puzzled, appreciation for connective leadership.

What do these leaders share that represents something genuinely new and responsive to the specific crises of our times? And what can we learn from them about the constraints imposed on individuals who have attempted to use connective leadership in a pre-connective world? To explore these questions, let's turn to a "thicker"[34] description of four of these special leaders.

Mohandas Gandhi and Martin Luther King, Jr.: Two Connective Pioneers

Although severely hampered by Stage 2 conditions, both Mohandas Gandhi (whose followers bestowed upon him the title of reverence "Mahatma," or "great soul") and later Martin Luther King, Jr., marched to connective drummers. Probably the least noted similarity between these two connective pioneers was their reluctance to accept the mantle of leadership.[35] Neither coveted the leader's role, nor did either ever run for political office.

Both Gandhi and King drew on a broad, new spectrum of leadership behaviors that often mystified Stage 2 friends and foes alike. Both sought to inspire constituents and opponents to take the moral high ground. Both linked their dreams and visions to those of other leaders. Ironically, they integrated spirituality and politics through strategies that demonstrated system savvy. Both were emergent Stage 3 leaders acting in a Stage 2 world.

The Radical Vision of Gandhi

The very core of Gandhi's teachings—passive resistance and nonviolence—contradicted the norms of traditional, authoritarian leadership. To many followers and adversaries alike, Gandhi's concept of passive resistance initially seemed oxymoronic, a naive pipe dream. How could a strategy so simple and gentle overcome Great Britain's military might?

Reared in traditional leadership models, many of Gandhi's would-be supporters struggled against their ingrained tendency to meet conventional power with equally conventional aggression. In practice, they would find that Gandhi's seemingly weak and contradictory concepts demanded extraordinary self-discipline and courage. Gandhi taught his followers that strength, not impotence, came from seeking the moral high ground. It also sprouted from the rich soil of community and human partnerships.

On some occasions Gandhi took extreme measures to communicate the meaning of his cause. Through self-disciplined fasts that brought him to the brink of death, Gandhi forced even his strongest adversaries to rethink their positions. He demonstrated that his goal of Indian independence transcended not only political and religious differences but even one's very life.

Where many only glimpsed weakness, Gandhi saw strength in leaning on, as well as helping, others. Believing that entrusting others with responsibility inspired them to discover new inner strengths, he left to associates the pragmatic implementation of his vision. He paid scant attention to financial and physical resources, casually expecting others to handle complex administrative arrangements. Gandhi, however, did not delegate these tasks in the traditional way, by frequently checking the details. Instead, he simply entrusted those more orderly and systematic than himself with such issues, including even his own physical care. They rarely failed him.

Gandhi was more intrigued by the role of teacher, educating his followers in the very broadest curriculum: from world politics to human relations to personal hygiene. At his ashram, Gandhi eagerly instructed his rural constituents on boiling water and many other intricacies of personal health, activities conventional politicians found strange for a moral and political leader. Some accused Gandhi of cynical posturing or escaping into trivial activities whenever serious political crises began to brew. Winston Churchill, interpreting such behavior as wily and manipulative, allegedly punned that Gandhi was the "greatest fakir" he had ever known.[36]

In his daily behavior, Gandhi contributed to others' tasks. He collaborated with them when he thought it would help and, like a vicarious parent, simply offered words of encouragement to those who sought his guidance as *bapu* (father or teacher). Using strategies that others associated with weakness and femininity, Gandhi helped—indeed he served—his supporters.

Gandhi focused on the human links shared by all people. Within his own Hindu community, he despised the caste system as a pernicious tool for separating, instead of connecting, people. Defying the age-old system, he drew supporters from the broadest social spectrum. To symbolize his acceptance of all human brethren, Gandhi publicly cleaned the latrines of "untouchables," pariahs in the Hindu caste system.

Where others sought separation, Gandhi grasped the need for connections. Much to the consternation of his Hindu supporters, he reached out to the Muslim "enemy." Unexpectedly setting aside the prohibitions of his Hindu faith, the deeply pious Gandhi dined with Muslims in a passionate, symbolic effort to convince Muslims and Hindus to work together for Indian independence. Unlike his Congress Party colleague Jawaharlal Nehru and Muslim leader Mohammed Ali Jinnah, Gandhi adamantly opposed the partitioning of India.[37] He sadly predicted the bloodshed and chaos that ultimately followed.

Gandhi had a special genius for dramatic gestures, *les beaux gestes,* and symbols that ignited imagination and stirred emotion. To protest Britain's proposed tax on salt, the septuagenarian, clad in his homespun dhoti, walked barefoot more than two hundred miles to the Indian Ocean. At Gandhi's insistence, he and his companions carried no supplies, entrusting their physical needs to both friendly and hostile villages along their trek to the sea.

Word of Gandhi's pilgrimage spread, attracting a retinue of international reporters. Finally, at dusk, he and his small entourage, followed by an expanding group of reporters, reached the shore of the Indian Ocean. Keenly aware that morning would provide better light for photographers, Gandhi waited until sunrise. The aging leader and his followers prayed through the night. At dawn, before the whirring newsreel cameras, Gandhi and his disciples waded into the sea for a ritual bath. Once back on shore, the frail leader bent down to clutch a small piece of caked salt in his fist. As the silent crowd watched, he slowly unclenched his fingers, revealing the salt, yet another symbol of India's struggle for independence. Then he quietly pronounced, "This is what the English would tax."[38]

Gandhi's simple, but deliberately theatrical, action drew world attention to Great Britain's plan to tax the salt that nature uses to season the oceans. That weekend, in darkened movie theaters around the world, millions of viewers instantly grasped Gandhi's meaning. Overnight, the Indian patriot's name and cause became household words.

Again and again, Gandhi chose just the right symbols and compelling gestures to convey his vision. In the waning days of British colonial rule, he deliberately and ironically selected an unlikely symbol, the wooden spinning wheel, to dramatize the critical role that simple, indigenous technology would play in India's future independence. This unexpected choice bemused some and baffled other outsiders. Yet, Gandhi's counterintuitive symbol communicated a profound message to his Indian supporters: India's independence would flow from rural crops, spun into clothing, freeing India from reliance on costly British imports.

Experience sharpened Gandhi's sense for the management of meaning through the drama of symbolism, costume, timing, and humor. Arriving by ship for an historic appointment with the British monarch, Gandhi shuffled down the gangplank, a stooped, frail figure, clad in his signature dhoti, open sandals on his feet. Grasping his walking stick and leading a goat (his sole source of milk), he greeted the waiting gaggle of international photographers at dockside. Later, when he emerged from his meeting with the king, reporters asked the Indian leader if he did not feel underdressed for the occasion. "Oh, no," Gandhi responded mischievously, "the King wore enough clothes and medals for the two of us."[39]

Toward the end of his life, Gandhi felt his constituency being eroded by more militant leaders, his own brand of leadership overwhelmed by Stage 2 tradition. Although many observers worldwide felt the emotional impact of Gandhi's example, few could completely decipher his profoundly revolutionary message. Almost predictably, Gandhi fell at the hands of assassins from within his own group. For Gandhi and later for Dr. King, it would take a martyr's death to prompt others to rebuild and expand their constituencies.

Martin Luther King, Jr., Apostle of Civil Rights

Another early connective leader, who appeared two decades after Gandhi, also preached nonviolence as a vehicle for overcoming oppression. Taking the moral high ground, Martin Luther King, Jr., argued, would ultimately change the social conscience of the nation. To the very end, he remained committed to nonviolent resistance. By the time he envisioned the Poor People's Campaign, however, King understood that effective protests would necessarily be "dislocative and even disruptive."[40] He held fast despite the sharp sting of mounting criticism from emerging black leaders who preferred decidedly more militant approaches. They too, along with many nonblacks, simply couldn't grasp the fundamental strength in King's connective style.

Gandhi's ideological heir emphasized other important dimensions of connective leadership as well: shared responsibility, networks of leaders, and a personal search for the meaning of one's life. King was a natural networker, a leader comfortable with groups of leaders and their constituents. His ability to communicate with a nontraditional constituency—with white liberals—was a major reason that both the National Association for the Advancement of Colored People (NAACP) and the Montgomery Improvement Association (MIA) wished to recruit him as their leader.[41]

Even physically, King demonstrated the importance of drawing others into the leadership process. Marching in Alabama, not out in front of the line but with arms linked in a phalanx of co-leaders, King and his colleagues all physically enacted their shared vision of racial equality. Here was brotherhood in action, community leaders together shouldering the responsibilities of leadership. Here were power and strength drawn from a collaboration transcending the narrow, egotistical individualism so fundamental to Stage 2 leaders.

The search for life's meaning and its linkage to purposes that exceeded his own personal existence were central aspects of King's leadership. He pondered "this challenge to be loyal to something that transcends our immediate lives."[42] In one speech, he reminded his listeners that "We have a responsibility to set out to discover what we are made for, to discover our life's work, to discover what we are called to do. And after we discover that, we should set out to do it with all of the strength and all of the power that we can muster."[43]

King's decision to speak out against the Vietnam War and his radical plan for the Poor People's Campaign—both choices destined to bring him greater criticism and personal danger—were prompted by his sense that evil must be fought at every level and at any cost. Even the sacrifice of one's life was not too great a price to pay. Dedication to such a transcendent mission would ennoble King and his followers.[44]

For King, as for Gandhi before him, Stage 2 posed serious barriers to the full realization of his connective dreams. It is not entirely coincidental that in the last phases of their lives, both men felt their support waning, with more militant colleagues calling their supporters to reject the subtler, counterintuitive power of nonviolence. The media, mired in Stage 2 thinking, heightened the sting of rejection by pronouncing King's nonviolent approach ineffective.

The Stage 2 leadership conditions prevented followers from grasping the significance of these pioneers' visions. In the decades since their assassinations, mystical reverence for these early connective leaders has grown so that their memory now shrouds their Stage 2 critics in obscurity. The expanding mythologies that swirl around these two figures offer evidence for the emergence of Stage 3, a stage in which we have begun to sense—if not yet completely comprehend—that such leadership styles open up new possibilities. Opportunities for a new vision of leadership exist not only in politics and government but in every leadership arena, from corporations and entrepreneurial ventures to educational, religious, and other nonprofit organizations.

Mikhail Gorbachev: A Transitional Connective Leader

After seven decades of individualistic, power-driven Communist leaders, Mikhail Gorbachev stepped to the helm of the Soviet

Union with a decidedly different leadership repertoire. Where his predecessors perceived only threats to their power, Gorbachev saw strength in truth and openness. His unprecedented call for *perestroika* and *glasnost* caught party apparatchiks and the average Soviet citizen off guard no less than unbelieving observers abroad.

Here again, we see the force of counterintuitive symbols. Gorbachev's seemingly simple concepts of perestroika and glasnost demanded nothing less than totally new attitudes and practices based on open self-appraisal of the Soviet Union. Political self-criticism, forbidden during the lifetime of most Soviet adults, threatened seventy years of authoritarian bureaucracy and self-protective censorship.

The change initially perplexed Soviet citizens, who had been raised on a diet of authority and power. The Old Guard, wedded to their ideology and privileges, resisted mightily. Optimism rose only cautiously among the larger Soviet populace, not yet ready to believe what seemed too good to be true. The older generation remembered the permanent stigma that early supporters of Nikita Khrushchev's reforms suffered in the wake of their leader's ouster. These chilling memories restrained any open endorsement of Gorbachev's radical proposals. Few stepped forward in unqualified support of this puzzling new leader.

Undaunted, Gorbachev began to dismantle the brittle Communist oligarchy. Gorbachev's connective leadership also stirred both hope and political resistance in other oppressed Eastern European countries.

Gorbachev's actions reverberated throughout the West. Turning traditional Stage 2 ideas of weakness into strength, Gorbachev reached across a forty-year abyss of enmity to find common cause with the United States, the Soviet Union's primary adversary. He initiated a rapprochement that caught Soviet and American political insiders totally off guard. In a televised address, Gorbachev assured the world, "We realize our interests, but we try to combine them with the interests of others."[45]

The Soviet leader quickly followed that staggering gesture with an equally electrifying offer to dismantle the powerful weapons of war, even if that meant taking the first unilateral step toward defusing the Cold War. In one stunning stroke, he revealed the power of a counterintuitive idea that echoed Gandhi and King: to disarm oneself before an armed opponent requires immense strength, not weakness.

Gorbachev's unanticipated overtures to the Soviets' Cold War enemies sparked confusion at home and uncertainty around the world. I remember visiting the Soviet Union in 1987 in the early days of the Gorbachev era. During that visit, I spoke with numerous Soviet academics and government bureaucrats, every one of whom expressed reservations about Gorbachev's efforts to change the Soviet Union. In my admittedly small sample, not a single person indicated wholehearted support for the new leader. Their wait-and-see attitude was palpable. On my return to the United States, my own colleagues and acquaintances were intensely interested in my impressions of Gorbachev, but to a person each one deeply suspected his intentions.

What was Gorbachev trying to do? How could his own people trust him when he extended his hand to the capitalist enemy? How could the NATO-pact countries believe this leader, who rejected the practices of Soviet predecessors known for measuring their authority by the number of warheads stockpiled in the USSR?

Initial distrust of the new Communist leader's surprising behavior gradually gave way to "Gorbymania" among the masses in West Germany and Great Britain, as well as in the United States. Ordinary citizens and political observers around the globe sensed that this new-style leader was offering a touch that the world sorely needed. Opinion polls indicated the genial Gorbachev easily could win political office in many of the non-Communist countries he had visited; however, his own nation, accustomed to more authoritarian rulers, remained skeptical. Clearly, it is easier to appreciate daring connective leadership enacted by the heads of *other* nations than by one's own leaders.

Economically drained by the endless arms race of the Cold War, and politically and militarily exhausted by the Afghanistan war, the Soviet economy came to a shuddering halt. The reforms of the Gorbachev period, often sabotaged by hard-liners and disbelieved by cynical, impatient reformers, placed additional burdens on the economically moribund system. In the process, the Soviet republics began to find their own voices and demand independence. Facing a major challenge, Gorbachev sought to create a new Soviet Union, a loosely connected network among previously annexed states, allowing each to select its own leadership. With the Commonwealth of Independent States, he drew new leadership candidates into the previously sacrosanct decision-making structures, while resisting others, like Boris Yeltsin, who would wrest and not share his power.

Still, the inevitable disruptions and chaos engendered by the complex transition to a market economy lengthened food lines and shortened consumers' patience. Caught between left-wing hard-liners and restive reformers, and misunderstood by a hungry and confused populace still trapped in a Stage 2 mentality, Gorbachev faltered.

Some will complain that Gorbachev did not move swiftly or broadly enough, both politically and economically, that his feet were more clay than his admirers recognize. Without gainsaying Gorbachev's mistakes and limitations as he moved in uncharted territory, history will probably acknowledge the monumental scale of the Soviet leader's accomplishment. Appearing at the ebb tide of Stage 2, in a country drained by seven decades of authoritarian, power-driven leadership, Gorbachev overcame the usual myopia of insiders to sound the call for a new leadership era, one that embraced cooperation instead of combat.

Perhaps Gorbachev's true measure will be read in his courageous use of connective leadership in an environment ill-prepared to accept these new behaviors. Without constituents who could respond to and support his connective mission, Gorbachev was destined to play a transitional leadership role. Nonetheless, this early connective leader's strategies have permanently reshaped the map of Eastern Europe—indeed, the course of world history. Historians ultimately may count the fact that Gorbachev catapulted his country across the threshold into the Connective Era as more important than the length of time he served as its official leader.

A Straw in the Stage 3 Wind: Chico Mendes, Political Ecologist

Francisco Mendes Filho, known to both devoted supporters and determined enemies as "Chico Mendes," grew up as a debt peon in the Brazilian rain forest. In 1976, incensed by the ravages that rubber barons inflicted both on the rubber tappers and the trees from which they drew their meager livelihoods, Mendes began to organize local workers.

Undaunted by plantation owners' ruthlessness toward *seringueiros* (rubber tappers), other forest dwellers, and the forest alike, Chico Mendes struggled relentlessly on two fronts: first to preserve the threatened rubber trees, and second to protect the dignity of the *seringueiros.* He led a nonviolent *empate*[46] (standoff) between his union and the ranchers of the Amazon. He fought to save the rubber trees for their own sake, as well as to provide a livelihood for both the tappers and the Indian dwellers of the Brazilian rain forest.

Mendes tramped through miles of forest, recruiting members for his rubber tappers' union. He sought the support of unlikely collaborators, from government officials to a group with the unfamiliar name of "environmentalists." Initially, Mendes didn't understand the ecological issues joining the Brazilian rain forest to a global web of consequences. The greenhouse effect, global warming, and the destruction of the ozone layer were not part of his initial concerns. Yet as he took his cause to private and government agencies, both within his own country and abroad, Mendes began to connect his own simpler vision of human dignity and forest preservation to the ecopolitical mission of environmental activists. By 1985, he had entwined the environmentalists' global dream with his own.

Mendes worked tirelessly to create a network peopled by illiterate rubber tappers, small farmers, government officials, politicians, and environmentalists. Eventually, he attracted educated aristocrats and articulate celebrities, who could publicize and fund his cause. Wearing a rumpled suit donated by an American church organization, he stubbornly lobbied officials, first in his own country and eventually worldwide. Unschooled in diplomatic protocol, he testified diffidently before international agencies, including the World Bank and the Inter-American Development Bank, to seek help before it was too late.

In an ironic twist, the efforts of this rural leader from the Brazilian province of Acre, close to the Peruvian border, led to a sophisticated "rain forest ball," sponsored by the Marchioness of Worcester and Imran Khan. Six thousand miles from rural Brazil, at the Leicester Square Hippodrome in London, society folks danced in "tropical dress" while they raised funds and consciousness for the rain forest of Brazil.

Mendes did more than enlist a highly diverse army of devoted supporters. Working with his own tappers, as well as with environmentalists and anthropologists, he developed the notion of an "extractive reserve," a preserve for forest dwellers, where rubber, Brazil nuts, and other indigenous fruits and medicines would be harvested in ways that sustained the forest. In October 1988, at his behest, the government finally declared a 61,000 hectare tract of land near Xapuri, traditionally used for rubber tapping, an "extractive reserve." In all, the government eventually created four extractive reserves. This monumental victory for Mendes's cause probably hurled the final insult at his enemies.

While environmentalists danced with aristocrats and celebrities at the rain forest ball, back in his own country, Mendes pragmatically reported to his rural supporters the death threats he had received. Land baron Darly Alves da Silva, convinced that Mendes's activities seriously endangered his holdings, had vowed to kill the rain forest champion. Mendes predicted he would not live to lead them for another year.

Five short weeks after the ball, on December 22, 1988, Mendes finished a card game with his bodyguards and headed out the back door of his family's three-room house to the outhouse. A hail of assassins' bullets tore through the forty-four-year old leader's head and heart, mortally injuring him and cutting short his efforts to preserve the Brazilian rain forest.[47,48]

Today Mendes' legacy is being carried forward by his cousin, Raimundo Barros, and Osmarino Amancio Rodriguez, along with their colleagues. In an historic meeting at Rio Branco, on Easter Sunday 1989, a new alliance was forged between the rubber tappers and Indians from tribes as different as the rubber-tapping Campa and Kaxinua and the last members of the Krenak, driven from their soil by huge state-owned corporations. *Ribeirinhos*—river people, harvesters of latex, gums, and natural tropical medicines—joined in an alliance with the rubber tappers, Indians, church leaders, environmentalists, and well-known Brazilian ecoactivists to rededicate themselves to their martyr's cause.

A report of the Rio Branco meeting reveals that the message of connective leadership is spreading. It also suggests, however, that resistance remains, even among the well-intentioned, who worried about the political connections these Brazilian activists have developed worldwide:

On the stage in the gym in Rio Branco, a rubber tapper wearing the *poronga*—a helmet fixed with a candle to guide him along forest paths in the predawn hours—embraced a Campa Indian amid the applause of the crowd at the symbolic expression of their new alliance. As Osmarino told the gathering, the situation has changed since Chico Mendes was killed. . . . His death showed the need for strengthened leadership throughout Amazonia, a broader political perspective and a robust organisational network. But the broader political perspective gestured at by Osmarino and by another *seringueiro* leader, Raimundo Barros (Chico's cousin) also represented a coming of age, one perhaps not entirely welcome to the first-world emissaries in Rio Branco.[49]

Still, the saga of Chico Mendes raises hopes for connective leadership, a straw in the Stage 3 wind. His change and growth are emblematic of the course taken by the entire environmental movement since the 1970s, which in turn echoes the worldwide transformation from Stage 2 to the Connective Era.[50]

Entering Stage 3: New Demands on Leaders and Constituents Alike

In this chapter, we have seen how the engines of change are pushing us simultaneously in different directions, toward both increased global interdependence and greater fragmentation born of diversity. In the careers of Gandhi, King, Gorbachev, and Mendes, we have begun to see, "through a glass darkly," the lineaments of a new form of leadership, one that holds far greater promise of meeting the challenges of this new era than the Stage 2 paradigm does. Nonetheless, the demands of this new era are not inconsequential for either leaders or supporters.

Because leaders and constituents are inextricably joined, there is no changing one without the other. Although this book speaks largely to the changes leaders must make, their departures from Stage 2 action and thought must be supported by constituents who can make complementary strides.

Becoming Leaders for Stage 3

Leaders who would deal effectively with Stage 3 issues must have the vision and skills to balance competing priorities. They must forge new solutions that integrate the economic, political, health, and educational needs of many diverse groups. Such leaders must bring both urban and rural, affluent and poor, as well as First, Second, and Third World constituencies into the dialogue. The problems Stage 3 leaders face demand working instrumentally, but ethically, with a loosely linked network of leaders and groups, even nations, to shape solutions to mutual problems.

Stage 3 leaders need to convince dissimilar, often antagonistic groups that theirs is a shared destiny in which everyone must contribute, and even sacrifice, for all to thrive. They must be capable of building bridges that span the competitive gulfs between organizations. Such leaders see the strength inherent in networks of leaders viewed as colleagues, rather than as competitors. A hallmark of their leadership is the capacity to transform interdependence and diversity from opposing into symbiotic forces.

Some emerging connective leaders already use dazzling connective skills to negotiate, persuade, help, nurture, collaborate, and contribute to the larger group enterprise. They devote themselves to suprapersonal causes and call upon their colleagues and constituents to make serious, but ennobling, sacrifices. Anita Roddick and Billy Shore (first met in Chapter One) are good examples of what we have been calling Stage 3 leaders. They comfortably negotiate the divergent interests of consumers, community groups, workers, shareholders, corporations, third-sector (nonprofit) organizations, governments, and financial institutions. They manage to function in the present without short-changing the future. They routinely bring unexpected parties into collaborative enterprises. They model the search for meaning in their own lives and create opportunities for others to find meaning in authentic experiences in organizations and community projects. (We look at such leaders more closely in Part Two.)

Evolving from Stage 2 Followers to Connective Constituents

The transition to the Connective Era remains troubled by the resistance of Stage 2 followers who fail to support would-be connective leaders. Even as the Connective Era dawns, followers everywhere have difficulty grasping the complexity of this new world that calls for long-term, intricate solutions.

For all the psychological and existential reasons we considered in Chapter Two, ambivalence toward leaders—even familiar Stage 2 leaders—is reflected in the rapid turnover among CEOs and wildly fluctuating approval ratings of political leaders. Even newly elected leaders have a hard time hanging on to the public's approval. While followers claim to want honorable, thoughtful leaders, they still desire quick fixes for even the most complicated problems. The Japanese press reports that business leaders long for a "political hero," a strong leader—"even if he should be a 'despot'"[51]—to surmount the country's woes.

Followers soon turn away from even the revolutionary heroes they sweep into office on a swelling tide of public esteem. By the end of 1995, Poland's once-idolized Lech Walesa had been swept from office. Russia's Boris Yeltsin saw his enthusiastic support sink from 85 percent in 1991 to 6 percent during the Chechnyan war in 1995 (lower than President Nixon's most disastrous Watergate levels).[52]

Even when supporters continue to idolize a leader personally, they express their ambivalence by disdaining the leader's policies and administrative minions. Nobel laureate Nelson Mandela received a 62 percent approval rating in 1995, but the public gave his government only a 40 percent nod.[53]

The media, through whose eyes the public glimpses and evaluates new leaders, still measure leaders by a Stage 2 yardstick. A quick scan of the comments of political pundits suggests that things have not changed that much since the days of Martin Luther King, Jr. Many followers would rather fight than switch to Stage 3.

Whether we want to acknowledge it or not, however, the old individualism of Stage 2 is evaporating. The individual destinies of leaders and supporters are tied willy nilly to the fate of the larger group. Global networks are needed to solve these common problems. Interdependence must supersede narrow individualism. Yet diversity produces new, more complex forms of individualism that pull in other directions. Only leaders who can use strong instrumental talents, integrated with both self-reliant and relational skills, will be able to harness the complexities and contradictions of these strong centrifugal forces.

Unaccustomed to the connective leader's demands for supporters to participate actively, rather than simply to criticize from the sidelines, Stage 2 followers stubbornly resist the unfamiliar strategies of the new leaders. They demand a voice but often shrink from the ongoing responsibilities that having a serious Stage 3 voice entails. Despite their rhetoric, many would-be supporters prefer to remain in the follower mode, passively reactive to paternalistic, Stage 2 leaders who will shoulder the burden.

Stage 2 followers have trouble understanding leaders who take the time to consult not only other leaders but also a broad set of constituents. In the search to quiet their existential anxiety, traditional followers continue to applaud leaders who make strong, rapid decisions, regardless of how ill-considered those choices may be. As we move clumsily into the Connective Era, "quick" and "tough" are still more acceptable to Stage 2 followers than consultative, considered, or connective action. To prepare for the Connective Era, followers need to develop a taste for sampling the perspectives of others, even when that process may delay decision making.

Effecting the transformation from Stage 2 followership to Connective Era constituency will also mean changing the way people think about the organizations to which they belong. The process involves loosening their identification with their home institution so as to make room for empathy, if not strong identification, with other organizations—even competitors. Given the diminishing likelihood that most workers will spend their entire careers within any single organization, that can only be a step in the right direction. Hard-line allegiance to political parties also needs to be softened to embrace the multiple, often competing needs of a complex society. In the age of globalization, constituents everywhere have to think about the behavioral and attitudinal flexibility required to become citizens of the world. Only supporters who can forego the security of authoritarian leaders and assume their legitimate share of responsibility will be able to break through the chrysalis of followership and emerge as full-fledged constituents.

As Stage 3 begins, the new winds of change are scattering our beliefs in the simple solutions that guided Stage 2 leaders and appeased their parochially defined followers. If we are to meet the challenges and reap the bounty of Stage 3, we need leaders with the savvy to braid multilayered interdependence with diverse needs for identity and expression. We also need not slavish followers but responsible constituents willing to assume their share of the burden.

In Part Two, we explore a detailed model of leadership that departs from traditional conceptions and fits more closely the transformed contours of the Stage 3 landscape. The Connective Leadership Model provides a way to make explicit the dimensions of this new form of leadership. The model translates the intimations provided by the early connective leaders seen here into a highly specific concept of what their example represents for their successors.

Part Two

The Connective Leadership Model

Figure 1. Connective Leadership Model.

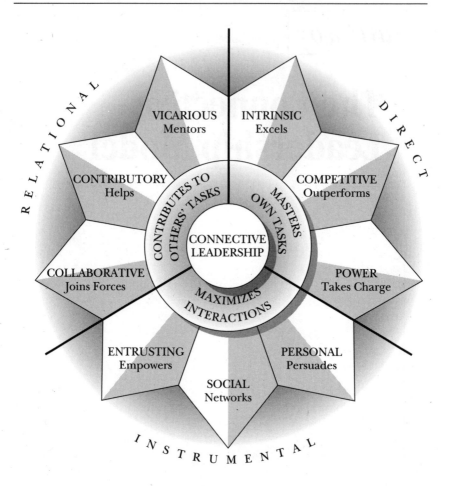

Note: Figure 1 was derived from the iterative interaction of theory and empirical research. Although we started with a linear theoretical model, repeated empirical tests of the theory, using factor, canonical, and correlational analysis, and other statistical procedures, eventually led us to the placement that is represented here. In statistical terms, each individual style is most closely correlated to its two contiguous styles (that is, one on each side), with the correlations dropping off quite regularly as one moves farther away from the focal style.

Chapter Five

Mapping Leadership Styles
Direct, Relational, and Instrumental

As practice is to policy, so style is to belief. Style is merely a consequence of what we believe, of what is in our hearts.
MAX DE PREE[1]

In previous chapters, we have explored the foundations of our images of leadership and demonstrated why radically new forms of leadership are a must in Stage 3, the Connective Era. We have also seen examples of early connective leaders, prophetic figures whose leadership strategies outstripped their followers' readiness to accept them. To advance to a more complete understanding of connective leadership, we need a conceptual tool, one that enables us to describe leadership behavior in greater detail.

This chapter and the three that follow provide such a tool, the Connective Leadership Model. The model helps us to analyze leadership and specific leaders in terms of their underlying behavioral preferences, called *achieving styles*.[2] Through experience and intuition, connective leaders have learned to use a wide range of these behaviors in ways that allow them to respond more appropriately to a Stage 3 environment. Since achieving styles are not the exclusive property of connective leaders, once the model is articulated then other aspiring leaders can learn to use them as well.

The Connective Leadership Model enables us to move beyond simple description by presenting a method that leaders can consciously and systematically use in several ways. The model allows leaders to assess not only their own leadership styles and those of others but also the leadership behaviors most needed in any particular situation and the leadership styles most valued in each organization.

This chapter first describes the intellectual impetus behind the model. It then reviews the early work on achieving styles and the intellectual process that eventually linked achieving styles to connective leadership. We then delineate the model, its empirical base, and three instruments developed to test and apply the model. Next is a description of how we learn to prefer certain styles and how these individual patterns of preferences, or achieving styles profiles, filter our perceptions of reality and thus often lead to inappropriate responses. The chapter illustrates the importance of situational cues and suggests how one can evaluate situations to determine the achieving styles demanded by different circumstances.

Finally, the chapter closes with a discussion of how organizations reward specific behaviors (organizational achieving styles) that reflect the values embedded in the organization's culture. While this chapter presents an overview of the model, the next three explore in depth the three sets of achieving styles—direct, relational, and instrumental—that constitute the model, with scores of illustrative examples drawn from the careers of real-life leaders.

Before presenting the overview, let me note three caveats. First, the model describes *how* people go about achieving their goals, not *what* their goals are. That is, achieving styles are the means, not the ends, that people use to accomplish their objectives. We might think of these achieving styles as implementation strategies, personal technologies, or simply the methods people learn early on and then consistently use to get whatever it is they want.

Second, most people develop a rather narrow repertoire of achieving styles, repeatedly drawing upon the same combination of behaviors even when they are inappropriate to the ends they are seeking. They consistently ignore other styles that may be more relevant in certain situations but that feel less comfortable to them. Most people repeatedly call upon the same two or three styles. In explaining the nine styles, however, I use the shortcut of describing people *as if* they were "pure" types who rely exclusively on one style.

Third, let's also remember that these styles are learned, usually early in life, and reinforced by a lifetime of successes and failures. Because these behaviors are learned, they also can be unlearned, altered, refined, and expanded. Therein lies the hope that leadership behavior *can* be changed and that most people can learn to act in ways that will make them more effective Stage 3 leaders.

From Ordinary Behavior to Leadership

Beginning in childhood, we all learn how to get things done, how to accomplish our goals. Given that we are raised by different types of parents and caretakers with different expectations and values, we don't all learn to emphasize the exact same behaviors. Some of us learn to confront tasks single-handedly, others learn to seek help; some learn to delegate, while others master alternative strategies for achieving their goals. Through trial and error, success and failure, we also discover combinations of strategies that tend to work for us. Achieving styles are simply behaviors for accomplishing our goals, social technologies or personal methods for engaging in the work of living and leading. When we are called upon to assume leadership responsibilities, these are the behaviors we bring to the leadership table.

The limited behavioral strategies that worked for us in non-leadership roles, however, may not be adequate to deal with the broader responsibilities that leadership brings. In social roles, as well as in technical fields, simple technologies may have to give way to different, more advanced methods for accomplishing our objectives. That is the role of innovation.[3] Swimmers, for example, may learn to dive by practicing independently, drawing on self-reliance and their own internalized standards of excellence. Those divers who move into leadership roles as team coaches must expand their narrow repertoire of achieving styles if they hope to mold other young athletes into a first-rate, dedicated team.

These ordinary behaviors that we all learn to some degree are the very same elements that leaders call upon to achieve their purposes. They are the source of leadership action. Few leaders are born with inherent expertise across the entire behavioral spectrum of achieving styles. True, some people, like Gandhi, seem to have a talent, even a genius for leadership. Yet most of the individuals who we would all agree were gifted leaders—exemplary or evil—had to learn new and expanded ways of achieving their goals when they assumed the mantle of leadership. Initially shy about speaking in public, Mohandas Gandhi laboriously taught himself to communicate his vision of an independent India through electrifying words and symbols.

Finally, world-class leaders, like world-class mathematicians, may come along only once or twice in our lifetimes. But just as we can teach most students to do math somewhat better than they would have done without instruction, so most people can learn to exercise leadership more effectively as well. Otherwise, why bother studying leadership, except to appreciate a mere curiosity that only giants exhibit? As the Connective Era calls for more leaders at every organizational and community level, we shall have increasing need for so-called ordinary people to learn the dynamics of leadership. The Connective Leadership Model, with its underlying array of achieving styles, can help to explicate the behaviors that leaders and the rest of us call upon to accomplish our goals.

The Early Development of Achieving Styles Research: The Link to Connective Leadership

To understand the Connective Leadership Model, it is useful to consider the original impetus for the research that eventually led to recognition of a pattern I now call connective leadership. A brief review of how some early research on achieving styles eventually drew my attention to that pattern will help to clarify the links between achieving styles and connective leadership.

The Impetus for the Early Research

The Connective Leadership Model grew out of earlier research on achieving styles begun in 1972 with my colleague Professor Harold Leavitt, of Stanford University.[4] Our research was prompted initially by an interest in differences between women and men in the behaviors they used to achieve their goals.

In the late 1960s, the work of psychologist Matina Horner generated considerable excitement about women's presumed fear of success in competitive situations.[5] Horner's research was designed to shed light upon equivocal results obtained from female subjects in earlier laboratory experiments on achievement motivation and performance conducted by psychologists David McClelland and J. W. Atkinson and their associates.[6] Women, it seemed, did not respond as predicted to their experimental manipulations. While the white, male students in the McClelland/Atkinson experiments reacted to achievement-oriented cues with increased achievement behavior, the results for women produced an inconsistent pattern, difficult to interpret.

Horner's work suggested that, in competitive situations, women had a "motive to avoid success," largely because success would lead to negative consequences, particularly from their peers. The same competitive situations, however, did not at all dampen men's motivation; in fact, they sharply increased men's achievement behavior.

We, however, felt that while women's resistance to overt competitiveness was indeed real, they were no more fearful of success than males. They simply went about it differently. We thought then, and still do, that women like to master challenging tasks, but they dislike perceiving themselves or being perceived by others as overtly competitive. We thought that women derived a sense of accomplishment not only from doing things well on their own but from working collaboratively and helping others with whom they identified, particularly their children and husbands, to achieve success.

A second stream of research, this one on gender differences in group decision making, contributed to our early interest in how people accomplish their goals. We were struck, for example, by some findings from organizational behaviorist Franklin Rubenstein's simulation of an industrial pollution situation.[7] In that experiment, subjects faced the choice of either reinvesting a portion of their gains to avoid polluting a river or simply using the river to make the most profit they could. In all-male groups, subjects tended not to reinvest to prevent pollution. Individual male "industrialists" competed against one other to squeeze maximum earnings from the river until its inevitable contamination curtailed further use. All-female groups tended to use a very different strategy. In those groups, all the subjects kept reinvesting part of their profits to prevent excessively polluting the river. This approach enabled the female subjects to continue benefiting indefinitely, albeit somewhat below the high but short-lived profit levels of their competitive male counterparts. Rubenstein's results strengthened our suspicion that men approached tasks directly, individualistically, and competitively, while women sought to achieve their goals more indirectly, collaboratively, and vicariously.

To test our ideas, Leavitt and I developed a survey instrument to measure the achievement behavior of individuals. We called that instrument the *L-BL Achieving Styles Inventory (ASI)*.[8] In 1973, we began to collect data, primarily from corporate executives but from other subjects as well, in the United States and numerous other countries, from Argentina to Taiwan.[9] Since 1984 alone, the revised and validated instrument has been administered to more than eight thousand individuals.[10]

By 1979, Leavitt had moved on to other research interests, and my own attention turned to the behavior of corporate and political leaders. I became particularly intrigued by the different combinations of achieving styles reflected in the behavior of leaders, both in our data base and in the world at large. This was the point at which the research on achieving styles became explicitly linked to the phenomenon later labeled *connective leadership*.

From Achieving Styles to Connective Leadership

Around that time, I began to notice several things about the behavior of a small number of leaders who appeared to be in close touch with a rapidly changing world.

First, this small set seemed to use more than the narrow band of achieving styles favored by traditional leaders and by people outside of leadership roles. Second, these leaders frequently used political, instrumental styles that bespoke an awareness of how groups and organizations (or systems) worked. They often favored various forms of instrumental behavior. Always aware of relationships and connections, they worked through large networks of associates, bringing others into the leadership circle in new, less authoritarian ways; they worked well with other leaders with similar, but not necessarily identical, goals; they used stunning, dramatic actions and symbols to communicate their vision. When necessary, these new leaders also used power and competitiveness like their predecessors. The political behavior of these new leaders, however, appeared to place greater emphasis on the good of the group rather than on the expansion of their own power. I began to think about this new leadership behavior as "connective" because it seemed to flow from a complex awareness and use of connections in all aspects of life.

These and other observations piqued my curiosity about the relationship between achieving styles and this new form of leadership. Only much later did I recognize their link to the various stages in leadership conditions. Eventually, I realized that although connective leaders drew upon the same basic achieving behaviors available to everyone, they used the entire repertoire not only more fully but in distinctively different ways. I also began to notice the parallels between the various achieving styles on the one hand and the forces of diversity and interdependence that were growing ever stronger at the societal level. Thus I began to conceptualize the full spectrum of achieving styles as a foundation for a Model of Connective Leadership.[11]

An Overview of the Connective Leadership Model

The Connective Leadership Model describes three general categories or sets of behaviors (achieving styles) used by individuals for achieving their objectives. The description of the model begins with the direct set, then moves to the relational set, and finally covers the instrumental set. Each set encompasses three styles, resulting in a full complement of nine achieving styles (Figure 1).[12]

The direct set is most closely related, at the societal level, to the various forms of diversity which prompt expressions of individualism. The relational set, with its emphasis on identification with others, is the counterpart of societal interdependence. Finally, the instrumental set provides a source of ethically rooted action that harmonizes the contradictory forces of diversity and interdependence represented by the direct and relational sets.

For ease of explanation, the nine styles are grouped into three sets. The groupings into sets should not be seen as impenetrable barriers, locking people into one set versus another. Not only are contiguous styles "kissing cousins," but some people prefer combinations of styles that draw from two or even all three sets. To deal with the complexities of Stage 3, connective leaders comfortably use the full palette of connective leadership styles in various combinations.

The Direct Set

The first set, the direct styles, focuses primarily on the tasks that individuals set for themselves. These styles, related to the forces of diversity, speak to issues of individualism and independence. People who prefer the direct styles confront the task or situation directly, rarely requiring intermediaries. They are particularly concerned with performance and perfection in carrying out their *own* objectives. They care primarily about exquisitely mastering tasks, their own performance, competitive preeminence, and control. People who prefer these styles tightly control the definition of goals and the means used to accomplish them.

Individualistic Stage 2 leaders, such as the late French president Charles de Gaulle, have a penchant for the direct styles. Connective leaders can and do use these styles when appropriate, but unlike Stage 2 leaders they don't necessarily select them as their first choice. Moreover, connective leaders refuse to be shackled by the limitations of this or any other single set of styles.

The three styles in the direct set are called *intrinsic, competitive,* and *power.*

These labels are probably self-explanatory, except perhaps for the *intrinsic* style. Even in the intrinsic style, only the label, not the behavior, is likely to be initially unfamiliar; in this style it is the content or intrinsic nature of the task that excites the individual. The challenge and importance of the goal captivate those individuals who gravitate toward the intrinsic style. Usually a clearly defined vision of the task compels their imagination, and their behavior follows in its service.

Given a project, people who prefer intrinsic action look to themselves, not others, to make it happen. The challenge of individualistically mastering a situation, task, or skill is what excites these individuals. Climbing Mt. Everest, starting a new company, organizing a new political party, discovering a new planet, painting a mural, developing a vaccine, designing new products and innovative manufacturing processes, giving a virtuoso performance, planning an elegant experiment: these are the stones against which intrinsic individuals strike the flint of their imagination and determination.

In striving to fulfill their own vision, intrinsic types are their own sternest critics, evaluating their performance against the most rigorous standards—usually against their own past attainments. Intrinsic types are oblivious to what others think about the nature and importance of their challenge or the quality of their performance. They don't particularly care whether their performance pleases or disappoints their audience. Instead, intrinsic types are guided by a strict, internal standard of excellence against which they measure themselves. "Good enough" never *is*, for intrinsic individuals.

Artist Diego Rivera, Italian filmmaker Lina Wertmuller, and choreographer Jacques D'Amboise all reflect the intrinsic sensibility when they attend more to their own standards of perfection than to those of their audiences. De Gaulle also marched to his own drummer, sometimes losing, sometimes regaining his followers, but always seeking direct satisfaction from striving for the fulfillment of his personal vision: a proud, free, and highly individualistic France.

The other two direct styles are quite familiar. The *competitive* style takes its name from the competitive individual's passion to outdo others. Being the best is what matters to competitive types, and competition is what makes their blood course. Their motto is the saying often attributed to the Green Bay Packers' former coach, Vince Lombardi: "Sure, winning isn't everything; it's the only thing."[13]

People who favor the *power* style are turned on by taking charge, coordinating, and organizing situations and events, resources, and other people. Power types may delegate tasks, but they always retain control over what and how things are done, as the behavior of many Stage 2 CEOs demonstrates. Individuals who gravitate to the power style give clear-cut assignments to others, provide detailed implementation plans, and set benchmarks and deadlines.

The Relational Set

The second set of achieving styles, the relational styles, is oriented toward the goals of others. These styles are related to the societal forces of interdependence. People who prefer relational styles easily take part in group tasks or contribute to other people's goals. They willingly relinquish control over both the means and the ends of accomplishment. Their intense identification with others—be they individuals (whether family or revered historical figures), groups (like football teams), or even institutions (such as a military academy)—enables them to contribute actively or passively to objectives established by others. In this way, relational individuals derive a strong sense of achievement, pride, and pleasure from their enthusiastic participation in the success of others with whom they identify, even when no personal relationship exists between them.

The relational set includes the *collaborative, contributory,* and *vicarious* styles.

People who use the *collaborative* style enjoy working with others on teams and joint projects. The synergy of the group gets collaborators going. They share in the glory and the hard work that brings success, but they also accept their share of the responsibility for failure. The bonds of friendship and camaraderie strengthen joint efforts and constitute an important part of the reward. The McNeil-Lehrer news team on public television reflected this style.

Contributory individuals are slightly different, deriving their satisfaction from helping other people complete their own chosen tasks. They recognize that the major accomplishment belongs to the other party, but they feel a sense of accomplishment from the piece they contributed. Later, we'll see an astounding example of contributory behavior demonstrated by mountain climber Mike Corbett, who helped his paraplegic friend, former park ranger Mark Wellman, fulfill his dream of climbing Yosemite's El Capitan.

People who prefer contributory styles are not necessarily prompted to help others because they lack the talent or determination to do it themselves. Rather, they derive a genuine sense of satisfaction from contributing to others' success. Of course, since each of the nine styles ordinarily is part of an individual's unique set of preferred styles (or profile), people who use contributory behavior in certain circumstances may under other conditions use direct styles to act on their own behalf.

People who prefer the final relational style, the *vicarious,* don't actually participate directly in other people's activities. Instead, they encourage or facilitate others' accomplishments. They act as mentors or fans, offering wisdom, cheering others on, and taking immense pride in the accomplishments of the people and groups with whom they identify.

Any parent who has ever watched a child perform on stage, make the heroic touchdown, or win a coveted prize can recognize the sense of achievement, seasoned with pride and joy, that vicarious individuals experience. Hadley Hemingway, first wife of American writer Ernest Hemingway, expressed that keen sense of identification with another's accomplishment that satisfies the vicarious individual's own need for achievement: "No, I don't write novels and stories n'so forth, but Ernest does, and that's practically the same thing."[14]

For vicarious individuals, a sense of accomplishment can develop even in the absence of a personal relationship with the one actively engaged in achieving a goal. Witness the pride and "connection" with their team that soccer fans demonstrate, or the intense connection that groupies feel with their idolized rock stars.

The research of Cialdini, De Nicholas, and associates on "self-presentation by association" suggests that some people receive a shot of self-esteem by identifying with and claiming association with a "winner."[15] This can happen even when their connection is as remote as that of a football fan cheering from an armchair a continent away. People quite distantly connected to a successful individual may enhance their own status by claiming the most tenuous connection to that person, for example, a shared birthdate. In a variety of ingenious experiments, Cialdini and his associates demonstrated the myriad ways in which individuals gain added status and "manage their public images indirectly by announcing their [sometimes trivial] connections with successful . . . others, thereby basking in the reflected glory of another's success."[16]

The Instrumental Set

The third and final set of achieving styles is called *instrumental* because people who prefer these strategies treat everything—themselves, their relationships, situations, and resources—as instruments for achieving their goals. People who gravitate toward the instrumental styles understand the subtlest human interactions and group processes, the most complex human systems. In organizations, they navigate well on the byways of the informal system, where friendships and all kinds of relationships move things along. People and politics fascinate instrumental types, who tune into the political process, sifting each nuance for meanings and possibilities. People who prefer these styles treat everyone, themselves and others, as instruments for accomplishing their ends. They retain control over goals but allow and even encourage others to shape the means to those ends.

Because they bend themselves and everything around them to their use, the behavior of instrumental individuals often resembles the kind of action Machiavelli recommended to the prince. When connective leaders use instrumental styles, however, their ethical commitment to altruistic purposes distinguishes them from the Machiavelli of *The Prince,* whose strategies held the taint of self-interest. This is why in Chapter One we called the connective leader's use of the instrumental styles "denatured Machiavellianism."

The three styles in this set are the *personal, social,* and *entrusting* styles.

The first of these, the *personal* style, involves using the self, a strategy that covers a lot of interesting territory. In their quest for achievement, individuals who prefer the personal style use every attribute and personal resource they have. Personal types call upon their intelligence and wit to draw supporters to their cause. They count on their charm, flair for high drama, physical attractiveness, sexual sizzle, family background and past accomplishments, and even the prestige of their alma mater to attract supporters. They use self-deprecating humor to offset the threat that their powerful gifts evoke.

Personal types are particularly adept at dramatic gestures and counterintuitive (unexpected or paradoxical) symbols that communicate their vision and enlist others in their cause. Their finely tuned sense of theater, sometimes even bordering on eccentricity, brings excitement, fun, and sometimes awe to their supporters.

Personal achievers frequently display exquisite timing and balance, taking action at exactly the right moment with just the right degree of flair. They unerringly select the perfect costume, replete with appropriate rituals, to communicate the importance and authenticity of their objectives. Deliberately selected by the British monarch to move India toward independence, Lord Viceroy Louis Mountbatten discharged his duties using the entire panoply of British pomp and circumstance. The intent of his personal strategies was to convince his Indian subjects that they still had a real Lord Viceroy.[17]

Personal types may sparkle with charisma as they convey their message to potential constituents. Their compelling performances captivate audiences, who readily enroll in their enterprise. The charisma and dramatic gestures of Gandhi and Mikhail Gorbachev won the hearts of global constituencies. As a presidential candidate, Bill Clinton's use of the town-meeting format to communicate directly with voters was a perfect example of personal behavior. Candidates Clinton and Al Gore used the populist symbolism of their campaign bus caravan to stir the political imagination of voters.

Negotiation and persuasion are the territory of personal types, who smoothly bring others around to a common point of view. People who prefer the personal styles perceive themselves and others, along with nonpersonal resources, as tools for brokering agreements. In the role of negotiator, personal types know exactly how to present themselves, how to time the offer, how to milk the drama of the moment. In a social environment where diversity at every level breeds conflicting interests, the capacity to use oneself and others to bridge these gulfs becomes increasingly valuable.

The other two instrumental styles focus less on charismatically using the self to enlist supporters and more on using relationships to get things done. People who prefer the *social* style cultivate and liberally use "contacts," always aware of how any new individual might fit into their larger scheme—if not now, maybe later. Faced with any task, social individuals immediately flip through their mental Rolodéx to identify people with the needed expertise, talent, experience, or other contacts. They build and maintain networks of associates that they call upon as the situation requires. Former president George Bush was noted for his use of long-time associates in times of crisis. In addition to the personal style, Bill Clinton uses social strategies, relying upon a vast network of associates and friends to advance his aims. The preinaugural economic summit of long-time associates and advisors he convened was a social type's quintessential event. For leaders who prefer the social style, it's *whom* you know, not *what* you know, that moves the agenda.

People who use the *entrusting* style behave somewhat differently. They simply expect everyone on their horizon to help them achieve what they consider their shared goals. They do not look for specific talents or experience, but they do take care to select capable candidates. The expectations entrusting individuals have for other people usually bear fruit, largely because their anticipation and trust stimulate motivation, stir creative juices, and buoy confidence. Entrusted with the leader's vision, the recipient responds with pride, creativity, and a sense of ownership.

Unlike direct types, who keep tight control over the goal as well as the path leading to it, people who use entrusting behavior simply have a goal that they expect others to share and help them reach. They comfortably seek counsel from others and usually leave their entrustees the choice of method. People who use entrusting behavior have complete faith that their associates will not disappoint them.

Part of the entrusting types' faith is based on their overall judgment of able helpers. Another part is founded on the entrusting individual's own mastery of the entrusting process, since entrusting others with one's cherished vision takes steady nerves and the ability to take risks. One CEO of a large retail chain spoke about the faith his organization places in the people to whom it entrusts multimillion dollar decisions. Although he acknowledged occasional, human qualms about the expensive risks involved, this CEO continues to entrust employees with enormous responsibilities.

Entrusting types know something else as well: entrusting others with one's vision works as a treasured gift that leaves the recipient indebted to the donor. This obligation creates tension and imbalance, which cannot be eased for the recipient except by reciprocation with a comparable gift: the fulfillment of the giver's expectations.[18] Recipients of such treasured gifts reach deep within themselves—to the very wellsprings of creativity, responsibility, and loyalty—to meet the giver's expectations and relieve their own indebtedness. In this way, entrusting types stimulate new ideas, as well as growth and leadership, in those to whom they entrust their goals. Parents who articulate coherent values but then leave it up to their kids to practice them, intuitively understand the special growth hormone that entrusting behavior contains.

How We Develop Preferred Styles

Through various experiences, most people eventually come to favor a particular combination of styles for achieving their goals. Some individuals' preferred styles remain confined within the direct, relational, or instrumental set, while others' preferences span two or even all three sets of styles. It's important to understand the origins of these preferences, because most of us have difficulty seeing beyond our own favorite styles. Poorly understood preferences can act as blinders that prevent us from developing a richer selection of leadership behaviors.

Learning Our Preferred Styles

The process of learning achieving styles most likely begins in early childhood. The satisfaction and frustration of our early needs make a significant impression on us. Primarily from how our parents and other caretakers respond to our calls for help, we begin to learn how to get what we need or simply want. The behavior of parents, teachers, and other role models is colored not only by their own achieving styles and general upbringing, but also by the cultural values prevalent during that historical period. Nor, as we saw in Chapter Two, is any generation immune to the universal existential forces that shape the deepest psychological needs. Within this broader existential and historical context, and mostly by trial and error, we discover how to influence both the people and events that structure our environment.

Learning the Direct Styles

Some parents don't believe their children should have their needs met on demand. They worry about spoiling them. Other parents may simply be too inattentive or busy to gratify very quickly their children's needs. Early on, these parents expect their children to do whatever they can for themselves, to do things without assistance or complaint. Such parents tend to raise children who prefer the direct styles, meeting their goals through intrinsic, competitive, and power styles.

Such parents make us feel good that we are so independent and grown-up, even when we're still quite small. We discover the zest of doing things individually, the satisfaction of being in charge of ourselves and our own little world. From caretakers like these, we learn at an early age to take pleasure in being responsible and doing things directly on our own. At a minimum, we learn that taking action ourselves usually proves better and quicker than getting others to do it for us. Consequently, we enjoy feeling self-reliant, competent, and in control.

For some direct individuals, the satisfaction that comes from mastering a task on their own, particularly when they do it perfectly, becomes its own reward. Challenges excite rather than intimidate people who develop a taste for the sweetness of intrinsic achievement.

Much of the time, intrinsic types don't have to be told when they have done something very well because they've developed their own very exacting standards. Mostly they keep measuring themselves against their own previous level of accomplishment, always striving to perfect their performance.

Other self-reliant individuals judge how well they have done by comparing themselves to those around them. They have learned to prefer the competitive style. Competitive action can be fun, particularly when we win the prize for being the best among a group of stellar performers. For some of us, winning makes our adrenaline run, and of course it usually brings us lots of attention.

Still other direct types come to feel that they can't really master a task unless they control every aspect of it. They learn to achieve individualistic ends through power. Coordinating, directing, and delegating don't seem very burdensome, and being the leader often brings them acclaim. In fact, being in charge exhilarates power types, who enjoy sipping the elixir of authority. This strategy helps them avoid the kind of dependence on others that they have learned to associate with delay and frustration.

Learning the Relational Styles

Parents who quickly and thoroughly fulfill our needs teach us that it is satisfying to do things for and with other people. We learn that relationships are a source of satisfaction and pleasure, even pride. We find that people like to do things with us, and it's fun to do things with them. These are the earliest inklings of collaborative behavior.

We also discover that positive results flow from identifying with others and their needs, a first step toward vicarious behavior. We see that people and their achievements are interesting and worthwhile.

As children, we also discover that each new skill we learn pleases our parents and other caretakers. The example of caretakers who willingly meet our needs reassures us that helping and working with others, particularly contributing and taking pride in other people's accomplishments (vicarious behavior), are achievements in themselves.

As children develop, many parents encourage and welcome their help in household and family activities. If the experience of helping others is positive, we learn a sense of accomplishment from collaborating or simply assisting others in their work, using contributory achieving styles. Not only that; we learn to trust others to help us, to work with us, and to take pride in our accomplishments.

These adults are comfortable role models, people we feel confident in emulating. We learn from their example that people do things together, that they can be counted on to share one another's hopes and dreams. All in all, relationships are satisfying and trustworthy. Doing things with and for people becomes a major source of pleasure and achievement. Growing up this way makes us comfortable with relational styles.

Learning the Instrumental Styles

Some parents don't respond quite so readily to their children's calls for help. Their slower, more measured response teaches us that we must work harder to entice or cajole people into meeting our needs. We learn to do special things to get their attention: cry louder, hold our breath, throw temper tantrums, smile, tease, laugh, and charm.

Early on we learn the elements of personal behavior. We dramatize our needs through gestures, rituals, and dress. We discover the importance of timing. Using charm and humor, sometimes rage and tears, we learn to wrap our parents around our finger. Their responses, in turn, teach us still other subtleties of using ourselves, as well as others, to get our way. Gradually, we become proficient at drawing others into our orbit to help us accomplish our goals.

Eventually we learn to use everything about ourselves—our intelligence, charm, wit, humor, poise, appearance, sexuality, past accomplishments, even our family background—to attract supporters to our cause. We discover how to use ourselves to persuade and negotiate with others to support us in what we want to do.

We discern that dramatizing ourselves, our activities, and our goals makes us more interesting to others, by exciting and attracting them to our quest. We learn to use symbols and unexpected gestures to surprise our audience and take away their collective breath. In this way, we enlist their eager support.

Besides using ourselves as instruments for fulfilling our goals, we realize we can use others in similar ways. Some of us develop social skills, identifying and cataloguing specific people for particular tasks. As new people enter our world, we include them in our network of potential associates and helpers. These are the recognizable behaviors of social types.

Some parents move very quickly to meet their children's needs, sometimes so quickly that their offspring don't have to do much for themselves. Their children learn that others will be there to help them satisfy their needs. These children learn to rely on everyone around them, with a trusting expectation that other people will willingly help them meet their objectives. They are learning to use entrusting behavior.

Success Brings More Success, and Some Limitations

Once we have developed a set of achieving behaviors that works for us, we tend to rely on it fairly exclusively. We learn to avoid those styles that brought us disappointment or failure in the past. Virtually without conscious thought, we call upon our trusted, reliable behaviors over and over as we manage our environment and get things done.

Success, confidence, increased expertise, and comfort reinforce one another. The more successful we are when we use certain combinations of behaviors, the more faith we place in them. The more confident we become about certain strategies, the more likely we are to rely upon them. The more we depend upon and use certain combinations, the more adept we become and the more comfortable we feel with those styles. Eventually, this cycle of success, confidence, increased expertise, and comfort leads us to rely on these familiar, winning styles and ignore the rest.

This cycle of reinforcement leads to considerable proficiency and ensured attainment much of the time. Nonetheless, it can easily trap us in a behavioral rut that limits our leadership possibilities. Paradoxically, our strengths can become our limitations.

Occasionally, a crisis or other unusual circumstance may prompt us to use different styles. If we are successful with these new styles, and if the crisis is severe or prolonged, we may begin to include those crisis-induced behaviors in our standard repertoire. More often, however, after the crisis, we revert to our old, familiar strategies, cutting ourselves a wedge of the same old pie, never knowing the treats we might have enjoyed by tasting styles we routinely disregard.

Achieving Styles Profiles: A Lens on the World

The limited set of achieving styles that most people use acts as a lens through which they perceive their world. This process has some problematical consequences.

Peak Styles and Profiles

That small group of styles, usually two or three, which people consistently draw upon regardless of the task I call their "peak" styles. Theoretically, the peak styles can be drawn from any part of the model, and in real life that happens fairly often. More commonly, however, peak styles are closely related behaviors, either all falling within one set or drawn from two adjoining sets. Data collected since 1984 from more than eight thousand subjects suggest that many people prefer styles that are closely clustered on the Connective Leadership Model.

The unique combination of preferred and underutilized styles constitutes an individual's achieving styles "profile." Much like our fingerprints, our individual profiles are distinctively composed of the peaks and valleys created by the styles we use frequently and the others we tend to avoid. The wider the band of favored styles, the greater our flexibility in responding to different circumstances. Individuals who are locked into a very narrow range of styles find their leadership potential severely restricted.

Connective leaders stand out from other people because they move easily across all nine achieving styles, using different combinations to respond to various circumstances. Their expertise with the complete set of achieving styles allows them enormous flexibility. In particular, their special use of instrumental strategies to diminish the contradictory effects of direct and relational behaviors gives them added versatility in a complex Stage 3 world.

Through the Lens of Achieving Styles: "Enacting" Our World

Our preferred achieving behaviors not only define how we respond to situations; they also affect how we perceive each new set of circumstances. Once we develop clear-cut preferences, we begin to define situations in ways that give us added opportunities—sometimes excuses—for using these comfortable strategies. By viewing the world through our achieving styles lens, we "enact" or construe the world to fit our favorite styles. As our trusted strategies become second nature, we tend to interpret the world in ways that allow us to use them as often as we can, even when they may be quite inappropriate, even dysfunctional.

A recent example comes from a humorous TV commercial promoting a particular bank. The ad pictures two male college roommates, one meticulously groomed and the other ill kempt. The neatly dressed young man describes himself as the more financially competent because he has opened a checking account with the sponsoring bank. When it turns out that his roommate has done the same, the neatly dressed competitor is temporarily dismayed. Then once more he describes his competitive edge: he can find his check book, while the messier roommate is frantically searching for his.

By enacting the world to conform to our peak styles, we can respond easily and comfortably—if not always successfully—to most situations. For example, intense competitors consistently see the world as a stage for competition, as our TV commercial demonstrates. Competitive types define most situations in competitive terms, which then gives them a reason to call upon their reliable competitive strategies. Avid collaborators, on the other hand, perceive most situations as settings that demand teamwork. Given a task to do on their own, collaborative types naturally reach for the telephone or e-mail to line up teams and draw others into their projects.

By defining the world in terms of our own preferred styles, we can feel perfectly secure about using them. This often works out just fine, because in many cases our definition is reasonably correct. Sometimes things work well even when we misinterpret the situation, because, by our behavior and attitudes, we convert our definition into a self-fulfilling prophecy. As sociologist W. I. Thomas[19] reminded us, the definition we impose on a situation often drives us to respond to it *as if* our definition were accurate. Our own reaction influences the responses of others, which in turn can transform the situation into what we thought it was in the first place.

In noncompetitive situations involving several people, for example, competitive individuals commonly define the situation as a contest. Their own competitive response, then, evokes a similar response from others. In this way, the competitive type's definition of the situation becomes a self-fulfilling prophecy. Ironically, this strategy occasionally gives the narrowly defined "expert" the edge over individuals who are similarly limited but to a different narrow band of behaviors and thereby forced to use an unfamiliar style.

Although behavior that creates a self-fulfilling prophecy sometimes leads to success, it can also cause problems. Let's return to the competitive type for another example. In situations where competition is inappropriate, competitive players come off very poorly, rejected and disliked by others. Competitive players also may have difficulty keeping their competitive strategies focused on their team's opponents, rather than on their own teammates.

More often than not, interpreting the world to conform to our own narrow band of styles leads to disaster. We act competitively even when the situation calls for collaboration, or we take charge, appearing egocentric and power-hungry, when we simply should have offered to help.

You may recall the trap former secretary of state Alexander Haig fell into during the tense hours following the 1981 attempt to assassinate then-president Ronald Reagan. Haig's famous televised message, "I'm in control here at the White House," sent negative shock waves through a nation of viewers who expected Haig to offer to stand by, rather than to step in and take over. Haig's misguided attempts to reassure the nation represented an unfortunate choice of achieving style, as well as what some of my executive-management students call a "CLS," that is, a "career-limiting statement."

It is not only competitive and power behavior that can get us into trouble. *Any* inappropriate achieving styles can do the same. For example, in a crisis, waiting for someone else to take charge when we should step forward can backfire. In such cases, the distorting spectacles of our achieving styles create severe myopia. When we use the full repertoire of leadership behaviors available to us, we can select styles more appropriate to the unique demands of the situation.

The Situation Will Get You If You Don't Watch Out

Everyone, especially leaders, has to confront complex situations, decide what to do, and then take action. That was true in Stages 1 and 2, and it remains true in Stage 3. What is distinctive about the present stage is that the complexity of situations is accelerating daily. Although the past few decades have brought extraordinary changes, the Connective Era is marked by a dramatic increase in the *pace* of change. If we continue to limit the range of leadership strategies we apply to these increasingly complex and more rapidly changing situations, we will surely lose the game.

In the intensifying crossfire between interdependence and diversity, even those situations that start out looking simple can grow much more complicated over time. Sometimes, the shift from simple to complex occurs very rapidly, as in crisis situations. In such cases, the capacity to adapt rapidly is critical.

Much of this volume focuses on the importance of the leader's ability to utilize the broadest range of achieving styles. Just as crucial, however, is the leader's capacity to interpret all the relevant *situational cues* in the surrounding environment that suggest the appropriate combination of achieving styles to be used. Connective leaders seem particularly adept at mapping their achieving styles strengths onto the achieving styles demanded by different circumstances. Leaders who can read the achieving styles cues embedded in each situation will have another advantage besides adapting their own styles: they can assemble the multiple, overlapping, or sequential work groups of people/leaders needed to respond to Stage 3 problems. For those who can't read the signals, to paraphrase the bogeyman warning from childhood, the situation will get you if you don't watch out.

Every situation provides cues, some obvious, others more nuanced, often quite contradictory. Cue sensitivity, that capacity to detect and interpret important signs in a messy situation, requires sharp antennae. Most of us think we're pretty good at reading even very subtle situational cues. Yet how often have we been surprised to learn that others in the same situation have understood the signals very differently? Think how frequently lawyers go wrong when they try to guess jurors' reactions to their arguments.

Sensitivity to cues is another hallmark of connective leaders. The behavior of connective leaders suggests that they are particularly sensitive to connections across a broad spectrum of people and events, even when their closest colleagues have been situationally myopic. Connective leaders can see how their own needs and goals are linked to those of others far beyond their circle of colleagues. They scan the situation for the connections that allow them to integrate seemingly conflicting ideas and goals.

Consider, for example, the congressional debate about affirmative action in the mid 1990s. As Republicans increasingly heated up their rhetoric about abolishing affirmative action, House Speaker Newt Gingrich, their political and intellectual leader, issued a very connective warning. The party, he said, "should spend four times as much effort reaching out to the black community to ensure that they know they will not be discriminated against, as compared to the amount of effort we've put into saying we're against quotas and set-asides."[20] Not surprisingly, Gingrich's congressional colleagues were somewhat taken aback. Unlike many of them, Gingrich could see the connections and read the complexities of the situation.

Assessing the Situation in Terms of Achieving Styles

At least six aspects of any particular situation are central to determining what kinds of achieving styles will work, either for the leader or the leader's group:

1. The nature of the task. For example, is it a unique event, like climbing Mt. Everest for the first time, or one that has been done before?
2. The importance of the task. Can the group survive if the task isn't accomplished? How perfectly must it be done for survival?
3. The nature and location of key resources. For example, do you need to negotiate to get resources or do you already possess what you need?
4. The condition of the internal environment in the system or organization where the task is to be performed. Are things in turmoil, or is life on an even keel?
5. The state of the external environment. Is the world outside changing rapidly, or do you see a crisis on the horizon?
6. The leader's position and longevity within the organization. Are you an "old hand" who knows how to get things done through the informal system, or are you a naive newcomer? Are you up high enough in the organization to wield organizational clout, or do you have to ask permission?

These are only a few illustrative questions. Each dimension of the situation requires in-depth analysis. Taking all six dimensions of the situation into account enables leaders to determine which combination of achieving styles will bring the greatest success. To build effective teams and organizations, Stage 3 leaders need to move beyond simply selecting the right combination of achieving styles for themselves in particular situations. They also have to evaluate the fit between the situational cues and the achieving styles represented by their constituents.

Simultaneously integrating six complicated dimensions of a situation is no easy task. Even people who recognize the importance of cues don't always know exactly where or how to begin. In leadership courses for corporate executives, I found that simply urging people first to be more sensitive to situational cues and then to relate them to their own achieving styles profiles didn't seem to help very much. Instead, we needed a straightforward, easy-to-use guide for recognizing and analyzing the often contradictory cues that punctuate complex environments.

The method should allow the leader or other user to analyze multiple aspects of any situation in terms of achieving styles. The results then could be matched to that individual's achieving styles strengths. Beyond improving their personal skills, leaders should be able to use this method for assembling the right mix of people to handle any specific situation. To help leaders deal with the organizational turbulence of Stage 3, rife with mergers, acquisitions and downsizings, the technique would need to take into account the relationship between achieving styles and other organizational factors.

After much debate and discussion, several graduate students in my Achieving Styles Research Group at the Peter F. Drucker Graduate Management Center[21] and I developed an instrument we call the *Achieving Styles Situational Assessment Inventory (ASSAI)*.[22] The inventory takes into account the six situational dimensions and provides a general guide for thinking simultaneously about all the contradictory forces in a situation. It is a learning template, not a permanent crutch to be used unremittingly and obsessively. For a simple example, using the ASSAI's results, a leader who is weak on the relational styles can see that a situation calling for such strengths requires the help of others who have those capabilities.

In a Stage 3 world, where fewer and fewer tasks are accomplished single-handedly, the inventory also can help leaders decide when other people are needed, and if so which ones, to contribute additional achieving styles.[23]

Organizational Achieving Styles: Reflecting the Culture

Just as individuals have unique achieving styles profiles, so do organizations have preferred sets of behaviors for which they reward their members. Some organizations recruit and reward hard-driving, individualistic, competitive members; others look for team players; and still others want people with system savvy, negotiating skills, and charismatic appeal. In a sense, the behaviors that organizations reward represent values promoted by their organizational culture.

Most of us have seen people whose achieving styles were out of sync with their organization. They were round pegs in square holes who often suffered from their lack of fit. Leaders whose achieving styles do not match the culture of the organization usually have difficulty leading, much less changing, their organizations.

Here too our experience in executive seminars and consulting situations began to suggest the need for an easy method to determine the behaviors most valued by the organization. The method also should reveal the fit between the leader's (and other organizational members') styles and the behaviors that the organization rewarded. To address this need, in 1982 another instrument was developed and tested: the *L-BL Organizational Achieving Styles Inventory (OASI)*, based directly on the original 1973 *L-BL Achieving Styles Inventory (ASI)* for individuals, described earlier in this chapter.

By mapping their own achieving styles profile onto the organization's profile, leaders can evaluate the fit between themselves and their organizations. They can also diagnose the areas of friction caused by a mismatch between their own leadership styles and the culture of the organization. Leaders will also find the OASI useful for matching the profiles of other organizational members to appropriate organizational functions and units.

Within units and at different organizational levels, the inventory (OASI) can determine the consistency with which behaviors are valued throughout the organization. As more organizations face the turmoil of mergers and acquisitions, their leaders will also need to be increasingly attuned to the fit between organizational cultures. There too, the OASI can provide useful insights.

The basis of connective leadership is the Connective Leadership Model, a group of behavioral strategies comprising nine individual achieving styles, grouped into the three sets: direct, relational, and instrumental. The parallels between the sets of styles used by individuals and the societal forces of diversity and interdependence make the model particularly relevant for understanding leadership in the Connective Era.

Seeing situations in terms of the distinctive combination of achieving styles that we have long favored may blind us to more appropriate behaviors in a given situation. It is a hallmark of connective leaders that they have a highly developed sensitivity to environmental cues that enables them to range freely and flexibly over all nine achieving styles as conditions demand.

By using the Model of Connective Leadership, as well as the various instruments for applying the model to themselves, their constituents, and organizations, aspiring leaders can increase their effectiveness in a Stage 3 world. Building on the overview in this chapter, we consider in depth each set of strategies underlying the Connective Leadership Model in the following three chapters.

Figure 2. The Direct Set of Styles.

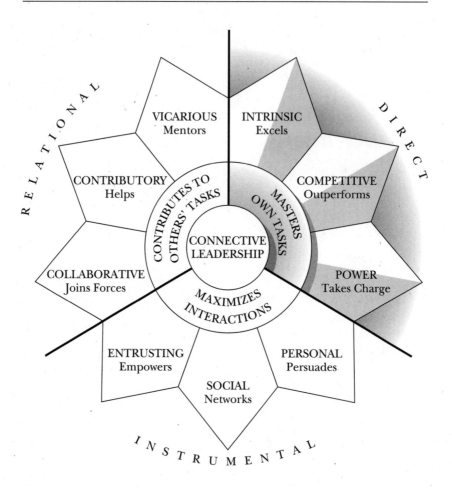

Chapter Six

The Direct Routes to Success

The Intrinsic, Competitive, and Power Styles

*I like what is in work—the chance to find yourself. Your
own reality—for yourself, not for others—what no other
man can ever know.*
JOSEPH CONRAD[1]

We begin our examination of the achieving styles that constitute
the Connective Leadership Model with the three direct styles:
intrinsic, competitive, and power. The direct styles are as American as Apple Computer.

These styles represent the core of American individualism.
They also foster innovation, creativity, diversity, and authoritarianism. In Chapter Three, we saw that the early American frontier,
with its isolation and rugged terrain, and later the immigration
experience favored strong, individualistic, self-reliant people.
These conditions groomed individuals who looked to themselves
and addressed their tasks directly, without counting on help from
others except in crises. Direct achievers expect, even prefer, to confront their world head on in their own way. They welcome the
enormous challenges of tasks, of competitors, and of situations.

Intent upon their own goals, direct achievers are very concerned
both with the *doing* or *mastery* of a task and with the *task itself*. They
perceive tasks as their own special challenge. For many direct achievers, the exhilaration of mastery and the beauty of the final outcome
are ends in themselves. Direct achievers also treasure their individuality, those qualities that set them apart from others. The current

141

flourishing of diversity around the world stems largely from a direct-achieving sensibility. Individualism, creativity, and innovation, characteristic of direct achievers, are the building blocks of diversity.

Let's take the words and actions of real people, many highlighted in the media, to provide illuminating glimpses of direct achieving styles in the world around us. Throughout the following chapters, we use portraits like these to provide flesh-and-blood examples of each achieving style.

For simplicity's sake, I've chosen to describe each of the nine achieving styles *as if* people used only one style. In real life, as I indicated in Chapter Five, people usually combine several strategies, often closely related ones (especially the contiguous styles), to form their unique achieving styles profile. If we listen closely to these exemplar achievers in the next few chapters, we hear traces of other, secondary styles that they use as well. Indeed, a number of these achievers reappear within and across chapters.

The Intrinsic Style

Let's begin with the *intrinsic* style, which, you will recall, focuses primarily on personal mastery or execution of a task. The task is seen as a challenge which must be met to perfection. The performance is measured against an internalized standard of excellence, not against the judgments or performance of others. The excitement for intrinsic achievers comes from the pleasure of the work itself, from excelling in the task, and meeting a challenge that they usually set for themselves. Indeed, the task is perceived as their personal challenge. People who prefer the intrinsic style see beauty in the flawless execution of a task. Like Joseph Conrad cited above, Andrew Carnegie is often quoted as saying "My heart is in the work."[2]

The Intrinsic Beauty of Achievement

For many intrinsic achievers, the sheer beauty of an achievement is what captures their heart. For them, nothing can compare to the breathtaking outcome of a perfectly executed task.

Arthur Kornberg, Medical Researcher

Arthur Kornberg, winner of the Nobel Prize in medicine, is a full-blown direct achiever. You can hear the cadence of the intrinsic style when Kornberg describes his impatience and excitement in solving a problem. For Kornberg, the outcome of outstanding performance is a special exuberance:

> I started observing rats when you fed them strange things that lacked certain vitamins and minerals. I discovered it was more gratifying to ask a simple question—in that case, one had to wait a few weeks before the rat manifested symptoms—and then observe a result. And then I got fascinated by biochemistry. . . . I heard about things like ATP and enzymes. . . . [At the National Institutes of Health] instead of waiting for weeks, one could within minutes see the consequence of an enzyme in action. . . . I don't think there's anything that matches the satisfaction of being able to formulate some question. It's a puzzle; it interests you; you have the means at your disposal, if you can generate them, to go about answering that question. When you've done it properly, you're the first person in history who has been able to resolve a basic fact of nature. And then, all around you, others are doing that, and pretty soon these little bits and pieces are put together, and suddenly something emerges that's very beautiful, very awesome.[3]

Jim Collins, Rock Climber

Like Nobel laureate Kornberg, intrinsic achievers often use poetic imagery to describe the psychic rewards of achievement. They talk of the "highs" that come with succeeding, particularly against strict, self-imposed standards of performance.

Jim Collins, reputedly one of the world's ten best rock climbers in the 1970s, described the emotions that characterize such a high:

> Some athletes call it the "White Moment." It's one of those special moments when every nerve in your body is focused on the here and now, and everything else is completely blocked out. I know of no other feeling that's quite so intense, and it is largely for those moments that I climb. Only then do I feel totally alive.[4]

Ronay Menschel, Politician

Contrary to the stereotype of politicians, the political world too has its share of intrinsic achievers who are intensely focused on the task. Ronay Menschel, one-time deputy mayor of New York City, described herself this way: "I'm just not interested in power. My interest is in getting things done and making improvements. What

I find exciting is discovering an inefficiency and making a change. . . ."[5]

The Exhilaration of Creativity

Creativity, another aspect of the intrinsic style, exhilarates many direct achievers. It is a potent attraction for individuals who seek out difficult challenges that require new solutions.

Randall Dougherty, Mathematician

Randall Dougherty exhibits the characteristics of a dedicated intrinsic achiever who experiences the inherent pleasure of doing a job that meets his own perfectionist standards. But even doing the task well is not the whole story. Intrinsic achievers reach deep within themselves to draw from the wellsprings of their creativity. Even as a teenager, Dougherty felt particularly exhilarated when he devised an elegant solution to a tough problem. As a Fairfax, Virginia, high school junior, Dougherty won second place in a national mathematics competition. In describing his usual strategy for solving mathematical problems, he alludes to the intrinsic achiever's special brand of satisfaction:

> [I usually look for a] trick solution, something that would make it real simple. Then if I cannot find one, I just work my way through. The elegant solutions are almost always the simple ones. I get a good feeling out of doing it.[6]

Individualism, Mastery, and Innovation

Expressing their individualism, mastering the task, and developing innovative solutions are the forces that drive intrinsic achievers. They reinforce one another.

William M. Brown, Inventor

William M. Brown, of Bedford, Massachusetts, invented a telephone that can be plugged into an ordinary electrical outlet. He describes the excitement of proving his own mastery: "One of my biggest joys has been the confidence I developed from knowing what I can and cannot do and how resilient I can be."[7]

Ralph Shimlian, Inventor

It is not surprising that inventors tend to be intrinsic achievers, searching for new ideas and innovations within themselves. Ralph Shimlian, founder and president of his own company, a first-degree black belt in karate, and a scuba diver, provides another snapshot of an intrinsic achiever.

Shimlian has designed many diver-propulsion vehicles used around the world, including an antishark device employed by the U.S. military as well as in the movie *Jaws*. When the Secret Service needed a silent, deadly, and easily concealed weapon to protect President Nixon on his historic trip to China, Shimlian created it. Shimlian likes to do it himself, unimpeded by the actions of others.

Raised in Santa Cruz, California, Shimlian competed in various team sports. As we might expect from an intrinsic achiever, Shimlian eventually gave up team sports for the individualistic sports of kung fu and Shoto Kan karate. Shimlian explains:

> I became disenchanted with team sports. I never liked depending on other members of a team. I preferred to do it on my own. I didn't want to lose a game because some idiot was looking the wrong way.[8]

Self-Reliance, Autonomy, Creative Integrity, and Perfection

Intrinsic achievers are usually very self-reliant, sometimes to a fault. They love doing things on their own. In fact, they believe they can do things better and faster without the help or interference of others.

Achievers who look inward for strength and direction usually feel most comfortable with intrinsic strategies. They yearn to be autonomous, masters of their own destiny. People who seek pure achievements and control over themselves, rather than power over others, frequently prefer the intrinsic style. Self-reliance, autonomy, creative control, and perfection are all-important to the intrinsic achiever.

Self-Reliance: Robert McFarlane

Learning self-reliance usually starts in childhood. Robert McFarlane, former national security adviser, gives us additional insight into the early independence training of intrinsic achievers:

> From the time I was young, I was told that to show uncertainty or vulnerability was a weakness. Crying was wrong. And if you were told to do something, like washing the car or homework or household chores, you were supposed to do it by yourself and not seek help. You were supposed to rely on yourself, not on others.[9]

Having learned early on to depend on themselves, adult intrinsic achievers may have difficulty looking to others for help.

Autonomy, a State of Being: Novelist Saul Bellow

Intrinsic achievers are oblivious to external standards of behavior, not only in their work but in the larger context of their lives. Oftentimes, intrinsic achievers describe this attitude toward their work as an inevitable, unwavering state of being. They are what they must be; they do what they must do. They are a cross between Abraham Maslow's[10] self-actualizer and David McClelland's[11] "high need achiever."

In a television interview, a reporter asked American novelist Saul Bellow if the fierce competition for a reading audience influenced his choice of subjects and literary style. Bellow's terse response reflects not only his disregard for competition, but also the intrinsic achiever's perception of a state of being that defines his persona: "I do what I do."

Creative Integrity, Internal Standards of Perfection: Diego Rivera, Lina Wertmuller, Jacques D'Amboise, and Norman Rockwell

Creative artists in many fields exhibit this same need for autonomy, often intertwined with rigorous internal standards of perfection and artistic integrity. E. B. White captured the essence of the intrinsic perspective in his poem, "I Paint What I See: A Ballad of Artistic Integrity." The poem describes the late Mexican artist Diego Rivera's response to Nelson Rockefeller's complaint that the mural he had commissioned for the Rockefeller Center in New York depicted not American political leaders and capitalists but socialist heroes and labor leaders instead. Rivera's truculent (and, as we can now see, intrinsic) response was:

> *"I paint what I paint, I paint what I see,*
> *I paint what I think," said Rivera,*

"And the thing that is dearest in life to me
In a bourgeois hall is Integrity."[12]

Internalized standards of perfection guide the intrinsic approach to a task. Indifferent to the evaluation—or accomplishments—of others, intrinsic achievers experience the thrill of accomplishment for its own, intrinsic sake. Their basic reward is the intense satisfaction derived from meeting the inherent challenges of the task and performing well, according to their own rigorous standards, not others'.

Lina Wertmuller, celebrated Italian film director, is guided by her internal aesthetic gyroscope. After producing two critically acclaimed but controversial films, *Swept Away* and *Seven Beauties*, Wertmuller produced several box-office flops in a row, including *A Joke of Destiny* and *Summer Night*. Despite these disappointments, Wertmuller remains steadfastly committed to her own artistic standards: "My first customer is myself. When I tell a story I like, I can sleep easy. I am sorry when audiences do not like it, but I have no choice."[13]

That others would be satisfied with something less or different is of little consequence to the intrinsic achiever. Jacques D'Amboise, protégé of the acclaimed choreographer George Balanchine, has described his obsession with artistic perfection, a drive that eclipsed his desire to please the audience. In a documentary film, D'Amboise insists, "I never cared about the audience. I just wanted to make the dance perfect."[14]

The self-critical impatience of the intrinsic achiever is evident in a description of American artist Norman Rockwell. One interviewer reports that when Rockwell

> painted one of his happy pictures, he often became upset with himself and fearfully anxious about doing his work faster and better. At such moments, he volubly disprized his talents and bemoaned the fact that he never could reach the perfection he aspired to.[15]

Perfection Outstrips Winning: Athletes Rick Carey, Larry Bird, Jeff Float, and Actor Harvey Keitel

It may come as some surprise that athletes, commonly viewed as relentless competitors, are often more concerned with doing something perfectly than outdoing their competitors. They can be among the heartiest of intrinsic achievers. For many athletes, surpassing others may be part—but not necessarily the key part—of meeting their internal standards of excellence. It is simply a step along the way.

U.S. Olympic swimming champion Rick Carey offers us a superb example. Dejected that his gold medal performance did not set a new world record, Carey could not conceal his disappointment from the media. Shocked by his lukewarm response to winning the Olympic prize, media reports chided Carey for his "attitude." The next day, Carey apologized to reporters and fans, who mistook his intrinsic response for poor sportsmanship (a curious form of mistaken identity).

In a TV interview following a successful game, Boston Celtics basketball star Larry Bird expressed the same concern with perfecting his own performance without regard to the competition: "I don't care about how good the others were. I just want to be the best that I can be."

This secondary importance of winning is characteristic of the intrinsic achieving strategy and distinguishes the intrinsic from the competitive, in which winning is everything. Another American swimmer who competed in the 1984 Olympics, Jeff Float, summed it up this way: "Winning is really not an end product. Winning is just a step to getting there. Winning is just the tip of the iceberg."[16]

Athletes are not alone in feeling that perfection is more important than winning. For actor Harvey Keitel, whose portrayal of mobster Mickey Cohen in the film *Bugsy* earned him an Oscar nomination for best supporting actor, a perfect portrayal is the crucial issue. Winning or losing an Oscar is far less important:

> Keitel insists that he was neither thrilled with the nomination ("I was so happy," he says sarcastically, "I went running down the street singing 'Zip-a Dee-Doo-Dah'") nor disappointed that he lost out to Jack Palance in *City Slickers*.

> "The only true recognition is in the work itself," he says. "You don't need to be nominated for an Oscar to be recognized for your work."[17]

Competition, an Impediment to Intrinsic Joy: Pianist Brian Ganz

For many intrinsic achievers, competition is actually an impediment to the untrammeled joy of a perfect achievement. Even collaborating or helping potential rivals achieve their goals is preferable to engaging in competitive combat.

Pianist Brian Ganz recalls that his teenage years were plagued by ambivalence toward playing in competitions. He describes a transcendental experience at the Queen Elizabeth International Piano Competition in Brussels, in the spring of 1991. He found himself sequestered for a week with eleven other finalists. The twelve pianists shared living quarters, ate together, and all practiced whatever piece was newly assigned that day, through which they would demonstrate their supreme worthiness for the prize. Ganz recalls that the anxious dozen gradually

> bonded in a spirit of mutual support . . . We shared our fears. We taped each other's performances. We played ping-pong and Frisbee. . . . One guy—who eventually won—was having trouble sleeping, so I loaned him a tape I had of ocean wave sounds. We were like a family. You can focus on the external trappings of success—and they are there—or you can concentrate on expressing your love of music or your love of whatever you're doing. For me, it comes down to a choice between anxiety or love. And I chose love.[18]

Ganz, who came away with a silver medal, actually earned something that he values far more. He finally understood the philosophy of his teacher, Leon Fleisher at the Peabody Conservatory in Baltimore, who repeatedly described to his pupil what I would identify as an intrinsic sensibility: "In music there are no winners or losers, only servants of a glorious and benign art."[19]

The Doing Is Its Own Reward

Intrinsic achievers see their accomplishments as ends in themselves, not as the means to glory and fame or as routes to other opportunities. In this regard, they are very different from instrumental achievers. Witness, for example, this scene at a press conference following a White House reception honoring Nobel laureate George Stigler, a University of Chicago economist. Gray-haired and scholarly, Stigler stepped to the podium and bent over the bank of microphones. A reporter asked, "What is your opinion of supply-side economics favored by this administration?" Without a moment's hesitation, Stigler easily responded, "A gimmick." Not surprisingly, the Reagan White House abruptly halted the press conference. With characteristic intrinsic indifference to others' opinions, Stigler explained: "They probably shouldn't have put me on [the air]. They were just trying to get a cheap bit out of my temporary notoriety as a prize winner. I'm not politically minded. I don't want a job."[20]

These snapshots, drawn from fields of endeavor as diverse as medical research, politics, art, and athletics, offer a montage of intrinsic achievers. Among the other qualities they share, intrinsic achievers simply love the very doing of their chosen work—and always aim for the beauty of a job perfectly executed.

Admittedly, the intrinsic style helps individuals to reach within themselves for remarkable virtuoso performances. Yet for leaders who prefer this style, their indifference to the opinions of others can deprive them of valuable external perspectives. Charles de Gaulle often suffered from this attitude. Insulation from alternative viewpoints can lead to serious, sometimes tragic, mistakes.

Leaders overly devoted to self-reliance also may forego needed help even when the task exceeds the capabilities of a single, albeit outstanding, individual. Their inability to look outside themselves may keep these leaders from bringing others affected by the decision into the action loop. In a world marked by interdependence, the consequences of ignoring others with mutual concerns can lead to complications down the road.

The Competitive Style

The *competitive* style is deeply ingrained in the American psyche. Americans are so enamored of competitors that we elevate them to celebrity status. C. Wright Mills caught the essence of our love affair with competition, saying that celebrity is

> the crowning result of the star system in a society that makes a fetish of competition. . . . It does not seem to matter what the man is the very best at; so long as he has won out in competition over all others, he is celebrated.[21]

Beating the Competition

Unlike their internally driven intrinsic cousins, competitive achievers exalt in measuring themselves against an *external* standard of excellence: their competitors' accomplishments. More than anything else, competitive achievers want to win, to be not so much excellent as *the best*. They won't settle for anything less than being numero uno.

Even when they are part of a team, competitive achievers compare their own contributions to the common goal with their teammates'. Although intrinsic achievers may talk about being the best, they are less concerned about doing better than others than about being the best that *they* can possibly be. For competitive achievers, however, doing their best is never good enough; true satisfaction comes only from doing better than everyone else.

Competitive achievers define the world as an endless set of contests. For them, excitement and zest for life flow from the competitive milieu. Not surprisingly, they do their best work when they can structure the situation as a competition, pitting themselves against other contenders. Everything from who wins the Nobel Prize to who gets the rarest roast beef at a banquet table to who sells the most insurance is grist for the competitive achiever's mill.

Mike Barrowman, Olympic Swimmer

For some athletes, an intrinsic approach is not enough. We saw the intrinsic obsession of swimmer Rick Carey, the Olympic gold medalist, who felt the anguish of failure inflicted by not meeting the time standard he had set for himself. Compare that picture to the competitive yearnings of another Olympic gold medalist swimmer, Mike Barrowman, who insists that concentrating exclusively on your own performance won't bring home the prize. Barrowman reports his own experience at the Olympic Village in Barcelona:

> Paying attention to your competitors is everything. It's the name of the game. . . . For instance, in the Olympic Village at Barcelona, I counted the number of steps from my room to the cafeteria. Then I counted the number of steps further it was for my competitors. And those extra steps were tucked away inside my mind, and I'd think about how they gave me an advantage. . . . Derailing your opposition is 99 percent of swimming.[22]

Barrowman insists that the desire to beat the competition separates winners from losers: "'He Who Wants It Most Badly Wins.' [The desire to win separates] the top 50 swimmers and the top 5."[23]

Ross Perot, Corporate Leader

Before his on-again off-again 1992 campaign for the U.S. presidency, Ross Perot mounted a "one-man crusade to make General Motors competitive again." In his outer office at GM, Perot reputedly hung Norman Rockwell's painting *Homecoming Marine.* The 1945 painting depicts the Marine with a Japanese flag in his hands, sitting in a garage surrounded by two youngsters and four men, to whom he is describing his war exploits. Perot reportedly explained that "the Marine is there to remind my GM visitors that we used to whip the Japanese right regularly. And if we ever decide we want to do it again in the car business, we can."[24]

Everything Is a Contest

Competitive achievers interpret virtually every situation as a combat in which they must pit themselves against worthy opponents. Contrast the intrinsic achiever's love of the activity itself with swimmer Barrowman's orientation that competition is simply a way of life:

> I'm not a swimmer as much as a competitor. I just chose swimming as my vehicle. It's a kind of energy . . . you might as well direct it. Otherwise, you wind up competing in parts of your life that you didn't want to, like relationships.[25]

Asked if he competes in relationships, Barrowman responded, "It does spill over sometimes. Those flames leap over the wall and enter areas you don't want them to be in."[26]

Competition colors virtually every action of the competitive achiever. At a residential leadership development program for the local presidents of a volunteer organization, I talked early in the day about connective leadership and achieving styles. I gave the participants my favorite quick-and-dirty method for identifying competitive achievers at dinner parties where all guests were served the same menu: watch for the person at your table who surreptitiously (or even brazenly) checks out everyone else's plate to assure himself that he has the largest and rarest piece of roast beef, the fluffiest and whitest garlic mashed potatoes, and the perkiest and greenest peas. (Incidentally, I have used *he* deliberately because research data indicate that men consistently score higher than women on the competitive style.) As luck would have it, dinner that evening was served with a set menu. As we all searched for our name plates at the dinner table, three women announced with considerable amusement that my quick-and-dirty competitive index had just been demonstrated. Apparently, dessert plates, each bearing a slice of dark, rich chocolate cake, had been set out as part of each place setting. One of the participants had approached the table, noticed his own dessert plate, then studied all the other pieces of cake at other seats. Without missing a beat, he reached for the largest piece of cake he could find and exchanged it for the one at his place. Ignoring his tablemates' amusement, he turned his measuring eye to the servings of roast beef that the waitress was placing before each guest.

James Watson, Scientist

Although the stereotype of scholars and scientists depicts them as immune to the competition that flourishes in the "real" world, insiders affirm that the competitive style knows no occupational boundaries. The unsparing description of the brass-knuckles contest to unlock the secret of DNA made *The Double Helix*[27] a national best-seller. Its author, Nobel laureate James D. Watson, became an international celebrity to millions of enthralled readers but persona non grata to many scientists within the research community. Watson's candid picture of his early conversations with colleague and fellow Nobelist Francis Crick vividly portrays the competitive achiever's propensity to shape situations as competitions: "Our lunch conversations quickly centered on how genes were put together. Within a few days after my arrival, we knew what to do: imitate Linus Pauling and beat him at his own game."[28]

Pauling was just one among a large cast of scientists whom Watson, a relative newcomer to the field, saw as targets of competition. Later, Watson describes his pleasure at the thought of outdoing Nobel laureate Joshua Lederberg, again on his own turf:

Particularly pleasing was the possibility that Joshua might be so stuck on his classical way of thinking that I would accomplish the unbelievable feat of beating him to the correct interpretation of his own experiments.[29]

For Watson, the race spurred his ambition, and everyone in his line of sight was perceived primarily as someone to outdo.

Joan Baez, Folk Singer

Like any other preferred style, the competitive style shows itself across situations, no matter how appropriate or inappropriate it is to the circumstances. Folk singer Joan Baez recalls how competitiveness spoiled her performance at a benefit concert in which a star-studded roster of musicians was raising money for a social cause:

> I turn the mike toward Chrissie, knowing my reputation for monopolizing it, and Sheena appears to our left. We are barely finishing up our little contribution when Sheena takes the mike with a quiet ferocity, leans away from us, hoards the microphone like a newly discovered family heirloom and sings our trio as a solo, leaving me leaning awkwardly toward the unavailable mike and Chrissie completely out of range. . . . The aggressive stars are reaching for microphones, and I don't feel like competing, so I turn around and head off the front lines and into the crowded stage.[30]

The competitive achiever has one preeminent goal: outshining everyone else. That is what counts.

Billy Wilson, Former Football Star

For the competitive achiever, not winning is to be avoided at all costs. The possibility of coming in second may even keep competitive achievers from entering the fray altogether. Former football star Billy Wilson refused to put his hat in the ring for a hotly contested coaching job when he thought he might be judged too old for the post. Under a banner headline reading "A Nice Guy Who Wants to Keep Finishing First," Wilson's decision was described thus: "Wilson says he has thought long and hard, but won't offer his name for consideration. He says he could not bear to see his name go down to the wire and then be rejected."[31]

American Competitiveness

As I write this chapter, the competitiveness of American industry is a hotly debated political issue. Every sector of the economy is scrambling aboard the competition bandwagon, drawing other segments of society along. The U.S. educational system, for example, is getting into the act in a very big way. A recent headline announced that the "Quest to Make U.S. More Competitive Could Be a Boon to Higher Education." Interestingly, the article describing higher education's role in "improving America's worldwide industrial competitiveness" also worried about maintaining the independence of the educational system. Competition and independence are "apple pie" American, even at the institutional level.

Competition is so American that even when we describe fun, we measure it competitively. On a recent hot summer evening, a TV newscaster reported the immense "fun" a group of sunbathers was having at the beach. He continued, "But the riders on the amusement park roller coaster say they are having even more fun." Even at the beach, winning remains a great American pastime.

Rethinking Competition as an Achievement Strategy

Despite its many attractions, competition has obvious drawbacks as well. Alfie Kohn argues that competition generates anxiety and prevents the efficient use and sharing of resources.[32] Trying to do well and trying to do better than someone else are very different processes. Trying to do *well* allows people to work together, sharing ideas, talent, and other resources to produce the best result. Trying to do *better* than the next person prompts not only anxiety, suspicion, and aggression but also an unwillingness to share the resources required to get the job done. At the very least, we need to reconsider our American passion for unadulterated competition. Let's take a close-up look at research that supports these conclusions.

Competition Versus Mastery Among Scientists

If we are to believe the growing evidence from studies of many different groups, competition per se fails to live up to its reputation as a key force in achievement motivation. In fact, the work of a University of Texas team headed by psychologist Robert Helmreich suggests that competition and achievement do not go so well together after all.[33] Helmreich and his group studied 103 Ph.D. scientists and engineers, all male, to see how their orientation toward work, mastery, and competitiveness related to their achievements (as indicated by the number of times other scientists cited their work). Helmreich and his colleagues found that the most successful scientists and engineers (that is, those whose work was most frequently cited by other scientists) scored high on the mastery and work measures, and low on the competitiveness scale. Similar studies of academic psychologists, business people (using salary as the measure of achievement), and college students (measuring achievement by grade point average) yielded comparable results.

Research on groups as diverse as fifth- and sixth-grade students, airline pilots, and reservation agents again produced a stronger relationship between success and mastery along with a clear work orientation than between success and competition. Again and again, Helmreich and his colleagues found the same unexpected result: competitiveness is linked to lower performance, not to high achievement.

These and other findings on the downside of competitive behavior that we discuss in the next chapter suggest that competition as an achievement strategy deserves some serious rethinking.

The Power Style

The third direct style, the *power* style, probably needs little introduction. Power achievers get their kicks from taking charge. They revel in bringing order out of chaos. They enjoy controlling and coordinating everything: people, tasks, resources, and situations. They have a knack for organizing and directing, whether the setting is the board room or the family picnic. They naturally expect to be in charge—of the corporate budget, the town hall, the PTA meeting, the TV remote control, or the thermostat on the king-size electric blanket. The power style attracts people who relish dominating the scene.

Power achievers naturally assume that they should direct and delegate certain tasks to other people in the chain of command who in turn should carry out their instructions. When they delegate tasks, power achievers see their actions as a legitimate expression of their power, and thus they usually retain overall control and leadership.

Leaders with strong power tendencies dominate the pages of history. Martin Luther, Napoleon Bonaparte, V. I. Lenin, Benito Mussolini, Winston Churchill, Charles de Gaulle, George Patton, Douglas MacArthur, Harry Truman, Indira Gandhi, and Margaret

Thatcher are part of a long list of power achievers who span time and geography.

Taking Control

Even when there is no formal reporting structure, power achievers act as if there were one, issuing orders, setting deadlines, and co-ordinating the activities of others. Power types tend to gravitate toward leadership roles. They simply see themselves as natural leaders. They also see the beauty in a well-coordinated performance.

Alexander Haig, Secretary of State

Power achievers perceive every situation as an opportunity to assume control. As we recounted in Chapter Five, following the attempt on President Reagan's life Secretary Haig proclaimed, much to the consternation of the White House, "I am in control at the White House."

Washington watchers were not particularly surprised. From the moment Haig was appointed secretary of state, his repeated efforts to augment his power base both dismayed the administration and prompted the media to dub him the "Czar of Foreign Policy." Haig's perception that he should step forward to take charge as Reagan underwent surgery probably gave his critics within the administration the perfect opening to engineer his demise as secretary of state.

In fact, some observers suggest that Haig's continued penchant for seizing power, often inappropriately, figured heavily in the public's rejection of his efforts to run for political office. Later we shall return to the important subject of the appropriate use of achieving strategies and cue sensitivity, because, as Chapter Five suggested, our achieving styles will surely get us if we don't watch out.

The Trappings of Power: Attorney General Edwin Meese III

Frequently, we can identity power achievers by their surroundings: sweeping corner offices, walls covered with framed awards and citations, even hunting trophies glaring glassy-eyed from their wall mountings. A *New York Times Magazine* article, aptly titled "Mr. Power," described Edwin Meese III's office during his term as U.S. attorney general:

In his corner office at the Justice Department, a private sanctum guarded by Federal Bureau of Investigation agents, Edwin Meese 3rd., the 75th Attorney General of the United States, has surrounded himself with symbols of the power he wields: a Border Patrol pistol; a United States marshal's badge; miniature police cars and helicopters. The office says much about the way Meese sees himself, for its motif reflects not so much the lawyer in Meese as it does the hard-nosed lawman: America's top cop.[34]

Meese's take-charge strategy, his determination to draw the organization toward his own central control, the language of authority and power, all come through very clearly in the article:

To "improve the management" of the 62,500-employee Justice Department, Meese is centralizing policy planning and budgeting under the control of a few trusted deputies. To implement his policy goals, he has organized key executives into small teams whose job it is to focus on Administration priorities. Meese and six top aides . . . [constitute] the 'command group' that meets every morning at 8:10 to map strategy.[35]

"Command group": the choice of phrase says it all.

Restructuring Relationships

Power players often restructure reporting relationships and responsibilities—a familiar strategy we recognize as "reorganizing"—to increase their control over people and events. At the highest level of government and industry, this behavior is readily observable.

Henry Kissinger, National Security Adviser

Henry Kissinger, national security advisor in the Nixon administration, had a taste for power that his staff understood and abetted. The description of aide Morton Halperin drawing up a plan to augment Kissinger's power within the administration offers a vivid inside view:

[Halperin] . . . took it upon himself to draft a broad memorandum that placed nearly all the power in the hands of the national security adviser.

Halperin understood the needs of his master as well as Kissinger understood the needs of his. The projected system gave Kissinger the power to decide the agenda for National Security Council meetings and also made him chairman of the review group that considered the various option papers prepared by the bureaucracy. Under the existing machinery, that function had been controlled by the State Department. In addition, Halperin's memorandum gave Kissinger direct authority to order State and other agencies to prepare option papers on specific subjects. . . . Under the proposed system, even the lower-level working groups for each geographical region would report directly to White House officials.[36]

The Practical and Symbolic Importance of Resources

Practitioners of power understand both the pragmatic and the symbolic importance of resources. Pragmatically, control over resources enables the leader to stymie or contribute to the flow of events, an ability that puts resource-needy others in the controller's debt.[37] Symbolically, resources create the *illusion* of power, which Machiavelli long ago recognized as even more important than power itself.[38]

Richard J. Daley, Political Boss

Richard J. Daley, longtime mayor of Chicago, was a master of accumulating and wielding resources both to signal and to enhance his political power. As Mike Royko details in his biography, even as a fledgling politico, he had studied the use of power:

Daley, at last, was where he wanted to be for the many years he had waited and worked. He was finally a member of the Cook County Democratic Central Committee, one of the fifty city ward committeemen and thirty suburban township committeemen who ran the party. He was not just another member, but much more. As the leader of a ward that had been, and would again be, one of the biggest vote producers for the party, he was part of the inner circle within the committee, made up of the leaders of the true "Machine" wards, who could always be counted on to deliver a big majority.[39]

The Beauty and Legitimate Use of Power

The power strategy is not used simply by people who relish power for what it can bring them personally. Stanford Business School professor

Jeffrey Pfeffer reminds us that power is a perfectly legitimate—in fact, essential—tool of organizational life.[40] Without it, organizations are rarely well run.

Nor are all power achievers "power hungry." Some simply see taking control as the obvious way to get things done. They assume overall responsibility for leading or coordinating the effort. As part of their take-charge posture, they confidently assign various parts of the task to others. Leaders who use the power style rarely shrink from seizing control when the situation calls for it, but they may take control out of the conviction that it is simply the right thing to do.

Norman Schwarzkopf, Army General

General Norman Schwarzkopf insists there are two basic leadership rules: "When you are placed in command, take charge" and "Do what is right."[41] For many power achievers, disorganization, chaos, or crisis trigger their need for order and control. Their natural response is to take charge.

Lillian Gallo, Marine Captain

For some power achievers, there is beauty in making things happen. A well-coordinated event represents an aesthetic harmony. Lillian Gallo, whom we meet again as the president of Los Angeles–based Gallo Entertainment, Inc., a TV production company, recalls her days as a Marine captain in the Korean War:

> What I loved and what I really felt good about was drill. As part of our training in Officers Candidate School, we took turns leading the company in drill. We were taught how to move a company of Marines. Practicing on the parade field, we learned how to give appropriate commands and how a company should execute them.
>
> There was something beautiful about giving a command and seeing an entire company of people move precisely to your command. Seeing all those people move as one was really a glorious sight. I remember the feeling . . . enjoying it (and wondering if I should).[42]

Mitch Snyder, Advocate for the Homeless

Power styles are not only for military types, political bosses, and business executives. A political activist who organizes members of a low-income community to demand better housing or equal employment opportunities may use this strategy as well. Although the activist utilizes power to attain certain political ends, the ends may be quite selfless: providing meals for the poor, protecting the environment, arranging medical care for the sick. In fact, some activists, while clearly taking charge, have been willing to sacrifice their own lives to make their political point.

A recent case involves the late Mitch Snyder, a Washington, D.C., advocate for the homeless. Snyder abandoned an established executive career to devote himself to improving the lot of the homeless in the nation's capitol. As we shall see in Chapter Eight, when Snyder's power strategy failed to secure an empty building to house his constituency, he rapidly shifted to an instrumental maneuver to attain his objective.

Although we may associate power with egocentric purposes, in fact achieving through power is a natural way of life for people with very diverse goals. Compare, for example, Mitch Snyder, who sought to commandeer a building to shelter the homeless, and Adolf Hitler, who strove to conquer the world to quench his own egomaniacal needs. Like all the other styles, the power style is driven by a broad band of motivations and goals. The behavior may look the same, but the motivations behind it and the goals toward which it is moving may be very different indeed.

Following Their Own Goals

Leaders who take naturally to power are not particularly concerned with enabling other people to accomplish their own ends. Their take-charge orientation prompts power achievers to push constituents to fulfill the leader's vision. And, in fact, some situations, like certain types of crises, call for a large dose of power action.

Leaders who can't sense when power (or, for that matter, any other specific achieving style) is called for are likely to lose their supporters' confidence. Rev. Bud Phillips, director of the Vancouver School of Theology, recalls a search committee's despair following an interview with the third candidate for the post of senior minister for the Central Church. One committee member declared, "It is as if they don't want to be caught leading!" What prompted that remark? In response to pointed questions about hypothetical leadership situations, the candidate "gave the impression that [he] understood himself to be 'an enabler' of the gifts and skills of the laity . . . but the people on the committee *knew* this congregation, and felt that an enabling ministry was inappropriate at this time."[43] Needless to say, the candidate was not offered the position. The inability to use power when it is called for can spell disaster even to the best-intentioned leaders.

Using power inappropriately has its serious consequences as well. Leaders who hold the reins too tightly are likely to impede growth in people to whom they delegate tasks. The predilection for tight control among leaders who favor power strategies can prevent others from developing ownership of their assigned task.

The three direct achieving styles—intrinsic, competitive, and power—describe the deepest core of American leadership, our favorite routes to success. They are clearly embedded in our history and in our national psyche, permeating our values and mores. We raise our children largely according to the direct achieving ethic. These behaviors also serve us well in crises, when we may need to impose order on chaos. As diversity and independence continue to erupt worldwide, an understanding of the direct styles will help leaders cope with the tensions that these forces generate.

The direct styles were a better fit, however, for the more isolated circumstances of a Stage 2 environment. As the world moves into Stage 3, direct achieving styles—undiluted and unaided by other achieving styles—won't be enough. In an interdependent world, leaders will need to work with associates from many other cultures that emphasize different achieving styles. In some cultures, such as those of China, Japan, Italy, and Argentina, the direct styles create the impression of hyperindividualism, egotism, selfishness, and insensitivity to the needs of others.

Relational styles, more oriented to the needs and tasks of others, offer leaders new opportunities to manage the interdependence of a Stage 3 environment. In the next chapter, we turn our attention to these styles many American leaders honor more in rhetoric than in reality.

Figure 3. The Relational Set of Styles.

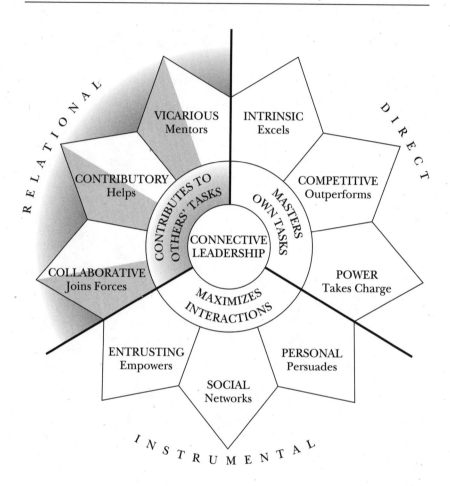

Chapter Seven

The Relational Path to Leadership

The Collaborative, Contributory, and Vicarious Styles

> *There must be not a balance of power but a community of power.*
> WOODROW WILSON[1]

The second set of achieving styles, the relational set, is paramount in many societies, among them Argentina, Singapore, and Egypt. In Stage 3, these are the strategies that leaders need to link themselves to other peoples' goals and visions. In contrast to the direct strategies that focus on one's own objectives, relational strategies emphasize participating in group goals and helping other people with their tasks.

It's important, however, not to be misled by the label *relational*. In traditional management jargon, the term *relational* means that an individual likes people and thrives on relationships. When management theorists contrast "people orientation" with "task orientation," "people orientation" has that relational meaning, liking or needing other people.

In the context of the Connective Leadership Model, however, *relational* means something quite different. It does *not* mean liking or even necessarily knowing people. Of course, individuals using relational achieving styles *may* certainly like and need people. It is just that liking people is not the important driving force behind their relational behavior. For relational achievers, it is *identifying* with people and meeting one's achievement needs through close or even distant relationships that is central. Thus, team members who can identify with one another, sharing the sweetness of the team's success and the bitterness of its defeats, are using relational styles, regardless of their affection for one another.

Identification, probably more than affection, subjects the golfer's caddie to a surge of elation or a downspin of despair, depending upon the golfer's final standing in the tour. Sports fans who savor their idols' victories identify with their admired achievers, so that they too are thrilled by every triumph and depressed at each failure. Each of these roles respectively—team member, caddie, and sports fan—represents a different type of relational achieving style: collaborative, contributory, and vicarious.

The Collaborative Style

Leaders who use the *collaborative* style prefer to accomplish their tasks within the milieu of a group. They believe that two heads are better than one. Given a task, collaborative achievers' first response is to assemble or join a team.

Collaborative achievers believe their best efforts are stimulated by the group's interaction. They find satisfaction, even excitement and motivation, in brainstorming with others. The synergy generated by group efforts is both the special fuel and the reward on which collaborative achievers thrive. Ordinarily, they strive to achieve smooth-working relationships with their teammates, but they do not shrink from open and vigorous debate on the issues. "Hot groups," those high-intensity, short-lived teams that frequently produce extraordinary results, exemplify the dynamic possibilities of the collaborative style.[2] They are particularly well suited to the temporary, fast-moving structures demanded by a Stage 3 world.

In contrast to both direct and instrumental achievers, who focus on their own goals, collaborative achievers easily accept or help fashion group goals. Because they also expect to share both the rewards and the penalties for the group's performance, "one for all and all for one" is the natural motto of collaborative achievers.

Collaborating Outshines Competing

Successful achievement demands appropriate allocation of resources, including ideas, labor, and material. Although Americans often prefer competing and acting independently to collaborating, a growing body of research indicates that collaboration leads to greater success than competition.

Competition Versus Collaboration Versus Independent Action

The research of University of Minnesota professors of education David and Roger Johnson[3] and their colleagues reveals the strength of collaborating in the classroom. Reviewing more than half a century of research[4] that compared competitive, cooperative, and individualistic classrooms, they found that:

- Cooperation led to higher achievement than did competition.[5]
- Cooperation was more likely than independence to be linked to higher achievement.[6]

Intrigued by the debate over the relative contributions of cooperation and competition to individual problem solving, Qin, Johnson, and Johnson reviewed forty-six studies published between 1929 and 1993.[7] They examined four different categories of problem solving: linguistic (using written and oral language), nonlinguistic (using symbols, math, motor activities, and actions), well-defined problems (with clearly specified operations and solutions), and ill-defined problems (lacking any well-articulated operations and solutions). On all four types of problem solving, members of cooperative teams outperformed individuals competing against each other, regardless of their age.

In addition to learning more about the topic they are studying, students in cooperative learning environments

- Feel more positive about learning
- Feel better about themselves
- Improve their capacity to take the emotional and cognitive perspective of others

These advantages occur despite differences in ability, social class, gender, ethnic background, and physical impairment. In the hands of skillful instructors, students in cooperative settings reduce their own sense of alienation and anger toward others generated in previous encounters.[8]

Still other evidence comes from the popular group problem-solving simulation Desert Survival, which repeatedly attests to the advantages of group over individual decision making. This well-known exercise presents the players with a crisis scenario in which they must imagine themselves the survivors of a plane crash in the desert. The analysis of decisions made by 4,116 individuals first on their own and later in groups shows that, overall, team decisions were decidedly superior to individual choices. Only 26 percent of the individual participants scored better than their teams. On "winning" teams (that is, those that outdid other teams according to the defined values of the simulation), only 13.1 percent of the individuals involved scored better than their groups. The evidence drawn from various sources strongly favors collaboration over individualistic competition.

Resolving Conflicts and Advancing Shared Visions

Collaboration turns out to be an important tool for resolving conflicts, particularly under certain circumstances. When problems are poorly defined or when stakeholders, especially those with differential power and resources, disagree on their definition, collaboration is an important method for untying the knot of dissension.

Collaboration, according to Pennsylvania State University professor Barbara Gray, is a "process in which those parties with a stake in the problem actively seek a mutually determined solution. They join forces, pool information, knock heads, construct alternative solutions, and forge an agreement."[9]

Collaboration incorporates two related processes for solving complex problems in an interdependent world: resolving conflicts and advancing shared visions. In Gray's view, collaboration allows the interested parties to work through emotion-laden issues to arrive at a negotiated settlement which all the stakeholders can accept. Each collaborator relinquishes some degree of sovereignty, while still preserving some power.[10]

Advancing a shared vision allows stakeholders to discover common values. These shared values, in turn, enable participants to develop plans for future joint responsibility for common policy issues. Multiple perspectives are joined to solve complex societal problems, within and between businesses, governments, labor groups, and communities.

By exploring their disagreements, stakeholders approaching the problem from different angles can find innovative solutions that transcend the limitations of their individual visions. Collaboration, according to this view, generates a "richer, more comprehensive appreciation of the problem among the stakeholders than any one of them could construct alone."[11] Because stakeholders generate the solutions only after in-depth analysis, and because they bring complementary perspectives and resources to bear on the solution, the quality of the solutions arrived at through collaboration is usually superior.

Resolving a thorny problem through collaboration brings participants additional longer-term gains. First, they begin to see each other as real people, with real concerns, rather than as stereotyped opponents. This new perception of one another leads to identification and empathy, which lay the groundwork for ongoing relationships and future collaboration.

Even the most skittish collaborators begin to discover that they have more in common than they previously thought. Commonalities in turn increase the collaborators' reservoir of goodwill, which they can then draw upon to settle other areas of disagreement.

Collaboration at Three Mile Island

The March 1979 accident at Three Mile Island (TMI), Pennsylvania, provides an example of successful collaboration among government agencies, technical experts, and ordinary citizens (serving as leaders at the grass-roots level). Immediately following the accident at TMI, the local residents were understandably concerned about the long-term health threat posed by the low but significant levels of radioactive material the damaged reactors had released into the atmosphere. Imagine the community's escalating concern when Metropolitan Edison, responsible for the nuclear reactors on Three Mile Island, announced plans for releasing into the atmosphere small amounts of radioactive krypton gas still trapped in the damaged reactor. According to Met Ed, the release of the krypton gas was necessary before experts could determine the degree of damage the reactor had sustained.

Despite the assurances of the Nuclear Regulatory Commission (NRC) that the released gas posed no threat to the community's health or safety, the citizenry remained unconvinced. Citizens' confidence in Met Ed and the NRC was at low ebb. Public meetings to discuss the environmental impact of releasing the krypton gas erupted in fierce debate. When the NRC announced the initiation of a community monitoring program, the notice fell on deaf ears. Then the U.S. Department of Energy appointed a technical working group (TWG), comprising representatives from the Environmental Protection Agency, the Pennsylvania Department of Environmental Resources (DER), the Pennsylvania State University, and EG&G Idaho, technical consultants to Met Ed.

The TWG was charged with creating a Citizens' Radiation Monitoring Program. It was designed to provide TMI-area residents with accurate and believable information about radiation levels during the period that the krypton gas was being released into the atmosphere. The basic assumption guiding the design of the program was that residents of the area would place greater confidence in information generated by ordinary citizens than by Met Ed or government representatives, whose credibility had disintegrated in the aftermath of the accident.

Each community within a five-mile radius of TMI nominated four citizens to monitor the radiation levels. The citizen monitors came from diverse occupations, social backgrounds, and age groups.

The Department of Energy donated the funds. The university designed the instruments and trained the citizens. EG&G Idaho, the EPA, and the DER provided technical expertise and staff. The citizens contributed their time, intelligence, and energies to track the radiation levels.

Each community created its own monitoring locations and schedules. Every day, the TWG reported the results the citizen monitors had charted. Within five months, the project was successfully completed, costing far less in dollars, person-hours, and frustration than anyone could have predicted at the outset. Met Ed received citizens' approval to begin the first crucial phase of the cleanup. Area residents obtained information that they and their citizen representatives believed was accurate and complete. With increased knowledge about nuclear power and community needs, acrimonious debates among all the stakeholders subsided and problem-solving dialogue increased.

The results of this complicated collaboration among government, communities, and the private sector demonstrated an important lesson: collaboration among initially antagonistic stakeholders, even on complex technical and sensitive social problems, can lead to technical and social economies. Many stakeholders whose mutual destinies are held hostage to the complex problems of an interdependent environment might look to the collaborative method for alternative, and often more cost-effective, leadership strategies.

Collaboration at the Top: Sharing Leadership

The benefits of collaboration extend far beyond the realm of conflict resolution. The goodwill and recognized commonalities sparked by collaboration can help leaders in the boardroom to work together long-term, resolving potential disagreements almost before they arise.

John French, Corporate Collaborator

The scion of a home furnishings dynasty, whom we shall give the pseudonym of John French, described the collaborative leadership history of the family company. French's grandfather established a furniture store just before the turn of the twentieth century. When the founder's sons inherited the business, they annually rotated the top corporate offices. Under their leadership, they created an upscale, service-oriented home furnishings company. Subsequently, the leadership structure was formalized into a CEO committee. From midcentury until 1990, the company grew nearly tenfold in size of workforce and sales.

John French explained the customary consensus that has enabled the third-generation family members to make critical, long-term decisions for the organization. He attributes the corporate committee's successful collaboration to the members' common background, particularly their having been introduced as teenagers to the business in low-level company roles. French suggests that joint ownership in the project plus respect for one another's positions are necessary ingredients for successful collaboration.

Nonetheless, disagreements occasionally arise within the French corporate committee. When they do, if one committee member vigorously dissents, that member's deeply held opinion usually prevails. Despite disparities in the coleaders' stock ownership, French explained, "We never vote our stock."

Other CEO Committees

CEO committees have a long and checkered history in American management. Few have been genuine substitutions for a single CEO. In 1903, Du Pont created a six-member executive committee to generate cooperatively crafted strategic decisions. Sears, Roebuck, in 1932, and later Hewlett-Packard, Caterpillar, Gulf Oil, and TRW experimented with an executive-office arrangement in place of an individual CEO.

In the 1960s and 1970s, the growth of conglomerates sparked a rash of variations on executive committees, some fashioned as the CEO's "cabinet." Mainstream organizations such as Ford, IBM, Dow Chemical, and Chase Manhattan joined the parade. By the late seventies and continuing through the eighties, a sizable number of disaffected companies jumped ship, returning to more conventional leadership structures.[12] Some, of course, had used the executive committee for inappropriate functions, and oftentimes the committee arrangement led to an endless round of meetings that generated more, not less, work.

Even at the very outset of Stage 3, whether they like it or not organizations are connected to a vast network of other organizations at home and abroad. Their own internal divisions are—or should be—interdependent also.

Now is clearly the time to reconsider the role of collaboration, not simply at lower levels of the organization but in the boardroom as well. A collaborative CEO function is not necessarily a universal substitute for the individual CEO, but it is a serious alternative road to organizational effectiveness. And although collaborative councils may not be the best solution for all organizations, they're probably worth another serious look.

Collaboration Versus Competition: Reducing Aggression and Violence

Collaboration has still other benefits, particularly as an antidote to aggression and hostility. Years of research have consistently shown that competition acts as a precursor to aggression and anger, while collaboration leads to agreement and friendship.[13] The well-known Robber's Cave experiments dramatically demonstrated that competitive games can ignite hostility and aggression among former friends.[14] Cooperation, on the other hand, served to dissolve even fresh hostilities. A recent field study conducted with Singaporean hotel managers and workers has confirmed that cooperative and competitive goals similarly affect the dynamics and outcomes of conflict in non-Western organizations.[15]

George Bush: Orchestrating Collaboration Among Former Enemies

Even on the international scene, collaborative leadership strategies can mute long-standing enmities, as former President George Bush discovered. In his Desert Storm showdown with Iraqi strongman Saddam Hussein, Bush used a collaborative approach to orchestrate a military response by a group of leaders many of whom had not spoken to one another in years.

This collaborative tour de force rested on a diplomatic and military alliance across a diverse set of unfriendly nations. Bush's finest hour in office drew on his ability to coalesce a group of former enemies to cooperate around new, if short-term, mutual goals. The need to collaborate meant shelving the intragroup hostilities, at least for the critical duration of the Desert Storm offensive.

Creating and Sustaining Cooperative Systems

While short-term collaboration among former foes is extremely important, sustaining longer-term cooperative systems deserves our serious attention, particularly in an interdependent world. If cooperation is so crucial, even for a nation seriously addicted to the opiate of complex individualism, how do we ever generate and sustain it without extinguishing our individualism? Or are collaboration, teams, and networks simply an idealistic dream?

The global network that collaborated to resolve the 1990 Gulf crisis offers some interesting clues as to how cooperation can work even among previously hostile members without extinguishing their individualism. But in an interdependent world, seriously addicted to complex individualism ourselves, how do we sustain the long-term cooperation that is the lifeblood of networks? Does cooperation occur only in crisis, and even then, only temporarily?

The field of game theory casts light on the origins and maintenance of cooperation. Research by Yale professor Robert Axelrod examines the optimal conditions for eliciting and sustaining cooperation, rather than hostility and retaliation.[16] Axelrod devised an ingeniously simple experiment: he invited various game theorists to write programs for a Computer Prisoner's Dilemma Tournament.

The Prisoner's Dilemma, a familiar instrument in laboratory research, allows players to seek either their own self-interest or the interest of the group. Pursuing one's self-interest involves the risk of winning or losing big, while cooperating offers somewhat lower, but more dependable, mutual gains. The game does not force cooperation. In fact, it permits players to exploit or mutually resist cooperating with one another. The game also recognizes that, as in real life, the players do not necessarily have totally opposing interests.

In Axelrod's study, game theorists in numerous disciplines submitted computer programs that competed in a round-robin computer tournament. To Axelrod's great surprise, the simplest program of all, "Tit for Tat," was the clear winner. (Tit for Tat involves an uncomplicated strategy in which the player starts by cooperating and subsequently merely mimics what the other player did on the last move.) A second round robin tournament, with sixty-two competing strategies, yielded the same result: Tit for Tat won again.

This led Axelrod to draw seven important conclusions about the necessary conditions for cooperation:

1. The emergence of cooperation requires the expectation of an enduring relationship, as in real-life work and family groups. One-night stands simply won't work, but the intensity of interaction need not remain constant.
2. The first tendrils of cooperative behavior are nourished by reciprocal cooperation on the second player's part.
3. The anticipation that cooperation will continue is important, but so is the recognition that noncooperation breeds more noncooperation, to the detriment of all. One implication is that even those who prefer cooperation must be prepared, on occasion, to go it alone and to use competitive or power strategies.
4. Once established, the cooperative efforts of a group can withstand the attack of a hostile, noncooperative group. A single

individual trying to cooperate with a noncooperative group, however, has very little chance of succeeding.

5. Successful cooperation requires assembling a large enough cadre of people with the cooperative, collaborative, and contributory skills to withstand a hostile assault.

6. Fostering continued cooperation requires that the principals have a reputation for toughness; that is, they will respond in kind to noncooperation. Clearly, direct-achieving strategies must always be available to back up cooperative relationships.

7. A willingness to entrust one's tasks to others and permit relationships to develop into a stable, if intermittent, system of reciprocity is a key ingredient in the recipe for sustained cooperation. Here we see the importance of individualism linked to instrumentalism, which (as discussed in the next chapter) entails social interaction, system savvy, and the ability to entrust and contribute to others. The skill to achieve goals through relationships that blossom into trusted, if episodic, alliances is an important stimulus to cooperation.

Collaboration requires deliberate nourishment and conscious effort to sustain it. Relationships built on trust, reciprocity, and mutual goals can help to create the conditions for collaboration that endure through time, even through periods of reduced or intermittent cooperation. While reciprocity is a key ingredient in collaboration, it is less central in the next style within the relational set, the contributory style.

Collaboration's Costs and Savings

Collaboration in various guises has sounded a recurring theme in the history of American industry. As we saw in Chapter Three, collaboration (sometimes configured as participative management) can be illusory, with far more sound than substance. Too often, authoritarian expectations have been wrapped in a thin coating of collaboration, a leadership M&M that has left a bitter aftertaste. Committees, the quintessential collaborative enterprise, have often drowned in quagmires of inaction. Consequently, it is not surprising that collaboration has been something of a distant second in American choices of leadership style.

Used with a connective sensibility, the collaborative style entails genuinely shared responsibility for success as well as failure. Within the context of the Connective Leadership Model, the flexibility, complexity, and nuances of each style are enhanced by the possibility of combining it with other styles. By drawing on the entire repertoire of achieving styles, collaboration takes on new meaning and opens new leadership options.

Connective leaders who weave the collaborative style into the fabric of their activities recognize the difficulties of leading through joint action, where no one party is the designated authority. They may call upon their instrumental skills to negotiate disagreements between themselves and their collaborators, or among a group of disagreeing stakeholders. Skillful connective leaders do not allow collaborative strategies, with their inherent tensions, to become a recipe for inaction.

The costs, both real and imagined, of collaboration in terms of speed and frustration are usually less than those of continued antagonism and competition. Each party only needs to contribute a portion, not all, of the needed resources. Pooling resources benefits everyone, since fewer resources are needed just to solve the problem than to resolve the issue *and* simultaneously battle all the other parties.

The expensive services of intermediaries, including lawyers, mediators, and key witnesses, are less likely to be needed. Research and development costs can be pooled effectively by several groups that work on related but different issues. Moreover, the less obvious but usually greater costs of inaction in the face of environmental, organizational, and political problems have to be counted as well.

The Contributory Style

The second relational style, the *contributory* style, is familiar to anyone raised in a family. We all recognize it as a traditional female way of doing things. Women routinely and effectively have used this style to assist their spouses, their children, and, when they worked outside the home, their bosses and charges.

Of course, the sphere of hearth and home, to which most women were limited for many centuries, bespeaks interdependence. It is therefore not surprising that women, long before men, seem to have discovered the strength of contributory strategies that work so well in an interdependent context. Unfortunately, in a world tuned to sexual stereotyping, the association between contributory behavior and the traditional female role has stigmatized this useful style, particularly as women have sought to move into front-line positions. Recently, however, intensifying global interdependence has been infusing contributory action with new strategic importance. If we examine contributory behavior without the filter of sexual stereotypes, we shall see some very strong and effective strategies just waiting for us to use.

Contributory achievers accept as their own the goals defined by others. Leaders who understand the benefits of contributory action feel comfortable helping others achieve their goals. There is mutual recognition that the overall accomplishment is appropriately attributed not to the leader, but to the person being helped.

Leaders who use contributory strategies recognize that identifying with others' goals and contributing actively to their tasks pave an important path to achievement. As we have seen, Mohandas Gandhi traveled to remote villages to instruct the inhabitants on important sanitation methods. By cleaning the latrines of the "untouchables," Gandhi simultaneously contributed to his constituents' needs and demonstrated his sense of identity with this stigmatized group.

Helping Others Helps Oneself

Helping others achieve their goals plants the seeds of reciprocity, which, as Axelrod has shown, is the basis of long-term cooperation.[17] When leaders facilitate others' desires without egotistically taking either charge or credit, they build a reservoir of goodwill and indebtedness available for the future.

The contributory style brings not only long-term benefits but immediate satisfaction. It inoculates leaders against the ravages of egomania, by offering them a lens for viewing the longings and needs of their supporters. Leaders favoring this style experience a genuine sense of achievement by contributing to someone else's successful performance.

Contributing to a Dream: Mike Corbett and Mark Wellman

An exquisite case of contributory achieving styles can be seen in the story of two modern American heroes, Mike Corbett and Mark Wellman. Let's consider Corbett's efforts to assist his friend Wellman fulfill a dream.

As a park ranger, Wellman was paralyzed in a fall. Yet he still yearned to climb the largest single piece of granite in the world, El Capitan in Yosemite National Park.

For seven years after his accident, Wellman's desire remained simply a tantalizing dream. It took the contributory action of Mike Corbett to turn that dream into a hard-won reality. The fact that Corbett, an accomplished climber in his own right, had climbed El Capitan forty-one times illustrates perfectly that contributory achievers commonly call upon the style out of strength, not weakness.

To give form to Wellman's intrinsic-achieving dream, Corbett first engineered a special pulley for Wellman to hoist himself up the thirty-six hundred feet to the summit. To prepare himself to use the pulley, Wellman doggedly trained in the gym for six months, practicing thousands of chin-ups every day.

Next, Corbett designed and sewed special canvas chaps to keep the "boss's" legs from scraping against the face of the cliff as Wellman was chinning himself more than seven thousand times to reach the top. In this historic effort, Corbett climbed ahead of Wellman to hammer in the anchors on which the paralyzed climber could hoist himself with his specially built pulley.

During the climb, as Wellman passed each anchor point, Corbett would slide down the cliff to retrieve the anchor and then climb ahead again to insert a new anchor. This remarkable contributory effort required Corbett to climb El Capitan the equivalent of three times. On December 8, 1991, as the climbers reached the top, spectators were overwhelmed by the unbelievable feat of a paralyzed climber chinning himself thirty-six hundred feet up the side of El Capitan.[18]

Most of the media attention went to the paralyzed climber. Corbett seemed perfectly content to have his own monumental effort viewed simply as a contribution to Wellman's achievement. In an unusual move, the U.S. Senate officially commended both climbers' heroic accomplishments. Climbing a sheer granite cliff in reflected heat that reached 126 degrees harks back to the "direct" exploits of our heroic frontier forebears, only this time contributory action made an intrinsic dream come true.

Political Spouses: Damned If You Do, Damned If You Don't

Some roles closely associated with leadership call for the deft touch of contributory behavior. Political and corporate spouses, speech-writers, and many professionals engaged in the helping professions all work within the limits of contributory roles.

As we suggested earlier, the family traditionally has been a set-ting for contributory behavior. The parent who feeds and bathes an infant and years later types that child's term paper is simply con-tinuing a pattern of contributory action. Although husbands and fathers also use contributory strategies within the family, women's contributory behavior has taken most of the spotlight.[19] Political families, who live under klieg lights, offer us a special example of the complexities associated with the contributory style.

Wives of political figures are old hands at contributory behav-ior. Depending on how they strike the balance between contribut-ing and taking charge, political wives—American first ladies, for example—find themselves either praised or pilloried. Balancing serious contributions and less visible background activity has been a difficult trial for many political spouses. In fact, knowing precisely when the contributory versus the vicarious style (or any other achieving style, for that matter) is appropriate is a serious issue for all of us, as we shall see later.

Eleanor Roosevelt

Eleanor Roosevelt's contributions to the career of her polio-stricken husband were both admired and reviled.[20] Campaign but-tons reading "Not Eleanor Either" reflected the recognition of her contributions to FDR's achievements, as well as the animosity her behavior aroused.

Extraordinarily shy by temperament, Eleanor Roosevelt man-aged to stay in the background during the early years of FDR's polit-ical career. Only after polio left the rising political star paralyzed was Mrs. Roosevelt forced into the spotlight to undertake many of the tasks her husband could no longer perform. She canvassed his political territory and accepted speaking invitations—which she dreaded—to keep his image alive in the voters' minds. During his presidential years, Roosevelt relied on the first lady's meetings with constituents to keep him in touch. He frequently referred to her as his "eyes and ears."

Rosalynn Carter

Like many other political spouses, Rosalynn Carter worked hard to project the "appropriate" helpmate image in her role as first lady. By concentrating on significant issues, she also tried to demonstrate her own personal strengths and echo the down-to-earth tone of the Carter administration.

As the wife of Georgia's governor, Rosalynn Carter had played a major role on the gubernatorial political team. To emphasize the seriousness of her new role as first lady, she instructed her White House staff not to brief reporters on her wardrobe. Whenever the press insisted upon highlighting the first lady's clothes and appearance, they were likely to suffer the consequences.[21]

Initially, the American public seemed to approve of Rosalynn Carter's serious approach. The first lady, however, soon found herself the butt of growing criticism after the media reported her regular attendance at cabinet meetings and her influence on staff shakeups:

> she has not been elected to any office. She draws no government salary. But Rosalynn Carter has become a powerful voice in the White House—and this week is no exception.
>
> Mrs. Carter has been meeting privately for the last few days with members of the White House senior staff as President Carter weighs the decision of who will stay and who will go in the shakeup of his administration.
>
> Mrs. Carter's press secretary says the First Lady will be involved in evaluating resignations submitted to the President by his Cabinet and other top-level appointees.[22]

This report and others detailing her contributions to the President's *core* tasks earned the first lady much negative ink and the dubious nickname of "Steel Magnolia."

Hillary Rodham Clinton

By the time Bill Clinton campaigned for the presidency, the role of American women had long been in transition. Reflecting that change, Hillary Rodham Clinton's performance probably has rewritten the rule book for American first ladies.

During her husband's presidential campaign, the media see-sawed between praise and censure for Hillary Rodham Clinton. They lauded her professional role as lawyer and child advocate but wondered if she would know her unelected "place" as first lady.

Every aspect of Hillary Rodham Clinton's persona came under intense scrutiny: her Wellesley/Yale Law School education, the length of her hair, her headbands, her disinterest in fashion, her maternal responsibilities, her many friendships, her influence on campaign policy. When she took the podium too intensely, she was warned off by a press corps who insisted she was overshadowing her husband. In the final days of the campaign, we saw a more demure wife on the speaker's platform, dutifully holding an umbrella over her husband's head as he spoke to the crowd on a rainy afternoon.

In the opening weeks of the Clinton administration, TV reporters highlighted the first lady's role at state dinners and meetings with world leaders. Was she actually discussing policy, and was this an appropriate function for the first lady, they wondered. The media pondered why the president's wife wanted to be referred to as Hillary *Rodham* Clinton. Did this signal a new foray into a separate identity?

With the announcement that Mrs. Clinton would spearhead the administration's health care policy task force, a torrent of media speculation flowed. Some commentators complained that it was unseemly for the president to appoint his wife to this critical task. That she had successfully undertaken a similar assignment during their Arkansas gubernatorial days was irrelevant, in their view.

Her virtuoso congressional testimony, unprompted by notes on the complexities of health care policy, won plaudits from Capitol Hill. Once again, however, the media sounded a not too subtle warning that the first lady was outshining the president. In fact, a national poll taken immediately following her testimony on the Hill revealed that a large percentage of those surveyed thought

Hillary Rodham Clinton was more intelligent than her husband. That same poll reported that a majority of those questioned believed the first lady could handle the presidency; however, a majority of these same respondents indicated they did not think she should run for the office. The subsequent debacle of the administration's health care plan brought a torrent of complaint about the first lady and the president.

The American public's response to Hillary Rodham Clinton's role in the administration's health care initiative reflects our ambivalence toward contributory achievement. We have a hard time considering the contributor a "real leader," so contributing is acceptable as long as it does not intrude noticeably on the official leadership sphere. When she delivered a strong speech at the United Nations Conference on the Status of Women in Beijing, the first lady was roundly applauded at home and abroad. She was, after all, discussing women's issues, an acceptable domain for the president's spouse, not too different from Jacqueline Kennedy redecorating the White House and Lady Bird Johnson planting flowers in the public parks of the capitol. If the contributor "steps beyond her role" and genuinely contributes to the leadership process, she evokes our ambivalence. We demonstrate our resentment in several ways: by attacking the contributor and diminishing her contribution, as well as by denigrating the leader to whose task she is contributing. Yet, as Mrs. Clinton has shown, such contributory behavior also wins the respect and affection of many admirers who welcome competent contributions to the complex tasks of Stage 3.

At this writing, the Whitewater scandal looms ominously over the first lady even more than over the president. Long before Whitewater, however, Mrs. Clinton had begun to avoid visible policy roles. The ambivalence she evokes underscores the complicated nature of this leadership option. Despite its potential dangers, contributory action still offers many potential benefits. As such, it is a leadership resource that we cannot afford to ignore.

Five Important Lessons

The Hillary Rodham Clinton case illustrates five important lessons about achieving styles generally and the contributory style in particular.

First, the contributory achiever is forced to strike a delicate balance to avoid upstaging the individual he or she is helping. This will be the case at least until a Stage 3 perspective becomes more widespread.

Second, the first lady's willingness to engage in contributory behavior vis-à-vis her husband, despite her known capacity for other achieving styles, reminds us that those who use the relational styles do not necessarily do so by default. Many, if not most, relational achievers are perfectly capable of achieving directly on their own or through the instrumental achieving styles we describe in the next chapter; however, under certain circumstances they deliberately choose to achieve by collaborating, encouraging, or helping others with whom they identify.

Third, as with other people encountered in this book, I am artificially disentangling one strain of Hillary Rodham Clinton's achieving styles repertoire simply to focus on that style. Although her participation in health care policy can be characterized as contributory, in other aspects of her first lady role she has made it clear she and the president work together as a team, using collaborative action. And, of course, her interaction with members of the health care policy task force, as well as with members of her staff, calls on a broad range of achieving styles.

Fourth, the association between traditional female roles and relational styles in many cases has prevented leaders, both male and female, from drawing on these useful styles. Paradoxically, those leaders who fearlessly use these styles—like Mohandas Gandhi, Martin Luther King, Jr., and Bulgarian political leader Elena Lagadinova (whom we meet in Chapter Eleven)—actually enhanced their leadership roles.

Offering one more illustration of a political spouse may help underscore a fifth lesson: the difficulty of selecting appropriate achieving styles for a specific situation. Here again, the contributory style is a convenient example, although the difficulty of matching styles to circumstances applies to the entire spectrum of achieving styles.

In the 1992 political season, Elizabeth Hanford Dole, wife of presidential aspirant Sen. Robert Dole, resigned her cabinet post as secretary of transportation in the Reagan administration to campaign full-time for her husband. The press immediately dubbed

the North Carolina native "her husband's Southern strategy."
Incensed feminists challenged her decision. The *Los Angeles Times*
reported, however, that

> putting her husband's career first has enhanced her reputation
> here [in Atlanta] as a woman worth listening to. . . . With her hus-
> band spending most of his time in Iowa and New Hampshire, Eliza-
> beth Dole is striving to reach voters in the 14 Southern states that
> will take part in the March 8 Super Tuesday primary.[23]

In 1995, Mrs. Dole requested a one-year leave of absence from
her duties as president of the Red Cross to participate in her husband's political campaign. Mrs. Dole announced that she would return to her Red Cross post full-time even, she hoped, with her
husband in the White House. This time the media reported her announcement without much comment.

Matching styles to situations is a complex task, as we saw in
Chapter Five. It is one that calls for sensitivity to situational cues
and the flexibility to recombine styles as the situation demands.

The Vicarious Style

Leaders who use the third style in the relational set, the *vicarious*
style, encourage and guide others to their goals. These leaders take
pleasure in the accomplishments of others, as if the success were
their own. They understand and identify with the dreams and goals
of other leaders, as well as their own constituents, be they company
employees, customers, voters, or political staff.

Vicarious achievers may offer encouragement or praise, but
they do not participate directly in the actual role tasks of the other
achiever. This is quite different from the way the contributory
achiever takes responsibility for a specific piece of the action.

Of course, we know that contributory and vicarious achieving
styles are closely related, so we expect some leaders to merge the
two sets of strategies. The parents of Olympic athletes commonly
exhibit both contributory and vicarious behavior in their devotion
to their offspring's success. Patriotic citizens, alumni loyal to their
alma mater, exultant parents of star students and athletes, faithful

fans cheering for the hometown team, even groupies at rock concerts: all exhibit vicarious behavior as well. They experience the deep-in-the-bones satisfaction that comes from the success of the people and institutions they love.

Vicarious achievers accept and identify with the goals selected by others. They also endorse the means that those others have chosen to achieve their objectives.

The vicarious style is akin to altruism, that willingness to give or even sacrifice the self to help others or a cause larger than ourselves. Such a style energizes constituents as well as leaders. Anita Roddick calls this the expression of "moral sympathy," with which the leader infuses the entire enterprise and everyone associated with it.[24] She understands the importance of leadership that

> has efficiency beyond [the leader's] self-aggrandizement, that takes in the bigger picture, beyond the wealth [that the enterprise is creating], and [focuses on] the joy there and the notion of a sense of community.[25]

Those leaders who understand and identify with their constituents' needs build loyalty and appreciation. Ross Perot tried to ground his 1992 presidential campaign in his "lifelong devotion to the individual." His electronic town meetings, featuring two-way communication between the leader and ordinary citizens, excited a frustrated public whose concerns and visions repeatedly had been subordinated to those of their political leaders.

Vicarious achievers nurture the real (and even sometimes imagined) relationship between themselves and their admired achiever. For some vicarious types, it is not even necessary to have a personal relationship with other achievers to draw pleasure from their success.

Arizona State University psychology professor Robert Cialdini's[26] research on how people use their connections, significant or trivial, with successful people to increase their own public image helps shed light on vicarious behavior.[27] Cialdini and his co-workers found that university students advertised their association with winning football teams by wearing some form of university insignia—a sweatshirt, jacket, or hat with the university's emblem—on Mondays following their football team's victory.[28]

While there is ample evidence that others' success is readily claimed through vicarious behavior, the picture regarding vicarious failure is less clear. When their team lost, the number of students sporting clothes with the school logo was considerably lower. In fact, students were likely to use the pronoun *we* when their team prevailed ("we won") but substitute the distancing pronoun *they* when their team suffered defeat ("they lost"). Cialdini interprets this behavior as an effort to "bask in the reflected glory of another's success while avoiding the shadow of another's defeat."[29]

Although football fans may be inclined to disclaim or ignore their team's defeat, parents and spouses commonly feel the pangs of their loved ones' blunders. How much vicarious achievers can dissociate themselves from the failures or successes of others may in fact depend on the closeness of the relationship.

Vicarious Mentors: Solving Leadership Succession

The vicarious style is an essential element in the leader's capacity to serve as mentor for aspiring successors. Identifying with the triumphs of others and feeling pride and a genuine sense of achievement from another's success help the leader to groom other leaders, including their own replacements. Stage 2 leaders, caught up in their own vision and the heady exercise of power, rarely worry about the problem of succession. The role of mentor holds little interest for them. When it does, it commonly takes the negative form of decapitating all heirs apparent.

When Leaders Fail to Act Vicariously: The Henry Fords

Some Stage 2 leaders, like Henry Ford and his namesake grandson, can't confront the inevitability of their replacement, even by their own kin.[30] Lee Iacocca describes the anguish he and other contenders for the Ford leadership mantle experienced at the hands of a mercurial Henry Ford II, who anointed and then annihilated a string of potential successors.[31] Suffering in the wings, however, doesn't seem to increase Stage 2 leaders' sensitivity to the problem once they ascend to the throne, as Iacocca's own reluctance to support a successor at Chrysler demonstrated.

Stage 2 leaders' addiction to intrinsic, competitive, and power strategies often makes it difficult for them to loosen their grip on the company's reins. They cling to the leadership role even when their own desiccated vision no longer supplies adequate organizational fuel. Blinded by their stubborn commitment to their original vision, some leaders find it impossible to adapt to the demand for change.

The elder Ford's resistance to innovation in his fading Model T was legendary:

> His dealers, watching the rise of Chevy and sensing that Chevy was listening to its dealers and customers as Ford was not, pleaded with him to change. He turned a deaf ear. By the early twenties the rumblings from the dealers were mounting. In particular they wanted changes in the ignition system. Some of them were invited to Detroit to meet with Henry Ford.
>
> "You can have them [the changes] over my dead body," Ford said. "That magneto stays on as long as I'm alive. . . ." At almost the same time some of the dealers asked Ford if he would vary the color of the Model T. "You can have them any color you want, boys, as long as they're black," Ford answered.[32]

For some Stage 2 leaders, it seems, even the subsequent foundering of a rudderless company is preferable to being outshone by a successor. Henry Ford's tyrannical treatment of Bill Knudsen, the Danish immigrant generally recognized as the "ablest man in the company" drove Knudsen into the arms of General Motors.[33] After driving Knudsen out of the company, Ford grumbled, "I let him go not because he wasn't good, but because he was too good—for me."[34]

When Stage 2 Leaders Can't Mentor: The Law Firm of Shea & Gould

The Fords were not the only corporate leaders unable to confront the succession issue. Recent examples abound. Family businesses, from Ferragamo to Gucci, take their succession battles to court. And law firms themselves are not immune.

One of New York's largest law firms, Shea & Gould, was founded in 1964 and disbanded in 1994, victim of the succession syndrome. Despite healthy revenues ($85 million in 1993), the firm could not resolve the leadership crisis that reportedly started in the mid 1980s. At that time, the founding partners, William A. Shea and Milton S.

Gould, began to turn power over to the next generation of lawyers, apparently without grooming any successors or preparing the organization for the transition. Accustomed to three decades of autocratic, Stage 2 patriarchy, the organization simply couldn't handle the leadership shift.

Once Shea and Gould renounced their veto power over the executive committee, the downhill slide began. From all appearances, the new leaders, Jerome Kern and Thomas E. Constance were more attuned to a Stage 3 world and tried to use more relational leadership styles. But the firm, mired in authoritarianism, found it impossible to move beyond their Stage 2 expectations. New York legal recruiter Lynn Mestel diagnosed Shea & Gould's problem as "too much democracy after too many years of dictatorship. They needed a Yeltsin."[35]

Being caught up in one's own power can blind the leader to the long-term leadership needs of the organization. Leaders who expect others to accept their vision but who fail to identify with the visions of others have great difficulty grooming the next generation of leaders. For followers, domination by entrenched Stage 2 leaders can atrophy their own leadership talents.

Anita Roddick, Founder of The Body Shop

Difficulty in envisioning the long term is fairly characteristic of Stage 2 leaders, who, as we have seen, have little patience for mentoring would-be successors. By contrast, Stage 3 leaders use vicarious and contributory strategies, as well as the entrusting style we explore in the next chapter, to address this task so crucial to the enduring success of organizations.

I caught up with Anita Roddick at Stanford Graduate School of Business, where she was spending several weeks in residence. I asked her about the succession issue for The Body Shop, since her own personality and values are so forcefully stamped on the firm's image. Her emphatic response:

> What I am trying to do in my company at the moment is to push
> it away from being personalized by me, as the [sole] visionary
> leader. I have to go through another decade of really planned
> thinking of how the leadership can be [extended to others] in the

company. . . . You've got to do it! There's no "How will you? How can you?" You just do it!

When she travels to various locations of The Body Shop, Roddick doesn't always check in to a hotel. Instead she bunks at the homes of her employees, staying up until the wee hours of the morning talking with them and their children about their hopes for themselves and their ideas for the company. She told me:

> I want to share information. I want to take the remarkable people I work with and bring them to my home, spend time with them, eat with them, greet them, walk at night with them, and have these wonderful, almost family-like gatherings with them.

Developing successors is an important mechanism for ensuring the long-term success of the organization. For Stage 3 leaders, the successor's success is also the mentor's achievement.

For Stage 3 leaders, the long-term health of the organization is also a tribute to their own foresight and ego strength. To most observers, it is clear evidence of the leader's commitment to goals that transcend narrow egoistic needs, proof of a profound altruism that nourishes individuals, organizations, and community.

Yet mentoring, an expression of the altruism embedded in the vicarious style, is not without tangible benefits to the mentor as well. Mentors no longer actively involved in their protégés' accomplishments still derive a sense of achievement through their protégés' success. Nor is vicarious achievement only manifested in warm and fuzzy feelings about the protégé. The most vital mentoring, in fact, often becomes a two-way street. Protégés contribute to their mentors' continuing success by keeping them informed about important new events, by protecting the mentor's reputation and fortunes, and by alerting the mentor to new professional developments.

The professor who serves on a graduate student's doctoral committee may maintain a long-term relationship with that student, taking pleasure and receiving some small degree of credit for the professional accomplishments of the protégé. It is not uncommon for the protégé to invite the mentor to participate in honorific activities, simultaneously enhancing both the mentor's and protégé's status.

Toward a Politics of Commonalities

The relational styles, so underutilized by Stage 2 leaders, have particular relevance for Stage 3. They help us move beyond a politics of differences to a politics of commonalities. They do so by offering strategies for dealing with the problem of interdependence in a world simmering with diversity. Because the relational styles always involve the act of identifying with others—even very different others—they make it possible for us to link our hearts and minds to the dreams that others cherish. They let us walk in other people's shoes and understand their perspectives as well as their goals. Relational styles help subdue the hostility that we often feel toward those who are very different from ourselves.

In this way, the relational styles enable us to build bridges between ourselves and others. In the process, they open an alternative route to achievement and community. In countries such as Japan that frown upon competition within the group, vicarious pleasure in the accomplishments of others creates a wellspring of strength for leaders.

Unfortunately, relational achieving strategies cause many Americans noticeable discomfort. Leaders afflicted by Stage 2 myopia see relational achieving strategies as a second-best choice, selected only by achievers who are too weak, too young, or too old to act independently.

Perhaps some of the uneasiness we Americans feel about these styles springs from relational achievers' willingness to accept others' goals instead of pressing their own. Except in crises, our culture does not teach us to experience the deep satisfactions embedded in relational accomplishments. Instead, it grooms us to seek the glory—and often the anguish—of individualistic action expressed through direct achieving styles.

Growing global interdependence has forced us to reexamine our understanding of cooperation and collaboration, as well as the meaning of pride in our peers' and associates' accomplishments. As we shed our Stage 2 blinders, we are beginning to glimpse the enrichment of spirit, rather than the imagined weakness, expressed in accounts of "my-son- (or daughter-) the-doctor's" accomplishments.

A new vocabulary suggests we are reassessing these relational possibilities. We've begun to translate *vicarious achievement* into *mentoring* (that is, guiding, encouraging, and taking pride in others' accomplishments). We are developing a new appreciation for mentoring, "employee involvement," and "union-management task forces," all concepts that rely on the relational styles.

Perhaps we are even beginning to understand the importance of nurturing successors and building community. As connective leaders demonstrate how to combine the direct, relational, and instrumental styles, we may learn some important new ways of leading. We return to this theme after completing our discussion of the instrumental styles in the next chapter.

The collaborative, contributory, and vicarious achieving styles allow leaders to contribute actively or passively to a group goal or to another's task. In a world marked by great diversity, relational achieving styles generate a politics of commonalities to replace the politics of differences. Stage 3 leaders appreciate the role of collaboration in reducing hostilities and increasing shared visions.

Relational styles are infused with altruism, mutual commitment, and moral sympathy. They offer the exhilaration of collaborating on a shared goal, contributing to others' dreams, and mentoring the next generation of leaders. They enlarge the leader's repertoire for nurturing successors, for building community, and for strengthening the long-term health of a many-splendored society.

Figure 4. The Instrumental Set of Styles.

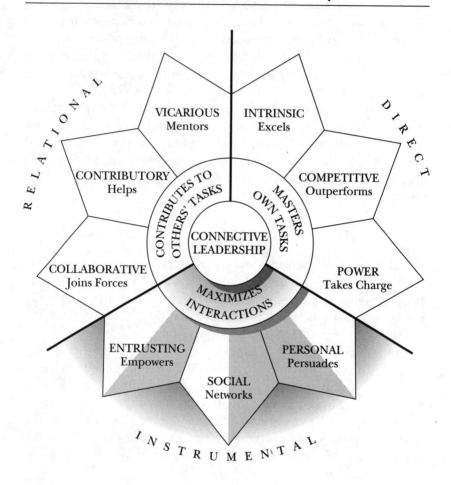

Chapter Eight

The Instrumental Road Less Traveled
The Personal, Social, and Entrusting Styles

*We have lots of people with tons and tons of responsibility,
whom I rely upon for everything. I look at myself as a
resource to them.*
WENDY KOPP[1]

Daring and discreet, or devious and dependent? Americans view the third set of achieving styles, the instrumental styles, through a multifocal lens. The reactions to the images they see range from attraction to skepticism and outright distrust. Because these styles conjure up Machiavellian manipulation, they leave many Americans quite ambivalent.

Like Machiavelli's prince, instrumental achievers know how to beguile us. They charm us with their clever wit. They draw us into their dazzling dreams. Yet, Americans have remained generally wary of these intriguing characters. We can't quite decide whether they are true visionaries or simply mad dreamers, or, in some cases, con artists.

We often wonder if the exuberant self-confidence of instrumental achievers is rooted in reality, or if it is just out-and-out braggadocio. When they assure us only we can do the job, their requests may raise suspicions that they value us primarily for what we can do for them.

Instrumental achievers have the social touch. They seem to know everyone, and the more renowned the better. Is it because others are naturally drawn to them? Or is it because they are just good, old-fashioned, manipulative social climbers?

True, the many political stratagems that Machiavelli recommended to the prince were designed to tighten the prince's control over his subjects. Even today, vintage Machiavellian behavior has the scent of self-interest. Still, Stage 3 leaders know that instrumental expertise can be used for the common good.

For connective leaders in a Stage 3 world, instrumental achieving styles offer a cornucopia of leadership strengths which are immensely useful, not just to the self-interested individual but to the larger community. The instrumental styles are important strategies for knitting groups of leaders with distinct missions and diverse constituents into mutually enhancing coalitions.

Instrumental achievers focus more on the *connections* rather than the *chasms* between people. Where others only perceive *distinctions* and *discord,* they see the *relationship* between ideologies and the *mutuality* between seemingly divergent groups. In a context of increasing diversity and multiculturalism, leaders who tap into common concerns and underlying values can help disparate groups chart their common ground. Such leaders also have the right touch for creating coalitions among large, diverse networks. Their instrumental sensibility drives them to transform divisive independence into unifying interdependence.

These leaders recognize the importance of information. Because they know and interact with many groups, instrumental achievers act as information nodes, receiving and passing along valuable knowledge that develops and integrates the different components of the system.

Instrumental achievers have a strong political sensibility. They are keyed in to who knows whom, who controls what, and how they do it. Their ability to tune into subtle group currents makes instrumental achievers experts in the complexities that flow from diversity. Social scientists would describe them as "process" people, specialists in social systems. They understand the subtle dynamics that inevitably percolate whenever groups gather.

It takes leaders with instrumental talents to build community. They know how to orchestrate community-level conversations.[2]

With great skill, they help groups sidestep the potholes along the route to communal goals.

Compared to direct achievers' near-obsession with the task, instrumental achievers focus on themselves, their relationships, and others to get what they want. They are maximizers, deftly making the most of their own and everyone else's strengths. They see untapped possibilities in people and situations. By maximizing everything about themselves, their relationships, and other peoples' talents, they easily bring people together to reach joint objectives.

Instrumental achievers calculate everyone's usefulness—even their own—for reaching their goals. Depending on which instrumental style they favor (and let's remember, they may use all three), these remarkable achievers bend their personalities and talents, their achievements, as well as their relationships with family, friends, colleagues, and casual acquaintances, into instruments for new accomplishments.

Instrumental achievers, like their direct neighbors, still want to define the goal, albeit with help from others. Instrumental achievers, however, are more likely than direct achievers to encourage others to design and carry out the implementation.

Three styles, personal, social, and entrusting, are the arrows in the instrumental leader's quiver. Because these instrumental styles are exceedingly subtle, as well as essential to leaders in a complex, interdependent world, we devote somewhat more time and space to them than the two more familiar sets of achieving styles. In this chapter, we visit with numerous leaders who are particularly adept at one or more of the instrumental styles, even when they also combine them with direct or relational leadership strategies.

The Personal Style

Among the instrumental set, the *personal* style is the most easily recognizable. Charismatic leaders introduced us to it even before Stage 3. Personal achievers use everything they have—their intellect, wit (often self-deprecating), charm, physical attractiveness, sexuality, oratorical skills, and persuasive talents, with a sprinkling of social status, past achievements, and the cachet of aristocratic lineage—to position themselves for new success.

Stage 2 Personal Achievers

John F. Kennedy: Camelot Revisited

President John F. Kennedy was the very model of a personal achiever. First as a beleaguered candidate and later as president, he used everything about himself to attract, cajole, and charm supporters. Kennedy's appealing image of youthful vigor, tanned good looks, a Harvard accent, and an All-American family—replete with stylish wife, energetic siblings, and a proud mother—transformed dubious voters into ardent supporters. His heroic, if exaggerated, exploits as a Navy PT boat commander reflected a macho spirit, while his Pulitzer Prize–winning book *Profiles in Courage* reflected a thoughtful intellect. His self-deprecating humor, a trademark of personal achievers, entranced the press corps who saw him through a Camelot mist.

Kennedy relied heavily on all of these personal characteristics and connections in his quest for high political office and later for presidential accomplishments. Like other personal achievers, Kennedy understood and used the power of his personal style to convince supporters to help him achieve his political goals. Unlike direct achievers, who try to do it all themselves or delegate portions of their tasks, personal achievers deliberately draw others into their magnetic field to join them in a mission requiring many hands and minds.

Henry Kissinger, Foreign Policy Virtuoso

Henry Kissinger provides a clear example of a Stage 2 achiever who utilized many aspects of his persona—notably his prodigious intellect, professorial status at Harvard, and quick wit—to move from the remote world of academia to the inner circle of world politics. Kissinger's memoirs chronicle the strategies he used to leapfrog from professor of government to advisor to New York governor Nelson Rockefeller, to President Nixon's special assistant for national security affairs, to secretary of state.[3] With wit and charm, Kissinger enthralled world leaders, political allies, and the international press, as well as a string of film stars whom he escorted to Hollywood galas. Kissinger's reply to reporters who inquired about his appeal to glamorous women revealed a personal sensibility: "Power," he growled good-naturedly, "is the greatest aphrodisiac."

Costume as Drama and Symbol

In setting the stage for success, personal achievers exploit the symbolism of dress, setting, and, frequently, theatrical props to enhance their mission and attract others to their enterprise.

FDR, Gandhi, and Nehru

President Franklin Roosevelt's cape and cigarette holder became the jaunty trademark that distracted the public from the physical ravages of polio that confined FDR to his wheelchair. These carefully selected symbols communicated the physically disabled president's vigor and ebullient self-confidence in facing the daunting challenges of the Great Depression and later World War II.

As we have already seen, Mohandas Gandhi, a master of most achieving styles, was a Stage 3 leader in a Stage 2 world. Keenly sensitive to the symbolism of costume, Gandhi replaced his Savile Row suits with the cotton dhoti of political prisoners. This symbolic act communicated two important messages: his identification with imprisoned patriots and the importance of India's self-reliance on indigenous resources (such as cotton) and labor.

Another Indian leader, Prime Minister Jawaharlal Nehru, always appeared in a high-collared jacket, the uniform of the Congress Party. His personal symbol was a single rose. Emulating his panache, admirers worldwide bought "Nehru jackets" in what became a fashion rage of the 1960s.

The Message of Uniforms: Castro, Arafat, and Hitler

Other leaders with a penchant for the personal style have used military uniforms to symbolize their mission and signal their resolve. Cuba's Fidel Castro and Yasser Arafat, leader of the Palestinian Liberation Organization, readily come to mind. Wearing (or rejecting) a uniform serves still other purposes, including setting oneself apart from the masses. Historians report that Adolph Hitler deliberately wore a military uniform when appearing among people dressed in business suits, and vice versa, to distinguish himself in every group.

Aquino, Mandela, and de Klerk

In a campaign that climaxed in a bloodless revolution, Philippine president Corazon Aquino's simple yellow dress became an emblem of her unvarnished integrity. It became a powerful symbol in the popular uprising that overturned the corrupt Marcos regime.

Campaigning for votes in South Africa's first multiracial democratic elections, African National Congress leader Nelson Mandela dressed in a distinctive dashiki signifying his party's heritage. Not to be outdone, incumbent President Frederik W. de Klerk wooed voters in what the *Los Angeles Times* dutifully reported as "Swazi gear."[4]

Personal achievers always seem to select just the right symbols to communicate and attract others to their cause. They also use *rejection* of highly charged symbols to communicate their message. Aquino's refusal to inhabit the predecessors' Mataplan Royal Palace conveyed the new president's determination to root out the corruption and greed (and discard the shoes) of the Marcoses.

The Seeds of Charisma: Drama, Symbolism, and Counterintuitive Action

Personal achievers' sharp sense of drama is not limited to the costumes they wear. They use many forms of symbolism, rituals, gestures, and timing with exquisite effect. They pinpoint just the right moment to make a dramatic entrance, launch an attack, or exit with flair. In so doing, their own persona becomes the magnet for attracting others to join their cause.

François Mitterand: The Art of the Beau Geste

Leaders who rely on personal behavior understand the impact of dramatic gestures. They are masters of the *beau geste,* those perfectly appropriate acts that capture the moment. To dramatize his concern for the victims of war-torn Bosnia-Herzegovina, ailing French president François Mitterand made an unexpected, one-day personal appearance in that country. The sight of the elderly statesman, valiantly braving his own physical infirmities to lend his presence to the cause of peace, touched an emotional chord worldwide.

Lord Louis Mountbatten, Last Viceroy of India

One particularly effective form of the *beau geste* is the counterintuitive gesture, an action that takes observers totally by surprise. Personal achievers rely heavily on counterintuitive gestures and symbols that captivate our imagination and permanently etch their memory in our psyches.

Catching us off guard with an unexpected act or symbol— sometimes spectacular, sometimes starkly simple—the charismatic leader ignites our imaginations and passions. Counterintuitive actions, with their built-in surprise, bypass our rational defenses and tap into the deep emotional reservoirs that followers bring to the leader/constituent relationship. Dazzled by the charismatic leader's ingenious manipulation of symbols, drama, and rituals, constituents find themselves in the leader's thrall.

As the last viceroy of India, Lord Louis Mountbatten used a palette of achieving styles, but particularly the personal style, to promote an overdue Indian transition to independence. Despite the fact that Mountbatten had come to preside over the transfer of power from Britain to India, he deliberately wrapped himself in costume and ritual to emphasize the legitimacy of this final viceroyalty.

Skillfully using elaborate ceremonies, military guards, medals, and the uniforms of his viceregal office, Mountbatten impressed and intrigued his Indian subjects with splendor and spectacle. Then, with breathtaking ease, he deliberately shattered the traditions of royal aloofness by reaching out casually and unpretentiously to his Indian hosts. By his simple, counterintuitive gesture, he signaled that he had chosen to act as their deliverer, not their dictator:

> [Mountbatten's] first announcement, that he and his wife or daughter would take their morning horseback rides unescorted, sent a shock wave of horror through the [Viceroy's] house. . . . The Indian villagers along the route of their morning rides began to witness a spectacle so wholly unbelievable as to seem a mirage: the Viceroy and Vicereine of India trotting past them, waving graciously, alone and unprotected. . . .

> He did something that no viceroy had deigned to do in two hundred years: he visited the home of an Indian who was not one of a handful of privileged princes. The viceregal couple walked into a garden party at the simple New Delhi residence of Jawaharlal Nehru. While Nehru's aides looked on dumb with disbelief, Mountbatten took Nehru by the elbow and strolled off among the guests casually chatting and shaking hands.[5]

These unexpected gestures caught the Indian leaders by surprise. By violating their rational expectations, Mountbatten's actions hit an emotional bull's-eye.

Jimmy Carter, a "People's President"

Ritual and pageantry ordinarily bedeck the inauguration of American presidents. In this highly ritualized procession, the newly inaugurated president with his first lady drive in the presidential limousine to a White House reception. Jimmy and Rosalynn Carter, unpretentious peanut farmers from Plains, Georgia, startled and captivated the nation by unexpectedly refusing the pomp and circumstance of official limousines. Instead, to the delight of the American public, they walked, hand in hand, down Pennsylvania Avenue.

Recalling it more than a decade later, President Carter revealed the intent behind this deliberate and counterintuitive gesture:

> One of the things we decided very secretly was that, after the inauguration ceremony, we would leave the limousine and walk down Pennsylvania Avenue just to show them that average American citizens were the ones that shaped the moral and ethical standards of our country and preserved it in times of tribulation and trial.[6]

Emperor Akihito of Japan

Another example of the counterintuitive gesture is provided by Emperor Akihito. Aware that many Japanese were questioning the relevance of the imperial family in the twentieth century, in his first address to his subjects the newly invested emperor purposefully chose symbolic language that evoked a major stir. In a sharp break with tradition, he spoke to his subjects using an honorific form of address.

Within the closed court of the imperial Japanese house, the essence of action is the symbolic gesture. Just as a classical drama can turn on the absence of a chair or the slightest abandonment of formal speech, the new occupant of the Chrysanthemum Throne made a revolutionary gesture in his first formal address. He merely added the honorific *san* in speaking of and to the Japanese people, something his father would have never dreamed of doing.[7] With this simple, unexpected, and thus all the more compelling act, the new emperor immediately delighted his audience and dampened their smoldering ambivalence.

Steve Jobs, Charismatic Entrepreneur

Through their choice of unique symbols and spectacular gestures, charismatic leaders convey a strong sense of personal authority that constituents find irresistible. As Apple Computer's cofounder, Steve Jobs's sense of drama provoked near-frenzied dedication among Apple employees. For openers, Jobs tucked the Macintosh design group, a small band of young computer hackers, into a separate building, Bandley 3. Next, he hung a pirate flag from the building's roof. This energetic entrepreneur intrigued his young protégés, a classic hot group, with his dream of a "computer for everyone."[8] At the 1994 Macworld Expo in San Francisco, Joanna Hoffman, a member of the original group (by then head of marketing at General Magic), recalled, "Steve was an inspiration, and I think all of us agree that his genius was unsurpassed."[9]

At the 1984 Apple shareholders' meeting, Jobs introduced the Macintosh with methodical, but playful, theatrics. He tantalized his audience with suspense and humor. With dramatic cadence, he described Apple Computer as a young David challenging the Goliath IBM. The audience resonated to each blow the brave young warrior struck.

Still shrouded in theatrical secrecy, the first Macintosh computer sat snugly in its canvas carrying case until the appointed moment. Only then did Jobs unveil the much-awaited Macintosh. The audience was astonished to hear a computer muse in robot-like tones, "Jobs was just like a father to me."

By then, the thirty-two hundred shareholders and employees were on their feet, cheering like rock fans at an outdoor concert. Not surprisingly, the press reported an amazing—or, in Jobs's vernacular, an "insanely great"—performance for a corporate executive.

When Jobs introduced his NeXT computer, he had an ordinarily blasé press begging for tickets. The entranced press expected a Jobs extravaganza, and that's exactly what they got.

Nascent Stage 3 Leaders: Martin Luther King, Jr., and Mikhail Gorbachev

Martin Luther King, Jr., strode the world stage in the best personal achieving tradition. The civil rights leader used his personal gifts in multiple ways to attract supporters to his historic mission.

Unlike many Stage 2 leaders who draw the world spotlight

tightly to themselves as individuals, King broke with this tradition. This early connective leader symbolized the importance of "brotherhood" by linking arms with fellow civil rights activists in his Freedom March through the streets of Selma, Alabama. That picture of Dr. King walking arm in arm with his fellow marchers was stark and powerful. Its impact came primarily through its contradiction of the customary images projected by more individualistic Stage 2 world leaders. King's personal symbolism still resounds down through the decades.

Mikhail Gorbachev startled Americans on his very first visit to the United States. Thousands of curious Washingtonians lined the streets of the capital to watch Gorbachev's motorcade wend its way to the White House. Without warning, the black limousine came to a sharp halt. The door opened, and out stepped the smiling Soviet leader, an unexpected contrast to his dour, aging predecessors. Gorbachev waved to the crowd, strode into their midst, shook hands, and kissed babies, much like the typical American politician.

In that one moment, Gorbachev's counterintuitive action communicated a reassuring message to wary Americans viewing his arrival on television. The emotional bond Gorbachev created with the American public that day laid the groundwork for trust and negotiation at the policy level, in those turbulent days leading to the end of the Cold War.

The Ultimate Use of the Self

Demonstrating a willingness to sacrifice oneself for the cause represents a special genre of dramatic gestures. For the personal achiever, it is the ultimate use of the self. In battle, some personal leaders are distinguished by their willingness to lead the charge, rather than issue orders to the troops from a protected command post.

What more dramatic use of the self can we imagine than the threat to fast to death to achieve one's purpose? Again, Gandhi offers us a quintessential example of personal action. In his determination to wrest an agreement of peace from warring Muslims and Hindus, the frail patriot undertook a death fast. When both sides saw that Gandhi's fast was threatening his life, they gave in to his wishes.

Activist Mitch Snyder

We left Mitch Snyder in Chapter Six, frustrated that his "take charge" (power) strategy wasn't working. There was no way that the federal government was going to donate an empty building to shelter the homeless. To make indifferent politicians and bureaucrats see the desperate plight of Washington's homeless, he resorted to the ultimate personal action, he vowed a Gandhi-like fast.

Each day his strength ebbed, until he gradually slipped beyond consciousness. Only then did the federal government finally agree to fund his $6 million haven for the homeless not far from the White House, and the activist was returned to health after a fifty-one-day fast.[10]

Snyder's behavior powerfully illustrates another important achieving styles dynamic: when a leader's action fails to achieve the goal, it is time to reassess one's choice of achieving styles. In Snyder's case, neither taking charge nor demanding federal resources—both power methods—had worked. Sensing the need for a different strategy to overcome bureaucratic resistance, he turned to personal action. We might say Snyder was listening to the situational feedback, or environmental cues, and—just as importantly—responding to them.

Reaching Out to the Opposition

Another category of counterintuitive gestures—reaching out to opponents—deserves special attention. Personal leaders are masters of the surprise rapprochement with long-standing enemies. They represent a stark contrast to Stage 2 leaders who use external enemies to build internal cohesion among their supporters. Personal types perceive potential alliances where others see only perpetuated animosities. Ignoring the divisions of race, party, religion, and nationality, they seek comrades and constituents through mutual goals.

This behavior often confuses their supporters. As a result, leaders who follow this course often discover that the fruits of these perplexing gestures may come at a dear price.

Anwar Sadat, Yitzhak Rabin, and Mikhail Gorbachev

In the fall of 1975, after years of stalemated bitterness and hostilities between Egypt and Israel, Egyptian president Anwar Sadat shocked the world by flying to Israel on a mission of peace. In that one breathtaking, counterintuitive act, Sadat melted away much of Israel's opposition and simultaneously provoked the realignment of the Arab League. His action permanently changed the course of Middle Eastern political history. It also set a precedent for the Palestinian-Israeli rapprochement two decades later. Of course, Sadat was taking a serious gamble in alienating his traditional followers; the venture ultimately cost him his life. Israeli prime minister Yitzhak Rabin's efforts, too, were to take a deadly turn.

After forty long years of the Cold War, without much fanfare Mikhail Gorbachev reached out to his American counterpart. The unexpected conciliatory gesture caught the world off balance, including both Gorbachev's own constituents and the U.S. government. Domestically, Gorbachev's critics worried that he was selling out; internationally, the Western allies responded with disbelief. But his counterintuitive gesture proved to be an authentic, and extraordinarily effective, personal action.

Bill Clinton Reaches Out

On the domestic level, President Clinton repeatedly has reached across the political divide for advice and support. His appointment of Reagan's press secretary, David Gergen, to a similar position within his own Democratic administration, as well as his selection of Republican cabinet members, reflects his comfort with counterintuitive gesture.

Behind the scenes, Clinton seeks wisdom and support across party lines, even from counselors uniformly shunned in the political arena. Not until after Richard Nixon's death did the American public learn that on several occasions Clinton had quietly solicited the counsel of the stigmatized Republican politician.

Frederik W. de Klerk

Son of a privileged Afrikaner family whose forebears settled in southern Africa in the seventeenth century, Frederik W. de Klerk was an unlikely candidate to dismantle apartheid. In fact, in 1948 his own father, Jan de Klerk, held a cabinet post in the National Party, whose platform promised to redesign society through the legalization of racial discrimination.

De Klerk himself held the flawless conservative credentials of an obscure minister of education when in 1989 the National Party caucus chose him to succeed President Pieter W. Botha. Earlier, in 1982, de Klerk had mollified the party's right wing, then threatening to secede, by vowing never to forsake the National Party's "own affairs," a familiar euphemism for apartheid.

This son of the elite Afrikaner class not only perplexed the black majority but also angered his own National Party by unpredictably reaching out to the black African National Congress. Anglican archbishop Desmond Tutu astutely observed that de Klerk's very conservative reputation "helped him to take actions that would be unthinkable, almost unacceptable, from somebody with a slightly more liberal hue."[11]

In one unexpected counterintuitive gesture after another, de Klerk announced that the future of South Africa lay not in maintaining apartheid but in dismantling it. His historic release of Nelson Mandela, the ANC leader imprisoned for twenty-seven years, brought the counterintuitive gesture to new heights. Not only was de Klerk reaching out to the traditional opposition, but he was deliberately setting in motion a process that could only lead to his own ouster as the nation's president. When the foregone conclusion of the election became official, de Klerk graciously saluted the new president:

> Mr. Mandela has walked a long road and now stands at the top of the hill. A traveler would sit down and admire the view, but a man of destiny knows that beyond this hill lies another and another. The journey is never complete.
>
> As he contemplates the next hill, I hold out my hand to Mr. Mandela in friendship and in cooperation. God bless South Africa. Nkosi Sikelele iAfrika (God bless Africa).[12]

The Role of Humor: Self-Deprecating Wit

Humor plays an important role in personal leadership behavior. Powerful personalities initially intimidate others or incite their resentment. Self-deprecating humor is a useful mechanism for reducing larger-than-life leaders to approachable human dimensions. It melts supporters' resistance to the leader's otherwise intimidating powers.

Abraham Lincoln: The Political Riposte

Abraham Lincoln was deservedly well known for his wit, which often poked fun at himself. In a heated moment of the now famous debates for the Illinois senate seat, Sen. Stephen Douglas angrily accused Lincoln of being two-faced. Without a moment's hesitation, Mr. Lincoln drolly responded, "Do you think if I had another face I would be wearing this one?"

Roosevelt, Kennedy, and Reagan

Many popular Stage 2 leaders, including Roosevelt, Kennedy, and Ronald Reagan, used self-deprecating humor to defuse opposition and charm supporters. With clever one-liners, all three deftly turned aside reporters' testy questions, leaving the press corps dissolved in approving laughter.

Roosevelt's famous "Fala" speech, in which he regaled the American radio audience with a hilarious litany of the dangers posed by his Scottie, was a brilliant retort to his political critics. Similarly, Kennedy's mockingly modest self-introduction at a state dinner in his honor ("I'm the man who has accompanied Jackie Kennedy to Paris") offers an oft-quoted example of his knack for using humor aimed at himself to charm others.

Ross Perot's Homespun Humor

In his 1992 campaign for the American presidency, entrepreneur Ross Perot laced his use of direct styles with a "down home" variety of humor to intrigue a disillusioned segment of American voters. Perot touted his impressive business exploits, as well as his personal wealth, as major qualifications for the presidency. Accused by his opponents of trying to buy the election, billionaire Perot wittily retorted, "Of course, I am. I'm buying it for the American people because my opponents have made it too expensive for the voters to buy for themselves." Homespun American humor and practicality were building blocks for the special form of charisma projected by this disarmingly unsophisticated candidate.

Charm and Persuasion: The Negotiator's Touch

"He can charm the fuzz off a peach" aptly describes an important dimension of personal behavior. This ability to persuade others involves first convincing oneself. This done, personal leaders may appear to be overly confident, egotistical, and ambitious. No doubt, some of them are. But mostly they simply persist in using everything they have to charm and persuade others to join their cause.

Negotiation and conflict resolution, of course, require more than persuasive charm. They also demand a special form of empathy. Earlier, we noted the personal achiever's capacity to discern an ally within an opponent. This same talent helps the personal leader understand the other party's point of view.

Personal leaders seem to maneuver and shift their position with considerable ease. Their nimbleness helps persuade opponents that moving one step closer to the "other side" is no sign of weakness or treachery.

In the war-torn Middle East, Arafat and Rabin have offered other examples of courageous conflict resolution. Braving intractable opposition from their own radical constituencies, the two Middle Eastern leaders, encouraged by Israeli prime minister Shimon Peres, repeatedly shifted ground. Eventually their negotiations created a framework for resolving their nations' deeply embedded disagreements. In this process, the historically hawkish Rabin gradually metamorphosed from a Stage 2 to a Stage 3 leader. Not all Stage 2 followers can make the same shift, as Rabin's assassination tragically reminds us.

Reinventing South Africa: de Klerk and Mandela

We return to de Klerk and Mandela as vivid examples of the personal achiever's negotiating skills: de Klerk in his determination to negotiate, Mandela in his charismatic persuasiveness. Even before signing Mandela's release from prison, de Klerk skillfully negotiated with his formidable opponent.

Once the freed Mandela resumed his leadership of the ANC, he and de Klerk doggedly negotiated an endless tangle of thorny issues. In his pledge of cooperation, Mandela recalled that for four years preceding the election he and de Klerk had "worked together, quarreled, addressed sensitive problems, and at the end of our heated exchanges were able to shake hands and to drink coffee."[13]

The Ultimate Persuader: Lyndon Baines Johnson

President Lyndon Johnson could persuade the most intransigent friend or foe to comply with his wishes. This ability to use himself as an instrument of persuasion was Johnson's congressional trademark.

As secretary to newly elected congressman Richard Kleberg, the twenty-three-year-old Johnson projected his own persona as if he, not Kleberg, were the congressman. Rather than buy the winter coat he desperately needed for the bitter Washington mornings, Johnson spent his first paycheck on a formal portrait of himself taken by the most prestigious Washington photographer. He inscribed one hundred photographs, which he sent to Texas constituents, as if *he* were the congressman and as if *they* had requested his picture.[14]

An instinctive instrumental achiever, Johnson masterfully flattered, cajoled, and often subtly threatened those whose votes he needed. Even as a college student, however, his persuasive charm had as many detractors as devotees. In fact, his college classmates greeted him as "Bull" Johnson, a shortened and sanitized version of his nickname for use in mixed company.[15] Like many other achievers who get stuck in their favorite, familiar styles, the president relied heavily—critics would say too heavily—on both personal and social action, which we describe later in this chapter.

Oratory That Stirs the Heart: Gandhi, King, and Jesse Jackson

Few things stir the heart like persuasive oratory that accompanies the personal style. It is a dangerous weapon in the hands of demagogues (remember Plato's suspicion of leaders who used rhetoric to stir their constituents' passions). Personal achievers usually hone their oratorical skills, sometimes to overcome initial shyness. Gandhi, who could move his listeners to tears, practiced for years to conquer his early dread of public speaking.

Some personal achievers learn the art of oratory in debating societies, others in the church. Through powerful oratory, Reverend King created the dream of a society unshackled from racial discrimination. The Reverend Jessie Jackson, similarly raised in the Baptist preaching tradition, brought a cheering audience to its feet at the 1988 Democratic national convention with his "lions and lambs" speech.

Leaders lacking oratorical skills have difficulty persuading would-be supporters, despite cogent ideas that more gifted speakers would easily use to electrify audiences. Many political candidates have lost their bids for high office because they lacked these crucial personal skills.

The Social Style

The second member of the instrumental set, the *social* style, shifts the spotlight from the persona of the leader to the leader's relationships. Rather than relying exclusively on themselves, these achievers utilize relationships with others as instruments to their desired ends.

Social achievers are cartographers who draw elaborate social maps in their heads. Everyone they meet becomes a pinpoint on that map. Each new acquaintance is entered into their mental data base, replete with detailed descriptions of the new entry's special talents and connections. Faced with a new task, social achievers search their social data base for those individuals whose specific characteristics match the task.

Not surprisingly, leaders skilled in the social style have a complex understanding of human interaction, all those encounters through which events unfold. They intuitively sense what makes groups tick. With system savvy, they tune into every nuance, interpreting and influencing those elusive processes that move things along in organizations. They keenly appreciate how human relationships dilute the rigidity of organizational structure and task. No other achievers can claim their expertise in group dynamics and the politics of social systems.

Social Networks: Lego for Grownups

Leaders who prefer the social style have a strong political sense. As you might expect, social achievers focus on the connective tissue between people and groups. Their political antennae guide them through the byways of the informal system that operates as a shadow structure inside every formal organization. Their feel for political subtleties evokes both awe and skepticism in observers accustomed to more direct approaches.

Based on personal relationships, informal networks inevitably arise to offset the cold rigidity of the formal structure. They are stitched together by the expectant thread of continued interaction. They provide counsel, affirmation, solace, privileged information, and access to related networks. Using their many contacts, social achievers seek and offer the latest information, a valuable resource in any organization.

Unlike the rigid hierarchies of formal organizations, the informal system may be composed of many loosely structured webs, outside the chain of reporting channels. More flexible than hierarchies, network segments can operate separately. They even break away temporarily for specific purposes and then regroup without damage, sometimes in new configurations—an adult version of Lego.

Informal networks operate both within and between complex organizations. Some social achievers simply form their own far-flung networks of associates who offer comfort and counsel. Leaders who favor social styles call on relationships without embarrassment, guilt, or discomfort. They recognize the informal system's role in disbursing important resources: advice, gossip (important intelligence concerning what's *about* to happen) and hard information, discretionary time, plus entrée to important people and places.

Since key decisions actually take shape in the organization's informal system, social leaders work their agenda through far-flung networks of associates. They value and nurture relationships within and beyond the boundaries of their own organizations, keeping in touch with long rosters of associates.

Ordinarily, social leaders are great telephoners and faxers, as well as dedicated note writers. George Bush, for example, is renowned for staying in touch. Even casual acquaintances, but particularly former associates, receive short notes and quick phone calls whenever Bush is in town. Social achievers understand that keeping in touch builds interpersonal capital, which can be drawn upon as circumstances demand. Their appreciation of relationships echoes the Chinese emphasis on "Guang-Xi," that is, whom you know and how you know them.

Kermit Campbell, Appreciator of Networks

The former CEO and chairman of Herman Miller, Kermit Campbell described to me a personal network of mentors and colleagues whom he regularly consults not for specific action advice but as sounding boards for his ideas. Describing his earlier career at Dow Corning, Campbell noted:

> I kept advancing through [Dow Corning], and along the way I started developing a network. In 1984, my first real breakthrough

into understanding what I was about and what I was doing was when I met George Land [author of *Grow or Die*]. It was almost a chance meeting. But he and I sat down just to get acquainted, and what was going to be a five-minute meeting turned into a three-hour session. Because we connected so much, our minds just came together. . . . At any rate, George Land has really become my mentor, and we continue to meet frequently. . . . But that network has continued to grow, and it includes people like Peter Senge at MIT. As a matter of fact, I just spent an hour and a half on the phone this morning with Peter Senge, and we've become very good friends. It's just one thing after another, and this network has evolved. It has helped me to see that my ideas were not really only *my* ideas, but were ideas for the future.[16]

When it came to decisions about specific operations within Herman Miller, Campbell consulted another informal network of people *inside* the company. He listened, asked questions, sought counsel, but took responsibility for making the final decision:

There are certain people whom I particularly respect. Of course, I respect all the people in the company, but on certain issues there are some that I feel have more to contribute than others. So, I sit down with my colleagues and talk with them about certain issues. . . . For specific decisions, I usually look for supporting information, but I don't look for answers outside of myself. I think, you know, that in my role the decisions have to be mine. So, I try to get the advice I need in a way that will help me make the decisions, but then ultimately it's my call.[17]

First, Whom They Know; Then, What They Know

Social achievers think in terms of connections, who can help whom, who is the expert on a certain issue, or who is that expert's expert. Given a tough chore, social achievers often attack the problem by thinking first about *whom* they know, then about *what* they know. They prefer gathering information through people, preferably experts, friends, and friends of friends, rather than through library or computer searches. They move through the chain of connections until they reach the ideal individual with just the right skills or contacts for the task at hand.

Lillian Gallo, Television Producer

The mental data base is the perfect emblem for the social achiever. In some fields, it is absolutely necessary. Producing films is such a field. It requires assembling short-lived teams of writers, directors, actors, composers, and other entertainment industry professionals. Knowing people in the industry and their special talents increases the chances of a successful outcome.

In the last chapter we met Lillian Gallo, but we looked at her experience in the Marines as an illustration of the direct approach. As an independent producer of films for TV, however, Gallo relies much more on the social style:

> Even before I was working in television, I would write down names from the credits of shows that I liked. If I thought the program was well written, I'd jot down the writer's name, for example. I still do this. I keep lists. As a member of an awards panel recently, viewing what is considered some of the best work in television, I found it an ideal time to save the data on who did what for potential staffing on future projects.
>
> The producer is the one who puts the team together and supervises every stage, from the writing of the script to planning the production, the actual filming, the post-production, to final delivery of the show to the network or cable company. As the one who hires key personnel, who in turn hire those in their departments, knowing who's who and who does what well is an important requisite for the job.
>
> I sometimes find myself eager to get good people I've worked with on other producers' projects. Does one need a good director, production designer, costumer, cinematographer, etc.? It's a help to those needing work, but also a service to other producers who always want to identify talented people.[18]

Gallo tells an amusing story that reflects her social instincts. When the 1994 Northridge/Reseda earthquake struck at 4:31 A.M., Lillian and her producer husband, Lew, jumped from their bed, grabbed bathrobes, and dashed downstairs to the back yard. A few minutes later, Lew decided to venture back inside to check for damage. Lillian, still reluctant to reenter the house, called after him, "Lew, just bring me my phone book." Spoken like a true social achiever.

Gallo is a good example of someone who integrates social behaviors with contributory and power strategies. And of course, all three styles are consistent with her role as producer.

Sharing Networks

Casual observers mistakenly think that *all* social leaders like to "collect" people. True, some social achievers do just that, not because of some obvious affinity but because of perceived usefulness. For most social achievers, however, adding newcomers to their network is just a way of life.

Social achievers do not jealously guard their roster of friends and associates. For them, networks are simply the fastest route to reaching anyone's objectives. They automatically utilize the same methods to help other people in *their* tasks, as well. They readily introduce people to one another. Once they identify the problem you are tackling, they quickly link you to people with similar interests or the appropriate expertise. Sometimes it takes several links in the chain to reach the perfect candidate, but the social leader works through a loosely coupled network to identify the ideal choice.

Often, social achievers bring you greetings from important people (to whom they are invariably "close"). And, mysteriously, these notable folks somehow always know you are the social achiever's friend. Meeting someone for the first time, social achievers establish connections by mentally scanning their vast list of acquaintances for mutual friends.

A colleague at another institution sends me unsolicited progress notes on her activities. Some time ago, she faxed me a letter she had received from a foundation program officer from whom she was seeking project funding. A handwritten note, at the bottom of the page, revealed her social route to the program officer: "My friend, Nancy, says she [the program officer] is very close to the Chairman of the Board/CEO and her recommendations generally are taken seriously."[19]

Many social achievers see everyone as potential "contacts," stops on the route to still other contacts. Social achievers rarely approach a contact cold. They work through other people. The colleague I just described wrote about still another project: "I have sent the proposal to 'Ms. Q' through 'Mary Jones.' So far I haven't heard anything. I want to do the study, but feel that [a collaborating colleague's] name carries more than mine with funders."[20]

Sometimes the person whose name is entered in the social achiever's address book can fulfill an immediate purpose. In other cases, this new acquaintance is included for some future, not yet obvious, use. Despite their casual attitude toward ideological or social differences among network members, social leaders are very selective in matching the person to the task. The lobbyist concerned with a special legislative proposal courts not just any staffer, but the one whose congressional boss can cast the vote spelling passage or defeat.

Reaching Beyond the Old Boy Network: Forming Coalitions

We recognize the phrase *old boy network* as the prototypical network of a close-knit circle of buddies. School, club, or church ties frequently laced the old boy network together. When a job needed to be done, those in good standing simply tapped into the network, which then took care of them.

Social achievers, however, take networking a step beyond the good old boys. In some respects, they resemble the personal achiever, who counterintuitively reaches out to the opposition, disarming foes and friends alike. The social achiever stretches across social and political boundaries to include a wide spectrum of network members. Differences in ideology, race, and nationality—key exclusionary criteria in the old boy network—are less important to social leaders than getting the job done. For them, the more diversity the better. Access to diverse groups only enhances their own usefulness as the thread lacing the pieces together. In fact, the *diversified* network is their natural medium.

Wendy Kopp, Coalition Builder

Wendy Kopp, founder and president of Teach for America, provides a good example of the social achiever's penchant for building coalitions. She also gives us a glimpse of a leader who transcends any one style or even set of styles. Indeed, Kopp has highly developed leadership skills. Starting as an intrinsic and power achiever, she gradually developed more social strategies, such as coalition building.

During her senior year at Princeton, Kopp conceived of a national teacher corps that required its members to commit two years to teaching in "under-resourced" public schools, both urban and rural. Kopp recalls,

> One thing I found personally inspiring was the idea of teaching (probably pragmatic idealism), assuming tremendous responsibility, having an impact on people's lives. My own personal interest made me think others would feel the same way. . . . I had this belief that college students were not just out for greed like they described us [in the 1980s]. That was a bunch of baloney. . . . But no one was calling on us to do anything to make a difference.[21]

Kopp and some of her Princeton classmates worked with the Foundation for Student Communication, an organization that created links between students and leaders. According to Kopp, while organizing a foundation-sponsored conference on educational reform the idea "popped into my head." She remembers,

> The students at the conference were simply outstanding. They were student leaders who . . . said they would teach. All of them said they would teach. I realized we needed a national teacher corps. I was looking for a senior thesis topic. I wrote a rationale and plan for the creation of a national teacher corps.[22]

After Kopp turned in her thesis, she "boiled it down to a 30-page proposal," which she sent to several dozen CEOs of major companies. As she described it, "A couple of them landed right." The day after graduation, Mobil awarded Kopp a $26,000 seed grant to get her started, and Union Carbide offered her the use of their offices for the summer.

Then Kopp set to work, calling upon her social talents to enlist a large circle of people whose help she needed to launch her teacher corps. According to Kopp,

> From the day I decided to do it, I was 100 percent convinced that it would happen. I was completely psyched that I would do it. I spent the summer meeting . . . people—in education, corporations, and school districts—getting feedback for developing plans and raising money. In the fall, I started hiring recent college graduates to make this happen.[23]

Since its founding in 1989, Teach for America, a privately funded, nonprofit organization, has established fifteen offices, run by eighty full-time staff, with an annual budget in 1996 of $5.2 million. As a young entrepreneurial innovator, Kopp saw the mission of Teach for America as "helping to transform the public education system." Besides meeting a widening circle of supporters, Kopp used her social skills to develop three related levels on which TFA works: the state policy level, the district teaching level, and the national public awareness level.

In the first four years of its existence, TFA placed twenty-four hundred candidates from the twelve thousand who applied. According to Kopp, "Teach for America recruits aggressively at two hundred colleges and universities across the country, selects corps members through a rigorous selection process, prepares them to enter the classroom through a national pre-service training institute, clusters them in school districts across the country that face persistent teacher shortages, and facilitates the creation of a support network."[24]

These highly motivated new teachers are inspiring children to work at what Kopp calls "the edge of their competence." TFA has placed their teachers in New York City, Los Angeles, Oakland, Houston, New Orleans, Baltimore, and Washington, D.C., as well as in rural areas of Georgia, North Carolina, Arkansas, Texas, and Louisiana.

We have already witnessed Kopp's talents as a social achiever. But her own evolution as a leader has seen Kopp move from a very hands-on, direct achiever, to a master of all the instrumental and relational styles. Here she describes her own development, from an intrinsic and power achiever to a more entrusting style, a style we describe more fully later in this chapter:

> As the organization has gone through several evolutions, [I've changed]. At the beginning, I was involved in everything, questioning everything. I was extremely hands-on in all areas, from raising money to designing the program. But now, I'm president of TFA, Inc., which is a holding company for three other programs: Teach, Learning Project, and Teach for America [each with its own president]. Some people might perceive that I am very hands-on. It's true. I have strong opinions about things. I'm only satisfied if I think it's right.

We've grown tremendously. There's no way to do that without empowering great people and believing in them. . . .

Finding great people is the most critical challenge we face. That is the number one challenge we face as an organization. The presidents of the three organizations, Richard Barth, Daniel Oscar, and Dan Porter, have been around for a long time. They're amazing people who rose to the top. Their job now is to cultivate amazing people underneath them. . . .

We have lots of people with tons and tons of responsibility, whom I rely upon for everything. I look at myself as a resource to them. More than that, I don't know. I'm not the kind of leader who is good at public speaking and whatever. Whenever I can get someone else to do the public speaking, I do.[25]

As an intrinsic and power achiever, Kopp liked to do everything herself. Then her social talents came into play, with the recognition that picking the right people was critical. Subsequently, Kopp moved to a more entrusting stance, where she could hand over tasks and simply count on others to do them well.

Social Achievers in an Interdependent World

Social achievers are completely at home in an interdependent world and in fact usually add to that interdependence by providing ties across various networks. In many societies, work is naturally accomplished through networks of trusted friends and family members. Americans have often rejected that sort of behavior as social climbing and name dropping, even nepotism; but gregarious, politically sensitive social leaders neither see it nor necessarily mean it that way. They simply feel quite comfortable using this crucial Stage 3 strategy, a strategy many Americans are only now beginning to appreciate.

The Entrusting Style

The last instrumental achieving style, the *entrusting* style, is closely related to the social style. Entrusting achievers believe the world is simply filled with people ready and willing to help them achieve their ends. Unlike social achievers, they don't worry so much about contacts and networks. They don't think very much about coalition building, either. They just assume that everyone in their orbit wants to get involved and help.

Unlike social types, entrusting achievers do not catalogue people according to specific talents and contacts. Rather, the entrusting achiever strongly believes that virtually everyone, given the chance, can meet a challenge, usually performing far beyond even his or her own expectations. It only takes the leader's respect and confidence to charge that individual's batteries.

Entrusting leaders consign their vision to their constituents, their paid staff, sometimes even casual volunteers, exciting and empowering those called upon to help. They feel comfortable placing their most important tasks in the hands of associates, whom they rely upon to fulfill their vision. Entrusting achievers are less egocentric than personal achievers, who see themselves as the ideal instrument for carrying out their own vision, albeit with the constituents' support.

Unlike the power achiever, who delegates a task to an associate with specific directions, the entrusting leader rather casually transfers responsibilities to supporters, without bothering to fill in the details. The entrusting leader simply outlines the goals and leaves the rest up to the other party. Entrusting achievers have a deep respect for the fruits of interdependence.

Getting the Most from Supporters

Entrusting behavior initially may arouse enormous anxiety in the individual expected to perform without any clear-cut guidelines. More often than not, however, the goal is achieved, with a crucial bonus: individuals entrusted with the task reach deep into their own resources to find a creative solution, unconstrained by the leader's specifications. Challenged by an unfamiliar task, their creative juices flow in ways that assignments from power achievers never provoked. People charged with an entrusting leader's task commonly discover they have much more to bring to their work than they originally thought, far more than simple ownership and responsibility. Their surprise and delight nourishes previously unrecognized wellsprings of creativity and self-confidence. The precious gift of the leader's trust is reciprocated by the designee's dedication not only to the task but to the entrusting leader.

Kermit Campbell: Inspiring Through Trust

Campbell, whom we met earlier, is a master of entrusting behavior. Ten weeks after he arrived at Herman Miller following thirty-two years spent at Dow Corning, Campbell eliminated the company's executive committee. He took this step to give people space to think for themselves and use their own creativity. During his time at the furniture design company, Campbell described his efforts this way:

> What I believe I have adopted not only as the mission of Herman Miller but also as my personal mission is to liberate the spirit of people, and certainly within Herman Miller I would like to liberate everyone's spirit. But to do that also as a father and as a friend. I want to help people to be liberated wherever they are because to me that's the real power of life, for people to be themselves, to throw off the constraints that we've placed on people from kindergarten on up and just to unshackle ourselves. I know that within Herman Miller there are great things that we never even dreamed about that are happening now.[26]

In place of the eight-member executive committee, Campbell had thirty people reporting to him. When I interviewed Campbell during his Herman Miller days, he described the new arrangement to promote initiative, responsibility, and creativity among the Herman Miller executive team:

> They are all doing their own thing, and most of the time I don't even know what they are doing, but I've given them the freedom to act within their area of influence. I have now what I call "roving executive committees." Max De Pree, in his book [*Leadership Is an Art*], talks about roving leadership. Well, I've adopted that, except that instead of roving leadership, I'm going to call them "roving executive committees." Literally scores of these little mini-executive committees are in existence at any given time, and I don't even know that most of them exist.
>
> I certainly am not a member of these ad hoc executive committees. But in a team of thirty people . . . [a few] will realize they have

common interests around an issue. They'll come together the day that they realize they have a need, settle the matter, make the decision, implement it immediately, and get on with life.

Some of the people are on multiple committees like that, making decisions that would previously have been funneled up through the organization, through group vice presidents and senior vice presidents and executive committees, which would have taken weeks or months or probably [would] never even have happened. Now we can do them in a matter of minutes. And, I don't even need to know about it. When someone gets into trouble or needs my help, then they call me.[27]

Campbell understands something important: trust that bestows freedom on others is essential to leadership. This trust is based upon a vision and values that the leader and supporters share, which allow the leader to entrust the task comfortably. The selected supporter, in turn, senses both faith and freedom in the leader's act. Campbell expresses it well:

So, it's a matter of trust. It's a matter of letting people know generally what the direction of the organization is. It's very much value-centered. This kind of an organization would never work if it were not based on values, because without values you don't have a North Star. You have to, to give this kind of freedom. So, the leader must be a value-based person, and the organization must be a value-based organization.[28]

"Peter Allen": Leadership by Expectation

Peter Allen (a pseudonym) is CEO of a large specialty chain known for high standards. He describes his company's approach:

Somebody said, "Gee, you guys do a great job of training." We don't do a very good job, but we pick pretty good people, whose parents train them pretty well. See, there's a big difference here. Our deal, hopefully, allows these people to be free agents and to react to things without thinking, "What does the rule book say?"

Mainly, it's the level of expectancy. In other words, if you are going to work here, this is what you have to do. . . . This is what [we] have to teach them: "You have to be nice to the customers, you have to respond to them." And they do it. It is a level of expectancy more than anything else.[29]

Allen is no reckless risk taker. He described the human reaction to this kind of risk taking:

It does [involve risk taking]. . . . It gets scary because there are so many moving parts: people making decisions, spending your money, committing you to things. If you stop to think about it, you think, "Oh, my golly, I need to have closer reins on that." And that's a very human reaction. I have it once in a while. But because we've run this thing this way all these years, we know that the energy and the good vibrations that it creates . . . drive this company. And so [I'm] going to continue to do that.[30]

An Entrusting Role: Orchestra Conductor

In some sense, any role that calls for contributions from others is a candidate for entrusting action. The more complex and extensive the tasks, the more likely that others will be needed. People who lead complex enterprises, and in particular subtle, creative, unprogrammable efforts, inevitably must count on others to help realize their vision.

Let's examine one particular role—symphony conductor—that calls for entrusting behavior.

Maestros Neville Marriner and Michael Tilson Thomas

Although they conduct their own interpretation of an orchestral piece, conductors must depend upon the orchestra members to carry out that musical vision. In a recent television interview, Sir Neville Marriner, the renowned British conductor, described the conductor's dependence upon the orchestra:

No orchestra wants to play poorly, but they respond differently to each conductor. The conductor who can articulate his musical vision but let the orchestra know he respects and depends upon their talent, skill, and effort usually gets a better performance than the genius task master who commands them to play exactly as he wants. The conductor who develops rapport with the orchestra, who makes it clear that he values and respects their contribution to his interpretation, is the one with whom orchestras love to play.

Michael Tilson Thomas, who debuted as music director of the San Francisco Symphony in the fall of 1995, insists that an orchestra should be

> a collection of talented individuals who create a vision together. [Tilson Thomas] described a recent rehearsal, as guest conductor, with the Chicago Symphony, of Tchaikovsky's Sixth: "Of course, they had played the *Pathétique* hundreds of times, but I wanted the feeling to be new, vulnerable. When we got to the second theme, instead of beating it note by note in the typical international schoolmaster way, I raised my hands into the air and gently indicated a breathing space that would precede this phrase, as if sung by a great soprano. At first they were baffled. I asked them to shape the familiar phrase by meeting me in psycho-acoustic space. . . . 'Let's breathe together, hold the first note slightly longer, and then let the melody gracefully fall away from it.' I couldn't make the music happen alone. We needed to share the feeling, we had to find that shape together, and we did. It was miraculous."[31]

This meeting of the minds, where the leader entrusts the vision to others who then make it happen, also occurs beyond the world of music and art. We see that managers in technical and industrial organizations use the entrusting style with equal success.

The Special Opportunities and Costs of Entrusting Behavior

The overall activity of management has been defined as doing things through other people.[32] Thus, whenever coordination or management is required, entrusting strategies are worth considering.

In situations where economic incentives or organizational power are limited, such as volunteer organizations or creative enterprises, the nonauthoritarian entrusting style is particularly effective. Offering individuals the opportunity to grow or contribute to a worthwhile endeavor—which touches the essence of entrusting behavior—is a powerful incentive.

Although entrusting behavior entails risk for all parties, entrusting leaders are not foolhardy risk takers. They select good people and then confidently let them make decisions, even very large decisions. Because those chosen for such assignments recognize the implied compliment, they rarely disappoint the entrusting leader.

Nonetheless, entrusting leaders can be misread as dependent or lazy. Joining entrusting with other styles substantially eliminates this misinterpretation.

American Ambivalence Toward the Instrumental Styles

Americans' devotion to meritocracy and individualism often conflicts with their use of instrumental strategies. From an American perspective, instrumental action smacks of everything from egomania, nepotism, and social climbing to manipulation, Machiavellianism, corruption, and dependency.

Despite the instrumental virtuosity many connective leaders display, these Stage 3 behaviors still can send a shiver down the American spine. That, however, is really *our* hang-up, because we view such behavior through the distorting haze of our own beloved direct styles.

We are quite myopic about the important leadership strengths offered by the instrumental styles, even when we routinely use these styles ourselves. For example, Americans fail to acknowledge the social component of requiring references in job and college applications. While explicitly rejecting nepotism, we still rely on recommendations from our trusted friends and associates in evaluating prospective employees, students, and even blind dates.

For an employer, confidence in choosing a potential employee comes from knowing that the candidate belongs to a group whose qualifications and standards he or she shares, like a union or an elite university. The group implicitly guarantees its members' performance. When necessary, the sponsoring group, be it family or fraternity, imposes sanctions. These implied warranties have an important social consequence: by claiming group membership, even strangers can count on a special hearing because we know their sponsors stand behind them. Perhaps even more importantly, the candidate feels constrained to uphold the group's standards, because to violate them means to lose the group's further endorsement.

Instrumentalism in Other Cultures

American reservations about instrumental action are not uniformly shared by other cultures. In fact, seen through the cultural spectacles of other societies, instrumental styles appear far less egotistical and narrow than the direct styles in which we take such pride. These more indirect, subtler styles focus on the group, rather than the individual, and widely distribute leadership and responsibility.

In cultures where family and ethnic communities loom large, the group exercises strong control over its members, who rely on relationships to ease their way, to open doors, and to offer otherwise unavailable opportunities. In societies as diverse as Italy and Japan, social action stitches the community together. Italian culture promotes working through others, influencing and drawing on a large network of family, friends, and associates—that is, the community—to achieve one's ends. In Japan, individuals who depend solely on their own achievements and attractiveness, foregoing an intermediary's introduction, find it difficult to penetrate any new group. The Japanese frequently interpret Americans' self-reliance as egotistical and insensitive. In China, too, emphasis on the group rather than the individual evokes respect.

Only recently have we begun to recognize that a tightly connected, global system responds most readily to interdependent strategies, involving trust and reliance on others. Gradually, we have begun to comprehend the legitimate centrality of networking and support groups. Coalition building and negotiating skills, so necessary in a world where escalating diversity creates different agendas, are finally being treated as serious organizational skills. In fact, the emergence of this new vocabulary signals our budding appreciation of these alternative strategies. More than that, however, the instrumental styles open up the path to community and the politics of commonalities.

Linking instrumental and relational strategies to newly invigorated direct styles offers the serious promise of community in a Stage 3 world. Yet Americans even now don't know quite what to make of instrumental behavior. We are dazzled by the daring of personal instrumental leaders, but we don't exactly trust these visionaries' dreams.

Americans are not much more comfortable with social achievers, people who seem to "collect" large networks of friends. Entrusting leaders present still another conundrum. Are they simply disguising their dependency by empowering others? Could they really do it themselves?

When the instrumental styles are seen from the perspectives of other societies, however, from Asia to Europe, the picture looks very different. The instrumental styles supply a foundation of trust that supports relationships. Societies where the instrumental styles are a way of life feel puzzled by American-style direct leaders. The challenge for the connective leader, then, here and abroad, is to reconcile these contradictory currents as we try to build an interdependent and highly diverse world community.

The instrumental road is the one less traveled by Americans. It is time we learned to drive it with verve.

Chapter Nine

Connective Leadership
More than the Sum of Its Parts

*Leadership [must have] efficiency beyond one's own self-
aggrandizement, that takes in the bigger picture . . . [and a]
sense of community, and the notion of moral sympathy.*
ANITA RODDICK[1]

The future of American institutions, both corporate and political,
depends upon our willingness to relinquish the tattered leadership
legacy of Stage 2. As the leadership paradigm shifts from independence to *interdependence,* from control to *connection,* from competition to *collaboration,* from individual to *group,* and from tightly
linked geopolitical alliances to loosely coupled global *networks,* we
need to encourage a new breed of leaders who can respond effectively to such conditions. To do so means reaching far beyond the
narrow set of strategies we now recognize as Stage 2 leadership.

The nine styles of the Connective Leadership Model, detailed
in the last three chapters, offer a wide spectrum of leadership
strategies. The model, however, opens up a still wider range of possible strategies when it is treated as a totality rather than as nine
separate pieces. In short, it becomes more than simply the sum of
its parts.

This chapter briefly introduces a few examples—there still
aren't very many out there—of present-day connective leaders as
a prelude to a section in which we consider how connective leaders differ from their Stage 2 predecessors in their use of achieving
styles. The third section of the chapter discusses how connective

leaders move beyond the nine individual styles and engage in the many synergistic possibilities that emerge from the model as a whole. In that section, I trace how Stage 3 leaders join their vision to others', build community through reciprocity and expectations of a shared future, transform passion for individualism into compassion for the group, harness their egos to societal needs, and engage in a lifelong search for meaning. I also examine how authenticity and accountability play a special role in legitimating the connective leader's unorthodox behavior. The fourth and last section of the chapter turns to two serious obstacles blocking the paths of potential connective leaders: traditional followers and the media, both trapped behind the walls of Stage 2 stereotypes.

Despite a Dearth, Some Visible Connective Leaders

Even as Stage 3 has edged into view, full-fledged connective leaders are still hard to find. Some leaders who now stride the corporate and political stage seem to be groping toward a vague, partially defined image of connective leadership; others, trying to move in that direction, are hobbled by resistance from various quarters. Occasionally, a Stage 2 leader ventures into a Stage 3 strategy, only later to backslide into conventional Stage 2 behavior. Because the cadre of compleat connective leaders is still small, occasionally I highlight a single example of connective behavior on the part of other individuals not necessarily included in their ranks.

Despite this dearth of Stage 3 connective leaders, a few are visible. By treading the unorthodox pathways of connective leadership, many of them have evoked media criticism, a topic we shall return to at the end of this chapter.

Anita Roddick, CEO of The Body Shop (whom we discussed in Chapter Seven and get to know better in Chapter Eleven), belongs in the connective category. She has created a global enterprise, based on "Trading with Communities in Need," linking First and Third World entrepreneurs and suppliers. In the process, Roddick imbues her entire company, from product line to bottom line, with a social consciousness. Employees and customers alike are drawn into her controversial crusades. This Stage 3 leader connects herself, her staff, franchisees, and customers to a host of global issues, such as protecting the rain forests, saving the whales, aiding Third

World and tribal nations, helping the homeless, and protesting violence against women, all of which bring interdependence and diversity into sharper focus.

Billy Shore, whom we've met before, founded S.O.S. (Share Our Strength). This nonprofit organization with headquarters in Washington, D.C., is devoted to helping the twenty million people who go hungry in America. Shore links a highly disparate set of activists, from food industry leaders to writers, scientists, and political activists, in a multifaceted campaign against hunger.

Wendy Kopp, whom we met in Chapter Eight, is another connective leader. She envisioned a massive network of individuals and organizations who would rebuild the American educational system. Her nonprofit organization, Teach for America, asks individuals to commit two years of their lives to teaching in urban and rural public schools that suffer from severely limited resources. Kopp picks top people and then relies on them to carry out TFA's mission, while she operates as a special resource to her entrusted staff. Linked to a broad set of leaders from many different fields, Kopp confers with these colleagues on issues they all confront, albeit in somewhat different situations. A hands-on type, this young connective leader keeps moving ahead with new ideas and new connections.

In the investment field, Robert Fisher, managing director of the Los Angeles office of Schroder Wertheim & Co., Inc., works seriously at breaking through the Stage 2 leadership mold. We see later in this chapter that his search for more complex levels of meaning and new leadership paths represents a departure from the ego-centered stance of Stage 2 leaders.

Pushing beyond Stage 2, Morton Meyerson, president and CEO of Perot Systems, has established an Intellectual Fitness Center to expose his people to an impressive set of experiences. Meyerson wants to satisfy their hunger for authentic experiences.

Some leaders, of course, are more adept than others at these unfamiliar strategies. Some use connective leadership effectively on certain issues, but not on others. In the international arena, Mikhail Gorbachev's startling his long-standing foes with an offer of unilateral nuclear disarmament demonstrated connective flair. Gorbachev's popularity with Americans skyrocketed, convincing many journalists that he could easily run for the U.S. presidency.

Nonetheless, this nascent connective leader couldn't quite cut it at home. Like most people born and raised under authoritarian Stage 2 rule, the Soviets responded to their leader's unorthodox connective ways with confusion and hostility. The Soviet people are not alone. Baffled Stage 2 followers everywhere are likely to ascribe all sorts of malevolent motives to such connective behavior from their leaders. At the end of this chapter, we return to this issue of perplexed followers.

How Connective Leaders' Achieving Styles are Different[2]

Stage 3 leaders depart radically from the behavior of many famous leaders of the past. In a general sense, this new leadership model focuses less on the individual personality of the leader and more on the group, in all its diversity and interdependence.

Unlike their Stage 2 predecessors, connective leaders do not need to be perceived as the supreme leader, the one and only, superior to all others. They do not need to outdo others or overwhelm traditional adversaries in order to succeed. They do not need to control all aspects of the enterprise, nor must they make all decisions independently and single-handedly. Consequently, connective leaders avoid getting trapped in the direct achieving set with its restricted palette of intrinsic, competitive, and power styles.

Distinguishing Features: Drawing on Specific Styles

Because connective leaders understand that leadership embraces all the varieties of behavior covered in the last four chapters, they combine many strategies to achieve their goals. Their conception of leadership reaches not only beyond the direct styles favored by traditional leaders, but even beyond the simple pastiche of competition and collaboration much touted in recent leadership literature.

Among the Stage 3 leaders I have observed, their most distinguishing characteristic is their willingness to call upon ethical instrumental action. With great virtuosity, connective leaders forge everything around them into tools for attacking complex situations. They use themselves as versatile leadership instruments, selecting just the right gestures and the perfect symbols to convey their message. Their timing is usually exquisite, their drama and rituals unforgettable. They cannily select the appropriate candidate to handle a particular problem. By calibrating the political temperature, they adroitly navigate treacherous political waters. Untainted by a self-serving addiction to power, their leadership is dedicated to the well-being of the group.

Drawing on these instrumental styles, Stage 3 leaders operate as brokers and matchmakers who bring together diverse people and organizations with common objectives. Using existing networks and assembling new ones where none exists, they serve as channels that connect very different kinds of groups. They negotiate alliances for themselves and others. Expecting everyone to share the burdens of leadership, connective leaders often behave as entrusters whose reliance on other people sparks self-confidence, creativity, ownership, and loyalty. Like charismatic magnets, they attract others to their cause through drama and symbolism.

Connective leaders perceive that interdependence means relationships of all kinds, among people, among organizations, and among nations. They therefore use relationships in multiple ways to accomplish their leadership tasks. They feel equally comfortable as members of the team, as behind-the-scenes helpers, or as facilitators and mentors. They establish relationships with dissimilar groups of people to accomplish mutual goals, and they help others do the same.

When they think it's called for, connective leaders can also use the direct styles with flair and flexibility. They lead the charge, push their own vision, and set exacting standards for themselves and others. Quite easily, they join the fray as fierce competitors, but always against external opponents, not their team members. While connective leaders ordinarily use instrumental and relational styles to negotiate, mediate, and persuade, they do not shrink from exercising direct power to bring opposing forces together.

This ability to use all nine styles prompts connective leaders to reach out to nontraditional supporters, often to those previously defined as the opposition. Ideological differences do not impede mutual long-term goals. John Sculley's collaborative agreements between Apple and long-time rival IBM provide an example of such behavior.

Another hallmark of Stage 3 leaders is their capacity to nurture personal relationships throughout their lives, with people in many fields and many places. For example, since his early adult years Bill Clinton has built relationships with legions of friends, many of whom are affectionately known as "FOBs" (for "friends of Bill").

Connective leaders also typically establish huge mosaics of less personal relationships. They develop joint ventures, partnerships, mergers, teams, projects, networks, and other types of temporary and long-term combinations. They arrange and join short-term alliances to accomplish joint purposes, and then move on to new challenges with other relevant allies. For each television production, Lillian Gallo of Gallo Entertainment, Inc., assembles a new group of cast and staff, some of whom may be old associates while others are brand new colleagues.

In contrast to Stage 2 leaders, caught up in their own strivings, connective leaders frequently act as mentors, taking special pride in the accomplishments of others, from colleagues to protégés, even in the successes of people not personally known to them. Esther Shapiro, TV producer and cocreator of the long-running TV series *Dynasty,* takes satisfaction in her role as mentor. Through Shapiro Entertainment, Inc., the company she and her collaborator husband founded, she encourages the careers of many young artists and family members.

In several ways, connective leaders raise charismatic leadership to new levels. They use counterintuitive or paradoxical gestures and symbols to communicate their vision. They use emotionally saturated symbols to communicate a powerful message. Both abstract and concrete symbols, such as Gorbachev's perestroika and Gandhi's spinning wheel, surprise and overcome the observer's rational defenses, hitting an emotional target. A keen personal sense of drama, ritual, costume, and timing can inspire and capture the hearts as well as the minds of potential supporters. Connective leaders use every aspect of their personal selves, from intelligence to family name, to help achieve their goals.

Flexibility Through Behavioral Options

Because these early connective leaders have access to the whole array of achieving styles, they can implement their policies innovatively and flexibly. At times, they entrust others to carry out, adapt, or elaborate their vision. By empowering people, they stimulate creativity, responsibility, and loyalty. Thus, Marcy Carsey, co-chairman/ executive producer of The Carsey-Werner Company, consistently sustained the creativity of many leading television figures in a series of award-winning comedies, from *The Cosby Show* to *Grace Under Fire.* At other times, connective leaders coordinate or facilitate the implementation process, often by just getting out of the way. Here, too, Carsey serves as a good example.

Connective leaders are seldom preternaturally wise and virtuous. The key to understanding their special brand of leadership is to look beneath the behaviors we have just listed to the styles that underlie them.

These styles in turn are nothing more nor less than learned behaviors. They are not the genetic property of a few rare and elite women or men. We learn them as we grow. Given any diverse group of very young children, we would not find many of these styles among them; but given any sizable group of adults, we would surely find all of them. It is not that connective leaders are special beings, born with the ability to tap into all of these styles, or that they necessarily had a more favored upbringing than other people. What makes connective leaders unusual is in part that they have learned—sometimes painfully—to draw upon the full range of strategies instead of just the narrow band that many of us employ. As we saw, it took many years of laborious practice for an initially shy Gandhi to perfect his extraordinary oratorical skills.

By spelling out a broad range of achieving styles potentially available to all aspiring leaders, the Connective Leadership Model can help us examine our own patterns. It also gives us a framework by which to evaluate the leadership images of our culture, so we can consciously decide which strategies we should learn and encourage in others.

Currently, as we know, the relational and instrumental styles are underutilized in our culture. It is worth considering what would happen if leaders broke through the constraints of the direct styles to use all three sets of achieving styles, particularly the styles in the relational and instrumental sets.

If most leaders were to expand their repertoires to include all nine styles of the model, that alone would enormously change leadership behavior. Indeed, given our deeply held belief in the narrow band of direct styles, such an unprecedented expansion in leadership behaviors would drastically transform our picture of what a leader really is. Yet the mere fact of having access to a wider range of styles by itself is only the first major step toward fully realized connective leadership.

The Synergistic Fruits of Connective Leadership: More than the Sum of Its Parts

A leader's consistent use of the entire range of achieving styles opens up another level of leadership awareness and behavior, a level that makes the model more than the sum of its parts. To appreciate more thoroughly the paradigm shift toward connective leadership, we need to examine several synergistic effects that flow from using the complete range. Using the whole rather than any specific styles enhances the leader's ability to deal with diversity and interdependence in their many guises.

A Feel for Interdependence

At the synergistic level, Stage 3 leaders gain a heightened sense of interdependence and of the changes and innovations necessary for coping with it. With many strategies to choose from, leaders can connect instead of conquer, collaborate rather than compete, entrust and empower rather than control, contribute rather than demand. Because they see strength in legions of leaders and constituents, they can comfortably seek and give counsel. They can feel pride without being directly involved. They can put together unusual alliances to accomplish their objectives through all kinds of connections—partnerships, networks, alliances, joint ventures, and mergers. They build or simply use existing social arrangements for interdependent action.

Billy Shore shows us how that approach works in practice. Once a congressional staff aide, Billy Shore abandoned his Washington insider post to found Share Our Strength (S.O.S.), a nonprofit organization that raises millions of dollars annually to help erase hunger and related nutritional problems. Perceiving, as no one before him had, the intersection between the private interests of the food industry and the public interests of hunger activists, he created an extensive network of chefs, restaurateurs, and suppliers, all focused on alleviating hunger in America.

In more than one hundred U.S. cities, Shore orchestrated "A Taste of the Nation," a series of fundraising banquets. Over five thousand chefs, representing many ethnic cuisines, prepared a great variety of foods—at their own expense—for more than sixty thousand guests. He also saw new connections between raising funds and creating a whole set of activities that bring still other people into his growing enterprise. This innovative connective leader pours the funds raised by "A Taste of the Nation" into a competitive grants program, in which yet another layer of experts and community members design and conduct different hunger-alleviating programs.

Shore believes that he has tapped into the latent desire of chefs and other food industry insiders to give something back to their communities. Convincing a chef to donate $1,500 worth of food and time is far easier, Shore insists, than persuading that same person to write an annual check for $150. The secret, he believes, lies in the rewarding human connections that personal participation brings with it. "People are just waiting," he told me, "to be shown a way to connect to the community, to get involved."[3]

Shore connects "circles of opinion leaders" to still other circles of opinion leaders, tapping into their networks and welcoming help from leaders in a vast range of fields. His uncanny sense of connections has led to the participation of an unlikely collection of professionals, from scientists to novelists, who support his crusade for the hungry. In this connective and collective brainstorming effort, writers offer to donate the rights to their best short stories and scientists to write articles that S.O.S. then sells to magazines and publishers. The royalties provide ongoing funding for S.O.S.'s operation.

Shore works on the premise that you "can show people there's a role for everybody, a way to give back to the community." His connective insight into the link between individual needs and public good is clear: "I tell my staff I want to build every program we do at the corner where public and private interests intersect."[4]

Connecting by Two-Way Arrows

The most obvious and important aspect of connective leadership is that it *connects*. It connects leaders to constituents, and leaders to other leaders, forming a community of shared actions, values, and responsibilities. Where Stage 2 leadership highlighted the leader's independence, in Stage 3 the emphasis is on the flow of *inter*dependent actions. This means connections between leaders and a diverse set of actors, among them the leader's constituents, other leaders, and *their* constituents. Although they are quite capable of independent action, connective leaders prefer to work through, with, and on behalf of others to attain their common objectives.

Traditional Stage 2 leadership patterns draw a *one-way* arrow from the leader's vision to the followers' support. Leaders such as Adolf Hitler, Charles de Gaulle, and Mao Tse-tung clung to their own visions, which they imposed, albeit in different ways, upon their followers.

In sharp contrast, connective leadership patterns draw many *two-way* arrows, running from the leader's vision to the constituents' support and back again, from the constituents' somewhat different vision to the leader's support. Connective leaders seek the points of intersection at which their own and their supporters' visions overlap. They actively support that middle ground and work to accommodate the rest. To attach constituents to their vision, connective leaders bring them into the leadership process, easily sharing both glory and responsibility.

When connective leaders attach themselves to the visions of others, they make room for all parties' deeply felt convictions without losing their own purpose and integrity. A good example is Chico Mendes, who, as we saw in Chapter Four, linked his concern for rain forest workers to the agenda of environmentalists worldwide. Like other connective leaders, Mendes's knack for integrating visions and values in the interests of all created an invigorated sense of purpose for him and his worldwide supporters.

Other two-directional arrows connect *networks* of leaders with one another. With shared commitment and responsibility, these networks of leaders combine their efforts to address common problems. James Burke, CEO of Johnson & Johnson, responded to the Tylenol crisis by organizing an alliance of pharmaceutical leaders to develop industrywide standards to prevent future product tampering.

The capacity to ally many leaders with many divergent visions is still another synergistic effect of connective leadership. George Bush tried a Stage 3 strategy to oppose the Stage 2 power grab of

Saddam Hussein. Bush connected an unlikely set of international leaders to join the effort. After Desert Storm, however, he reverted to his customary Stage 2 posture. This example serves as a reminder that crisis situations can push even Stage 2 leaders temporarily to move beyond their limited strategies. Only a deeper understanding and consistent use of the entire range of available styles takes a leader to a fully realized level of connective leadership.

Stage 3 leaders push the envelope to meld divergent views. They reach out to former opponents in order to create a larger community that will pursue more comprehensive goals. Gorbachev gave the world a startling example of this ability in his dramatic efforts to breach the chasm between the Soviet Union and its Cold War opponents.

For connective leaders, the route to group cohesion is mutual problems and goals, not mutual enemies and fear. Thus, Wendy Kopp saw the plight of American schools as the rallying point for both young college graduates and large corporations. She seeks to create alliances and combinations to deal with their commonly shared problems.

Individuals who use connective styles, geared to an interdependent world, make decisions that address the interests of the whole group. In organizations, this means taking an "organizational," "institutional," or "system" perspective. Rather than favoring one division of the organization or playing it off against another, connective leaders search for solutions that will benefit all parties.

Even leaders who officially represent defined segments of the system can act as connective leaders. They do so by fitting their own group's interests into the overall well-being of the system. They avoid playing competitive, zero-sum games against leaders representing other units. They promote positive, community- or system-embracing values. They preserve the best of traditional values and integrate them with other values that emerge from new conditions. The Ben and Jerry's ice cream enterprise intertwines the founders' beliefs with local values. These corporate leaders act out their values in various ways, both through their corporate giving pattern and through an annual New England–style celebration that reciprocates their shareholders' and local citizens' support.

Peer Groups More than Hierarchies

Because they perceive complex connections among people and organizations, connective leaders do not focus on vertical relationships and hierarchies. In fact, they see their environment as networks of peers rather than hierarchies of ranks. Egalitarian and horizontal structures, with no one giving orders and no one snapping to attention, appeal to connective leaders.

Connective leaders like to build enduring relationships with other leaders. They undertake joint enterprises as partners or collaborators, both intermittently and in steady, ongoing relationships. They are more likely to think of others as "colleagues," "collaborators," "partners," "constituents," and "supporters" than as "superiors," "bosses," "followers," or "subordinates."

Because they can work easily with peers, connective leaders frequently seek counsel from colleagues and experts. They value advice. They do not, as so many politicians do, use advisors as political pawns to legitimate their agenda. Kerm Campbell, for example, calls on a large roster of other CEOs, researchers, and philosophers to help him with new concepts and serious organizational issues.

Interdependence, Reciprocity, and a Shared Future

Because connective leaders recognize the importance and inevitability of interdependence, it is not surprising that they often turn necessity into a virtue. They do not try to maximize their freedom to make whatever decisions they want. Quite the reverse: they work actively to build a sense of long-term interdependence with others. They assiduously follow the universal law of reciprocation, the law that psychologically obligates each of us, if we receive a gift, to repay it.[5] Connective leaders' gifts of trust, collaboration, sponsorship, encouragement, and behind-the-scenes assistance set the reciprocation dynamic in motion. Their behavior in turn becomes a model for other members of their interdependent environment.

Reciprocation, crucial to interdependence, thrives on the expectation of an enduring relationship. Because they conceive of collaboration in the very broadest and longest terms, connective leaders encourage expectations for a common future. For groups to flourish, they need a strong sense of identity and an expectation of a shared future. These in turn nurture reciprocity and altruism.[6] Once set in motion, reciprocity, a sense of identity, and expectations for an extended relationship lay the foundation for community. Long-term collaboration springs from members' sense of an abiding connection with the group.

For their part, connective leaders nourish an underlying belief in the value of community writ large that sustains everyone. That belief then generates the willingness to sacrifice short-term, individual interests for long-term, group survival. It is a belief that community members carry with them as they move from one temporary organizational structure or alliance to another. They see themselves as part of a kaleidoscopic, loosely linked community, members of multiple related groups and organizations with enduring connections.

Resources for the Future

It takes a long-term, community perspective to spend current resources to prevent possible future problems. Because connective leaders build collaborative arrangements for the long term, they are willing to do just that. They commit part of their current resources to protect the future, despite a keen awareness that supporting more popular, short-term efforts will yield more immediate kudos. Their acute awareness of the link between present and future prompts connective leaders to measure all current options in terms of the future flexibility they offer. "If we do this now," they ask themselves, "will future course corrections still be possible?"

During her term of office, former San Francisco mayor Dianne Feinstein allocated funds to retrofit Candlestick Park for earthquake resistance. Several months after Feinstein's successor took office, the devastating Loma Prieta earthquake rumbled through San Francisco. As luck would have it, the quake struck in the opening minutes of a World Series game being played at Candlestick. Sixty thousand spectators were spared injury and death by Feinstein's earlier, look-ahead decision.

Mort Meyerson of Perot Systems has seeded a number of company programs, including the Intellectual Fitness Center, whose fruit he does not expect to harvest in this season or even the next.

His time horizon is far greater than that of most Western executives. Meyerson says,

> Right now the jury is out. I think that we've done a lot of things which have prepared us to be very successful. But you can't find it right now in looking at our track record. Part of this has to do with what time zone exists. I live in a twenty-year time zone, where almost anything is possible.[7]

Meyerson is very clear about the risks such long-term thinking entails, particularly when dealing with financial analysts whose time zone extends only to the next quarterly report.

Connective leaders' awareness of the interdependence between present and future leads them to craft near-term solutions that won't preclude future choices. Frances Hesselbein, former executive director of Girl Scouts USA, saw the long-term need to revitalize her enterprise by diversifying the traditionally white middle-class organization to reflect the diverse character of contemporary America. In "managing for the mission," Hesselbein always insisted on measuring short-term tactics by the yardstick of future flexibility. Intrinsic visionaries, with their insight into how large organizations really work, can operate effectively in that way.

An Eye for Diversity

In addition to a feel for interdependence, a second synergistic effect that flows from the Connective Leadership Model is a sharpened eye for diversity. Unlike their predecessors, connective leaders perceive diversity as the door to opportunities, rather than the lid to Pandora's box. They conceive of diversity in the very broadest terms. Their antennae search out the demographic diversity that is embedded in age, gender, racial, ethnic, and other minority groups. They also resonate to organizational diversity reflected in temporary structures and loosely connected alliances, as well as in different organizational contexts, spanning public-sector bureaucracies, for-profit firms, and nonprofit organizations. Because connective leaders know they need many different kinds of resources to satisfy a world thirsty for innovations, they welcome diversity in all its forms as a reservoir of new possibilities.

From human diversity, connective leaders create a multi-stranded human cord strong enough to support the most complex enterprises. Using their instrumental talents, they tie together divergent groups, weaving and repairing the connective tissues among people and organizations. Here, connective leaders are distinctly unlike Stage 2 leaders who, fearing that diversity will dilute their homogeneous constituencies, seek to exclude anyone they perceive as different.

The human linkages created through connective leadership ultimately build a sense of community, where respect for individual differences and responsibility toward the group go hand in hand. Exploiting the strengths of diversity, connective leaders build community and entrust a wide range of people, many unlike themselves, to share the burdens of leadership.

Because connective leaders can easily shift leadership gears, they welcome the new possibilities that sprout in and between all organizational forms, the new and the old. They are at home in networks, in loosely coupled alliances, on task forces, and in other temporary organizations, as well as in longer-lived arrangements. Their flexibility sharpens their eye for the connections among issues, ideologies, and goals that take root in the various soils of the public and private sectors.

A Different Understanding of Power

Connective leadership utilizes many varied forms of action, giving Stage 3 leaders a different understanding of power than their Stage 2 counterparts. For connective leaders, power is not a limited pie. It is wonderfully elastic. It can be divided without shrinking. Using the resources of diverse parties only makes the pie taste better and last longer. Connective leaders understand that their own power actually expands as they empower others. For them, power is a negotiating process, not a personality trait, much less a commodity to be hoarded.[8] Consequently, they prefer negotiation and persuasion to conflict and threat.

From a connective vantage point, negotiating means that each party brings different resources to the bargaining table. Connective leaders recognize that those with the most relevant resources will gain power—at least for the moment. Here too, the different talents, skills, and knowledge of a diverse set of contributors are relevant and appreciated. Unlike their Stage 2 predecessors, connective leaders are comfortable with a reality in which no one party permanently monopolizes the power market.

Compared to their controlling predecessors, Stage 3 leaders see power in strange places: in sharing, in compromising and negotiating, in helping and seeking help, in working together, in entrusting others, in altruism and self-sacrifice—and far less often in authoritarian, individualistic behavior.

Harnessing the Leader's Ego

Stage 3 leaders know when and how to harness their own egos to the group's goals, even to the group's survival after the leader has stepped aside. This emphasis on the group's future prompts connective leaders to take seriously their mentoring responsibilities toward potential leaders. They "grow" leadership at every level, a sine qua non for strong organizations.[9] Unlike Henry Ford, Sr., who destroyed every heir apparent, connective leaders are much more likely to ensure an array of seasoned candidates ready to assume the leadership mantle when the moment arrives.

Anita Roddick provides a Stage 3 example in this context. She consciously grooms successors, in part by reducing the social distance between herself and others in her organizations. Her approachable demeanor toward other associates of The Body Shop (and their families as well) diminishes the organizational divide between current and future top management.

Many students of traditional charismatic leadership point to the important role of a strong ego in the leadership process. Strapping the individual leader's ego to community goals does not cause the leader to dwindle into an egoless nonentity. In fact, a reasonable measure of ego and character, mixed with supra-egoistic goals, produces a heady leadership recipe. Connective leaders frequently use that combination to address the needs of a diversified but interconnected constituency. Wendy Kopp certainly is not short on ego, as her steadfast reliance on her own insights clearly indicates. Yet her healthy ego does not require Kopp to speak as the sole public voice of Teach for America. Whenever possible, she prefers to let others do the public speaking for the organization.

A Lifelong Search for Meaning

Several connective leaders I have interviewed shared a third intriguing characteristic. They were embarked on what I can only describe as a search for meaning. Because they combine their long-term perspective with a sensitivity to the complexity of connections everywhere, they envision their lives as a continuous search for deeper, more comprehensive meaning. Expectedly, their search goes in many directions, ferreting out the connections that others might overlook. For some, the search begins in response to a trauma or loss. For others, it comes about in response to a challenge.

Regardless of what prompted their search, these connective leaders constantly seek greater insight into themselves and others. They search for challenges that extend their understanding. They seek out new ideas and linkages between the new and the old. They experiment, with reading, with education, with travel, with athletics, with conversations, proactively trying many different paths to stretch themselves and discover innovative ways of being and acting. As we shall see, they also invite others to join their search and broaden their horizons.

Robert Fisher: A Continuing Transformation

Robert Fisher, managing director of Schroder Wertheim's Los Angeles investment office, continues a lifelong search that began when a high school shoulder injury ended his hopes for a professional career in baseball. Fisher described the process:

> Athletics were always my thing. However, if you were athletic, you were considered a dumb jock. And that's how I grew up thinking of myself, as a dumb jock, until my athletic days were over because of an injury. I was confronted . . . with a whole kind of rethinking about who I was and academics and about what I was going to do with my life. . . . I think it's a gradual process, and it starts with necessity. . . . I really had very little doubt that I would have a professional [athletic] career, and of course when that is taken away and the reality sets in, you know that it's going to be academics and learning that are going to get you somewhere and so you grudgingly go in [that direction].
>
> I don't think, though, that the transformation is complete even today. . . . I don't think that the transformation . . . will ever stop.

That's the essence of life. It's the same thing that drove me to go to [a particular seminar, where we first met one another—Author], because you want to learn. I think that is the legacy, one of the most significant legacies, of that experience. I took it into myself. I internalized it by being on a constant search for more knowledge.[10]

Not content merely to *be* a leader, connective leaders consciously explore the meaning and the practice of leadership, always trying to reach a higher level of understanding and performance. At one point during our interview, Fisher reached into his briefcase to recover a chapter from Robert K. Greenleaf's *Servant Leadership*. He had also photocopied a 1994 op-ed article by Václav Havel in the *New York Times*. Fisher took time to inquire about my reaction to *Servant Leadership* and to Max De Pree's ideas about leadership. In a similar vein, Kerm Campbell maintains an ongoing dialogue about leadership and organizational innovation with a broad range of associates in and out of academia and the corporate world.

Morton Meyerson: A Lifelong Journey

Meyerson, too, is engaged in an ongoing search, for better ways to run his organization, for innovative products, for more creative ways to serve his customers, and for the deepest meaning of life. Meyerson's latest efforts to stretch himself and his associates are focused on Perot Systems' Intellectual Fitness Center (IFC), run by historian Luis Martin:

> There is another side to the equation. . . . If you have smoking cessation programs and weight reduction programs, etc., and if you're into preventive health care, ultimately you'll pay less money for health care. . . . That generally is accepted on the health side. But there is nothing equivalent on the intellectual or the soul side. So you have a fitness center where you have aerobics or can lift weights, but there is no similar thing for the mind and for the soul. So we set up an Intellectual Fitness Center.[11]

Meyerson and his wife, Marlene, both participated with a group of Perot executives in a three-day retreat in Taos, New Mexico, sponsored by the IFC. There, under the guidance of a geologist, the retreat members hunted for fossils in a creek bed. With the help of a sculptor, they made clay masks. In discussion groups, they probed their own and others' thoughts and feelings on the Vietnam War and other sensitive topics. Meyerson describes his experience:

> I was in a session with three other people in the company whom I hadn't worked with . . . but whom I knew kind of vaguely. Into the third day, I had insights into them as people that could not have happened under any other circumstance. I could not have sat in a business room or a conference center. . . . I could not have guessed. Anyway, one of these people that I've known for eighteen years is the most hard-nosed pragmatic manager. He looks like a battling Rambo when he approaches projects. He started talking in one of the sessions on Vietnam. . . . In one moment, I saw that there was a real person in there, and he wasn't all armor. . . . He was more than just a knight in armor.[12]

Meyerson's search has brought humility to a man brimming with confidence. He offered a modest disclaimer about leadership:

> Let me say for openers: unfortunately for you and your book, I am discovering that the more experience I have, that the more things I try, the less I know about it; which is disconcerting, because in the technology world where I've lived most of my life, there is relative certainty, even in the uncertainty of putting systems in. At least you know if it works or if it doesn't work. And I've spent most of my career in the nether world between those spots where technicians live, which is binary in terms of if it works or not, and where most human beings don't operate that way at all. There are thousands of inputs, and it's intuitive. The two sides of your brain don't operate on the same inputs. And I've more or less motored in between those two worlds. . . . I've tried dozens of things like this [the Intellectual Fitness Center programs], and the best I can tell you is that there is no clear picture. . . . To me, to think about different possibilities on how to improve things and to question tradition and the status quo is very interesting. . . . I'm continually reminded it's a work in process. There is no completion.[13]

Meyerson is no starry-eyed dreamer. His own special combination of thoughtful pragmatism finds expression in many customer- and product-oriented ways. At the same time, he argues that people have a "genetic need for authentic experiences and they reject inauthentic things." Bringing others the opportunity to engage in authentic experiences is part of Meyerson's ongoing quest. The example set by such connective leaders' emphasis on wider meaning makes constituents feel seriously engaged in a mission infused with purpose, not simply yoked to meaningless "grunt work."

Authenticity, Accountability, and the Leader

Meyerson reminds us that people resonate to authentic experiences. They also respond to authentic leaders. Authenticity is a quality difficult to define but immediately apparent to the observer. It is more often sensed than seen or heard. Authenticity conveys that the leader is committed to a cause that transcends his or her individual egoistic needs, a cause that benefits the larger community. The cause can take many forms, from a higher quality of television entertainment to a new vaccine to eradicate a dreaded illness.

It appears that when leaders fully commit themselves to the cause and demand the same from supporters, their authenticity magnetizes supporters and ignites their dedication. Authenticity seasons the behavior of leaders with credibility and inspiration. It is the special ingredient that helps supporters decipher the motives behind their leader's actions. Without it, constituents cannot affirm a leader's selflessness and commitment. Instead, they will interpret the leader's behavior as suspicious, even phony. When potential constituents detect the faintest signs of inauthentic behavior, they hold back, wary and aloof.

Although authenticity has been vital to leaders in all eras, it has special significance for connective leaders, whose broadened repertoire of strategies leads to complex, often enigmatic actions. Compared to the behaviors of their Stage 2 counterparts, their decisions and actions may seem unorthodox. Constituents need to feel the bedrock of the connective leader's authenticity to sustain their belief and support. Thus, authenticity helps connective leaders move flexibly without incurring the cynicism or wrath of their constituencies.

Moreover, because connective leaders take the entire organization or community as their responsibility, their actions do not always favor their regular, close-in constituents. In fact, on occasion the connective leader's natural constituents may find themselves on the short end of the leader's decision. It is at such points that a connective leader's authenticity provides an essential bulwark against the suspicion of abandonment and betrayal that the leader's own group may be feeling.

Authenticity is especially crucial to connective leaders for still another reason. Because connective leaders frequently do unusual things that may look Machiavellian, authenticity provides constituents with a corrective lens. Through the glass of authenticity, they can see that their leader's Machiavellianism is of the benign kind: nonselfish instrumental action in the service of all. A deceptive or cynical use of such instrumental behavior might fool some of the people some of the time, but it won't fool anyone for long. Without authenticity, the power of that instrumental style dissolves into a murky pool of self-serving manipulation.

This is not to say that the leader's interests may never be served. Since they are always aligned with the group's interests, the leader along with all other community members is likely to benefit. This, as we see later, is often misinterpreted by the watchful media. But self-interest is neither the primary effect nor the motivator of the connective leader's actions.

A complicated relationship exists between authenticity and the Connective Leadership Model. First, our distrust of manipulative behavior requires a strong dose of authenticity to help the instrumental styles gain the confidence of constituents. Yet without the power to communicate effectively and a strong dash of charisma, both of which flow from the personal style, authenticity may earn our respect but not necessarily our devotion. Second, the decisive individualistic leadership actions associated with the competitive and power styles are less often called upon by connective leaders, who tend to reserve them for crisis situations. When an *authentic* Stage 3 leader does temporarily shift into those styles, constituents are more likely to accept it as appropriate. In short, authenticity by itself cannot carry the day. It needs the very connective leadership styles it enhances to prove compelling to constituents.

Roddick talks about leadership that "has efficiency beyond one's own self-aggrandizement, that takes in the bigger picture of the wealth there, and the joy there, and the notion of a sense of community, and the notion of moral sympathy."[14]

She recalls learning about a conversation with the King of Bhutan, who responded to an inquiry about Bhutan's gross national product by saying: "Don't talk to me about my country's gross national product. Talk to me about my country's gross national happiness." Connective leaders, tuned in to the higher needs of the human spirit, tend to think in such terms.

Savvy constituents usually can sense correctly when a leader's behavior is driven by unbridled egotism, hypocritical opportunism, or just plain weakness. They also commonly know when it is motivated by some worthwhile greater purpose. For example, Gandhi's Indian supporters understood that his seemingly quixotic and varied tactics—fasting to wring agreement from opponents, cleaning untouchables' latrines, and meeting heads of state—all served his greater purpose of moving India toward self-reliance and freedom.

Still, authenticity is not a guarantee against misunderstanding. As we shall see, the media frequently misread the behavior of connective leaders. Moreover, Stage 2 leaders whose own more individualistic behavior is confined to the direct styles may be unable to comprehend that instrumental action can have ethical and altruistic motives.

Authenticity and Sacrifice: The Chance to Ennoble the Self

Connective leaders commit—and in some cases even sacrifice—themselves to their cause, inspiring constituents to move beyond conventional levels of followership. They also demand sacrifice from others, thereby offering constituents serious opportunities to ennoble themselves. Such self-sacrifice, the ultimate use of the personal style, is exemplified in its most extreme form by Mitch Snyder's near-deadly fast that pushed the Reagan administration to donate a shelter for the homeless.

An important paradox is embedded in the leader's demand for sacrifice. When we are inspired to sacrifice for a larger cause, we usually feel more enhanced than diminished by what we give up. We ourselves change and grow as we sacrifice for a cause greater than ourselves. In meeting such challenges, we ennoble ourselves. Small wonder that those leaders who demand the most from us, as connective leaders almost always do, leave us feeling the most enriched. Such leaders help their constituents realize their full potential, or in Maslow's terms, to move toward "self-actualization."[15]

In the ideal case, the connective leader's posture toward self-sacrifice provides a prism which illuminates authenticity. When their own actions are authentic, such leaders can guiltlessly entreat constituents to sacrifice for a larger purpose. They can make this enormous demand because they know that they themselves are ready to sacrifice as much or more.

Moreover, when the connective leader's call for sacrifice is palpably authentic, constituents intuitively know that the leader is offering them an opportunity to extend and enrich themselves. The connective leader is beckoning them to taste the satisfaction that flows from selfless devotion to a larger cause.

When, on the other hand, a leader's call for sacrifice is seen as *inauthentic*, watch out! Readers may remember when former Chrysler president Lee Iacocca announced he was taking only one dollar in annual salary to demonstrate "equality of sacrifice."[16] That gesture inspired Chrysler workers to accept hefty pay cuts to ensure the survival of their troubled company. Later, revelations that Iacocca had quietly arranged for lucrative stock options and other financial benefits in lieu of his regular salary struck a chord of betrayal among Chrysler workers. In that case, inauthenticity seriously tarnished the leader's rising star.

Authentic connective leaders display little interest in personal gain. With rare exceptions, they reject the opportunities for personal wealth that sprout around leadership roles. When connective action earns leaders international acclaim, those who do succumb to the temptation of personal aggrandizement invite ultimate rejection by their communities.

Thus Egyptian president Anwar Sadat's indulgent lifestyle, supported by wealth allegedly stockpiled while in office, led many Egyptian citizens to discount his spectacular international accomplishments. Decades after his assassination, many Egyptians continue to denigrate Sadat's contribution to peace despite the international symbolism of the Nobel Peace Prize. Some even cynically question the motives underlying Sadat's connective rapprochement with Israel.

Where Accountability Counts

Because a Stage 3 world connects everyone and everything, few secrets remain. Abetted by willing informants, the media scrutinize the lives and legends of leaders. The unorthodox behaviors of connective leaders are difficult to interpret. Consequently, connective leaders bear a special burden to explain themselves. They must be prepared to demonstrate accountability for their actions, even actions taken long before they assumed the mantle of formal leadership.

A commitment to accountability keeps the connective leader's feet to the fire. For better or worse, in this interdependent environment even the actions of people long ago or only remotely associated with leaders can cast a shadow over their integrity. Accountability may not be enough to protect the connective leader against all accusations and misinterpretations, but combined with authenticity it offers some modicum of help.

Authenticity and accountability are twin imperatives for Stage 3 leaders. Those leaders who try to implement the Connective Leadership Model find their efforts enhanced by grounding their decisions and actions in authenticity and accepting the responsibility for explaining their leadership strategies.

What Stands in the Way?

Like early adopters of any new technology, the first practitioners of new leadership models are bound to face difficulties. Pioneers in every field have always taken risks, and innovation is not without its pains and failures. We should hardly expect, then, that the first connective leaders should find themselves sailing on smooth seas. Particularly in the opening phase of Stage 3, numerous barriers continue to impede the connective leader's path. Passive followers and significant segments of the media, still encumbered by Stage 2 perspectives, constitute two of the most difficult barriers.

Confused Followers

Elsewhere I have suggested that old-style followers, raised on a Stage 2 diet and caught in their existential fears, don't know quite what to make of connective leaders. Traditional followers expect to follow, to wait for directions, to implement the leader's vision. Yet to live in a world marked by interdependence and diversity, followers too have to change their behavior and move more swiftly. They have to make the leap from passivity to proactivity, an enormous challenge.

Constrained by traditional concepts of leadership, traditional followers frequently press nascent connective leaders to return to the more familiar controlling styles. Even at the cost of their own oppression, frightened followers draw security from the devil they *do* know. This was the trap into which the initially promising leadership bid of President Cory Aquino fell. In the corporate world as well, some connective leaders have been undone by initially enthusiastic staff and advisory boards who demanded more conventional leadership at the first signs of trouble.

In this transition to Stage 3, we see evidence of supporters' bewilderment not just in the United States but in many other countries as well. Centuries of history with take-charge leaders have done little to prepare most of us to shoulder the responsibilities of Stage 3. From the Philippines to Poland, ambivalence toward new leadership styles abounds.

In country after country, newly emancipated citizens blame their old-guard, authoritarian leaders for their blighted lives. They want the old ones *out*. Yet, once they're out, many constituents, not sure of what kind of leaders they want *in*, recall the old ones to duty. They seek leaders who use direct styles because that offers a comforting illusion of control, even if the control crosses the line back into subjugation. Ironically, in Poland and Bulgaria, after initially ousting authoritarian Communist leaders, voters elected many of them back into power. In the inevitable upheaval after the overthrow of a controlling leader, followers may question whether the pain of the new is any better than the agony of the old. Gorbachev too fell victim to such ambivalence.

Admittedly, Stage 2 leaders project certainty about their own vision, a certainty that both reassures and energizes followers, particularly in times of crisis. By contrast, connective leaders' willingness to incorporate multiple visions, to collaborate, negotiate, and generally bring others into the leadership process may appear weak. Yet there is no evidence that connective leaders shrink from toughness. In fact, as research suggests, a willingness to collaborate, combined with a reputation for toughness, often makes one's opponent more willing to cooperate.[17]

The defense minister of Afghanistan, Ahmad Shah Masood, the former *mujahedeen* commander, has been celebrated as "the Afghan who won the Cold War." Hailed as a world-class guerrilla leader, alongside Mao Tse-tung, Ho Chi Minh, Che Guevara, and Marshal Tito, Masood is even more remarkable for his Stage 3 behavior. According to the *Wall Street Journal*, Masood's "great achievement has been to make the various ethnic groups of northern Afghanistan, burdened by centuries of mutual suspicion, work together toward a common goal."[18] Although Masood will fight when left no alternative, his clear preference is for negotiation and consensus building.

For active constituency to replace passive followership will take considerable effort. Given the existential and psychological roots of our human quest for leadership, we cannot expect to find any easy method to finesse this transition. Yet an understanding of these deep-seated forces can help us move from the passive dependency of followership to the active responsibility of constituency. Requiring supporters to meet the same standards of authenticity and accountability as leaders would be a big step in that direction. As connective leaders draw more supporters into the leadership process, more and more followers will have to move from passive follower to active constituent, and then perhaps to connective leader.

The Media: Sustaining Resistance to Stage 3 Leaders

Again and again, followers' confused response to connective leaders is sustained by the media, still trammeled by Stage 2 expectations. Their addiction to omniscient, controlling leadership leads the media to frame their analyses of corporate and political leaders in terms of their own existential anxieties. In a 1995 *International Herald Tribune* article, one analyst complained about Bill Clinton:

> We gave up a long time ago on Mr. Clinton as father figure. He is president as gifted teenager, elevating his undisciplined, incomplete, searching personality to a management style. The problem with this president is that he never stops learning.[19]

The media's dedication to the narrow band of direct styles makes them question the maturity and machismo, even the vision, of any leaders who seek out new ideas. Clinton has received an even heavier barrage of criticism for his propensity to consult widely before acting. Using a Stage 2 lens, the media view as a weakness his tendency to give and take, instead of stubbornly defending his initial position. They see his efforts to shape umbrella policies to cover diverse groups the same way. The media complain about congressional gridlock as well. Thirsty for the reassurance that saturates authoritarian decision making, the fourth estate has repeatedly misread consultation, collaboration, and compromise as indecision.

The media seem baffled by leaders who reach out to the opposition to accomplish a goal. This type of instrumental action is easily misinterpreted as pure Machiavellian opportunism or weakness. House Speaker Newt Gingrich has felt the sting of such criticism for forging alliances with "the enemy." His creation of a Republican task force to reconsider the GOP's position on wetlands, endangered species, and other environmental issues evoked much skepticism. It was not particularly surprising, either, that reporters responded cynically to Yasser Arafat's first tentative efforts to negotiate with then–Prime Minister Yitzhak Rabin. The media's initial analysis focused primarily on Arafat's lack of resources and weakening support among Palestinians, rather than on the courage it took to face the wrath of many followers as he took his first connective steps.

Leaders who work for the good of the group are not necessarily inauthentic because they manage to survive and prosper along with the group. This distinction often gets lost in the media's rush to judgment about leaders who try to lead in innovative ways. Although we have highlighted the willingness of connective leaders to sacrifice themselves to a higher cause, clearly the preservation of a leader who can help the group achieve its objectives is a far more useful outcome.

Because the media still lampoon and bait those leaders who attempt Stage 3 strategies, many fledgling connective leaders become too discouraged to persist. Connective leadership is not for the faint hearted. Until we develop the conceptual tools, as well as the stomach, for supporting emerging connective leaders, we shall continue to suffer from the persistence of uncertainty, confusion, and ambivalence.

Despite these caveats, the future for connective leaders is far from bleak. The examples we have seen of nascent and emerging connective leaders—with more to come in the next chapters—give us ample evidence of the vitality of the new connective thrust. As the effects of diversity and interdependence continue to shape our lives, the orientations and talents of these leaders will become more and more appropriate.

While Stage 2 leaders limit themselves to the direct set of achieving styles, connective Stage 3 leaders prefer to use the whole range. They break through the constraints imposed by the direct styles to combine them with new perspectives drawn from the relational and instrumental styles. By drawing on all nine styles, connective leaders can move flexibly and innovatively through the interdependent Stage 3 world. That, however, is just the first step toward becoming a fully realized connective leader.

The second and crucial step is to engage the synergistic effects of such leadership: seeing and making connections where others don't; viewing diversity as a valued reservoir of resources; harnessing the ego to the high purposes and burdens of the group; translating passion for individuals into compassion for the group; and setting oneself and others on a lifelong search for authentic experiences and greater understanding. This is how the Connective Leadership Model becomes more than the sum of its parts.

Part Three

Bridging to the Stage 3 World

Chapter Ten

The Connective Organization
Matching Leadership and Organizational Styles

All of humanity's pursuits are connected, after all, and we
remain ignorant of those connections at our peril.
WARREN BENNIS[1]

In the dynamic landscape of Stage 3, organizations take many new and varied forms. New, small, transient organizations, as Bennis and Slater predicted in the 1960s, will stand alongside older, larger organizations, now battle-scarred from mergers, acquisitions, downsizings, flattenings, and bouts with reengineering.[2] Leaders face many challenges as they work to build and revitalize organizations that can work effectively in a Stage 3 world, a world both buffeted and braced by the tensions of interdependence and diversity.

The old leadership models, barely effective in Stage 2, offer no new approaches. New leadership models can expand our thinking about fresh, innovative ways to meet these organizational challenges, but they have to offer more than theory and hope. Lacking empirical data, models are nothing more than lifeless skeletons. To address this issue, the next two chapters depart from the two previous parts of this book by introducing survey research findings based on the Connective Leadership Model.

This chapter draws an empirical picture of the achieving styles used by men and women in corporate leadership roles (upper- and middle-level managers), as well as by entrepreneurs. The managerial findings allow us to determine if the connective leader's expanded palette is being used by managers at different levels. The data on entrepreneurs shed light on how their connective leadership potential can be put to work inside large organizations. In the concluding section of the chapter, I shift the focus to the achieving styles of whole organizations, to the behaviors valued and rewarded by organizations and inculcated through their cultures. There, I explore what happens when the personal technologies or achieving styles used by individuals and the behaviors valued by organizations are in or out of sync with one another.

The Organizational Challenges of Stage 3

The challenges confronting organizational leaders in Stage 3 are indeed daunting, even to the most intrepid. Organizational restructuring has bulldozed away much worker morale and loyalty, along with many levels of management, and thousands of jobs. Unexpected layoffs have shattered many workers' expectations of secure, lifelong careers within a single organization. The loosened bonds between workers and organizations have increased worker disaffection and raised turnover rates. And the continuing trend toward downsizing and cost-cutting offers little likelihood that either organizational paternalism or worker loyalty will return soon, if ever.

Motivation and Belonging Amidst Alienation and Diversity

In a context of rapid change, uncertainty, and alienation, leaders face an uphill struggle to reassure and inspire employees, to spark motivation, and to articulate meaningful organizational purposes. The vastly different backgrounds, values, and talents of an increasingly diverse workforce make the task more difficult. If they are to avoid being torn apart by the contradictory needs of various constituencies, leaders will have to bridge enormous cultural divides. They will have to create a sense of community in which a mosaic of organizational members can feel included and impelled to make their special contributions to the total enterprise.

In a globalized economy, the answer may lie within the problem itself. Savvy organizational leaders can exploit the strengths inherent in diversity. The many perspectives, languages, knowl-

edges, and values of a diverse workforce can be used to the organization's advantage. This approach requires leaders with an eye
for diversity and a feel for the strength of interdependence. A strategy based on diversity, you will recall from Chapter One, drives
Voice Processing Corp., whose forty employees speak thirty languages. Similarly, where the organization's customers and stakeholders also represent diversity, leaders can draw on the knowledge
within their own variegated workforces to understand their achieving styles. Where few individuals span the complete range of behaviors, by combining the strengths of different team members the
leader can assemble effective, flexible teams to meet a wide range
of organizational objectives. This is putting diversity and interdependence to work for the organization.

New Organizational Structures:
Dealing with Organizational Diversity

The need for innovative organizational designs tests leaders' ability to
move beyond traditional hierarchical architecture to new organizational forms. In Stage 3, leaders are called upon to deal with the
organizational diversity represented by networks within and between
organizations, one-time or sequential outsourcing arrangements,
short- and medium-term alliances, and collaborative efforts with competitors. The challenge is not to restore old organizations to their former strength and glory but to redesign them so they can confront an
unknowable future. This is where a connective leader's feel for interdependence and long-term perspective come seriously into play.

Although our emphasis has been on fast-changing, short-lived
alliances, let us by no means throw longer-term alliances out with
Stage 2. Stage 3 leaders who sense the growing permeability of established organizational walls are more likely than their predecessors
to build longer-lasting connections as well, without feeling violated.

American Express came to this awareness slowly and painfully.
Only after they had lost more and more market share to competitors did AmEx finally announce it would follow the trend to "co-
branded" cards. This marketing device tempts customers with an
array of goodies for every dollar charged on the card.[3] Previously,
AmEx had limited its co-branding ventures to AT&T. Through subsidiaries Lehman Brothers and Smith Barney, AmEx did issue cards

with their brokerage accounts. That effort skirted the larger possibilities available through retail purchases of consumer goods. By the time AmEx got around to joining the connective parade, VISA/MasterCard had already issued more than twenty-eight million co-branded cards, through Citibank, Household Bank, Associates National, Chemical Bank, and Banc One.

Leaders who actively seek such connections have a knack for Organizational Lego. Aficionados know that the goal of this serious game is to connect pieces of one organization with parts of another and then take them apart when the task is done, reusing some components and adding new ones to build an ongoing series of structures. They also know how to look *within* their own organizations to restructure them into malleable forms responsive to changing demands from clients, customers, and other stakeholders. Leaders who can do this will be building a rapid-reaction capability to cope with a constantly changing environment.

Diversity at a Distance: Offshore Employees, Unseen Stakeholders

Diversity and interdependence pose still another challenge for organizational leaders. Here the challenge comes from the tenuous connections between parent organizations and their offshore employees. Other unnoticed stakeholders beyond the organizational walls, such as community residents concerned with health and safety, also pose potential issues. Organizations that ignore cultural diversity and interdependence do so at their peril.

Union Carbide learned that painfully expensive lesson in Bhopal, India.[4] The 1984 toxic chemical explosion at Union Carbide's Bhopal plant killed more than two thousand people and injured more than three hundred thousand others. Many of the injured suffered permanent injuries. The company's neglect and ignorance of their indigenous Indian workers and stakeholders played a large part in the tragic consequences.

Transforming Competitors into Collaborators

In an interconnected world, competitors need to be viewed differently as well. Increasingly, competitors are proving valuable collaborators, as Apple Computer belatedly discovered. In its infancy,

Apple's chaotic and innovative cofounder, Steve Jobs, made a strategic decision: the Macintosh computing platform would stand alone, unlinkable to other non-Apple computers and unlikely to be cloned. For a short time this strategy succeeded, especially with Apple's original target market, education, where students and educators could work in splendid seclusion or hook up to other Apple/Mac users. Indeed, in those early days, many Macintosh buffs regarded their isolation as a quixotic badge of honor.

In a very few years, technological change and the need for connectivity overtook Apple's individualistic, Stage 2 strategy. Many Macintosh users who relished their machine's virtuosity became frustrated when their Macs couldn't talk to their colleagues' computers. Third-party vendors offered a variety of stop-gap devices to let Macs talk to other computers, but these proved less than ideal. By the time Apple finally recognized the connectivity problem, Wall Street analysts and users too were convinced that Apple had taken far too long to change. (Sony had a similar experience with its Beta format for videocassette recorders.)

Later, in a move that symbolized both their customers' need to function in an interdependent environment as well as their own corporate redirection, Apple signed an historic cooperative agreement with IBM. That pact eventually led to the Power Mac and the Power PC. Even a few short years before, few industry analysts would have predicted such a collaboration between those two aggressive competitors. As of this writing, Wall Street continues to speculate about whether this long overdue strategic redirection can sustain Apple as a viable, independent company.

The moral for organizational leaders is simple: competitors can be less dangerous and far more useful as collaborators. A viable connective approach can transform competitors not into smoldering, subdued enemies but into formidable collaborators. The point is not to avoid competition, but to enhance it by combining it with other strategies. By taking such connective action, former competitors increase the possibility that collaborating and contributing to one another's success will open new horizons for both.

Leadership Succession: New and Old Versions

The challenge of leadership succession bedevils many organizations. Traditionally, the succession issue has centered either on new, younger leaders to replace retiring chiefs or on avoiding the loss of enterprising stars who might move to greener pastures. Although those forms of succession will surely continue, in Stage 3 succession means something else as well. In a world where diversity also signifies a multitude of organizational forms, leadership succession means building a cadre of leaders who can head them. During their careers, these new leaders can expect to lead many different kinds of organizational structures, from short-term alliances to more stable partnerships and joint ventures.

John Gardner[5] argues that organizations of the future will require the exercise of leadership at all levels, not just at the top. Without such dispersed leadership, too much depends on too few, and organizations remain hobbled by their inability to grow the next generation of leaders.

Both kinds of leadership succession set organizational challenges for leaders. Here too, people with connective styles, with their long-term perspective, their sense of the community's future needs, and the capacity to yoke their egos to organizational goals, make particularly attractive leadership candidates.

Innovation: Can Entrepreneurs and Intrapreneurs Help?

In Stage 3, the need to innovate will only escalate. The ability of organizational leaders to lead innovatively and to encourage innovation among their colleagues will further separate Stage 2 from Stage 3 leaders.

Innovation has always been a hallmark of entrepreneurs. Entrepreneurs, however, have usually represented something of an enigma for Stage 2 organizations. More often than not, Stage 2 companies drove entrepreneurs away, vilifying them as troublemakers, too egocentric to be good team players. Employees with entrepreneurial bents were often disdained as internal competitors or marauders, on the prowl for organizational booty. Those who created both internal and external networks of supporters risked being labeled "political" or worse yet "entrepreneurial." In large part, resistance to entrepreneurial co-workers arose more in response to their disturbing instrumental styles than to their more familiar, out-and-out Stage 2 competitive and power strategies.

Only recently has entrepreneurship regained legitimacy within large-scale organizations. In fact, the term *intrapreneurs* was deliberately coined to diminish the political stigma and emphasize the creative energy such entrepreneurial individuals instill in large organizations.[6] The new vocabulary may also reflect a gradually increasing comfort with instrumental action.

Managers concerned about dwindling motivation and innovation have begun to encourage intrapreneurship alongside team-oriented approaches. In fact, some intrapreneurs gather around them high-spirited teams, or hot groups, determined to create something new and wonderful despite the oppressiveness of their bureaucratic homes.[7]

Interestingly, research on the achieving styles of full-fledged independent entrepreneurs reveals them—particularly female entrepreneurs—to have leadership profiles with a distinctly connective cast. In contrast to the valleys and peaks we see in corporate managers' style profiles, the leadership profiles of these entrepreneurs are surprisingly balanced, with strong scores on all nine achieving styles.

Given what entrepreneurs set out to do, their achieving style profiles make perfect sense. Entrepreneurs are the Jacks and Jills of all trades. They do whatever has to be done, using their achieving styles as personal technologies, applying different combinations to different problems. Drawing on their own intelligence, initiative, and energy, they take charge of every step, from envisioning the new product or service to raising capital to marketing the final product. Nor do entrepreneurs usually stop there. They create large networks of associates and participate in community projects, from the local school board to the chamber of commerce. With keen political savvy, they sponsor important public events to shine the spotlight on their entrepreneurial ventures. In other words, entrepreneurs use whatever achieving styles are appropriate to woo success. They adapt their innovating personal technologies to meet all the requirements of their entrepreneurial role. Consequently, they enjoy well-rounded achieving styles profiles that would make any connective leader proud.

Does that mean that entrepreneurs are really connective leaders? Unfortunately, the answer is "not very often," since most entrepreneurs are usually too committed to their own egoistic vision to move to the synergistic level of supra-egoistic behavior we described in the preceding chapter.

Still, we might ask if there is any way to capture the benefits of the entrepreneur's connective leadership propensities within established organizations. The short answer is "yes," but only if entrepreneurs can move beyond their self-orientation to the point where the synergistic effects of connective leadership kick in. Both organizations and entrepreneurs would be well served by catching entrepreneurs early, when they are still sufficiently cash-shy to be tempted by offers of organizational capital. Then they might direct their leadership skills within the organization instead of heading off to seek their fortunes. Putting young, energetic entrepreneurs in charge of new units that need innovation, flexibility, and political savvy, as some companies have done, can accomplish two goals: create a connective edge for the organization and give entrepreneurs time to mature.

Innovation and Discontinuity: Changing Scientific and Personal Technologies

Innovation is too important, however, to be left entirely to the entrepreneurs and their intrapreneurial relatives. The complexity of Stage 3 calls for much more. Some analysts describe our current era as the age of discontinuities,[8] in which things change so completely that our practiced ways of doing things no longer work. Indeed, the propensity to fall back on our tried-and-true methods keeps us from attempting new ways more appropriate to the realities we face.

Richard Foster, a director of the management consulting firm McKinsey & Co., suggests that innovation can be used as a basic method for renewing organizations and employees.[9] He warns us that innovation is risky and frightening because it requires us to relinquish the still-viable method by which we have achieved our current success. Nonetheless, Foster argues convincingly that we must be willing to abandon our most successful technologies, even as they continue to work for us, if we are to develop innovations more appropriate to the future.

Clinging to old technologies until they reach their limits and investing only in incremental improvements represent a sure-fire strategy for ending up behind the curve. Unfortunately, too many organizations are still led by risk-averse Stage 2 leaders, who stick stubbornly to the trusted organizational and personal methods that have brought them success in the past.

The USDA: In with the Old, Out with the New

A case in point is the world-renowned, century-old U.S. Department of Agriculture, with its national network of agricultural colleges.[10] In the 1960s, using chemical pesticides and herbicides, and building massive dams to irrigate previously arid land, the USDA ushered in the Green Revolution. The discoveries of agricultural scientists enormously increased acreage yields, promising thereby to eradicate hunger. Hailed worldwide for its miraculous accomplishments, the agricultural establishment confidently believed it was traveling along just the right track.

Eventually, however, consumers and environmentalists began to notice some unforeseen side effects of the Green Revolution:[11] streams and soil contaminated by petrochemical pesticides and herbicides, deforestation, soil erosion, and salinization.[12] At first the traditional, closely knit agricultural science establishment dismissed the criticism, clinging to its fundamental axiom: "If it ain't broke, don't fix it." Perplexed and unresponsive to the growing chorus of complaints, the embattled agricultural science community circled its wagons.

While the USDA clung to its seemingly tried-and-true technologies, the world around it did not stand still. Nonagricultural scientists, trained in chemistry, biology, and physics, began to turn their attention to agricultural problems. Locked into their long and successful tradition, agricultural scientists steadily lost ground to these new "disciplinary" people with their strange new concepts and technologies. In 1972, the National Research Council[13] issued a stinging critique of traditional agricultural science, ushering in more than two decades of frantic efforts by the agricultural research community to reestablish its preeminence.

The message couldn't be clearer. Those organizations still caught in the thrall of their old technologies will find themselves in a serious, and sometimes fatal, catch-up mode.[14] "Success," it has been said, "teaches all the wrong lessons."

Innovation in Personal Technologies: Managing High-Tech Projects

The lesson to be learned from the USDA applies to the question of individual leadership as well. In Chapters One and Five, I suggested that achieving styles are essentially personal technologies that we all use to achieve our goals. Leaders who have relied for past success on the direct achieving styles, or even on the relational styles, will find these personal technologies insufficient for leading the organizations of the twenty-first century.

Risky as it may feel, calling upon instrumental and relational styles to invigorate the more familiar leadership technologies of intrinsic, competitive, and power strategies is a triple-barreled approach to innovation. Adding new achieving styles ammunition to the leadership armory represents innovation in its own right. These new leadership approaches in turn stimulate innovation and responsibility in constituents and competitors-turned-collaborators.

The world of high technology provides a good illustration of the importance of new personal leadership technologies. High-tech R&D organizations often must cope with sprawling, complex projects that call for innovation all along the line. The research findings of E. C. Williams[15] shed intriguing light on how new leadership technologies can work in such settings. In a study of seven corporations awarded contracts by the U.S. Department of Defense, Williams investigated more than one hundred factors that might account for managers' success in bringing large, technology-based projects to completion on time and on budget.

Conventional management thinking suggests that large projects should be subject to strict management controls. Williams, however, found that as project size increased, management controls became *less* effective in ensuring the project's success. Leadership strategies, rather than mechanical control systems, were more likely to yield success in complex projects. In fact, Williams showed that both personal and entrusting leadership strategies (through which managers charismatically attracted and inspired team members, while leaving the implementation up to them) were significant predictors of success.

More surprising at first glance was still another finding: managers who used vicarious behavior also had a positive effect on the project's outcome. Encouragement and praise, rather than direct and controlling supervision, were more likely to bring success.

Williams came up with another intriguing and unexpected finding: holding the complexity of computer software constant, advanced technical training was *negatively* related to success. In other words, technical leadership was less important than connective managerial leadership. Confronted with complicated, large-scale projects, entrusting managers who relied on their staff to take the project and run with it, without detailed guidance and monitoring, were more likely to bring these massive projects to successful conclusions.

On a large-scale project, micromanaging is an exercise in futility. Too many details and too many people are involved. Instead, inspiring responsibility and innovation all down the line is much more likely to work. Giving those on the front line a sense of ownership and pride increases their motivation. It also energizes team members to try innovative solutions in uncharted territory. Williams found that managers who relied upon Stage 2 power strategies, controlling and micromanaging all aspects of the operation, were unlikely to bring their projects to successful completion.

Competitive leadership didn't work either. Managers who needed to prove their superior competence, who put their ego ahead of the project, got poor results from their people. In fact, there was a clear negative relationship between the use of competitive and power leadership styles and the successful completion of large, complex high-tech projects. In all seven firms, the use of new connective technologies helped the managers to lead much more successfully.

In short, Stage 3 leaders face formidable organizational challenges, from rekindling motivation to dealing with diversity born of new workers, new organizational forms, and new offshore employees and stakeholders. Innovation will be needed on every level. Yet, the innovations brought by rapidly changing technology present their own problems for organizational leaders.

To meet these challenges, leaders will need to make appropriate changes in their personal technologies, that is, the achieving styles spectrum they call upon to reach their goals. Entrepreneurs and intrapreneurs have the raw materials to fashion an appropriate response to Stage 3, but only if they move to the synergistic level of connective leadership.

Can American Organizations Generate Connective Leaders?

Are American organizations really likely to encourage connective leadership, either at the top or any other level? Are members anywhere in the organization learning the skills needed for connective leadership? Can they combine at least some direct, instrumental, and relational styles? Do people who rise to upper-management positions look more like connective leaders than people below them in the organization?

Let's examine the clues provided by a large study we conducted between 1984 and 1995 in the Achieving Styles Project at the Peter F. Drucker Graduate Management Center of The Claremont Graduate School. We collected data on more than eighty-five hundred corporate employees, from upper-level managers to nonprofessional, nonsupervisory, and clerical workers. All of these individuals completed the *L-BL Achieving Styles Inventory*,[16] a forty-five-item questionnaire in which they indicated how frequently they used the nine achieving styles. Here we discuss the findings on more than fifty-one hundred[17] upper and middle managers, 3,126 men and 2,041 women, in the United States.

The Achieving Styles of Upper-Level Managers

First, let's review the good news about upper managers, whose achieving styles profiles give us some cause for encouragement. Contrary to the profile of Stage 2 leaders, who wedged themselves almost exclusively into the direct set (intrinsic, competitive, and power), these upper-level managers report they combine high levels of intrinsic and power behavior with only slightly lower levels of all three relational styles (that is, collaborative, contributory, and vicarious). In short, these senior managers are perfectly able to take control, but they know how to share power and offer technical and political help, as well as encouragement. They see collaboration as a more effective method for accomplishing tasks than traditional unalloyed power and competition.

In fact, the findings on competition are both interesting and quite unexpected. Although their competitive level was still somewhat higher than the competitive scores of employees at six lower organizational levels, these eleven hundred upper-level managers gave competition a surprisingly low rank: eighth out of the nine styles, only slightly higher than the social style. If anything, we probably ought to worry a little that these executives seem to reject competitive styles so emphatically.

Scores for the collaborative, contributory, and vicarious styles were almost as high as those for the intrinsic and power strategies. Among the instrumental styles, entrusting was the favorite of these upper managers. Although they ranked this very useful strategy for encouraging responsibility only sixth out of nine, upper-level managers did give it a stronger vote than employees at all other organizational levels.

The bad news is that senior managers rate the personal and social styles decidedly lower than the intrinsic and power strategies. They also rank them below all three relational styles. In fact, members of the next three organizational levels below upper management—middle managers, first-line supervisors, and professional non-supervisory personnel—all rate the personal style higher than these senior managers do.

These findings suggest that when senior managers want to motivate co-workers, they rely more on their formal power and authority, as well as on their relational efforts to support others. Regrettably, they ignore all the enormous potency of the personal style, with its charisma, drama, and symbolism.

Worse yet, for these senior managers the social style is the least attractive choice, although the upper-level managers did give it a higher absolute score than those lower in the organizational hierarchy. These corporate leaders don't much like this key set of strategies that connective leaders use for constructing networks and mobilizing the informal system. Unfortunately, social behavior too remains quite unappreciated at all organizational levels.

In sum, senior corporate managers, like generations of their forebears, still prefer to use I'm-in-charge methods. They seem, however, to have tempered their own competitive tendencies somewhat and increased their ability to help other people achieve their goals, so there is some reason for optimism here.

These senior managers feel quite comfortable as team members. The upper managers in this study said they spent a fair bit of their time helping others accomplish their assignments, sometimes by taking a background role but also by playing mentor. When it comes to the instrumental styles, as we have seen, these upper-level managers are still quite hesitant. Yet these are the styles that help leaders attract others, develop networks, and work through the tangled brush of the informal system. Fortunately,

these senior managers seem somewhat more willing to try entrusting styles, behaviors that unleash creativity, loyalty, and responsibility in constituents and other leaders.

The Achieving Styles of Middle-Level Managers

The achieving styles profiles of middle managers closely resemble
those of managers at the top. Like their upper-level colleagues,
middle managers rank intrinsic and power in a first tier, well above
all the remaining seven styles. Their second tier is composed of the
contributory, collaborative, and vicarious styles. Within the relational set, there is some indication that the middle managers prefer contributory behavior, particularly over vicarious or collaborative
action. That is, these middle managers feel more comfortable helping others complete their tasks than acting as mentors or team
members. They may not feel they have the time, skills, experience,
or formal status to play the mentor role.

Conventional wisdom would argue that middle managers lack
interest in collaboration because they are still climbing the organizational ladder and trying to distinguish themselves from their
teammates. This line of reasoning would suggest that middle managers consequently act in more self-interested and competitive ways
than their higher level co-workers. This turns out *not* to be the case.
In fact, middle managers appear to be considerably less competitive than their upper-level colleagues. Surprisingly, middle managers report an even greater dislike for competitive behavior than
do senior managers.

An important distinction emerges when we take gender into account. As we see in Chapter Eleven, there are strong differences between men and women on competitiveness. Female managers, both
senior and middle-level, give the competitive style their lowest rating. Both senior and middle-level female managers reject competition more emphatically than males at these managerial levels.

Within the male group, while middle managers fall considerably below their senior male colleagues, they favor competition far
more than their female middle-level peers do. This difference by
managerial level holds up only among men. That is, women's dis-
taste for competition is so intense that there is no difference between female upper and middle managers.

Another interesting distinction appears between leaders who have made it to the top and those still climbing the ladder. Middle managers use personal behavior with far greater frequency than their upper-division colleagues do. Rather than behaving competitively to make their way in the organization, middle managers rely on their personal skills. They act as charismatically as possible, calling on their intelligence, wit, interpersonal talent, educational backgrounds, and previous occupational roles to gain recognition.

There are some gender differences here too, with middle-level women somewhat less comfortable than men about using personal styles. Yet these middle-level women are still markedly more willing to use these personal strategies than senior managers, male or female.

The entrusting style works quite the other way for middle-level managers, who are noticeably less likely than senior managers to rely on their staff to carry out important tasks without looking over shoulders. Perhaps while managers are still on the way up, it is more difficult to entrust to others crucial tasks whose successful completion might decide their next promotion.

These research findings reveal both similarities and differences in achieving style preferences among present-day senior and middle corporate managers. Both upper and middle managers readily use the intrinsic and power styles, as well as all three relational styles: collaborative, contributory, and vicarious. In addition, they consistently reject both competitive and social behavior.

Senior managers, however, seem better able to deploy entrusting strategies, while middle-level managers prefer using themselves instrumentally, instead of entrusting their tasks to others. We might interpret the instrumental self-use of middle managers in the following way: lacking a reservoir of organizational authority to call upon, middle managers may feel safer falling back upon inner personal resources. Once the organization confers sufficient authority on the upper-level managers, they are less likely to call upon their personal resources.

Perhaps we should interpret the senior managers' diminished use of personal behavior, at least in part, as a "status marker." If one has "arrived," then one demonstrates that new status by relying on newly acquired power and authority, rather than on personal influence. One way of testing this hunch is to look at people who do not supervise others, such as nonsupervisory professional workers.

That group is professionally well regarded, but its members lack organizational authority. Interestingly enough, professional non-supervisory workers rank the personal style third, much higher than any of their managerial co-workers. If we look farther down the organizational ladder, clerical and nonprofessional, non-supervisory employees rank personal strategies higher than their managers do. Clerical workers rank it fourth, and nonprofessional, nonsupervisory workers accord it fifth place.

These findings suggest that as individuals move up the organizational ladder, they are less likely to use charismatic behavior to persuade others to help them. Apparently, the talent and skill necessary for the personal side of connective leadership exist at lower organizational levels. As individuals climb the organizational ladder, they seem to set those skills aside, relying more on the formal authority that comes with more senior positions.

The flamboyance of charisma admittedly can be risky. Perhaps at lower organizational levels, where the stakes are not so high, people are more willing, or sometimes even forced, to take such risks. As organizational belt-tightening increases, high-salaried senior positions become disturbingly scarce. Let's also not forget the old corporate symbol, the gray flannel suit, somber and conforming, that traditionally signaled managerial risk aversion.[18]

Do Our Managers Have What It Takes to Become Connective Leaders?

I have argued that connective leadership demands the use of all nine styles, with special emphasis upon the instrumental styles. In light of these research findings, do we have the makings of connective leadership at all organizational levels? The positive news, as I have suggested, is that at least two of the three direct styles and all three relational styles are easily used by leaders at different levels of the organization. The less familiar styles, entrusting and personal, appear to depend upon level.

People seem to grow into the entrusting style, while unfortunately they outgrow the personal behavior. Perhaps most disturbing, the social style is seriously underutilized. Yet that style is absolutely crucial in an interdependent milieu. It is the best available mechanism for creating the networks from which multiple alliances can be forged.

Despite our society's enormous emphasis on it, competitive action seems to have fallen into disfavor, most likely in response to the organizational mantra of teamwork. Maybe, just maybe, competitive behavior will not be terribly missed in Stage 3, especially if organizational leaders can integrate more of the instrumental styles with their already meshed direct and relational strengths. In general, though, using the entire array of achieving styles is a better route to connective leadership.

Overall, our research findings suggest that organizations still have some way to go before they can claim victory in the development of connective leaders, particularly in terms of the ethically based instrumental styles. The intrinsic and power styles, along with the collaborative, contributory, and vicarious strategies, appear to be in good health. Among the instrumental styles, so apropos for an interdependent environment, entrusting behavior seems to be the prerogative of senior managers. The personal style appears to be the province of corporate citizens without much formal authority. The competitive and social styles have few takers willing to admit that they can or do use them. And we know from our other observational studies that the styles people report they use are indeed the ones that observers confirm they actually do employ.[19]

For all styles to be encouraged at every level, we need to think about using the organization's culture and reward systems to encourage the use of new strategies. Otherwise, the learning that takes place in the lower ranks of the organization, particularly about instrumental styles, is jettisoned when individuals reach the higher rungs of the organizational ladder.

Without encouragement, the entrusting behavior that senior corporate executives apparently have begun to use fails to diffuse throughout the organization. And the charisma, excitement, and inspiration of the personal style have difficulty making their way into the boardroom. Perhaps as the exigencies of Stage 3 become more evident, the benefits of organizationally focused instrumental action will also become more widely appreciated. Then senior managers may feel more comfortable managing with the styles they demonstrated in their earlier middle-level years.

Organizational Achieving Styles: Cultures, Values, Rewards, and Discontinuities

So far, this chapter has focused on individuals and their personal achieving styles. But organizations have their special achieving styles too, styles that their cultures, consciously or unconsciously, inculcate in their members. That is to say, organizations characteristically reward certain kinds of achieving behavior and punish or ignore other kinds.[20]

An organization's pattern of achieving styles constitutes an important aspect of its culture, along with its embedded traditions, beliefs, and rituals. Together, they reflect the organization's values and shape its members' expectations about how they are supposed to behave. This spectrum of expected behaviors in turn shapes the organization's reward system, encouraging members to behave this way and discouraging them from behaving that way. An organization's achieving style profile can give us a quick-and-dirty fix on both its broad culture and the reward system it uses to enforce it. In the process, the profile can also specify the personal technologies that the organization underrewards or overrewards.

Discontinuities in Preferred Styles

An organization's achieving styles profile can also reveal four kinds of possible discontinuities that may be brewing:

1. Mismatches between individual behavior and organizational norms
2. Mismatches between individuals and their organizational roles
3. Mismatches between the preferred styles of given individuals and those of the others in their current or aspired-to group
4. Still other mismatches among the interpretations ascribed by different units to messages from their organizational leaders

By exploring these discontinuities in achieving styles, we can gain insight into ways to remedy or at least understand them.

Organizational Culture and Individual Achieving Styles

Organizational culture both comforts and controls its members.[21] It comforts them by generating a familiar context for organizational life and offering membership to those who conform. At the same time, organizational culture controls members by constricting the range of behaviors and attitudes that are valued and rewarded. As the uninitiated in any organization soon discover, violating cultural norms is a sure route to disaster.

Strong and pervasive though it may be, organizational culture is extraordinarily difficult to describe. Culture is much like atmosphere: you can't grab a handful of it, even when it's all around you. Yet it is both real and pervasive. We sense an organization's culture the minute we cross its threshold. Where one high-tech organization prides itself on traditional establishment behavior, buttressed by a clear set of dress and behavioral codes, another is equally insistent about its own nonestablishment ambiance. Such differences in cultural "fog" can be picked up by organizational achieving styles profiles.

New members of organizations quickly learn both the explicit and implicit values and norms of their new culture. They soon understand that those who join up with the culture are more likely to be rewarded than those who march to a different drummer. From an achieving styles perspective, individuals whose styles do not mesh with the organization's are likely to face serious difficulties, if not expulsion.

Some organizations value a narrow range of achieving styles, some a very wide array. Some reward competitive- and power-oriented behavior. Others may focus on teamwork, negotiation, networking, and mentoring. Some actively, albeit unconsciously, punish employees who engage in those same behaviors. Furthermore, while individuals can usually sense when their behaviors don't quite fit the organization's style, they often don't know why or what to do about it.

I once conducted a seminar on leadership and achieving styles at a Managing Your Career Day alumni program at Stanford's Graduate School of Business. Before the seminar, everyone filled out the individual *L-BL Achieving Styles Inventory*. Then we discussed the leadership model that underlay it, along with the fit between an individual's profile and the styles valued by his or her organization.

Afterwards, a young woman (whose name I no longer remember), assistant to the president of a large HMO, approached me and confided:

You know, I've always felt I didn't fit into my organization, but I never knew quite why. Now, I understand. They want everyone to collaborate, never to stand out, never to take charge in any obvious way. Everyone has to agree, or at least pretend to. If you try to present another point of view, they don't think you're a team player. But I like to do things, and I don't like to wait for the whole group to get its act together before I can move. I feel stifled that I can't speak out and always have to "go along to get along."

Several months later, I learned that she had left the organization voluntarily in search of a better fit. Explicitly examining the lack of fit between her own achieving styles and the organization's could have helped this young woman and her boss to address the tension more constructively. That tension was probably also being experienced by other members of the organization. Using the Connective Leadership Model to clarify the organization's values and expectations could have a salutary effect for leaders and staff throughout the organization.

Individual Achieving Styles and Organizational Roles

In the preceding example, the discontinuity was between an individual's styles and the styles valued by the organization. A similar mismatch can also occur between an individual's style and the style demanded by a particular role in the organization. It may be difficult for a collaboratively oriented person to function in a job that requires lots of competition, like sales manager. Because the expectations for roles are expressed through the organizational culture, it is often difficult to determine where one begins and the other ends. Difficult as role expectations and cultures are to disentangle, the Connective Leadership Model, with its underlying achieving styles, may be one good way to illuminate them.

Discontinuities Across Individuals: Current and Future Group Membership

The model also can highlight issues that arise from the consonance or dissonance between an individual's achieving styles profile and those of his or her colleagues. What happens, for instance, when there is a sharp difference between the achieving styles profile of middle manager John Jones and the aggregate profile of his current work group? Further, what happens when there is a sharp difference between Jones's profile and the collective styles of the senior managers whose ranks he aspires to join?

On the issue of fit between an individual's styles and the collective styles of the group to which that person aspires, my research data on women in middle-level managerial positions suggest a paradoxical pattern. Women commonly exhibit higher relational and lower competitive scores than their male peers. That kind of achieving styles pattern is often interpreted as inappropriate for top jobs because it is not sufficiently competitive. As a result, female middle managers are passed over for promotion to senior positions. The paradox shows up at this point: once promoted to senior positions, their male colleagues start learning to decrease their competitiveness and increase their relational skills. The result is that the newly promoted males eventually become corporate cross dressers, closely resembling the women whom they bypassed.

Organizational Messages, Mixed and Misread

Some discontinuities stem from the messages leaders send to their people. Intentionally or not, leaders are constantly transmitting all kinds of signals about the sorts of achieving styles they want. Their signals, however, must always pass through human perceptual filters, and those filters are powerful interpreters of reality. And of course it is not the message sent but the filtered message received that determines how we act and react.

Unfortunately, but not unexpectedly, messages about desired achieving styles commonly are misread, creating yet another level of discontinuities. Messages communicated by organizational leaders may be different for different levels, or simply heard that way by recipients. Moreover, people in different functional areas may interpret these messages in diverse ways, usually in light of their beliefs about how rewards are actually distributed. By using the framework of connective leadership, we can begin to develop a handle on how we might deal with this form of organizational discontinuity.

The CEO, for example, may be signaling approval of teamwork, but the signal may be picked up differently by different groups, especially if their tasks are dramatically dissimilar. The sales department may read the message as encouraging team members to share contacts with one another (that is, increase their use of the social style). The engineering department may hear the message as support for their highly collaborative brainstorming sessions.

To complicate matters, that message may also be differentially interpreted as we move down the organizational ladder. Here is a short case that might shed some light on such communication problems:

At an undergraduate liberal arts college, both the president's and vice president's responses to the organizational achieving styles questionnaire (OASI) indicated that above all else the school rewarded collaborative and vicarious behavior.[22] The behavior was manifested by a high degree of teamwork among faculty and close, individual mentoring of students. The college's deans, down one administrative level, agreed that teamwork was rewarded, but they further felt that entrusting others and contributing to other peoples' tasks were also highly prized.

The faculty, on the other hand, read the organizational messages differently. They believed the college really wanted them to build their professional reputations through publishing and presenting their work at conferences, that is, to act intrinsically, competitively, and personally. They also felt the college encouraged personal and power behavior, such as getting elected to offices in professional associations and powerful campus committees.

Secretaries and other clerical staff held still another view of what the top wanted. They thought the college would reward them for using the social style, by networking and accomplishing things through a web of personal relationships. As it turned out, most of the secretaries had indeed learned the ropes from personal contacts with one another. In fact, there was no other way for them to learn how to prepare academic papers or process travel vouchers.

Leaders of student organizations were the only group who tended to agree with the president's and vice president's views about which achieving styles the institution supported. Presumably, these aspiring young leaders, viewing the top officers as role models, accepted their values. Moreover, these student leaders felt that taking charge (using the power style) was also highly valued and rewarded. They could point to their own success at the college as evidence.

To some degree, all of these interpretations are probably correct. Much like the allegorical blind men touching different parts of the elephant, people in different organizational positions may "touch" genuinely divergent realities. While top management may view its reward structure as though it were consistent throughout the organization, in fact very different achieving styles yardsticks determine rewards in separate functional areas and levels. Moreover, the increased diversity of the Stage 3 world is exacerbating communication problems. The diversity of gender, ethnic, racial, and other backgrounds creates a series of cultural filters through which organizational messages must pass.

These divergent interpretations need to be resolved by organizational leaders in consultation with leadership at every level. The connective leadership framework can become useful here to help examine, realistically and without personal acrimony, the demands and options available to all organizational members. Concepts and vocabulary that focus on behavior, not on personality characteristics, can help structure a more objective evaluation of such problems. They also help identify which achieving styles patterns should be rewarded to help fulfill the organization's mission.

Discontinuities: A Diagnostic Cue

Once identified, these many forms of discontinuity can be useful diagnostic cues, particularly when widespread throughout the organization. For example, a "productivity" or "morale" problem may be traced by a serious disagreement between the aggregated individual profiles of the employees and the organization's own profile. Careful analysis may then reveal that the organization's leadership is recruiting inappropriate people for its mission or miscommunicating which behaviors and values it genuinely regards as important. On the other hand, the organization may not be adequately socializing the new recruits to the organization's expectations. Or it may be that although the individuals and the organization value the same kinds of behaviors, the individuals are giving the organization far more than they feel the organization actually rewards.

In some circumstances, leaders must ask how big the gap really is. Does it represent over- or underperformance? Does the gap exist across the board, or only among certain groups? And how long can the organization continue that way without serious mishap? Large or multiple gaps between the members' group profile and the organizational profile usually indicate a significant morale problem among the troops.

Some Consequences for the Individual

Our analysis suggests that achieving styles have consequences for both individuals and organizations. As we have already seen, individuals whose achieving styles profiles diverge greatly from those their organizations value probably cannot expect to receive many formal rewards, such as promotions, salary increases, and choice assignments.

For people whose profiles diverge significantly from their organization's profile, several options are available. First, they can learn to modify their own individual profiles to fit better with the profile their organization rewards. That takes training and a desire to change. That can also be experienced as anything from "knuckling under" to "just learning the ropes." Second, they can try to alter the organization's reward system. That amounts to changing the whole organizational culture to fit one individual's preferences. A good many CEOs have gone down in flames trying to do just that. And third, "divergents" can depart the scene, looking for another organization whose reward system offers a better match.

Some individuals with divergent profiles derive greater satisfaction from the subjective rewards of being different. Although these nonconformists may feel undervalued or unloved in their organization, they still may exult in what they believe to be their unique attitudes and styles. In fact, some individuals maintain their identity primarily by being at odds with every group they enter. In social psychology, those folks have usually been labeled "chronic deviants," a phrase itself imbued with implicit values.

Organizational members with divergent achieving styles profiles sometimes perceive themselves as the "conscience" of the organization. They may thus perform a valuable service. While they may never receive formal organizational rewards, such individuals usually measure their success by a different, more subjective metric.

Marching to an Internal Drummer: The Case of Marylou

The week I arrived at The Claremont Graduate School, a female student in the Public Policy Program, whom I shall call Marylou,

asked to speak to me about the summer job she was just completing. Marylou, a bright, lively twenty-seven-year-old, was clearly troubled. She had just spent the summer working as a leadership intern
at a not-for-profit foundation that focused on educational problems of minorities.

At the outset, Marylou told me, her excitement had soared at
the prospect of using her public policy knowledge and her passion
for helping the "underdog." The situation rapidly deteriorated into a disaster. As Marylou described her experience, after a short
time on the job she discovered that the foundation was making
many hypocritical and inept decisions. When she tried to push the
organization to live up to its official goals, she met with indifference and outright hostility.

At the time that she talked to me, Marylou was trying to resolve
a painful dilemma. The foundation had offered her a six-month
extension, and Marylou was agonizing over her decision. Should she
continue to push the foundation toward its lofty goals and suffer the
pain of its hostility and foot dragging, or seek another position in a
"better" organization? Eventually, Marylou decided to move to a social service agency, which she believed held itself to higher standards
of integrity and compassion.

About four months later, I received another call from Marylou.
By this time, she had discovered that the agency was really no better
than the foundation. Again, Marylou felt alienated. Again, she found
herself—in her view—acting as the conscience of the organization.

You can guess the rest. Several years later, the local newspaper
ran a story about the conflict between a nearby low-income neighborhood, home to a small group of ethnic minorities, and a local
private school, which was threatening to displace the community
members. And there was Marylou, leading the charge. Although
her ethnic background was different from her neighbors', she had
chosen to live in their midst to symbolize her commitment to their
cause. As we might imagine, it was Marylou who, incensed at the
school's plan to demolish the community, mobilized her neighbors
to fight their impending ouster. This time little David beat Goliath,
successfully fending off the private school, its feisty president, and
a retinue of lawyers.

I often think of Marylou with her indomitable spirit and
admirable devotion to the needs of others, trying to push every
organization she encounters to move to the synergistic level we

discussed in Chapter Nine. She will probably go through life seeking organizations whose causes she believes in but whose reality will fall somewhat short—at least without her help.

Here the issue is not so much a lack of fit between Marylou's specific achieving styles profile and that of the organizations she joins. It seems that Marylou naturally zeros in on that vulnerable point at which the organization could, or in her view should, move on to the level where the important synergistic effects of the Connective Leadership Model come into play. Because she gravitates toward the role of gadfly, it is highly unlikely that Marylou will receive the formal promotions and rewards of the organizations she tries to change. Nonetheless, I suspect that Marylou probably feels adequately rewarded by the respect and affection she earns from her sympathetic but less assertive co-workers and from the larger community that applauds her altruistic determination.

Nonconformists Within the Organization: Mavericks and Radicals

Not all individuals with divergent profiles end up leaving their organizations. In fact, some organizations view a sprinkling of nonconformists as useful sources of criticism and creativity. IBM in its earlier days did that. The younger Thomas Watson is said to have once read an essay by Kierkegaard about the wild ducks of Denmark. When the ducks migrated in, many local people fed and nurtured them so well that many of them did not migrate out again. Well fed and cared for, they became tame. But a few ducks could not be tamed. They always followed their instincts, migrating out when the time came. Watson, impressed with what he had read, decided that IBM needed some untamable "wild ducks," people who could not be tamed into quiescence by fat organizational rewards. The story goes that Watson decided to salt the whole organization with a few such wild ducks. To help do so, he established the IBM Fellows program, a program which grants a few outstanding individuals the freedom to do whatever they please, without organizational control.

In the IBM case, the organization bestowed special symbolic rewards. In other situations, informal rewards such as colleagues' respect for their wisdom or integrity may be sufficient recognition for those whose achieving styles deviate from the organizational culture yet contribute to its welfare.

Other individuals, or even whole groups, whose achieving styles are radically different from the organization's may see themselves as the "house radicals" or mavericks. Sometimes, these mavericks may be regarded simply as troublemakers or egocentric *enfants terribles*. At other moments in the organization's (or larger society's) history, such individualists may be openly admired as heroes. Their rebellion against authority may blaze an achieving styles trail that others would like to follow if only they dared.

One more important point here: some individualists understand that reshaping themselves to conform to the organization's norms would be both undesirable and futile. They recognize that remolding themselves in the organization's image would drain their two most valuable possessions: their creativity and their integrity.

Some Consequences for the Organization

The organization, no less than its individual members, faces choices when mismatches exist between individuals' achieving styles and the organization's culture. One of these choices concerns whether the organization should or should not strive to eliminate such differences. What are the prices and prizes of tolerating nonconforming individuals and small groups? Alternatively, what is the cost/benefit ratio for nurturing conformists?

Conformity, whether in achieving styles or other aspects of group behavior, encourages organizational stability. It helps keep chaos in check. Departures from traditional ways of thinking and doing can threaten tightly controlled, homogeneous organizations. The organization, through its cadre of conforming members, can be counted upon to behave in expected ways, providing predictable services and products. In such organizations, leadership succession may be relatively smooth because the criteria and mechanisms for succession are clear, and potential candidates abound.

On the other hand, organizations that reinforce consistent patterns of achieving styles may be less tolerant of novel ideas. Such conformity-demanding organizations would also be courting the even more serious danger of banishing creativity in order to eliminate disorder.

Encouraging the valuable individual whose achieving styles profile doesn't fit the organization's is a complex task. Perhaps connective leaders, who understand the strengths an organization gains from diversity, can help the creative nonconformist find an organizational niche. Better still, let them create a sheltered niche, from which both the nonconformist and the organization may reap rich dividends in creative actions.

Beyond paying a high price in creativity, conformity-seeking organizations run other serious risks. Organizations that ignore the warnings of those who view the world through other glasses do so at their peril. Those individuals may be the only ones able to foresee an impending crisis or a new opportunity. Their divergent profiles, when accepted, serve as an organizational shield against a "groupthink" mentality.[23]

Over time in any organization, cultural inertia sets in. The culture remains deeply rooted, but the individual members and the external environment move toward a newer reality. As organizational tensions, including those generated by diversity and interdependence, fragment the cultures of organizations, leaders need new conceptual tools for handling the problem. An explicit exploration of these gaps can lead to a reevaluation of just which styles are wanted by both the organization and its members. Organizations may then find ways to make room for the Marylous of the world, respecting their contributions and benefiting from their perspectives.

Stage 3 presents leaders with impressive challenges, as we have enumerated in the first section of this chapter. The concept of connective leadership might give us a leg up on these challenges—if organizations can fold such leadership into their structures.

Research findings indicate that connective leadership is slowly seeping into the American corporate workplace. Data on more than five thousand corporate managers reveal that they have some distance to go to catch up with entrepreneurs (who seem to have the makings for connective leadership, if only their unremitting focus on their own visions can be enlarged).

Instrumental action is gaining very slowly. The data also hold a surprise about the classic Stage 2 favorite, competition. It is losing ground in corporate management, especially among women.

Perceptive leaders can learn much from assessing the achieving style profiles of organizations themselves, above and beyond (but also in interaction with) those of individuals. The discontinuities between organizational and individual styles have hidden benefits as well as more obvious costs. These complex discontinuities, some reflecting diversity and differences, challenge leaders to manage with creativity and style. In the next chapter, we look at how female leaders meet these and other organizational challenges.

Chapter Eleven

Women Leaders

An Oxymoron? Or Does Gender Make a Difference?

The Punic Wars left a large part of the business of the city in the hands of women. They managed.
JESSIE BERNARD[1]

In Part One of this book, I talked about the American leadership images that represent our ego ideal, that is, an ideal construct of what we all *would* be if only we could. That ego ideal, I have suggested, draws on a very limited set of behaviors that we now recognize as the direct achieving styles.

These direct styles emphasize power, competition, self-reliance, and a belief in one's own abilities. They also stress mastery and creativity, along with rigorous internalized standards of excellence. For many people, these qualities virtually define leadership. They also closely mirror our traditional notion of masculinity. This association of leadership with masculinity raises the question of how female leadership enters the picture.

Only recently has female leadership begun to shed the onus of oxymoron. A compendium of leadership research[2] concludes that there are no consistent differences between men and women in leadership traits or effectiveness, although different contexts may trigger or suppress female leadership.[3,4] Many studies suggest that the leadership behaviors of women and men in similar situations are virtually impossible to differentiate from one another.[5,6] A more recent meta-analysis of 162 studies of gender differences among leaders, however, concluded that women were more likely than men to share decision making and lead collaboratively.[7]

Some research on female leadership suggests that the nature of the task may make a difference. One review of differences in leadership between men and women reported that groups engaged in creative tasks do better when led by a woman.[8]

Other research indicates that even when male and female leaders act similarly, they tend to be evaluated differently, with men often being rated as more effective than women.[9,10,11] A review of more than eight hundred research reports on female leadership drew several conclusions:

- Beliefs and attitudes about women in leadership roles have gradually begun to change
- Despite enduring stereotypes, few behavioral differences can be consistently documented
- Perceptions about women's effectiveness as leaders are mixed and conflicting
- Differences in subordinates' perceptions of male and female leaders show up much more in laboratory simulations than in real-life organizations, where associates' ongoing relationships with women leaders penetrate the mists of stereotypes.[12]

Recent decades have so transformed the social and political context of women's leadership that one scholar recommends simply discounting most of the earlier studies of sex differences in leadership.[13] In this chapter, we first trace the recent shifts in female leadership patterns. We then turn to some current examples of female political and corporate leaders in the United States and abroad. Finally, to discern the underlying behavioral dynamics, we present our research findings on the achieving styles of more than five thousand men and women in the corporate world.

The Connective Leadership Model suggests some new avenues of exploration into the nature of female leadership. The association of the direct styles with "masculine" qualities raises the question of whether women prefer achievement behaviors represented by the other segments of the model. If so, might female leaders have something distinctive to offer in the connective era? Would their preferred styles fill out the complement of strategies that connective leaders need? Or are female leaders in reality not so very different from their male counterparts? This chapter explores these issues.

Women as the Embedded "Other"

Female leadership holds special relevance for the twenty-first century. The reasons for this are tied to the essential issues of interdependency and diversity. For generations, women have lived in *embedded* roles, roles intimately interwoven into the warp and woof of the social context. By their very embeddedness, women serve as links between other roles, between generations, between institutions, between the public and private domains.

Within the family, women join rivalrous siblings to one another, to indulgent parents and doting grandparents, as well as to a network of cousins, aunts, and uncles. Women reach beyond the private arena of the family to connect children and parents not only to school and church but to the larger community as well. As psychiatrist Jean Baker Miller has argued, women's lives are structured by connectedness and relationships.[14] Their roles form the nodes in the larger net that we recognize as the interdependent social fabric. Interdependence is second nature to women.

Still, as Simone de Beauvoir understood so well, women have always been the "Other."[15] In a world whose institutions were shaped by men to accommodate men (my own mother regularly claimed, "It's a man's world"), women have clearly represented the diversity factor. Where women's sexuality was seen as their most prominent attraction, it was celebrated: *vive la différence.* Yet more recently, when this disparity was used to plead special needs (for flextime in the workplace, parental leave, or other measures), it has sparked resistance and anger.

The contemporary resurgence of the women's movement has brought a sharpened sense of individuation, independence, and legitimation to women's differentness. Growing pride in their "difference" and determination to demand their fair share of society's bounty have thrust women into the vortex of the social storm. Their quest for acceptance of their diversity has been the template for similar claims by other minorities across a broad spectrum of diversity. Women have frequently joined forces with other diverse

groups to confront the pressures arising from their common position as "others."

Consequently, women are no newcomers to the complications
generated by interdependence and diversity. Their experiences,
for better or worse, put them uniquely in sync with the complexities of a Stage 3 world. As such, women represent an important
source of potential leadership.

Female Leadership in the Postwar Period

The transition from Stage 2 to Stage 3 has been presaged by the
emergence of female leaders in the years since World War II. The
war became a watershed on the domestic front as well as in international affairs. During the war, American women made unprecedented inroads into the paid labor force. Not only did more
women than ever before enter standard female occupations, but
they also gained access to traditionally male jobs, particularly in
defense plants churning out planes, tanks, and other wartime
armaments.[16] In unpublicized but unambiguous military roles,
women also flew convoys and decoded enemy communications
close to the front lines.[17]

With the approach of demobilization, though, women would be
elbowed aside for returning veterans, despite numerous surveys
attesting to their desire to continue working. In fact, one United
Auto Workers' (UAW) survey found that 85 percent of their employed female members preferred to continue working in the postwar period. Moreover, 98.5 percent of the single women, 100
percent of the widows, and 68.7 percent of the married women in
the UAW study reported they would continue to work outside the
home "if a job were available."[18] Nevertheless, as early as August 1944,

a disproportionate number of female employees were being laid
off. In aircraft parts plants for example, although women
amounted to 42.2 percent of the total working population, they
constituted 60.2 percent of the workers laid off. In the aircraft
engine plants, while women were 39.2 percent of the workers
employed, they were 86 percent of the layoffs. In the truck and
agricultural implements industry, women were 13.1 percent of the
work force, but 51.6 percent of the layoffs.[19]

Historians who reviewed the records of grievances preserved at the Labor and Urban Affairs Archives at Wayne State University concluded that "for the most part women war workers *expected* and *did not especially resent* being laid off as cutbacks marked the end of the war. What they did resent and what several filed grievances against was that they were not rehired in accordance with their perceived seniority when the plant was reconverted to postwar production, sometimes as early as one or two years later."[20]

In the Baltimore shipyards, union bosses promised women they would be rehired if they patriotically relinquished their high-paying jobs to returning servicemen.[21] Those who complied learned later that the promise would never be kept. The mass media urged women to return home to hearth and husband.

The disarmament period introduced an extraordinary era of togetherness that wrapped women in a domestic cocoon. Their leadership talents were corralled within the family arena, or at best within volunteer activities. Not until the late 1970s did economists even begin to measure the considerable contribution women's volunteer activities made to the nation's economy.

For much of the postwar period, women remained a rarity in leadership positions, both in corporate boardrooms and congressional corridors. Scant attention was paid to women's invisibility or the limited leadership opportunities reflected by that exclusion. A century earlier, the abolitionist movement had sensitized women to the importance of suffrage; now it took women's experience in the civil rights movement to draw their attention to their own social condition. In 1963, just as women were beginning to question the limitations in their own lives, Betty Friedan's landmark book *The Feminine Mystique* catalyzed a period of consciousness raising and political activity for women's rights.[22]

The next three decades witnessed a torrent of scholarly and polemical work that fueled feminist political action. The scarcity of women in leadership positions gradually became a very hot topic. "Alas," the establishment responded, as it had to so many other minorities, "there simply are no women with the proper credentials for leadership." The pipeline was alleged to be empty.

The educational system, the tributary along which young males were navigated into positions of power and prominence, had by contrast served as a white-water rapids for women. As late as midcentury, only 20 percent of American college graduates were women. Even they, however, were underrepresented at the higher levels of the corporate, political, and academic worlds. By 1960, female lawyers numbered barely 7,500, or 3.3 percent of the entire field. Nationwide, there were 16,000 female physicians, or 6.8 percent of the medical profession, and only 7,400 female engineers (0.9 percent).[23] Women held less than 4 percent of congressional seats, with most inheriting their roles as political widows. Women leaders were still perceived as anomalies.[24]

Those women who managed to enter the charmed circle of male leadership on their own, such as Ukrainian-born and Milwaukee-educated Golda Meir, paid the price in terms of their feminine image. Israeli prime minister Ben Gurion, unwittingly combining praise and denigration, described Golda Meir as "the only real man in my cabinet." Meir subsequently served as Israel's first and only female prime minister. Not surprisingly, like her male contemporaries, she used Stage 2 strategies with authority.

Attitudes toward female leadership remained generally negative during the early postwar decades. Study after study reported an unwillingness among both men and women to work for female bosses. Even when resistance to women bosses was not explicit, researchers reported, descriptions of ideal managers and male personality traits coincided while differing dramatically from those of females.[25] In 1972, a national survey of attitudes toward male and female managers revealed that the five personal characteristics of corporate leaders most valued by Americans were analytical ability, decisiveness, consistency, objectivity, and emotional stability—all qualities stereotypically associated with masculinity.[26]

Several laboratory studies of male college students in the 1950s indirectly but pervasively influenced attitudes toward women in leadership roles. Harvard psychologist Robert F. Bales studied how male college students behaved in laboratory task groups.[27] In the Laboratory of Social Relations at Harvard, Bales and Slater[28] observed that two types of leaders emerged in these all-male experiments: the "idea man" or task leader, who helped members focus on the group's tasks, and the "best-liked man" or socioemotional leader, who bound up the emotional wounds commonly inflicted by the work group.

Extrapolating from these laboratory findings on male undergraduates to men's and women's family roles, Harvard sociologist

Talcott Parsons theorized that men acted as task leaders, women as socioemotional leaders.[29] Parsons' extrapolation was simple and structural: men would be the breadwinners, and women would attend to the emotional needs of the family. In this way, Parsons reasoned, disagreeable competition between men and women would be avoided.

This interpretation, consonant with prevailing sex-role stereotypes, jelled into social science dogma. As such, it exerted an influence far beyond the halls of academe. Later studies of male and female behavior in *same sex* groups, however, failed to reveal any differences between men and women subjects in the number of task-oriented behaviors they displayed.[30]

That women's task-oriented behavior in all-female groups looked no different than the behavior of men in all-male groups was puzzling, given observed differences between men and women in mixed-sex groups. Some analysts later interpreted this as evidence that women could in fact perform leadership tasks, but that they had been raised to stifle such "unfeminine" behavior while in the presence of men. This explanation fit with sociologist Mirra Komarovsky's[31] work on female college students, which reported in 1953 that young women deliberately acted helpless and lost athletic competitions to young men so as to protect their romantic possibilities.

A host of nonlaboratory studies focusing on men and women leaders in comparable positions and engaged in similar activities failed to identify differences between the sexes in leader effectiveness, motivation, personality, or leadership styles.[32] Still, some studies suggested that successful female managers tend to exhibit more masculine or androgynous behavior.[33] Contemporary researchers Jan Grant[34] and Ann Gregory[35] have attributed those results to successful female managers' emulating male, rather than female, role models.

A somewhat confusing picture emerged from such research. On average, women were said to exhibit different preferences than men, leaning toward the socioemotional style associated with femininity. At the same time, those women who, like Golda Meir, did achieve leadership positions in a predominantly male environment were said to exhibit "masculine" leadership tendencies. They were the exceptions who conveniently proved the rule—simultaneously vindicating traditional notions of leadership and ingrained skepticism about the "typical" woman's ability to fill a leadership role. Yet the study of women leaders *within* female groups hinted that perhaps the gender difference was really a difference in social context.

Two decades of work by scholars, activists, and policy makers have begun to make some discernible differences in the way we think about women leaders. In a cross-generational study of female leaders who shaped the American women's movement, Astin and Leland concluded that these leaders viewed power and leadership through a different lens than did men and earlier women leaders.[36] They believed in collective action based on empowering others, largely by creating and working through networks. The female leaders acknowledged the support of other women with whom they worked toward mutual goals. For these female leaders, power was perceived as energy—not control—generated and shared with others. Astin and Leland identified the processes these leaders used to initiate revolutionary social change: "They identified problems and accepted complexity as both a challenge and an opportunity. They developed a network of like-minded people and worked together within and outside the system to transform it. Their specific qualities and strategies emphasize clarity of value, listening to and empowering others, and doing one's homework. Their styles rely greatly on self-awareness and interpersonal and communication skills."[37]

In this description we hear echoes of what we call the collaborative, contributory, and vicarious styles, along with conscious use of all the instrumental strategies. This picture provides a significant contrast to the direct styles and the individualism associated with Stage 2 leadership. But is this really a gender difference, or is something else happening here? We can explore that question by turning to an examination of some recent female leaders.

Portraits of Recent Female Leaders

In recent decades, political activism and consciousness raising have dismantled many serious barriers to female leadership. Circumstances have changed sufficiently to promote a small but respectable number of women to visible leadership positions in a number of arenas. In the United States, we have witnessed Geraldine Ferraro run on a major party's presidential ticket and Sandra Day O'Connor and

Ruth Bader Ginsburg take seats on the U.S. Supreme Court. Meanwhile, a hardy crop of female executives and entrepreneurs has appeared in the corporate and not-for-profit worlds.

In the United States, the greatest gains in female employment since 1983 have come in managerial and professional occupations. By 1991, the number of women employed as executives, administrators, and managers had climbed to an all-time high of 6,064,000, representing 42 percent of people in those fields and a 9 percent increase since 1983. American women of color have also made headway, but their gains have occurred more slowly. Only 1 or 2 percent of senior, executive-level officers are women, but limited samples from Fortune 500 companies reveal that 83 percent of those women executives were at the vice-presidential level or above. Women entrepreneurs have been making their mark as well, with a 57 percent increase in the number of women-owned businesses from 1982 to 1987.[38] These American figures are far more optimistic than international statistics. The International Labor Organization indicates that women hold only 14 percent of managerial and executive jobs around the world.[39]

On the international stage, an increasing number of first-time female heads of state have appeared. Iceland, Ireland, Nicaragua, and Sri Lanka have elected female presidents, and as of this writing women are serving as prime ministers in Norway, Pakistan, Rwanda, and Sri Lanka. Some female leaders, including India's Indira Gandhi, the Philippines' Corazon Aquino, and France's Edith Cresson, had limited success in top national leadership roles. In Pakistan, Benazir Bhutto has clearly had her ups and downs, and Tansu Cillar has been in and out of the Turkish prime ministership several times. Some female heads of state, like Kim Campbell in Canada, have not lasted very long.

Nonetheless, between 1988 and 1995 the number of women in parliaments worldwide dipped 7 percent, according to the Inter-Parliamentary Union. This drop is attributed largely to the decrease in female parliamentarians among former Soviet bloc countries, where the communist system of quotas for women has been eliminated in the post–Cold War era.[40]

What are these twentieth-century women leaders like? What kinds of achieving styles do they favor? Are we any more likely to find connective leaders in their midst than among male leaders?

Political Leaders

Among female political leaders, the results are mixed at best. Some, like Margaret Thatcher, exhibited direct achieving styles even more extreme than those of their male colleagues.[41] Others, like Cory Aquino, initially attempted more connective strategies, but lacking support they soon fell back into the old, familiar, direct mold of their male counterparts. A few less well known potential female leaders have gone on to blaze new trails.

British Prime Minister Margaret Thatcher

Few would dispute that Great Britain's first female prime minister, Margaret Thatcher, is a legend in her own right. The longest-tenured British prime minister of the twentieth century, Thatcher crafted a political era that bore her unmistakable stamp. Even after her rout from office, Thatcher has continued to influence British political events from behind—and sometimes still in front of—the scene.[42]

Convinced that Thatcher's unpopularity would cost the party the national election, the Tories engineered a palace coup. Ironically, after her ouster, the party regulars were forced to enlist Thatcher's help to shore up the vulnerable candidacy of her successor, John Major. In the final days of a sagging campaign, Thatcher vigorously stumped for Major's election. Many credited Major's victory to Thatcher's enduring ability to persuade constituents.

Although Thatcher later freely and publicly criticized her successor's performance, she unexpectedly offered her support in a gesture that many felt rescued Major from a vote of no confidence. Nonetheless, in her autobiography, Thatcher was not beyond assailing Major as someone ill at ease with "large ideas."[43]

How would we characterize Margaret Thatcher in terms of achieving styles? Is she a connective leader? Hardly. In fact, Thatcher more closely resembles the archetype of the Stage 2 leader, one who takes control, issues orders, "gets the facts, and takes the decision." In a post–prime ministerial TV interview with Barbara Walters aired in the United States, Thatcher readily revealed her own Stage 2 perspective when she insisted upon the "insurmountable" differences, rather than the common ground, among members of the European Economic Community. When Walters asked the former prime minister if she still felt her opposition to a common currency among the European Union nations had been warranted, Thatcher replied, "I was totally, totally correct. It is inconceivable that countries so different as the European nations involved could use a system that works beautifully in the United States." Thatcher's own words eloquently underscore her Stage 2 emphasis on the differences, rather than the similarities, among potential members of an interdependent alliance.

From its opening chapters, Thatcher's autobiography suggests her preference for the direct styles, power, competition, and solo action. In her first twenty-four hours as prime minister, Thatcher recalls, she viewed choosing her cabinet as "one of the most important ways in which a prime minister can exercise power over the whole conduct of government."[44] She comments, with considerable regret, on the political constraints under which her choices necessarily were made. More, not less, power would have suited her.

In numerous passages in the autobiography, Thatcher reveals the primacy she accords winning. She recalls with special fondness a few lines from a speech given by her husband, Denis Thatcher: "The desire to win is born in most of us. The will to win is a matter of training. The manner of winning is a matter of honor."[45]

Again and again, Mrs. Thatcher expresses her preference for autonomy, a mark of the intrinsic and power styles. Unlike even many Stage 2 leaders, Thatcher seems to welcome the loneliness at the top that accompanies power, accepting isolation as a natural companion to power and autonomy. She writes, "Being prime minister is a lonely job. In a sense, it ought to be: you cannot lead from the crowd."[46]

Indian Prime Minister Indira Gandhi

Indira Gandhi, the first female prime minister of India and leader of the Congress Party, also exemplified a Stage 2 approach. During the Cold War, Gandhi opted for neutrality at best; at worst, she played off the United States and the Soviet Union against one another to enhance her own position.

Initially, Gandhi seemed to be following in the political footsteps of her father, Jawaharlal Nehru, the first democratically elected Indian prime minister. When Gandhi took over the prime ministership in 1966, it soon became evident that she was forging her own path.

Many hailed Gandhi's early political success in permanently splitting the Congress Party, a coalition of "old-line Congress king-makers" and state politicians her father had worked a lifetime to forge. She demonstrated diplomatic skill and military might by intervening in the 1971 Pakistani civil war, which ultimately resulted in the founding of Bangladesh. This action also signaled India's position as the primary military presence in South Asia. Still, Gandhi's Stage 2 leadership ultimately crippled her efforts on behalf of Indian democracy and undermined her international legacy. The leader of more than 700 million Indian citizens for over fifteen years (1966–1977 and 1980–1984), eventually Gandhi was turned out of office after adopting authoritarian "emergency" powers, which she used to run the country as a dictatorship from 1975 to 1977.

The alleged emergency resulted from a court judgment against Gandhi for election fraud. Refusing to surrender her political position, Gandhi assumed dictatorial powers: invalidating the court ruling against her, imprisoning thousands of her political opponents, muzzling the press, and undercutting the independent Indian judiciary. These and other authoritarian abuses ultimately led to her political defeat in 1977.

In her second term of office, from 1980 to 1984, Gandhi once more exhibited a penchant for imperious leadership, power, and manipulation. A recent biographer describes Gandhi as the opposite of her father, seeking confrontation rather than consensus, seeing disloyalty and crushing it where others might have seen diversity and encouraged it.[47]

During the early 1980s, Prime Minister Gandhi instituted severe measures to control population growth. When her handling of a water-rights dispute among Punjabi Sikhs escalated the problem into a full-scale rebellion, Gandhi ultimately quashed the protest by a bloody military attack on the Sikhs' sacred Golden Temple. Many political observers attribute Gandhi's subsequent assassination by two of her bodyguards, both Sikhs, to the disastrous Golden Temple massacre.

Irish President Mary Robinson

The leadership behavior of Irish president Mary Robinson offers an example of a female leader acting connectively and being sharply criticized by followers stuck in a Stage 2 quagmire. Robinson reached out in quick succession first to Britain's Queen Elizabeth and then to Irish Republican Army spokesperson Gerry Adams, president of Sinn Fein. This connective action incited the ire of leading Unionists, as well as political leaders in London and Dublin.

Unfazed by a blistering denunciation from co-patriots, as well as from British Prime Minister Major, President Robinson declared, "I have come here [to West Belfast] because I have already had indications of the community's vitality, self-development, and spirit and strength. This is my opportunity to come to listen, to see and to learn, and to value what you have here in this community in West Belfast."[48]

Much to the chagrin of her critics, Robinson focused on the special gifts of the opposing constituencies, rather than on the gulfs between them. Regretting that "people saw West Belfast entirely in political terms," Robinson pronounced her own assessment: "There is a very resourceful, witty, warm, loving, caring community, and I saw that in a very real sense."[49] Despite the criticism, Robinson's connective outreach was the model for the subsequent historic rapprochement between Britain and Northern Ireland.

Bulgaria's Elena Lagadinova

Elena Atanassova Lagadinova, former member of Parliament and president of the Committee of the Movement of Bulgarian Women, practiced connective leadership long before the concept had a name. An agrobiologist and plant geneticist by training, the young researcher was initially in her element studying slides and writing scientific papers. Despite her celebrity as an adolescent guerrilla partisan during World War II, she unpretentiously followed her first love: science.

Convinced that they needed both her people skills and her popularity, the Bulgarian Communist Party approached Lagadinova to run for a parliamentary seat in 1965, a few years after she received her doctorate. Lagadinova described how she cried for days at the thought of giving up her beloved science. Despite her personal preference for an academic career, the young scientist reluctantly started a new life that would take her on a leadership journey for more than two decades.

Lagadinova grew up amid family values of patriotism and dedication to communist ideals. Her father had been a respected Bulgarian Communist Party member. Her mother had died in 1934, when Elena was barely four years old. The preadolescent Lagadinova, along with her father and three brothers, had joined the guerrilla movement, working with the underground throughout the grim days of World War II. Her experience with the Nazi enemy revealed the dark side of leadership to the young patriot. The Fascist militia retaliated for her family's guerrilla activities by torching their home. Later, the Nazis tortured and killed her second elder brother. Yet even that personal trauma did not stop the twelve-year-old from riding on horseback to deliver crucial messages to the Bulgarian resistance fighters.

Drawn reluctantly into the Communist Party leadership, Lagadinova quickly earned the respect of her peers. By 1966, she had entered Parliament. In 1968, Lagadinova was elected president of the Committee of the Movement of Bulgarian Women, a post she held for the next two decades.

I first met Elena Lagadinova in Sofia in 1980, at a conference cosponsored by the U.S. National Science Foundation. The Cold War was still icy, but Lagadinova showed little patience for political impediments to collaboration. With pragmatic enthusiasm, she assured the conferees, "Do not worry about ideology and government barriers. The work we have to do for women in both of our countries is too important for that. We shall manage together!" The skeptical American visitors, initially on guard against communist manipulation, soon learned her word was as true as her vision.

The second time I met Lagadinova was in 1985, during the United Nations Conference on the Status of Women, in Nairobi. There, the conference delegates elected Lagadinova rapporteur, testimony to how much she was esteemed by an immense international network of policy makers, political activists, and academics.

Almost immediately, a crisis sparked by a shortage of hotel rooms threatened to send many of the nongovernmental organization (NGO) representatives packing. Lagadinova quietly intervened. A master of connective leadership, she did her work without fanfare, connecting the representatives of the beleaguered delegates with conference officials and other key decision makers who could smooth the way. Once a resolution had been reached,

Lagadinova happily joined the former antagonists—both the Kenyan government minister who had spearheaded the room ousters and the two spokespeople for the homeless delegates—in a reconciliation lunch.

In the summer of 1987, I found myself in Sofia for a second visit, this time as a consultant to the Ministry of Science and Technology, as well as the Women's Committee. Elena Lagadinova, it turned out, was now my official host. Although every minute of my formal schedule was full, that didn't constrain my energetic host, who kept adding "just one more appointment" to my schedule. The new appointments ranged from government ministers to poets, artists, and priests.

Late one morning, after several meetings, Lagadinova announced that the Bulgarian prelate, a member of the Bulgarian Orthodox Church leadership, was expecting us at two o'clock. That puzzled me, given the party's and state's official suppression of the church. Within the hour, she announced that the prelate wanted us to come even earlier to meet the papal nuncio, who was also arriving from Rome. This unlikely set of connections was typical of Lagadinova: bringing together a Communist Party leader, the spiritual leader of the Bulgarian Orthodox Church, a senior representative of the Roman Catholic Church, and an American professor.

The prelate's explanation dispelled some of the mystery surrounding his connection to Lagadinova. Although religion was anathema to the party, Lagadinova had empathized with the plight of young Orthodox priests who clung to their religious vows. They knew her as a friend for whom human connections loomed much larger than party directives. Quietly, as a young party functionary, she responded to their pleas for help. The prelate was one of those who, as a priest many years before, had sought her help and advice. Over the years their friendship had grown quietly despite official party disapproval.

One last vignette about Lagadinova illustrates how heavy a price can be paid by connective leaders in a Stage 2 milieu.

Irrevocably committed to humanistic ideals that knew no party labels, Lagadinova ran into conflict with leaders from party and state after the November 10, 1989, political change. In the waning days of Bulgarian Communist rule, party and state officials mounted a campaign to force Bulgarian citizens of various ethnic backgrounds to take Bulgarian names. After the political transition, the issue heated up once again. Lagadinova was running into conflict with certain leaders from the party and state about various aspects of the change. One of the conflicts revolved around the party's demand for a new change of names among the ethnic Turkish-speaking Bulgarians—changing Arabic names to Bulgarian or vice versa, Bulgarian names back to Turkish. Lagadinova denounced the intervention, taking a stand in favor of personal liberties. She insisted that it was up to the individual to decide whether to have a Bulgarian or a Turkish name: "What an absurd idea for people to have to give up their own names, be they Bulgarian or Turkish! We are people proud of our heritage. For centuries Christian Bulgarians, Mohammedan Bulgarians, Bulgarian Muslims, and Bulgarian Turks have lived and worked in good neighborly relations. Why can't they continue to live and work together as before?"

In a 1995 letter, Lagadinova described her role in the post-November discussions:

At that time, some internal forces and also some external interested parties brought forward anew the issue of name changes which had by that time already abated. The aim was to charge the situation further, to cause destabilization through inciting antagonistic feelings and . . . conflicts in society. [This was attempted] through the injection of additional tension between people in the regions where Greek Orthodox Bulgarians and Moslem Bulgarians (the ethnic group of Turkish-speaking Bulgarians, and so-called Mohammedans) have lived for decades in full harmony. The issue was brought to the surface of the tide sharply, aggressively, contrary to the norms of civil behavior, although by that time many of these people had voluntarily already taken their Bulgarian names and some even had turned to Christianity.

So it was at that time that in the course of a discussion with the Party leadership I declared myself against any administrative intervention in this very delicate and intimate matter. What name would one choose to bear—a Turkish or a Bulgarian one—should be an issue of personal aspirations and personal motivation. We have had enough of self-interested and careeristic manipulation of this issue by certain politicians at the expense of this part of Bulgarian citizens.

Of course, after the change at the end of 1989, I being consistent in my convictions and deeds, demanded prompt action, however not chaotic, not an unweighed . . . action with grave and irreversible consequences in the future. Prompt action was needed on many of the issues concerning the approach, methods, goals, etc. Naturally, I ran into conflict with the leaders of the Party and the State. I became "inconvenient," and I immediately submitted my documents for retirement.[50]

Like other authentic leaders, Lagadinova sacrificed her career on the altar of an ideal, in this case a connective commitment to diversity amidst interdependence. In the bitter aftermath of this struggle, Lagadinova lives quietly with her husband outside the political spotlight.

This is an often-repeated scene. Connective leaders reach out. Their Stage 2 comrades and constituents don't get it.

Corporate Leaders: Private and Third Sector

Over the last two decades, female corporate leaders have emerged in increasing numbers, despite the barriers that ordinarily have kept women from the boardroom. Many of these new corporate women, however, are quite indistinguishable from their male counterparts in their conventional leadership styles.

Within this select group, Katherine Graham, CEO of the *Washington Post,* learned the hard way to be a direct-achieving leader, when the death of her publisher husband unexpectedly thrust her into the leadership role. A recent biography details her transformation from a vicarious, if intimidated, housewife, into an entrusting (by default) neophyte publisher, to a competitive, power-driven CEO.[51] Estee Lauder, of cosmetics fame, as well as Donna Karan, whose design empire helps shape the American fashion industry, also come to mind as examples of female leaders who rely on the direct styles.

Are connective female leaders, then, the corporate exception rather than the rule? To explore that question, let us consider three other female leaders of large organizational enterprises.

Anita Roddick, The Body Shop

In earlier chapters, we met Anita Roddick, founder and CEO of The Body Shop, who has received enormous media attention.[52] Yet most of Roddick's analysts have focused on her "controversial" values and "unorthodox" business practices. Here, instead, we measure Roddick against our connective leadership benchmark.

The daughter of Italian immigrants to Great Britain, Roddick initially established her small company in 1976 as a means of supporting her family. She quickly determined that her organization would be guided by holistic principles. (Not coincidentally, that holistic approach, along with a concern for caring and contributing to others, was a cornerstone of the women's movement in the sixties and seventies.[53]) As Roddick describes it,

> We took a holistic view of business, one in which we saw ourselves not just as creators of profits for shareholders, but as a force for good, working for the welfare of our staff, for the community and ultimately for the future of the planet itself. . . . We believed that it was possible to shift from a value system of ever-increasing profits to one in which core values were concerned with human and social issues and were founded on feminine values like love and care.[54]

Roddick's dedication to larger social issues does not insulate her from hard economic realities. As she herself indicated: "It is, of course, the luxury of our healthy earnings that allows us to pursue an aggressive policy of social and environmental activism. Although we [Roddick and her husband, Gordon] wholeheartedly support all our campaigning, we would never sanction any of it if we could not afford it, or if it somehow endangered the future prosperity of the company."[55]

Nor does Roddick's holistic approach mean that she doesn't set high expectations for her employees, her franchisees, and their staffs. Some of them call themselves "the Grateful Dead," that is, grateful to Anita, but dead from working so hard.[56] We hear the echoes of a self-confident leader's entrusting style, a leader whose high standards push her constituents to heights beyond their own expectations. Corporate lunchroom posters urge The Body Shop workers to "Think Frivolously" and "Break the Rules." It's hard to imagine not feeling a surge of creativity when the company itself is urging employees to shatter traditional thought patterns.

Roddick imbues the corporate culture with her own personal values. She claims she is looking for the "modern-day equivalent of those Quakers whose successful businesses made money because they offered honest products, treated their people decently, worked hard, spent honestly, saved honestly, gave honest value for money, put back more than they took out, and told no lies."[57] This is a tall intrinsic order, but one that Roddick consistently tries to fill.

Although Roddick has a clear personal vision and core values—intrinsic qualities—she also has the connective capacity to recognize fully the values dear to others, whether or not they coincide with her own. Her ability to link her own vision with those of people she encounters is clearly captured in The Body Shop's policy of allowing every employee to devote four hours monthly to volunteer work furthering some social cause. The particular cause is of the individual employee's own choosing, but the volunteer work is performed on company time and paid for from company coffers. In the process, Roddick relies on her entrusting judgment that employees will carry out, and even enlarge, her vision beyond her own original expectations.

One afternoon during her visit to the Stanford Graduate School of Business, Roddick emphasized to me the need for moral leadership in the corporate world. She looks for leadership, she says, in "unexpected places," in ordinary people. Yet she laments that "we don't have a system for celebrating [moral leaders]. Any man or woman who sticks his or her head out like a giraffe isn't seen as a leader in the community. They're seen as an irritant, a revolutionary, maybe anarchic. Anyone who challenges the status quo or the sacred cows of business or education or all those institutions which are so moribund . . . is diminished and made silly or menial."[58]

With over thirteen hundred mostly franchised outlets in forty-five countries, Roddick doesn't just let nature take its own organizational course. For example, though franchisees have great autonomy, the need to bring a recognizable identity to The Body Shop stores worldwide required some degree of corporate control. To do this, The Body Shop head office requires that all stores act in a manner consistent with the company's environmental consciousness, including painting store interiors dark green. Eventually, Roddick also became concerned that allowing each store to select its own social campaigns was fragmenting both the company's image and energies. As a result, she decided that headquarters would determine which social issues were to be supported companywide. Corporate headquarters then would supply educational flyers and pamphlets for stores to distribute to its customers. But the company still maintains a hands-off policy regarding the choice of social and political issues to which individual employees devote their company-subsidized volunteer efforts.

Within the business community, Roddick is often perceived as a maverick. She earns this image rightfully because she consistently integrates her political and social values with her everyday work decisions. At Stanford, she shocked, delighted, and outraged various audiences with her views on power, shareholders, and even penises. She told one startled audience: "The trouble with society is the power of the penis."

In Roddick's view, part of the problem is the expectations the media have for leaders:

> Media, I think, are one of the greatest protagonists of diminishing the role of heroes and leadership in our society. . . . They'd be more comfortable if my husband would say it, but they are not comfortable in listening to me talk about corporate crimes or about empowerment or new paradigms of business. . . . It's a cynicism which pervades everything. It seems to me when you become outspoken, when you are altruistic in an environment that doesn't celebrate . . . humanity in any way, in which business has not played a compassionate role, the media do not know what to make of you as a leader.[59]

With the panache of a personal achiever, Roddick dresses and acts the part of the maverick. Letting her full head of dark curly hair escape in a thousand directions, Roddick refuses to "dress for success." Instead, her costume consists of oversized shirts, boots, blue jeans, and occasionally a skirt. Looking more like a flower child of the sixties than a corporate titan of the nineties, Roddick uses her own appearance as a constant embodiment of her values. Her physical persona, words, and actions underscore her commitments, deliberately personifying The Body Shop's values for customers, franchisees, staff, stakeholders, and media. From an achieving styles perspective, we would have to give Roddick high marks on the personal style, for using herself as an instrument to enlist a worldwide constituency, not only for her products but for the many causes she supports.

Roddick's connective inclinations can also be seen in her relations with Third World suppliers. Her Trading with Communities in Need initiative in Third World countries relies on genuinely collaborative relationships with contractors in developing countries, rather than simply donations from corporate profits. Other firms send manufacturing offshore in search of cheaper labor costs; Roddick deliberately takes an unusual approach. She looks for natural products and services that Third World groups can readily provide and then contracts to pay them at world-market rates. In collaborative arrangements, Roddick nurtures small working units, often family businesses, in the developing nations—or what she calls "the majority world."

Roddick spends almost half the year traveling, visiting stores, and scouting for natural products she can order from these majority-world entrepreneurs. She visits tropical rain forests and meets with indigenous, often tribal, experts, who share their knowledge of natural ingredients. Then she negotiates joint ventures between these Third World partners and The Body Shop. Roddick happily combines social and personal leadership strategies.

Fortunately for The Body Shop, this Stage 3 approach fits an even broader market segment of today's young, environmentally conscious shoppers than it did in the company's early years. The result: a balance sheet that records $338 million in annual sales.[60]

The media, dubious of corporate leaders who benefit financially while acting connectively, raise questions about The Body Shop's virtue. Controversy swirls around whether any of the company's ingredients has ever been tested on animals. Nonetheless, Roddick remains determined to prove that an organization can do well while doing good, can be connective as well as corporate. Using the full spectrum of achieving styles, Roddick doggedly works to connect her Stage 3 vision to her operations, her employees' and customers' vision to her own and hers to theirs, and her company's well-being to the good of a global society.

Marcy Carsey, The Carsey-Werner Company

Marcy Carsey is perhaps the most powerful low-profile female in the entertainment industry. As co-owner and executive producer of The Carsey-Werner Company, an independent production enterprise in Studio City, California, she has been described as "the most financially successful television producer in history."[61] This accolade actually underplays her achievements, which spread far beyond the financial end of the business.

In collaboration with partner Tom Werner, Carsey has produced a string of hit shows on network television, including *The Cosby Show, Roseanne, A Different World,* and *Grace Under Fire.* In an unprecedented achievement, Carsey-Werner swept the top three annual rankings in the 1988–89 season, with *Cosby* number one, *Roseanne* number two, and *A Different World* number three.

Carsey and Werner are probably recognized most for the quality, creativity, and artistic integrity of the productions that bear the Carsey-Werner imprimatur. The esteem in which they are held by the industry is reflected in the many awards they have won: the Emmy, the Golden Globe, the People's Choice Award, the NAACP Image Award, the Peabody, and the Humanitas Prize, plus a host of other awards for producing responsible television.

For Carsey, keenly attuned to a Stage 3 environment, diversity is something to be actively sought, not avoided. For her, diversity is the life blood of creativity:

> To me, there's always a force at work toward nondiversity that you constantly have to work against to achieve diversity. . . . Whom are you relying on to execute ideas, whom are you relying on to come up with ideas, whom are you relying on to feed off for yourself, to surround yourself with? There is always a push toward uniformity that we have to struggle against. . . . Most people's natural instinct is to hire people that they are familiar with, that sound like them, . . . that they can connect [with] somehow, in background or mindset or whatever. That is kind of a human nature thing, and you have to fight against that all the time in ourselves, as well as in the people whom we hire, who are then going to be hiring other people. [We try] to reach for the broadest spectrum of points of view and personalities and backgrounds.[62]

When Carsey doesn't find diversity, she creates it. As she explained further during an interview in her office in Studio City: "Bill Cosby taught us that if it doesn't exist, grow your own. If you can't find a writer who is of a different background or a different ethnic origin or a different gender, then the obvious choice for the show you're doing is to grow your own, train them yourself. Or find a playwright, for example. That's what we love doing: finding somebody from another endeavor, another medium. And if they're willing, [we] bring them into this and see if they can grow to love this form."

As a connective leader, Carsey understands the catalytic effect of bringing people together, of creating a collaborative enterprise in which people find creative expression. In running the business, she draws on the social style, using the antennae of an impresario to gather talented people around a common purpose; but Carsey also resonates to the intrinsic style's excitement about the creative task:

> I know I love running a business because I love gathering people together to do good stuff. Just the bare bones of it. I love the fact that people come together and bring their skills and work together. And something from nothing comes out of it, and everybody, hopefully, goes home feeling good about that. It's hard, and it's a struggle sometimes, but you always keep your eye on the goal. What do you want to do? What is this all about? It's about living gracefully, doing it gracefully. . . . And it's about the end result, which is, sometimes, as often as we can make it, wonderful television. And that, to me, is fabulous! Working with people you like—it's wonderful!

Despite her head-turning achievements, Carsey remains an unpretentious straight shooter. Unimpressed by power and posturing, Carsey's résumé and the company "brochure" reflect this unassuming attitude. Her official biography appears on a plain piece of paper, no letterhead, no graphic design.

She readily talks about her childhood in Weymouth, Massachusetts, where she and an older brother were raised by a father who worked in the shipyards and a mother who would have loved to have had a nonvolunteer job. In less than 125 words, the résumé paints Carsey's background in sparse, New England simplicity: from her undergraduate degree in English literature (cum laude) at the University of New Hampshire, to the establishment of her own production company in 1980. That start-up became The Carsey-Werner Company when Tom Werner became her partner the next year. The brochure is equally understated, three simple pages. In a world where hype is king, Carsey seems refreshingly unconcerned with image.

Carsey has the connective hang of things. She easily moves across styles, from intrinsic to power, to social, to entrusting, to collaborative action, and back again. She brims with the animation of an intrinsic achiever when she describes her work:

It's all just about the work that you do and the process by which you do it. The fun you have doing it, or the positive stuff you put out there by just doing it and failing and succeeding and failing and succeeding, and just doing it. I think it's all lovely!

Carsey's language reflects the cadence of the intrinsic style. Rigorous internalized standards, so central to intrinsic achievers, constitute the Carsey-Werner mission: for every show "to be worthy of its airtime." Words like *fun, excitement,* and *love* keep popping into her description of how she and Werner feel about their work:

. . . We love doing what we're doing. We will always love it because everything we do is new. So, you can't get tired of doing what you're doing when every show you do is a whole new experience and a whole different thing.

As an intrinsic achiever, Carsey resonates to diversity and interdependence. But she is many other things as well. Carsey finds meaning not just in work but in the varied aspects of life. She sees the connections between artistic creativity and a full, multidimensional life:

You know what? I just want to go home early. I have kids to raise. I have a husband, and I want a life. . . . I want everyone else to go home early, because I don't think people are happy if they're. . . . Well, it's more than that. I also think they're not as good at what they do if they're not leading a life. If they don't have a fulfilling, wonderful, creative, happy, joyful, varied life, then what are they bringing to the creative process?

Apparently, Carsey was well known in her early years at ABC for rushing up and down the halls at 6:30 P.M., calling out "Go home! What are you doing here? Go home!" Peter Roth, who now runs Fox Television, still likes to remind Carsey of her ABC antics.

Like other connective leaders, Carsey sees the connections among talents, processes, and purposes. The connections are to be made for a higher purpose, for the goal of the creative enterprise itself. When I asked Carsey whether she would prefer to concentrate on the creative end and leave the negotiations to others, her reply highlighted the importance of a larger purpose:

No, it's very comfortable for us. We learned at ABC (where we both worked before forming our partnership) . . . that negotiation is not separate from the creative process . . . because it's all intertwined. All negotiation—I learned there—is two people after what they're after. . . . They have wants and desires that overlap, and some that don't overlap. But it's the coming together: I'm bringing this, and you're bringing that. And how do we come together so that I'm happy coming out of it, you're happy coming out of it, and neither of us feels that we've just lost an arm? If that works, then you're off and running to make the ideas work. . . . It's about what ideas this person can help you put across. It's about the larger thing, always, for everybody.

As part of her connective approach to leadership, Carsey entrustingly assumes others will naturally rise to her level of expectation. When they don't perform, she takes responsibility as the leader, rather than blaming others. Carsey sees her leadership role as being a "catalyst" for others. Although she expresses it differently, Carsey simply expects those around her to be as intrinsic as she is:

Sometimes I expect too much. I forget to tell people a certain thing that I expect, especially that I expect people to be self-starters. I expect people to be independent. And I expect them to revel in that independence and that self-determination, that impetus. Sometimes, people don't realize, because they've come from working in another kind of company, that that's what we want, and I've neglected to tell them. Sometimes, they actually don't like it. Sometimes I assume too much about what people know about how to work because it seems so natural to work this way.

Unlike some Stage 3 leaders, Carsey admits little interest in grooming successors to carry on the company. Organizations, including her own, must take a back seat to the product, in this case the creative enterprise: "We're so product centered that I don't think either of us has built this company in order to have a company that lives forever. I think we've built a company in order to have a creative product that lives forever." Carsey carries the same philosophy into anticipating new collaborations, new productions, new hits, and new adventures.

So far, we have concentrated on female leaders in the for-profit part of the corporate world. But as I suggested earlier, not-for-profit organizations are a promising place to seek out connective leaders. We have already met Wendy Kopp, founder of the flourishing not-for-profit organization Teach for America, and Billy Shore, who established S.O.S. We now visit Frances Hesselbein, another leader who brought a connective approach to a large, nonprofit organization.

Frances Hesselbein and the Girl Scouts

The media have examined every aspect of Frances Hesselbein's leadership except perhaps the most important one: her connective talents. During the 1980s, as executive director of Girl Scouts USA, Hesselbein galvanized this establishment organization through connective virtuosity. During this period, rival organizations worked feverishly to maintain their regular constituencies or to poach on GSUSA's mostly white middle-class membership. Seeing connections rather than calamity in diversity, Hesselbein deliberately reached out to include girls from low-income and minority families.

Hesselbein assumed the stewardship of the Girl Scouts in 1976, determined to staunch an eight-year membership hemorrhage. She began immediately to "manage for the mission," with results that are now legendary.

Before Hesselbein, the GSUSA had served primarily a white, middle-class clientele: the young girls who were the "target audience" and their mothers, who acted as volunteer staff but were also considered adult dues-paying members. A rather small, paid, professional staff mirrored the white, middle-class demographics of the membership.

Now, however, the GSUSA was facing a phalanx of serious competitors, including the Boy Scouts, eager to recruit girls to fill their dwindling membership ranks. Not least among GSUSA's rivals were the public schools themselves, busily updating their extracurricular programs with new after-school activities for children of mothers in the workforce. To complicate matters, as more mothers joined the ranks of paid labor, the pool from which the GSUSA ordinarily drew adult volunteers rapidly shrank.

Hesselbein developed a quietly revolutionary and connective vision, which ingeniously provided a solution to declining membership. She set out to make GSUSA a truly diverse organization, to serve all girls, as its original constitution intended. Along the way, she enlarged the long-standing array of Girl Scouts programs, which had emphasized good grooming, sewing, cooking, and party hosting, to include mathematics and computers, previously considered male territory. In the process, Hesselbein stretched the occupational horizons of the young scouts.

Hesselbein also devised special programs to attract girls from low-income ethnic and racial minority groups. She gave the GSUSA publications a dramatic facelift, one that reflected the interests and aspirations of these new young members.

But Hesselbein didn't stop there; racial and ethnic diversity became a goal for the adult volunteers and paid staff as well. She could see the unnoticed connections, she told me, between GSUSA and people who "had never been considered [by the Girl Scouts] for volunteer roles: non-Brownie mothers, young women and men without children, young businesspeople, older Americans, retired women and men interested in the growth and development of young people." By connectively expanding the criteria for volunteer membership, Hesselbein cleverly opened the adult ranks in the GSUSA to an army of new recruits. Between 1976 and 1990, she grew her adult volunteer base from 650,000 to 788,000 and the girl membership ranks from 2 to 2.5 million. By the time she left to become CEO of the Peter F. Drucker Foundation for Nonprofit Management in New York, 10 percent of the adult volunteers represented minority groups, as did 15 percent of the Girl Scouts, a 300 percent increase in minority representation from the previous decade.

Turning diversity and interdependence to the advantage of the behemoth volunteer organization brought Hesselbein under the media spotlight. A 1990 *Business Week*[63] cover story hailed her as a not-for-profit corporate leader who could teach for-profit CEOs a few new management tricks. But where did she learn this connective touch?

On a late spring afternoon in Claremont, California, Hesselbein reminisced about her childhood. Born near Johnstown, Pennsylvania, she was raised by a mother who traced her lineage to members of Charles Wesley's religious dissenters. On her father's side as well, she was descended from clergy (her paternal grandfather was a Disciples of Christ minister). But it was her grandmother, with her "treasure house" of stories—actually small morality plays—who had the greatest influence on the young girl's character. From her grandmother, she learned the secret of diversity: "not to have favorites, to recognize that everyone is valuable."[64]

Like many connective leaders, Hesselbein did not grow up yearning to be a leader. In fact, as a teenager, she dreamed of writing poetry, maybe even plays. Married at age twenty-two to John Hesselbein, Frances joined right in the family filmmaking and photojournalism business. In a family business, she learned a simple collaborative and contributory lesson: everyone helps out.

Radiating zest in that spring afternoon talk, Hesselbein defined leadership as a "matter of how to be, not how to do it," adding: "It's your own qualities and character. What you are moves into the job. You express yourself in your work. You grow along the way."

When I asked Hesselbein what she thought were the most important qualities for a leader, she framed her answer in recognizably connective language: "Integrity, a sense of ethics that works full-time, and [the capacity] to communicate with all your partners and constituents." She also touched on authenticity:

> Everyone in the organization watches to see if you mean what you say. You have to deal fairly and equitably with everyone. The leader has to have a moral compass. When a decision has to be made, the leader with integrity and commitment to the mission has to deliver a clear and consistent message.

> The leader has to be the embodiment of the mission, of the institution. You have to be faithful to the mission—you can't be slightly faithful to it one day and 100 percent faithful the next. High visibility is a price tag of leadership, and you have to be comfortable with it.

Hesselbein brings this connective orientation to her newest role as president and CEO of the Drucker Foundation. Although she is keenly aware of her young organization's mission, she doesn't believe the leader necessarily has to be the one to envision it. She described her belief that leaders can attach themselves to an already articulated vision:

> Leaders search until they find an enterprise with a mission they can be committed to. Everything flows from the mission. In my life, for the second time, I am immersed in an organization with a mission I believe in passionately.

Hesselbein's example demonstrates that commitment to a mission helps connective leaders draw a diverse group of constituents together around a coherent, consistent goal. And in connective fashion, she describes the importance of "serv[ing] different constituents with different needs. [They all] have to coalesce around the mission. The most exciting part of leadership is finding ways to communicate vision and mission, to bring people together, to recognize their contributions." Here, the forces of diversity and interdependence reinforce one another.

Many corporate leaders find it difficult to motivate paid employees. In an organization where fewer than 1 percent of the GSUSA's 788,000 adult members were paid staff, Hesselbein understood that energizing "volunteer power" was an even stiffer task.[65] At the Drucker Foundation, where she still relies largely on volunteers, she continues to practice leadership by expectation. Expressing the strong expectations of entrusting achievers, Hesselbein described her strategy for creating productive, dedicated volunteers: "A leader in the nonprofit world looks at every volunteer with the same expectation as you do with a valuable staff member: a very professionally written job description, orientation and training for the job, recognition, and performance appraisal. You treat them with respect."

The nonprofit world offers many leadership challenges. Depending upon volunteers' effort, time, and money can be a chancy thing at best, but Hesselbein relentlessly works at developing a connective edge.

Women's Achieving Styles: *Vive la Difference?*

There are indeed outstanding women leaders, and many of them behave connectively. But are they typical? What about the "new" women in leadership roles? How do their achieving styles profiles compare with those of their male counterparts? Are they any more or less likely than men to be connective leaders?

Until the early 1980s, data on corporate leaders from the Achieving Styles Project confirmed what other researchers had also found. In the United States, male and female managers looked surprisingly alike, with only one persistent difference: women were far less likely than men to act competitively. This gender difference in competitiveness remained consistent across cultural lines. Even in societies such as Taiwan, where the overall level of competition exceeded the U.S. level, women scored significantly lower than men on the competitive style.

The picture has begun to change since 1984. The ongoing survey of achieving styles of American corporate leaders described in Chapter Ten revealed a fault line snaking through the old sex-role stereotypes. The changes I found between these 2,041 women and 3,126 men, however, were not always what I expected.

The Direct Styles

Women Surpass Males in Task Orientation

First, in contrast to past descriptions, like those of Parsons and Bales,[66] that males are more task-oriented than females, I found that female managers were far and away the more intrinsic group. (Recall that the intrinsic direct style concentrates on the challenges of task mastery and excellent performance.) True, both male and female managers favored the intrinsic style above all other achieving styles. Still, something new was happening: women had taken a decided lead in this department.

Because this finding departed sharply from previous results, I looked more closely at these data, breaking the male and female groups into upper- and middle-management groups. Not only were female upper managers more task oriented than their male counterparts, but even female middle managers outstripped their male peers in their preference for intrinsic action. A separate analysis of the achieving styles profiles of managers in thirteen countries revealed the same pattern.

Competition Remains a Hard Nut to Crack

As noted a moment ago, pre-1984 data suggested that competitiveness was the only achieving styles difference between male and female managers, with men clearly outdistancing women. That gender difference on competitiveness remains very clear in more recent data. In fact, the largest achieving styles difference between men and women corporate leaders stubbornly continues to appear in the competitive scale.

Once again, we broke the data down by managerial level. Both upper- and middle-level male managers rated themselves significantly more competitive than did either of the two female groups.

As we saw in Chapter Ten, the upper-level males were noticeably more competitive than the middle-level males. There was very little difference in competitiveness between the upper- and middle-level managerial women. That is, regardless of managerial rank, women are less driven by competition than men. In fact, female managers ranked the competitive style smack at the bottom of their preference rankings, ninth out of nine.

The male results held a curious surprise. Despite their stronger preference for competition compared to women, male managers did *not* rank the competitive style among their top three preferences. In fact, as we saw earlier, senior male managers ranked the competitive style quite low (sixth out of nine), and male middle-level managers ranked it close to the bottom (eighth out of nine). Perhaps male leaders are gradually loosening their hold on competition. The recent emphasis in American business schools on teamwork may be having an impact after all.

Power: What's Good for the Gander

When it comes to the power style, what's good for the gander is gradually becoming good for the goose. Power appears equally important to female and male managers.

At the highest corporate level, both men and women use the power style with equal and considerable frequency. Both groups rank it second, after intrinsic. According to their own reports, both upper-level men and women engage in power behavior more frequently than their middle-level subordinates do. Power, it seems, comes with corporate position, and top-level females are no less likely than top-level males to use it with relish.

The Relational Styles: Males Invade Traditionally Female Territory

The relational styles—the heartland of interdependence—allow us to resonate to other people's visions and dreams, to collaborate in group enterprises, as well as to encourage, coach, and take downright visceral pride in others' accomplishments. In general, next to the intrinsic and power styles, both male and female corporate leaders look quite favorably upon the relational styles, but here too there are some surprises in the data. Sex stereotypes would lead us to believe that women prefer to accomplish tasks through relationships, but do the research findings point to a connective leadership advantage here? Unfortunately, the answer is a resounding no. Women seem to be rejecting their relational edge.

According to the subjects' self-reports, all three relational styles are used more frequently by men than by women. Moreover, it is the very top level males who call on these styles more often than more junior managers.

Men Gain the Collaborative Advantage: The Status Shield

In general, male corporate leaders seem to have the collaborative advantage over their female colleagues, although collaborating receives a fourth rank from both female and male managers, particularly those at the very top of the organization. Male upper managers report they use their collaborative skills with slightly higher frequency than female upper managers, but the difference is not very great.

Male upper-level managers, however, give a significantly higher score to collaborative than do *either* male or female middle managers. Compare this to the behavior of female upper managers, whose use of collaborative behavior exceeds only that of female middle managers.

What these collaborative data seem to be telling us is that upper-level managers feel more comfortable collaborating than do middle-level managers. Upper status, based upon both managerial position and gender role, allows the leader to collaborate, without being perceived as soft or inadequate. Still, leaders who lack adequate formal status, either managerial or gender, are likely to collaborate less, presumably for fear of appearing weak.

Contributory Action for the Highest Levels

The second relational style, contributory, fares quite well among both female and male corporate leaders, who rank it third out of nine. Here again, however, when we examine how often managers report they use contributory behavior, we see the same pattern as in the collaborative style: upper-level males report significantly greater use of contributory than middle-level groups of either sex. Female upper managers also indicate that they use contributory strategies more frequently than either of the middle-level managerial groups.

Only the difference between the two female groups, however, is statistically significant.

The same status shield that I described for collaborative behavior presumably operates here as well. That is, once managers move into senior leadership positions, they feel their senior status protects their collaborative behavior from being mistaken for weakness.

In fact, in both the collaborative and contributory cases, upper-level managers probably get *extra* credit from their subordinates for choosing these styles. Subordinates recognize that their bosses could simply fall back on their formal authority to require compliance. So those upper-level managers who do choose to use more relational styles are more likely to be perceived as "good guys."

Among their peers, collaborating and contributing, rather than competing, probably bring similar rewards to upper managers: goodwill and appreciation. Senior managers, who traditionally have expected ruthless competition from their peers in other parts of the organization, probably value the stress reduction that flows from these more relational styles.

Vicarious Territory: Overrun by Males

Women traditionally have held title to vicarious achievement. Women's encouragement and pride in their children's and spouses' accomplishments have been legendary. Women's tendency to take pleasure from the achievements of others has been ridiculed, despite the critical emotional and political vitamins their support provided.

As long as vicarious behavior was seen as the province of women, it was generally denigrated as passivity, born of an inability to achieve independently. Stereotyped in this way, the strength of character with which vicarious achievers transcend more narrowly based egocentric concerns rarely received recognition.

If vicarious behavior has been the traditional territory of females, do women in organizations maintain that hegemony vis-à-vis their male colleagues? Apparently not. Here too males are invading an established female province. Male upper managers seem to be far outdistancing both upper- and middle-level female managers and their male subordinates.

According to their self-reports, male senior managers rely on vicarious strategies significantly more often than do women at that level. Female senior managers call upon the vicarious style significantly more often than their female subordinates do, but surprisingly, even male middle managers are more likely than female upper managers to feel comfortable with vicarious action.

It is difficult to interpret these changes. Do they mean that men are finally being freed from repressive societal and organizational expectations, freed to follow a more natural impulse? Or do the changes suggest that men recognize the value in these traditionally female behaviors and have the organizational clout to use them with impunity?

Sadly noteworthy is the negative showing of female middle managers, who trail way behind the three other groups in vicarious behavior. Higher gender status (that is, maleness) seems to promote the use of this style in organizations. The status shield seems to be in play here, too.

Despite the fact that women's socialization ordinarily emphasizes all the relational styles,[67] female managers apparently are relinquishing their vicarious skills in the organizational setting. We can only speculate that this pattern reflects women managers' efforts to avoid being perceived as traditional females. Males, protected by their higher gender status, presumably find it less threatening to commandeer this style, with all its built-in mentoring capacity. In addition, as I suggested earlier, if women have not had mentors as they climbed the organizational ladder, they may not have learned how to be a mentor for others. Or they may feel no strong obligation to "do unto others what was not done unto them."

As the organizational world grows more diverse and complicated, fledgling managers will need all the advice and encouragement they can get from experienced senior leaders. If those women who advance through the managerial ranks are unwilling or unable to act vicariously, to collaborate or contribute readily to others' success, they may be depriving more junior managerial candidates of important training and support. They are also foregoing a distinctive learned advantage that their male peers have begun to use with skill and flair.

Male upper managers, in contrast, seem to be integrating the intrinsic and power styles with all three relational styles while downplaying competition. Still, these senior male managers have yet to embrace instrumental action wholeheartedly. They are particularly wary of the personal and social styles, which can help integrate the *inter*dependency embedded in relational styles with the *in*dependence and diversity available through the direct styles.

The Instrumental Styles: Still the Road Less Traveled

In earlier chapters, I noted that the three instrumental styles—personal, social, and entrusting—sorely needed in an interdependent, diversity-riven environment are undervalued in American organizations. Our survey results support the suggestion that these three styles are still resisted by American managers, although as we shall see there are some interesting differences across these groups.

Avoiding the Personal

The personal style, you may recall, is a mark of charismatic leaders, whose dramatic gestures and counterintuitive use of symbols, rituals, and dress attract constituents to their cause. Leadership lore places charisma firmly at the core of leadership behavior. Yet the male and female corporate leaders in our study were equally and emphatically unenthusiastic about this useful type of Stage 3 action.

The most surprising finding about the personal style was the very low rank it received from both groups, seventh place out of nine. The highest rank accorded this style was a rather weak sixth out of nine, given by middle-level managers, male and female alike. Female top-level managers ranked personal a cool seventh, and their male colleagues gave it an even chillier eighth-place ranking. Clearly, women corporate leaders are no more inclined than their male counterparts to develop this aspect of connective leadership.

Social Surprises

The research findings on the social style are even more unexpected. In an interdependent world, where networking has become a sine qua non, we would have expected these managers to report considerable enthusiasm for building organizational networks. On the contrary, our data suggest that both male and female corporate leaders find the social style even less attractive than the more charismatic and dramatic personal strategies.

Perhaps trying to put the lie to the stereotype that women get ahead through relationships, female managers report they reject such strategies. They emphatically avoid the social style, ranking it eighth, just one place above their most rejected style (the competitive). And both top- and middle-level male managers rank the social style at the very bottom of the heap. Clearly, these women managers are not much more likely than the men to use this key component of connective leadership, one that helps leaders build needed alliances and networks in an interdependent environment.

Women Entrust More than Men, but Reluctantly

The final instrumental style, entrusting, offers still more unexpected results. Entrusting, you will recall, involves expecting those around you just naturally to help you achieve your goals. This behavior tends to encourage creativity and ownership, empowering even those who initially may feel they are ill-prepared to undertake the assignment.

The first unanticipated result is that the corporate women in our study, particularly those at the highest managerial level, used entrusting behavior significantly more than men.[68] These findings run contrary to the stereotype of female bosses hovering over subordinates as they complete their tasks. That's the good news for women and connective leadership.

The bad news is that even these top-level women rank this important connective leadership ingredient only sixth out of nine. The other three managerial groups, middle-level women and upper- and middle-level men, were consistent in ranking entrusting action slightly lower, placing it seventh out of nine.

One possible explanation for top-level corporate women's greater use of entrusting strategies may be related to their own experience in climbing the organizational ladder. Senior male managers, who are the most likely and valued mentors in organizations, have customarily selected male protégés, leaving upwardly mobile females to find their own way. Their bosses simply expected them to do the job.[69]

Consequently, women, much more than their male peers, have been forced to fall back on their own resources. Left to fend for themselves, many women know that leading by expectation works. Those women who eventually make it to the top may be more likely to think that others can or should be able to do the same.

The Next Generation

Up to now, we have been considering the achieving styles patterns of adult women already engaged in corporate leadership roles. What can we expect from the next generation of female leaders? Other researchers have found intriguing gender-based differences in the achieving styles of student leaders.[70,71,72]

One study of sixty-two female class presidents found that these young leaders favored the intrinsic, power, and collaborative styles.[73] Another study of young women student leaders also reported that they liked best of all taking charge (that is, using the power style) and mastering the task themselves (acting intrinsically). Next, these young female leaders favored the collaborative style, which was strongly linked to other leadership behaviors such as "experimenting and taking risks," "envisioning the future," "enlisting others," "fostering collaboration," "strengthening others," "setting the example," and "planning small wins,"[74] all key aspects of connective leadership.

These younger leaders contributed to the success of others, and they entrustingly expected others to pitch in and do their part. Much like the adult female corporate leaders in our own research, these student leaders were least comfortable with the competitive and social styles. And in a study that asked followers to evaluate female leaders, those leaders who were viewed as empowering and transformational were likely to emphasize collaborative leadership strategies.[75,76] The next generation seems to be on the connective track.

To return to the question, "Does gender make a difference?" the answer is yes, but in a highly complex way. Reviews of the literature on female leadership provide a complicated picture. In general, the actual leadership behavior of females is virtually indistinguishable from men's, when context is held constant. Sometimes the nature of the task makes a difference. But mostly it is the *perceptions* of female leaders' behavior, not the actual behavior, that vary, and then too mostly in laboratories, rather than in real-life organizational settings.

In interviews with female corporate leaders, we see considerable evidence of a connective sensibility that informs their leadership behavior. But in these opening days of Stage 3, American male and female corporate leaders still have a long way to go in hitting their connective stride. At present, few are putting the leadership know-how of ethical instrumental action to work, although the women managers do seem slightly more willing than their male counterparts to entrust and empower others.

Although we do not have comparable achieving styles data on a large sample of female political leaders, with some exceptions (such as Mary Robinson and Elena Lagadinova) the ones who have captured public attention seem even more stuck in Stage 2 than their male counterparts. That observation raises an interesting question: do corporate women, who don't have to stand for popular election and don't need a broad-based electorate, find it easier to use connective leadership styles? Or, put another way, do voters have stronger expectations for political leaders to demonstrate the John Wayne syndrome?

The sketches of Anita Roddick and Frances Hesselbein pose provocative questions about women corporate leaders. It is, perhaps, not simply coincidental that their major constituencies (customers, members, volunteers, and staff) are predominantly female.[77] Marcy Carsey, however, is co-leader of an organization with both male and female employees. Her creative work speaks to an audience without gender, race, or ethnic limitations. Perhaps the road to successful connective leadership is more open to women in the corporate and nonprofit world than in the political arena. Much work remains to be done before a clear answer can be given to this important question.

Although the data on female leadership raise many new questions, we can take some hope from the next generation of female leaders. Research on their achieving styles suggests that these young female leaders seem to know how to combine entrusting strategies with intrinsic and power styles. The future of connective leadership appears to be in good hands.

Perhaps as constituents begin to recognize that connective leaders can be both tough and tender, courageous and comfortable, leaders will be encouraged to build both instrumental and relational styles into their repertoires. Still, the true challenge of connective leadership for both men and women will be integrating all nine styles and using appropriate combinations, with authenticity and accountability, as each situation demands.

Our look at female leadership, particularly among the next generation, takes us almost full circle. In the final chapter, we close the circle by returning to the serious issues that connective leaders, like other kinds of leaders, must face: life, death, and the search for meaning.

Chapter Twelve

Connective Leadership and the Serious Issues

Life, Death, and the Search for Meaning

> *Man is perishable. That may be; but let us perish resisting,*
> *and, if nothing is what awaits us, let us not act in such a*
> *way that it would be a just fate.*
> ÉTIENNE PIVERT DE SÉNANCOUR[1]

For hundreds of years, the subject of leadership has troubled and intrigued pundits and practitioners, as well as the rest of us. By now, one would think, that issue should have been exhaustively mined and thoroughly understood. Yet we continue, decade after decade, even century after century, to think, debate, and write about leadership.

The reasons for this unending interest are undoubtedly complex, far too complicated to be dispatched briefly here. But we rarely consider one central reason for our relentless curiosity: that the ongoing excavation of the leadership concept is part of a deeper search for the meaning of life, a search for how each of us mere mortals fits into the larger picture. As we examine the shards of our psycho-archaeological findings, we seek clues to the enigma of our human condition, all the way from the earliest stirrings of history to the current emergence of Stage 3.

In some inchoate way, we sense that despite our Odyssean search leadership remains an immanent, mysterious process. The continual reemergence of the issue reaffirms that it is a crucible, forcing us to refine our understanding of ourselves and of the changing world in which we live.

I have alluded to this deep layer of the meaning and purposes of leadership throughout this book. We encountered it directly, in Chapter Two, early in our exploration into the psychological and existential foundations of leadership. We met it again in Chapter Nine in our discussion of the synergistic effects of connective leadership. We have glimpsed it several times in the stories of leaders whose words so often point to larger purposes that underlie their view of organizational and political life. Now we return to the theme of leadership as a serious issue of human existence, this time from the vantage point afforded us by the concept of connective leadership.

A Return to Fundamentals:
Our Human Duality and Where It Leads

When I began to think about this book several years ago, the winds of change were little more than gentle zephyrs. Never could I have predicted how quickly they would accelerate into hurricane force. During the course of this writing, the rising global storm has virtually blown away the old boundaries of Eastern Europe and cracked the foundations of entrenched power structures in many other parts of the world. Meanwhile, the winds of change from Asia gather increasing force as their influence blows across the world.

At the height of this great global storm, some nations broke apart, others were born, and still others drastically changed their political structures and ideologies. In the aftermath, the organizational skyline has also changed, with new and different organizational architectures suddenly appearing alongside the old familiar forms.

Paradoxically, this sweeping change has revealed not so much something new as something we can now recognize as quite ancient and irreducible: the fundamental duality of the human condition. Becker (and Kierkegaard before him) reminded us of the existential paradox: human beings are "half animal and half symbolic . . . a condition of *individuality within finitude*" (emphasis in original).[2] Becker eloquently explains:

> Man has a symbolic identity that brings him sharply out of nature. He is a symbolic self, a creature with a name, a life history. He is a

creator with a mind that soars out to speculate about atoms and infinity, who can place himself imaginatively at a point in space and contemplate bemusedly his own planet. This immense expansion, this dexterity, this ethereality, this self-consciousness gives to man literally the status of a small god in nature. . . . Yet, at the same time . . . man is a worm and food for worms. This is the paradox: he is out of nature and hopelessly in it; he is dual, up in the stars and yet housed in a heart-pumping, breath-gasping body that once belonged to a fish and still carries the gill-marks to prove it. . . . Man is literally split in two: he has an awareness of his own splendid uniqueness in that he sticks out of nature with a towering majesty, and yet he goes back into the ground a few feet . . . to rot and disappear forever. It is a terrifying dilemma to be in and to have to live with.[3]

As symbolic beings, each of us is constantly aware of our unique, but painfully finite, individuality. We yearn to express our symbolic nature, particularly our noblest capacity for heroism and even the ethereality which Becker describes. At the same time, we remain entrapped by our biological limitations. For us, as for all other species, there is no escaping the inevitability of death. Such is the irreducibility of the human condition even as we enter Stage 3.

Every time we act, we must make choices. Those choices are driven by different yearnings and calculations that may oscillate, over different periods of our development, between the interests of self and the interests of others. We must also make choices in terms of expected results or worthy aspirations. Stanford University professor James March argues that

there are two great traditions for understanding, motivating, and justifying human action. The first sees action as based on expectations of its consequences. The second sees action as based on fulfilling the obligations of personal identity. The first tradition speaks of incentives and desires. The second tradition speaks of self-conceptions and appropriate behavior. The modern ideology of human choice is overwhelmingly in the first tradition. Modern theories of choice teach us to evaluate our alternatives by calculating their expected consequences and to choose the alternative with the highest expected value. . . . [The second tradition involves] a conception of human reason based on fulfilling personal identities and a logic of appropriateness [versus] a conception based on expectations and a logic of consequences.[4]

These two bases of choice raise different questions:

> Within [the second] tradition, a decision maker asks: What kind of a person am I? What kind of a situation is this? What does a person such as I do in a situation such as this? Actions are matched to situations by rules associated with an individual's identity, or self conception. . . . The essential feature of the vision is that decision makers are imagined to have identities and to try to fulfill those identities by acting in ways that are consistent with them. The human condition is seen as consisting in the confirmation of self through discharging the obligations of proper behavior in situations that arise. . . .[5] In the end, perhaps, humans establish their claims to uniqueness not so much by responding to the demands of consequences as by responding to the demands of identity.[6]

The choices we make, based either on a logic of consequences or a logic of appropriateness, express who we are and what we are about. The significance of these choices becomes greater to us over time, as we shall see.

The Epicenter of the Human Dilemma

For centuries, philosophers, playwrights, psychologists, and other observers of the human condition have placed the terror of death at the epicenter of the human dilemma. For Zilboorg,[7] Fromm,[8] Becker,[9] and many others, it is the fear of death, forever lingering in the shadows of our lives, that generates the most profound human consequences.

The pervasive fear of death sends us on a four-pronged search directly related to leadership:

- First, the terror of death compels us to search for leaders, gods, and belief systems—religious, political, scientific, and artistic— to protect us. Leaders and gods do so, in part, through the illusion of their omniscience and control that diminishes our fear.[10] Ideologies perform comparable functions.
- Second, that fear also sends us on an endless search for life's meaning.
- Third, it forces us to keep seeking life-expanding experiences that will, at least temporarily, obscure the ever-present fear.

- And ultimately, it sets us on the most challenging search of all: the search for ways to transcend our finite selves by somehow leaving a permanent footprint in the shifting sands of immortality.

The Self and the Other: In Search of Complex Understanding

Psychologists and psychoanalysts often describe our lifelong quest for more and more complex meaning as one that oscillates between a focus on the self and a focus on the Other. University of Chicago professor Mihaly Csikszentmihalyi describes the process in the following way:

> . . . building a complex meaning system seems to involve focusing attention alternately on the self and on the Other. . . . But complexity consists of *integration* as well as differentiation. . . . Just as we have learned to separate ourselves from each other and from the environment, we now need to learn how to reunite ourselves with other entities around us without losing our hard-won individuality.[11]

While there is disagreement about the exact number, timing, and content of the stages involved, Csikszentmihalyi insists "there is a consensus among psychologists who study such subjects that people develop their concept of who they are, and of what they want to achieve in life, according to a sequence of steps."[12] Human development itself is a dialectical process between self and Other. This process moves in alternating stages as we seek increasingly complex meanings of life.[13]

In early life, as the self begins to emerge, there is intense concentration on physical comfort and survival, security, and self-recognition. Then, even as very young children, our attention is drawn to the outside world. We become engaged in absorbing its meanings and gradually adapting to the norms of the larger community. In adolescence, our focus on peers reaches a crescendo, before we oscillate back in early adulthood to a focus on ourselves, this time as mates, as parents, as workers.

A later stage in the developmental process, closer to midlife, brings us back to what Csikszentmihalyi calls "reflective individualism." It is here, as maturing adults, that we introspect about who we are, what we have done, and the nature and limits of our own worth. In this stage, we dig into issues of personal authenticity and integrity. We strive to settle the score with our egoistic selves. This introspective period keeps us focused primarily on ourselves, aloof to the outside. The innate urge for self-development grows stronger, driving us to the next level, in our unending quest for ever more complex understanding.

In late midlife or even later, the anguish of isolation and our common biological destiny now firmly anchor us to the world we share with others. We become more or less reconciled to our physical limitations, particularly as aging exacerbates them in ourselves and others. We reorient ourselves to the wider world, more confident, more self-defined, more aware, and usually more accepting of who we are and how we shall express that identity. This stage marks our reentry into an enlarged external world.[14]

It is a time to resolve the struggle between action based on the logic of consequences versus action based on the logic of identity. In this mature stage, often as grandparents, we are finally ready to seek something beyond simple reintegration with others.

We can now open ourselves to purposes beyond our narrow egoistic needs, new purposes in which we find our most important identity. In our search for meaning, we are finally prepared to commit ourselves, even sacrifice ourselves if necessary, to broad, supra-egoistic, perhaps even universal, purposes. The serious ills of the world—war, poverty, homelessness, environmental hazards, and the violation of human rights—now seem to beckon our wholehearted dedication.

Intimations of our own mortality urge us to express our symbolic nature, our truest identity. The drive to know and express our truest self reaches its peak in this mature stage, as we search for our most complex meaning.[15] Now we must also come to grips with our inherent duality. So once again we engage in distinguishing ourselves, this time not from others but from ourselves. By calling forth our most heroic, altruistic, noble selves willing to dedicate, perhaps sacrifice ourselves, to larger societal causes, we distinguish our symbolic from our physical being. In this way, we separate the egoistic self, so caught in the personal well-being of ego and body, family and career, from the supra-egoistic beings that we now yearn to be. In this way, we also try symbolically to conquer death and transcend our own mortality.

Naturally, not everyone moves across the "spiral of ascending complexity."[16] Those with overwhelming survival needs may never move beyond the very first plateau. Others become permanently enmeshed in their own careers and families. Still others, whose lives are cut short, may not get the chance to travel the full trajectory. As Csikszentmihalyi reminds us, "these stages do not necessarily reflect what does happen, or what will happen; they characterize what *can* happen."[17]

In sum, the dynamic of our individual development launches us on a journey toward increasingly complex levels of meaning. It engages us, albeit often unconsciously, in a "dialectic tension, [an] alternation between differentiation on the one hand and integration on the other."[18] Thus more and more complex levels of meaning make sense to us as we progress in our personal development, alternating between a focus first on ourselves and then on the Other. Eventually, our commitment to a logic of appropriateness urges us to fulfill our most central identity, the most noble aspect of ourselves.

Throughout this book, we have described another dialectic, this one at the societal level, that oscillates between the Stage 3 forces of increasing diversity, with its emphasis on individual identity, and interdependence, with its focus on the collective Other. Not coincidentally, this societal dialectic parallels the developmental process in individuals. Both shift their foci, back and forth, between the self and Other, between the individual and the larger group. So at the very root of our human condition as individuals, we find processes that both mirror and drive the escalating societal forces of diversity and interdependence that characterize Stage 3.

The Role of the Leader Redux

From this perspective, we can see that the overarching task of leadership is to help us connect these two dialectics between self and Other, one functioning at the individual level and the other at the societal level. If we can connect the societal dialectic between diversity (focused on individual identity) and interdependence (emphasizing the collective Other) to our individual developmental dialectic (between self and Other), we will finally understand the complex meanings of life to which our personal developmental dialectic has been dedicated.

It is at this point that our incessant scrutiny of leadership begins to fit into the existential puzzle. The awareness of death, particularly our own but the death of beloved others too, ticks incessantly at the center of our human struggle. Because "death is a *complex symbol*"[19] of our most troubling fears about loss of control, saturated as it is with so many levels of meaning, it continues to engage our curiosity, even as we push it deep into our unconscious. Leadership, itself a complex symbol of security and control, allows us to spread a bright cloth of conscious, life-affirming possibilities over the unconscious, dark table of feared death.

Leadership turns our attention away from our personal death and directs it instead to a conscious discourse about pervasive societal issues, a discourse that allows us to deal symbolically with our unconscious personal fears. In this discourse, contemporary threats—nuclear annihilation, urban violence, human rights violations, hunger, homelessness, economic meltdown, environmental decay, and a host of other arm's length problems—serve as surrogates for our much closer, more fearsome existential uncertainties. In this way, leadership helps us, at least temporarily, to prevail over our unconscious anxieties.

In short, the role of the leader exists and has always existed to meet the complex pressing needs of the human condition. If leaders didn't exist, we would create them. We often do, of course, particularly because they respond in at least four ways to our profound existential needs.

The Illusion of Control and Security

First, leaders weave for us the illusion that they can indeed solve the problems that currently beset us. Leaders help to quell these surrogate anxieties by the reassurance their larger-than-life images project on our mental screens. Their profound self-confidence, whether real or simply imagined by needy followers, creates for us the conceit of control, certitude, and safety.

Some leaders, such as Franklin Roosevelt in the Great Depression, bring order out of chaos and restore our sense of balance and safety. Other, often malevolent, leaders, such as Adolf Hitler, build their dominance through the creation of chaos which they manipulate.[20]

Coherence and Complexity

Second, through the visions they project, leaders bring meaning and coherence to the confusion of life. The best leaders teach us increasingly complex layers of meaning that help us to integrate the twin dialectics, individual and societal, between self and Other. The actions and symbols Gandhi chose—from his protest walk to the sea, to his own daily spinning of cotton, to his washing the untouchables' latrines—demonstrated that link between personal action and societal results.

In some cases, the leader's vision comes preattached to a complex belief system, sometimes religious, other times political, scientific, or occasionally artistic. These systems of belief, these ideologies, still our terror and comfort us, offering reassuring explanations of the anomalies and ambiguities of life. Like our mother's reassuring explanations of thunder and lightning when we were children, they touch us with new understanding. They enable us to cope with the growing complexity of our own existence in a constantly changing world.

Only in crisis, when embedded ideologies no longer can explain the erupting reality, do these explanations fail.[21] It is then that we are most receptive, even vulnerable, to the call of new, charismatic leaders.[22]

Life-Expanding Experiences

Third, by articulating and legitimating grand purposes, leaders help their constituents to engage in life-expanding experiences. At times, these growth experiences immerse us in an enormous range of activities, both painful and pleasurable, from learning a new language all the way to exploring our galaxy and landing someone on the moon. Some of these experiences drive us inward to our very core; others push us outward into the hustle and bustle of the world around us.

Leaders remind us that there are endless lessons to be learned, endless developmental steps to be taken. By liberating the spirits of those around them, leaders teach us to set ourselves and others free. By their model of authenticity, they send us searching for that bedrock within ourselves on which to erect our lives and through which to engage our environment. By his example, Sir Edmund P. Hillary challenged not just his own team to scale Mt. Everest; he also inspired successive generations of climbers to ascend many other mountains, both physical and spiritual.

By challenging us, these experiences force us to expand every dimension of our lives. Absorbed in this developmental search, first within ourselves, and then within others and the world around us, we barely notice the fear of death slipping below our angle of vision.

Ennobling Opportunities: The Call to Commitment

Fourth, leaders identify and orchestrate opportunities for us to ennoble ourselves. Challenged by our leaders to commit to a cause larger than our own egocentric beings, we are offered a special opportunity. It is our chance to act with nobility, to perform beyond our greatest expectations, possibly even to transcend our own mortality.

By accepting that challenge, by committing to a larger cause, we move toward three desirable goals:

- First, we enrich our lives by our willingness to sacrifice for a supra-personal cause, adding a "thickness" of meaning found nowhere else.[23]
- Second, by unreservedly devoting ourselves to causes greater than ourselves, we free ourselves from the narrow quarrels of life, from the tyranny of egotism, and from the need to be more perfect than we can ever be. Paradoxically, in the act of immersing ourselves in the greatest expression of Other, that is, some larger purpose, we emerge as our most unique selves.
- Third, by acting with courage and heroism, we symbolically face down death and sweeten its sting. We experience what Csikszentmihalyi describes as "flow" or "the optimal experience."[24]

Through such efforts, we achieve the ultimate integration of diversity and interdependence. Occasionally, this also leads to immortality, the voice of a distinct individual remembered for all time. In this symbolic way, we may finally elude death's grasp.

Martin Luther King, Jr., challenged his people to sacrifice themselves to the cause of equality. He challenged a nation to disentangle itself from the noose of racial divisiveness. King's courage and wisdom transcend his physical death, leaving behind an enduring model of leadership.

What Can Connective Leaders Add?

Connective leaders, like other leaders, respond to these deep human needs, but they serve them somewhat differently. In contrast to their Stage 2 predecessors, their receptivity to new concepts and more complex ways of leading causes us to recognize new truths and even more complex meanings. Their recognition of connections among diverse people, contradictory ideologies, and seemingly unrelated events helps them and their constituents to move beyond a politics of differences to a politics of commonalities. Their own actions call upon many different, unorthodox kinds of behavior, way beyond the currently favored combination of competition and collaboration. They draw their strength from a broad repertoire of leadership behaviors. Their benign instrumental, political sensibility endows them with fresh leadership insights and strengths.

We have seen examples of leaders who help to define what this new leadership is, but as we have noted, full-fledged connective leaders are still hard to find. Consequently, in the following sections, I am writing not only about the characteristics of existing connective leaders but also about the qualities of connective leadership that ideally can flow from such a conception of leadership.

Integrating and Encouraging Multiple Visions

Connective leaders, like all leaders, offer a vision to allay contemporary problems. But unlike Stage 2 leaders, they rarely think theirs is the one best way. They believe in their own vision, but they are willing to amend it with the insights of others. They welcome diversity as the wellspring of creativity and complex truth.

Because they do not guard their vision with proprietary zeal, connective leaders can also entrust its implementation, even its expansion, to others. As part of this process, connective leaders encourage the leadership potential of others.

Chico Mendes widened his vision to incorporate a global environmentalist agenda. As we saw in Chapter Four, he encouraged others to join the leadership process, to elaborate his vision and its practical implementation. In doing so, Mendes prepared his constituents to see new possibilities. Consequently, after his assassination, his cousin Raimundo Barros, Osmarino Amancio Rodriguez, and their colleagues were able to forge new alliances among Indian tribes at the historic 1989 Rio Branco meeting.[25]

Accepting Ambiguity, Rejecting Orthodoxy

Connective leaders solicit diverse viewpoints because they can deal with the ambiguities that Stage 2 leaders usually perceive as threatening. Consequently, connective leaders have no need to demand orthodoxy from themselves or their constituents.

Connective leaders' comfort with ambiguity allows them to respond adeptly to the heightened complexity and rapid change of Stage 3. Such an environment demands that decisions be taken with much less than perfect knowledge. Leaders who can tolerate ambiguity recognize that partial information, lurking within the shadows of ambiguity, may be the critical signal to change strategy.

Connective leaders handle ambiguity by accepting, seeking, and interpreting new information from many sources, by preparing for contingencies, and by using a broad set of leadership strategies. They consult widely, despite the objections of Stage 2 critics, who often misread this search as indecisiveness. Their search for new interpretations and their rejection of orthodoxy prompt connective leaders to respond more flexibly to rapidly unfolding situations.

Assembling Changing Coalitions

Connective leaders are particularly expert in orchestrating multiple coalitions. Because they do not demand orthodox allegiance to their entire agenda, connective leaders willingly accept help from coalition members on some issues while respecting their refusal on others.

These Stage 3 leaders welcome opportunities to form alliances among multiple organizations, even those that Stage 2 leaders would have viewed as competitors. Wendy Kopp creates alliances among former antagonists to reclaim the nation's schools. These leaders who are at home in Stage 3 also forge links between the most improbable allies and engage them in the most unlikely actions. When Billy Shore connects circles of leaders from many different spheres, from food to poetry, he clearly exemplifies this dimension of connective leadership.

Helping Passive Followers Become Active Constituents

In contrast to Stage 2 predecessors, connective leaders guide supporters along the unfamiliar footpaths of leadership. They recognize that constituents, encouraged to experience their own leadership gifts, not only lose their fear but actually find their own strength and creativity.

Connective leaders do not need the contrast of weak followers to highlight their strength. They prefer to transform passive followers into active, responsible constituents, inviting them into the circle of leadership. By casually entrusting their goals to others, without controlling the details, they encourage supporters to spread their own leadership wings.

Unlike Stage 2 leaders, connective leaders don't need to demonstrate their ability to outdo other leaders. In fact, they enthusiastically join other leaders, both recognized and emerging, in accomplishing common goals.

In the past, our existential bondage locked us into the passive role of followers, forever seeking leaders to guide us through life's treacherous shoals. Our readiness to abdicate our own power, even actively offering it to Stage 2 leaders, has spawned dictatorships and hobbled democracies. Only our ambivalence toward leadership has offered some limited protection. It is that same ambivalence, unfortunately, that has kept some potential connective leaders from actively seeking leadership roles.

To loosen the existential bondage that invites tyranny, we must be willing to share the responsibilities of leadership. Stage 3 promises to be a coming of age for followers maturing into constituents, and ultimately into leaders. Constituency, after all, entails active responsibility, even the traumatic liability of leadership. Connective leaders' readiness to welcome constituents as leaders, to help them assume an appropriate portion of responsibility so that they may learn without being overwhelmed, will ease the way.

As Stage 3 advances, constituents will have to look to themselves, not just to others, to solve problems that affect the entire community, from the community of the company to the community of nations. Connective leaders will need to welcome these partnerships and promote alliances among diverse networks of constituents, neophyte leaders, and established leaders. And when the leadership burdens become too heavy, as they frequently will, fledgling leaders and other constituents must steel themselves against backsliding into Stage 2, in the vain hope that the established leaders will do it all.

Complex Meanings, Fused Dialectics

Because connective leaders see connections everywhere—in the relationships among people, parties, institutions, and ideologies—their visions are much richer than the visions of Stage 2 leaders. Consequently, the meanings of life that they bring to their constituents are deeper, more abundant, and more diverse than those of traditional leaders.

Because they value and seek out new connections everywhere, Stage 3 leaders are themselves engaged in an endless search for greater meaning, for better causes to serve, and for more authentic ways to achieve them. They are the ultimate role models for the constituents who accompany them. At Perot Systems, Mort Meyerson not only pursues greater meaning for himself; he invites his people to join him in these life-expanding experiences.

More than that, connective leaders can help us to integrate the societal dialectic between diversity and interdependence, a dialectic that pulls the world in many conflicting directions. We have seen how diversity makes claims for the individual, how interdependence speaks for the collective Other. We now know that dialectic is mirrored at the individual level by the tension between self and Other. Connective leaders can help interpret and resolve those parallel tensions, in part by drawing upon the widest range of leadership behaviors. Using themselves and others as the instruments for reconciling these twin dialectics, connective leaders light up the Stage 3 sky with an explosion of possibilities.

Moving Beyond Individualism to a Politics of Commonalities

The connective leadership perspective raises entirely different questions than those posed by Stage 2 leaders. Stage 2 leaders asked, "Who will follow me? Who will support my dream? Who is different from us? Who is our enemy?" Connective leaders ask instead, "What are our challenges? What are our dreams? Where is our common ground? What can we do for and with each other?" Connective leaders' thirst to conquer is focused on problems, not on people or nations. That thirst is slaked not by aggression and violence, but by a mixture of persuasion, collaboration, and trust.

Connective leaders move beyond narrow individualism, welding the advantages of diversity to the benefits of interdependence through political, instrumental savvy. Through a politics of commonalities, connective leaders move beyond individual differences to the similarities among the needs and dreams of many groups. They focus on the common ground, the connections among people, not on the contrasts and chasms that separate them. Of course, connective leaders recognize the differences, but they welcome them as a source of multithreaded strength. By loosening the bonds of individualism, they use diversity to brace interdependence, to stimulate innovation, and to serve the needs of all. For these reasons, if for no other, connective leaders are our best hope for achieving renewal through interdependence.

Stage 2 leaders dealt very differently with the distinctions among people and groups. They ranked them from good to bad, important to trivial, central to peripheral. They led by dividing and conquering. They constructed hierarchical organizations to separate groups, whom they then could treat differently. Stage 2 leaders believed that some groups should rule, while others obeyed. They used common enemies to unite their troubled followers.

The connective leader views the world through a much wider-angle lens, raising a host of very different questions. "How can we make room for everyone around the table of human reconciliation? How can we integrate the greatest number of human goals? How can we use our human differences to live together more harmoniously and productively? How can we construct organizations with the least bureaucracy and the most responsibility? How can we bridge the gulf between organizations? How can we bring together overlapping networks of leaders?"

These are questions born of an interdependent sensibility, of a regard for the whole. These are the concerns that touch the higher levels of human development, that promise our lives real meaning.

Connective leaders, reaching beyond themselves to institutional and societal goals, offer us the hope of community. Through community, we find the fundamental sense that we belong, that each of our contributions, our histories, and our unique perspectives is valued.

Some observers predict that the world is destined to fragment into oblivion. Connective leaders, by contrast, offer the possibility of binding the very widest range of talents, needs, cultures, and dreams into productive, nurturing community. At every level of society and at every organizational rung, connective leaders are needed to meet this transforming challenge.

Connective Leaders and Pressing Societal Problems

To be useful, the Connective Leadership Model ultimately must offer more than intriguing theoretical possibilities for solving problems we have yet to confront. Connective leaders must proffer realistic strategies for dealing with serious here-and-now problems: population, hunger, crime, homelessness, environmental degradation, education, immigration, violence, and too many more. In earlier chapters, we described several leaders who are doing just that. For example:

We met Billy Shore, from Share Our Strength, who connects ever-widening networks of chefs, restaurateurs, food wholesalers and retailers, scientists, and novelists to raise money and consciousness about the hungry. With Shore's orchestration, one innovative project after another is generating solutions to local hunger.

We met Wendy Kopp, from Teach for America, who has used connective strategies to tackle the seemingly intractable problems of educating our youth. Her efforts have attracted the commitment of young and old, rich and poor, politically indifferent and politically active. Schools that have suffered for decades from limited resources are beginning to respond to Kopp's connective leadership approach.

We met Frances Hesselbein, who transformed Girl Scouts USA by opening its doors to girls from multiethnic and multiracial backgrounds and to new cadres of adult volunteers. We have seen her offer innovative, life-expanding experiences to low-income girls, and chances for ennoblement to adults searching for purpose and community.

Kerm Campbell, Anita Roddick, Mort Meyerson, Lillian Gallo, Robert Fisher, and Marcy Carsey all show us different connective ways to restructure and run successful businesses. And despite all the stereotypes that distort our vision of Hollywood, the entertainment industry offers us an unusual model, a field that creates temporary kaleidoscopic structures to exploit the artistic community's creative diversity. At its best, the industry's artistic expression makes us reflect on the human condition, in all its comedic and tragic guises.

There are still other possibilities for connective leadership to combat societal problems. Those entrepreneurs who can refocus their dedication from personal to larger community enterprises have the leadership skills to act connectively. In 1984, the world watched entrepreneur Peter Ueberroth coordinate an enormously diverse Olympic enterprise, with unprecedented success.

In the political arena too, some leaders already perceive that the enormity of the social problems we face begs for a more connective approach. Some, like Chico Mendes, Mary Robinson, and Elena Lagadinova, who can reach across party and ideological lines to solve problems troubling the entire community, be it a rural village or a bustling metropolis, can make mountains move.

Closer to home, connective political leaders are beginning to reach across partisan boundaries to support candidates with whom they share common goals and perspectives. Here and there, a nascent connective sensibility is appearing. For example, the 1994 California congressional elections provided an encouraging example of this new Stage 3 perception taking hold, with Richard Riordan, Republican mayor of Los Angeles, endorsing the Democratic candidate for the U.S. Senate, Dianne Feinstein.

Hunger, education, low-income kids, adults seeking belonging and meaning, and corporate turmoil are just a start. Other serious social problems too, like homelessness and crime, child abuse, domestic violence, immigration, the environment, even human rights and world peace, can bend to the imperatives of new leadership initiatives—given half a chance, given a sufficient cadre of connective leaders, given committed constituents.

Of course, we would be naive to think that problems decades in the making will yield readily to *any* arsenal of new leadership strategies. Clearly, connective leadership—or any other kind of leadership, for that matter—is no panacea for our social ills.

The enormous diversity of Stage 3 requires a multitude of approaches to make the pieces fit. Connective leadership is only one important possibility. But other elements are needed too. In an age of information, we need effective and responsible strategies for communicating new ideas, debating new issues, and crafting new solutions. An enlightened media could help explain and ease the difficulties of the transition to Stage 3. So could a strong and diverse set of values that embrace the entire spectrum of human cultures. But these are topics for other books.

Because the underlying reasons that compel us to worry about leadership are part of our human condition, it is unlikely that we shall ever stop pondering the leadership issue per se. In each era, however, the pragmatic societal ills we confront as surrogates for our deeper concerns, and the context in which these problems arise, continue to change. So as each historical stage gives way to the next, the pragmatic question of *which kind* of leadership will best serve us must be asked anew. As Stage 3 emerges, clinging to our familiar, Stage 2 leadership patterns is a sure recipe for disaster.

Inevitably, our human anxieties leave us vulnerable to inauthentic leaders who promise us snake oil as the elixir of life. Connective leaders, who communicate authenticity and accountability through their clear dedication to non-egoistic goals, are the ones more likely to lead without falling prey to corruption and self-deception. Their examples teach us to beware of self-serving leaders who crave power so desperately that they cannot distinguish between virtue and corruption or recognize the larger causes that serve us all. More reluctant leaders, like Gandhi and King, who struggle between their disinclination for personal acclaim and their sense of duty—leaders whom we are virtually forced to draft—remain a safer bet.

The quest to understand leadership is endless. We persist in our search because it goes to the heart of the human condition: our dual human nature, as symbolic and physical beings. As physical beings, we base our actions on a logic of expected consequences. As symbolic beings, we act on a logic of appropriateness. It is the logic of appropriateness that enables us to express our most mature identity.

Leaders help us to deal with the epicenter of the human dilemma, that is, our terror of death. This fear launches us on a search for leaders, gods, and belief systems. It propels us to search for the meaning of life through authentic experiences. Most importantly, our fear of death prompts us to transcend our finite being by leaving behind an immortal contribution.

Human development is marked by sequential stages, alternating between a focus on the self and Other. After repeated oscillations between self and Other, we eventually reach a mature introspective period. Only then are we ready to move beyond our limited, physical, worldly self to a wholehearted dedication to the Other, to societal, sometimes universal causes.

The muffled intimations of our own mortality impel us to express our symbolic nature. They call forth our most noble, heroic self, willing to commit, even sacrifice, our self, if need be, to some larger cause. This moves us toward the most refined expression of self. Now we strive to differentiate the self not from Others, but from our former narrowly focused self. We move toward new levels of meaning, where dedication to a logic of appropriateness dictates the expression of our most admirable identity (what Machiavelli called "virtu"[26]). Finally, we connect our own developmental alternation between the self and Other to the societal dialectic between diversity and interdependence.

Leaders help us to link these twin dialectics, one deeply individual, the other broadly societal, by burying the fear of death below our level of consciousness. In this way, they free us to commit ourselves to life-affirming possibilities that, not coincidentally, act as surrogates for our most profound unconscious concerns. Our commitment to end war addresses our unconscious fears about our own death; our dedication to eradicate world hunger embraces the unacknowledged anxieties about our own starvation; our willingness to sacrifice in the name of human rights speaks to our own deepest needs for equality and freedom. By presenting us with societal challenges, leaders show us the way to ennoble ourselves, to transcend death, symbolically, by these immortal contributions to life.

Connective leaders fulfill all these leadership functions in highly distinctive ways, ways that address the tensions generated by diversity and interdependence. True, they are imperfect; and true, our ambivalence often keeps us from following them in their uncharted adventures. Still, connective leaders offer the best available model for us to emulate. With an eye for diversity, they integrate and encourage multiple visions; accept ambiguity and reject orthodoxy; and assemble changing coalitions where followers can shed passivity for active constituency, eventually to emerge as leaders themselves. With a feel for interdependence, they recognize subtle connections among people, events, institutions, and ideologies; move beyond individualism to a politics of commonalities; and take on serious societal problems. They do all this not to slake their own thirst for power, but to satisfy their constituents' hunger for meaningful productive lives.

While connective leaders have much to recommend them, from time to time they, too, will inevitably falter. When Stage 3 dilemmas stymie them, rejecting these new leaders or demanding that they revert to Stage 2 behaviors will not produce useful solutions. A highly diverse and interdependent world may be frustrating, but regression to Stage 2 leadership is a foolish hope, a luxury we simply cannot afford.

Everywhere around the globe, in every organization, in every neighborhood, it is within our power to convert the tensions between diversity and interdependence into constructive, innovative forces. We can make this choice to integrate our individual growth with the larger issues of our Stage 3 world. Our individual and societal destinies are on the line. The opportunity is ours to seize. In Stage 3, this bold choice may well be our last real hope for gaining the connective edge.

Notes

Preface

1. To ensure that the self-report instruments reflect real-world behavior, detailed observational behavioral studies have been and continue to be conducted under the aegis of the Achieving Styles Project, at the Peter F. Drucker Graduate Management Center, The Claremont Graduate School, Claremont, CA 91711.

Chapter One

1. Havel (1994).
2. Diversity takes many forms at many different levels, from the multinational to the individual. By *global diversity*, I mean the pluralism of nation-states, where a multiplicity of nations—some new and others newly rearranged, along with old, established nations—all coexisting and interacting, seek to create or maintain their distinctive identities.

   Organizational diversity is a multidimensional concept. There is organizational diversity that arises from the process by which new organizations emerge, others merge, some disappear, and still others simply transform themselves to meet changing circumstances. The processes involved are essentially similar to those that generate multinational diversity; however, they operate at a different structural level.

   Organizational diversity also refers to different structural forms of organizations (that is, stable hierarchies, enduring networks, temporary alliances, partnerships, teams, etc.) or different organizational sectors (for-profit, not-for-profit, public versus private). The term also includes organizations with diverse orientations or goals (secular/sacred, political/aesthetic, etc.).

   Demographic diversity refers to the distinctive characteristics exhibited by different demographic groups, such as sex, race, and/or ethnic background. In some instances, the demographic characteristic also leads to a cultural identity shared by the individuals exhibiting that characteristic (race, ethnic group, religion, physical handicap, sex, sexual orientation, etc.). Political-action groups or ideological groups may then arise, in which members perceive themselves as a constituency devoted to protecting or asserting their political or legal interests. In political-action terms, this type of diversity may have a cultural component and thus be thought of as *cultural diversity*. In this context, *diversity* often carries an "equal opportunity" connotation.

   Diversity also exists at the individual level. *Individual diversity* refers to the unique set of skills, talents, abilities, and gifts that any specific individual embodies.

   My use of the general term *diversity* includes all of these expressions of the emergence or maintenance of a self-conscious and distinctive identity.

3. Havel (1994).
4. Havel (1994).
5. Bellah and others (1985).
6. Drucker (1969).
7. Morison (1981).
8. Wright (1993).
9. For a discussion of post-heroic leadership, see Bradford and Cohen (1984a). See also Bradford and Cohen (1984b).
10. Friedman (1995), p. 15.
11. Lipman-Blumen (1973).
12. O'Toole and Bennis (1992). See also Handy (1992).
13. Brandt (1994).
14. For an interesting perspective on how often we have misjudged the potential effects of technology, as described by economist of technological change and Stanford professor Nathan Rosenberg, see O'Toole (1994).
15. Other forms, such as short-lived "hot groups" that work on challenging tasks or arise in crisis, will become more common. See Leavitt and Lipman-Blumen (1995).
16. For a prescient view of factors generating temporary organizations, see Bennis and Slater (1968).
17. While nationalism creates fragmentation, it also sounds a call to come home, an invitation to belonging.
18. Stewart and others (1993); Deveny and Suein (1994); Parrish (1994).
19. Banks and others (1993); Cook (1989).
20. The spread of power to previously disenfranchised groups has also brought a shift in the conceptualization of how the larger society should encompass new, diverse groups with different cultural and experiential backgrounds. For an analysis of the shift from assimilation, or the melting-pot model, to acculturation, see Thomas (1992).
21. Selz (1994).
22. For an expansion of this position taken by Steinbrunner, see Wright (1993).
23. Lipman-Blumen and others (1994).
24. U.S. Department of Labor (1994).
25. Mitchell and Oneal (1994).
26. Personal interview with Morton Meyerson, August 13, 1994, Los Angeles.
27. De Pree (1989).
28. Personal interview with Kermit Campbell, March 25, 1994, West Hollywood, California.
29. In his less well known work *The Discourses*, Machiavelli articulated a strong ethical and democratic prescription for leadership, which envisioned leaders devoted not to the selfish acquisition of political power but to the community's well-being (Machiavelli, [1513] 1970). Unfortunately, because the manipulative Machiavelli of *The Prince* is more widely read than the more principled Machiavelli of *The Discourses*, any action smacking of "Machiavellianism" continues to prompt revulsion.

    For an interesting commentary on the two faces of Machiavelli, see B. Crick's Introduction in Machiavelli ([1513] 1970), particularly "So Many Machiavellis" (pp. 13–17). See also Dunn and Burns (1995), pp. 41–44.
30. For a discussion of the difference between followers and constituents, see Gardner (1990).

31. Greenleaf (1977). See also De Pree (1989).

32. In an oft-quoted remark, Justice Potter Stewart said, "I shall not today attempt further to define [obscenity]; and perhaps I could never succeed in intelligibly doing so. But I know it when I see it." *Jacobellis* v. *Ohio*, 378 U.S., 184, p. 198, 1964 decision.

33. Badaracco and Ellsworth (1989).

34. For this particular insight, I am indebted to my colleague the late Professor E. Webb, Stanford University, Graduate School of Business, who read an earlier version of this chapter.

35. Gardner (1990).

36. For an interesting interpretation of the universal law of reciprocation, see Cialdini (1984). According to the law of reciprocation, the tensions aroused by receiving an unsolicited gift cannot be reduced until the recipient repays the gift giver with a comparable or better gift.

37. Leavitt and Lipman-Blumen (1995).

38. Bennis and Nanus (1985).

39. For a discussion of women as connective leaders, see Lipman-Blumen (1992a).

Chapter Two

1. Freud (1935).

2. A few exceptions exist. The Konds and the Nuer have been described by Bailey, who reports that the Konds of highland Orissa in India in the nineteenth century were primarily autarkic, that is, fiercely independent and unwilling to accept any individual as their acknowledged leader. Bailey quotes Evans-Pritchard's description of the Nuer: "They strut about like lords of the earth, which, indeed they consider themselves to be. There is no master and no servant in their society, but only equals who regard themselves as God's noblest creation. . . . Among themselves even the suspicion of an order riles a man and he either does not carry it out or he carries it out in a casual and dilatory manner that is more insulting than a refusal. (Evans-Pritchard 1940:182)." Bailey (1988), p. 38.

3. Gibb (1947); Bass (1990).

4. Bennis and Nanus (1985), p. 4.

5. Weber (1947).

6. For a recent treatment of the sociological and psychological theories of charisma, from Mill and Nietzsche to Weber, Durkheim, Mesmer, Le Bon, Tarde, Freud, and Lifton, as well as for case studies of Adolph Hitler, Charles Manson, and Jim Jones, see Lindholm (1990).

7. For an analysis of the relationship between the leader's self-confidence and the followers' devotion, see Chemers (1993).

8. Weber ([1925] 1946), p. 4.

9. Avolio and Bass (1988); Conger and Kanungo (1987).

10. Bailey (1988).

11. Bennis and Nanus (1985); Tichy and Devanna (1986); Leavitt (1986); Conger and Kanungo (1987); Kouzes and Posner (1987); Conger (1989); Nanus (1992); House and Boas (1993).

12. Burns (1978).

13. Bass (1985).

14. Greenleaf (1970), p. 7.
15. Weber ([1925] 1946); Wolff (1950); Barnard (1938); Gardner (1990).
16. Barnard (1938); Simon (1947); Weber (1947).
17. Kipling ([1893] 1920).
18. For an analysis of how experienced civil servants can undermine the most senior political appointees who head their agencies, see Heclo (1977).
19. Frieze and others (1978); Deck (1968).
20. Frieze, Olson, and Russell (1991); Frieze, Olson, and Good (1990).
21. Frieze, Olson, and Russell (1991); Frieze, Olson, and Good (1990).
22. Roszell, Kennedy, and Grabb (1989).
23. The concept of existential uncertainty advanced here should be distinguished from Søren Kierkegaard's notions of both subjective and objective dread. According to Kierkegaard, "Subjective dread is the dread posited in the individual as the consequence of his sin, . . . the dread which exists in the innocence of the individual, a dread which corresponds to that of Adam and yet is quantitatively different from Adam's. . . . By objective dread . . . we understand the reflection in the whole world of that sinfulness which is propagated by generation" (Kierkegaard, [1844] 1957, pp. 50–51).
24. I use the term *existential anxiety* to refer to *un*conscious processes, which are rarely brought directly to the surface of human consciousness. In twentieth-century literature, the works of Camus, Kafka, and Hesse depict anxiety as a more conscious phenomenon, in which their protagonists seek to escape the suffering induced by a sense of meaninglessness and isolation. See Camus (1960), Kafka ([1930] 1943), and Hesse ([1927] 1947).

    The poem "The Age of Anxiety," by W. H. Auden, depicts the conscious anxiety experienced by four characters during the war. Although their anxiety is related to a sense of their own valuelessness, their inability to experience love, and their loneliness, Auden indicates that the roots of anxiety are deep in the social processes evident in "this stupid world where / Gadgets are gods." Nonetheless, in this same poem Auden touches on a deeper wellspring of anxiety, closer to my own concept of existential uncertainty: "The fears we know / Are of not knowing. Will nightfall bring us / Some awful order?" (Auden, 1947, p. 42). Incidentally, it is interesting to note that composer/conductor Leonard Bernstein translated Auden's poem into a symphony, which saw its premier in 1949.

    In modern classical and existential philosophy and religion, anxiety also represents a central concern. Spinoza's concern with fear, which he defines in contrast to hope, prefigures later work in theology and philosophy, but does not directly address the issue of anxiety. Theologians from Niebuhr to Tillich to Heidegger have wrestled with the role of anxiety in human existence. Tillich conceptualizes anxiety as the human reaction to the awareness of the possibility of nonbeing—a concept that itself involves not simply the cessation of physical existence, but death of spiritual and psychological meaningfulness, as well. See Spinoza ([1677], 1910), Niebuhr (1941–1943), Tillich (1944), and Heidegger ([1927], 1962).
25. The following argument was first advanced in an earlier work (Lipman-Blumen, 1984). For a more recent and revised treatment of this question, see Lipman-Blumen (1993).
26. Zilboorg (1943).
27. The next several paragraphs draw heavily from Lipman-Blumen (1993).

28. Becker (1973), p. 11; Shaler (1900).
29. The concept of anxiety in twentieth-century psychological literature takes on a clinical orientation, which is related to, but clearly distinct from, the meaning presumed in this chapter. For an excellent summary of psychological theories of anxiety through midcentury, see May (1950).
30. Perrow (1984).
31. Lipman-Blumen (1984).
32. The concept of control and the "illusion" of control have been central, in various ways, to most of the social and behavioral science disciplines. In recent years, however, these concepts and their contextual meaning have been the subject of serious criticism. See for example Stam (1987).
33. Lipman-Blumen (1984).
34. Meindl, Ehrlich, and Dukerich (1985).
35. Becker (1973), p. 23.
36. For a discussion of how such "truths" or "discourses" are developed, see Barthes (1957) and Foucault (1980, 1983).
37. Leavitt (1951).
38. Bailey (1988).
39. Robin Lane Fox writes, "Alexander had been concerned for his own fame. He founded cities to perpetuate it and patronized an historian, the kinsman of Aristotle, to spread it. Legend began early, some of it at his own encouragement" (Fox, 1980, p. 33).
40. Malinowski (1955); see also Malinowski (1992) and Mauss (1979).
41. Leavitt (1951).
42. Kissinger speech presented at "Turning Strategic Vision into Operational Reality," 1989 Top Management Forum (Paris).
43. Dahlburg (1993).
44. Lash (1971); Cook (1992).
45. Goodwin (1987).
46. Garrow (1986).

Chapter Three

1. Gans (1988).
2. H. Ross Perot's 1992 presidential bid inspired 19 percent of voters to choose him against stiff odds. Perot's entire quixotic effort warmed the direct-achieving cockles of the American heart.
3. In the frontier environment, the landowner and his family cleared and farmed the land and raised cattle, sheep, pigs, and chickens to meet the family's needs. Besides sharing the farming and animal chores, the farmer's wife attended the children, prepared meals, preserved food, cleaned house, spun cloth, and sewed the family's clothes from products created on the farm. The American farm family was a highly effective, self-contained entrepreneurial unit, where producers and consumers were one.
4. For Thomas Jefferson, education was the key to the farmer's independence. Jefferson worried lest the American farmer, through lack of education, slip into the servitude that had trapped the European peasant. The far-flung agricultural extension system, an out-of-school educational system that still exists in more than two thousand American cities and towns, was part of the Jeffersonian legacy to protect the American

farmer's independence. It is no psychological accident that American agricultural policy continues to revere the small farmer. In so doing, we are safeguarding the kernel of our fundamental leadership model.

5. James Madison, Thomas Jefferson, and Thomas Paine, along with many of their copatriots, worried that the new Constitution still did not adequately guarantee individual freedom. Thus the Bill of Rights, adopted in 1791, spelled out additional individual rights in painstaking detail.

6. Many immigrants had left behind European bosses who vigorously fought their workers' propensity to drink and revel. According to one study, in the era from 1766 to 1876, workers in Birmingham, England, observed Mondays as a holiday to be spent in the "alehouse enjoying drink, bar games, entertainments, 'pugilism,' and animal fights" (Zuboff, 1984, p. 32). See also Reid (1976).

   According to Zuboff and Reid, drinking on Monday was simply the continuation of the weekend festivities. Still, the more independent European workers came to America in search of better jobs, better working conditions, and better wages. For detailed treatments of this period, see Rodgers (1978), the three-volume work by Boorstin (1973), and Wren (1979).

7. Zuboff (1984), p. 35.

8. Many labor historians interpret these rates as the combined effect of "the ambivalence and enduring orneriness of American workers . . . [and] the increasingly severe pressure that employers and managers brought to bear on dysfunctional, uncontrolled, and irregular behavior" (Zuboff, 1984, p. 34).

9. It was not uncommon for workers to be fined as much as half a day's wages for talking, singing, or missing the starting whistle (Zuboff, 1984, p. 34).

10. Skilled machinists and hand workers continued to work in the same factories right through the turn of the century (Hounshell, 1984).

11. The puddler's job was to stand before an open furnace, turning a thick molten liquid into steel.

12. Both skilled workers and laborers engaged in heavy manual work. The difference between skilled and unskilled labor, according to industrial historian Shoshana Zuboff, was not intellectual versus manual labor. Instead, the "difference lay . . . in a content of rationality of participation for skilled workers versus one of total indifference for laborers" (Zuboff, 1984, p. 40). These were the grim conditions under which workers labored in America. See also Samuel (1977).

13. Samuel Slater, a textile engineer, and Moses Brown, a wealthy Quaker merchant, opened the first American textile factory in Pawtucket, Rhode Island. Slater introduced the "Rhode Island system," first at the Pawtucket mill and later at another factory, in Fall River, Massachusetts. For a more detailed description, see Wren (1979) and Marburg (1941).

    Robert Owen, British entrepreneur turned reformer, introduced legislation to bar children under age ten from British factory employment and to prohibit night work for children. In 1819, a watered-down bill was passed that set the minimum child labor age at nine years and limited even this prohibition to cotton mills (Wren, 1979). See also Owen's autobiography (Owen, [1857] 1967).

14. Foner (1979); Dublin (1975).

15. Cochran and Miller (1961); Ware (1959).

16. Bernard (1981), p. 47.

17. Twenty years later, by 1920, that figure had increased to 42 percent of all eighteen- and nineteen-year-old women. See Rodgers (1978); U.S. Bureau of the Census (1943); Smuts (1960).

18. This figure ignores work "taken in" at home by married women in dire economic straits.

19. Workers were well aware of the toll that their physical exertions took on their lives. In the steel mills, puddlers rarely lived to be more than fifty (Samuel, 1977).

20. For an interesting treatment of trade union history during this period, see Golden and Ruttenberg (1942). For an analysis of later trade union efforts, see Schlossberg (1994).

21. For more detailed descriptions of trade unions' response to the "driving method" of supervision, see Hobsbawn (1964); Nelson (1975); Slichter (1941); Ulman (1955); Montgomery (1979).

22. McKelvey (1952).

23. Rodgers (1978), p. 27.

24. Copley (1923); Kakar (1970); Halberstam (1986); Brooks (1955); Nevins and Hill (1954, 1963).

25. The term *scientific management* was actually coined by Boston lawyer Louis D. Brandeis, who used Taylor's arguments to fight the 1910 request by Eastern railroads for the Interstate Commerce Commission to increase their freight rates. At first reluctant to accept such an "academic" label, Taylor eventually adopted the term himself, even using it as the title of his famous book, *Scientific Management* (Taylor, 1911b). Many of the components of Taylor's scientific management philosophy were first described in the work of earlier industrialists, writers, and inventors, such as British "computer" inventor Charles Babbage (1792–1871), French engineer Charles Dupin (1784–1873), and *American Railroad Journal* editor Henry Varnum Poor (1812–1905). But Taylor's articulation of scientific management brought the pieces together with coherence and a unifying philosophical perspective (see Wren, 1979).

26. "Second class men" were divided into two categories: men who were able but unwilling or too lazy to perform the task, and men who were physically or mentally unable to do the job. The first category, according to Taylor, were not worth hiring. The second group would be given tasks appropriate to their abilities, thereby allowing them to perform as "first class men" too.

27. Taylor's method emerged from meticulously analyzing the work of pig-iron handlers, whom he described as "so stupid and so phlegmatic that [they] more nearly resemble[d] . . . the ox than any other type." Such unthinking workers, Taylor argued, "must consequently be trained by a man more intelligent than [themselves]" (Taylor, 1911b, p. 59).

28. For more detailed descriptions of Taylorism, see Thompson (1922); Littler (1978); Braverman (1974); Nelson (1980).

29. This interpretation was made by James Campbell Quick (personal communication with author, February 17, 1995).

30. When prepublication excerpts from Taylor's groundbreaking book *Scientific Management* appeared in *The American Magazine* in 1911, novelist/social reformer Upton Sinclair penned an indignant letter to the editor: "[Mr. Taylor] tells us how workingmen were loading twelve and a half tons of pig iron and he induced them to load forty-seven tons instead. They had formerly been getting $1.15; he paid them $1.85. Thus it appears that he gave about 61 per cent increase in wages and got 362 per cent increase

in work. I shall not soon forget the picture which he gave us of the poor old laborer who was trying to build his pitiful little home after hours, and who was induced to give 362 per cent more service for 61 per cent more pay" (Sinclair, 1911).

31. Taylor (1911a), pp. 244–245.
32. These restrictions were not removed until 1949 (Wren, 1979).
33. For a vivid description of Ford's application of Taylorism, see Halberstam (1986).
34. Halberstam (1986), p. 87.
35. Braverman (1974).
36. Halberstam (1986).
37. Weber ([1925] 1968).
38. Weber ([1925] 1968), pp. 215–216.
39. Tillett, Kempner, and Wills (1970).
40. Mayo (1933).
41. Roethlisberger and Dickson (1939).
42. Marrow, Bowers, and Seashore (1967).
43. Maslow (1943).
44. Wilson (1955); Whyte (1956).
45. Sloan (1964).
46. For an interesting analysis of the opening salvo of the American student revolution, see Lipset and Wolin (1965).
47. Freeman (1975).
48. Freeman (1975).
49. Halberstam (1986).
50. Pascale and Athos (1981); Ouchi (1981).
51. Vroom and Yetton (1973).
52. Stead ([1902] 1972). University of California, San Diego, communications professor Michael Schudson reports that the earliest interviews appeared in American newspapers in the mid-nineteenth century. Before that time, "Much reporting remained nothing more than the publication of official documents and public speeches, verbatim. Reporters often talked with public officials but they did not refer to those conversations in their news stories" (Schudson, 1994). See also Shaw (1994).
53. Lublin (1994).
54. McGregor (1957).
55. Lublin (1994).
56. Bellah and others (1985), p. 6.
57. "The high cost of a family business" (1993).
58. Gerard (1990).
59. Speech at Stanford Graduate School of Business, October 22, 1990.
60. Giamatti (1990).
61. For an interesting analysis of baseball's place in American culture, see Will (1989).
62. "Oliver North" (1987), p. 35.

Chapter Four

1. Braudel (1981).
2. For an interesting view of how small changes in one part of a vast system create chaos in parts far away, see Gleick (1987).

3. Perrow (1984).

4. Drucker (1989).

5. Drucker (1989), p. 20.

6. Russell (1990), p. C1.

7. Duchêne (1994).

8. The seven ASEAN members are Brunei, Indonesia, Malaysia, the Philippines, Singapore, Thailand, and Vietnam. Vietnam joined in July 1995.

9. Richardson (1995).

10. Richardson (1995), p. 9.

11. For an analysis of the shift from assimilation, or the melting-pot model, to acculturation, which values the different cultural and experiential backgrounds of diverse groups and individuals, see Thomas (1992).

12. Well into the 1990s, those expectations remain only partially fulfilled, still waiting for new leaders to champion them. In 1991, the average family income finally reached $28,428, taking most of a decade to inch up 8.25 percent, despite the increasing prevalence of both partners in the paid labor force.

13. For a trenchant analysis of the rise of Pentecostal spirituality and the reconfiguration of religion, see Cox (1995).

14. Toffler (1990), and remarks made at a presentation by Harvey Cox, Santa Monica, California, November 2, 1994.

15. "Catholic church" (1995).

16. *Gallup report no. 288* (1989).

17. Gallup (1992).

18. Cox (1994).

19. Nor is this search for solid, if constrained, religious guidance limited to the United States. The rise of religious fundamentalism, worldwide, has grown enormously in the last decade. In fact, Islam is reported to be the fastest growing religion in the world, with one billion adherents and counting (Murphy, 1993). In North America alone, adherents to the Muslim faith increased from 291,200 in 1980 to 2,642,000 in 1993 (*World Almanac*, 1980; 1993).

    For an overview of the history and growth of Islam in the United States, see Marty (1985).

20. In the most expensive trial in American history (*People v. Raymond Buckey*), the director and teachers of a California preschool were charged with multiple instances of sexual abuse. The eventual dismissal of all charges following a hung jury left parents, as well as prosecutors, frustrated and furious (Timnick, 1990).

21. Wycliff (1990).

22. O'Reilly (1994); Porter and McKibbin (1988); Schlossman, Sedlak, and Wechsler (1987); Leavitt (1992).

23. Meyer (1990).

24. A few law schools, such as New York University Law School, are already responding with lawyering programs that teach negotiation, interpersonal relationships, and nonlitigious ways to resolve disputes.

25. Leavitt (1986); Tichy and Devanna (1986); Nanus (1992). For a reaction to the overreaction to vision and related mission statements, see Fuchsberg (1994).

26. Lewis (1989); Burrough and Helyar (1990); Bruck (1988).

27. Rose, Christian, and Nomani (1995).

28. A more recent analysis by Ohmae (1995) suggests that the conventional wisdom about MITI as the guiding force behind Japan's economic "miracle" is erroneous.

29. As we've noted above, the European picture tilts in a different direction. European managers foster commitment within and even between their organizations, but their tendency to worry about the subtleties and postpone decision making often undercuts the strength that their sense of community inspires. They nurture interpersonal relationships in organizational settings, often spending hours over business lunches cementing personal connections; however, the outcome of these interactions is rarely tied to a production schedule. So productivity remains a problem, albeit somewhat differently shaped, for European managers. I am indebted for this observation to Bram Flippo, of Avery Dennison, Materials Group Europe (personal communication, May 1994).

30. Fuchsberg (1994).

31. A new study reports that Los Angeles school children have one-fourth less lung capacity than children living in less polluted areas. The deteriorating environment not only affects human health; it also kills forests, streams, and wildlife. The degradation of the environment casts a long shadow over generations yet unborn.

32. An interesting example of an attempt to reconceptualize the issues of nationalism and ethnicity is embodied in the Institute for Multiethnicity and Transnationalism, at the University of Southern California, Los Angeles.

33. Max Weber argues that charismatic leaders arise in times of distress, with the new leaders offering radical solutions to the problems the community faces (Weber, [1925] 1968).

34. Geertz (1973).

35. For a description of Martin Luther King, Jr.'s, resistance to assuming the leadership role first of the Montgomery branch of the NAACP and later of the Montgomery Improvement Association, see Garrow (1986).

36. Collins and Lapierre (1975).

37. Shirer (1979); Collins and Lapierre (1975).

38. Collins and Lapierre (1975), p. 62.

39. Collins and Lapierre (1975), p. 62.

40. Garrow (1990), p. 31.

41. Garrow (1986).

42. Garrow (1990), p. 24.

43. Garrow (1990), p. 34.

44. Garrow (1990).

45. Televised speech, December 9, 1987.

46. After the initial success of the 1976 *empate*, at least forty-three more standoffs were organized to prevent the chainsaw clearing of more than 1.2 million hectares in Brazil.

47. Revkin (1990); Hecht and Cockburn (1989a); Cockburn (1989); Hecht and Cockburn (1989b); Carroll (1991).

48. In December 1990, a jury convicted Darly Alves da Silva for planning the slaying and his son, Darci Alves Pereira, for firing the shotgun that killed Mendes. Father and son were found guilty of first-degree murder and sentenced to nineteen years in prison.

49. Hecht and Cockburn (1989a), p. 18.

50. In the summer of 1995, French president Jacques Chirac announced France's intention to conduct tests of nuclear weapons under the Mururoa Atoll in the South Pacific. The French, who have no environmental movement, were taken aback by the worldwide protest to their announcement. Thomas L. Friedman interpreted Chirac's move as an expression of Gaullism, "a form of psychotherapy, an ideology invented by Charles de Gaulle to rebuild French dignity after the excruciating humiliation of being defeated by the Nazis and liberated by the Americans. The Gaullist in Mr. Chirac says that France, as a self-proclaimed Great Power, must maintain an independent nuclear option and an independent military identity. Therefore, it will test the newest weapons in its nuclear arsenal. . . . And if the rest of the world doesn't like it, well, all the better. That is the fun of being a Gaullist. I detonate, therefore I exist" (Friedman, 1995, p. 15).
51. Nakamura (1995), p. 9.
52. "Kremlin bets" (1995); Benkelman and Page (1995).
53. "Thumbs up" (1995).

Chapter Five

1. De Pree (1989).
2. The term *achieving styles,* rather than *achievement styles,* was deliberately selected to convey a sense of the action used in the pursuit of goals.
3. For an interesting discussion of the need to relinquish old technologies, even when they still work well, in order to succeed in innovating, see Foster (1986).
4. From 1972 to 1979, Leavitt and I ran several parallel research groups, usually one at the Stanford Graduate School of Business and the other in Washington, D.C. After 1979, Leavitt moved on to other research interests, and I continued the achieving styles research, first with a group of students in Washington known as the East Coast 3, and later with an ongoing research group composed of graduate students at The Claremont Graduate School, Claremont, California.
5. See the seminal work of Horner (1968).
6. McClelland, Atkinson, Clark, and Lowell (1953).
7. Rubenstein (1971).
8. *L-BL* stands for "Lipman-Blumen" (Jean) and "Leavitt" (Harold J.), the originators of the model.
9. The ASI has been translated into eleven languages, from Arabic, Bulgarian, and Chinese to Thai.
10. Since 1979, the ASI has undergone fourteen revisions to ensure its psychometric adequacy. Extensive reliability, validity, and predictive ability tests have been run on the ASI. For additional technical information see Lipman-Blumen (1991, 1987; 1988). For early conceptualizations and results, see Lipman-Blumen and Leavitt (1976); Lipman-Blumen and others (1980); Leavitt and Lipman-Blumen (1980); Lipman-Blumen, Handley-Isaksen, and Leavitt (1983).
11. For an earlier treatment of the relationship between connective leadership and achieving styles, based on the L-BL Achieving Styles Model, see Lipman-Blumen (1992a).
12. For a more technical discussion of the statistical and psychometric properties of the individual *L-BL Achieving Styles Inventory* (ASI) and the L-BL Achieving Styles Model that it reflects, see Lipman-Blumen (1991, 1987; 1988). For descriptions of earlier

versions of the model and research findings based on that model, see articles by Lipman-Blumen, Leavitt, and their graduate students in endnote 10 of this chapter.

13. Although often attributed to Vince Lombardi, according to the *Oxford Dictionary of Quotations* (4th ed., 1992) this statement apparently was first made by Vanderbilt University coach Henry "Red" Sanders in *Sports Illustrated* (December 26, 1955). The Oxford source indicates that Lombardi presumably told an interviewer in 1962, "Winning isn't everything, but wanting to win is."

14. Gioia (1992), p. 29.

15. Cialdini and De Nicholas (1989). See also Cialdini, Finch, and De Nicholas (1990).

16. Cialdini and De Nicholas (1989).

17. Collins and Lapierre (1975).

18. For a discussion of gifts and reciprocity, see Cialdini (1984). See also Mauss (1979).

19. Thomas (1951).

20. Corbett (1995), sect. A, p. 1.

21. The Achieving Styles Project is housed at the Peter F. Drucker Graduate Management Center, The Claremont Graduate School, Claremont, CA 91711.

22. Since it is beyond the scope of this volume to present in detail a technical instrument and the method for scoring it, here I briefly sketch an overview. Built around six key dimensions of the situation, ASSAI allows an individual to consider simultaneously many contradictory aspects of the situation. The user responds to a series of yes/no questions that have been previously assessed by a panel of achieving styles researchers to determine the styles most appropriate under the yes and no conditions. The scoring method integrates and weights the contradictory clues. Combining all facets of the situation, ASSAI produces an achieving styles profile that is most appropriate for the circumstances, ranking the styles from the most to the least suitable.

23. This can be accomplished using the ASI to derive individual achieving styles profiles of all relevant candidates.

Chapter Six

1. Conrad ([1902] 1994).

2. Andrew Carnegie, in personal letter to William Dihl, mayor of Pittsburgh, Nov. 15, 1900.

3. "'Something emerges,'" p. 1.

4. Collins (1990), p. 43.

5. Klemesrud (1978), p. C37.

6. Feinberg (1977), Metro p. B1.

7. Bleakley (1983), p. 72.

8. Hanner (1978), sect. V, p. 1.

9. Dowd (1987), pp. 1A, 10A.

10. Maslow (1943).

11. McClelland (1967).

12. Rodman (1939), pp. 291–292.

13. Park (1989).

14. Televised documentary, 1988.

15. Walton (1978), p. 3C.

16. Leavy (1984), p. 47.

17. Wartofsky (1995), p. 24.
18. Sherrill (1994), pp. G1, G10.
19. Sherrill (1994), p. G10.
20. Osnos (1982), p. C15.
21. Mills (1956), p. 80. For an interesting treatment of celebrity, see Braudy (1986).
22. Sherrill (1994), p. G10.
23. Sherrill (1994), p. G10.
24. Mason, Mitchell, Hampton, and Frons (1986), p. 60.
25. Sherrill (1994), p. G10.
26. Sherrill (1994), p. G10.
27. Watson (1968).
28. Watson (1968), p. 27.
29. Watson (1968), p. 92.
30. Baez (1987), p. 15.
31. Bricker (1978), p. 1D.
32. Kohn (1992).
33. Helmreich, Beane, Lucker, and Spence (1978).
34. Jenkins (1986), p. 19.
35. Jenkins (1986), p. 19.
36. Hersh (1983).
37. Lipman-Blumen (1984). See also Pfeffer (1981).
38. Machiavelli ([1513] 1977).
39. Royko (1971), p. 57.
40. Pfeffer (1981). See also Pfeffer (1992).
41. "Newsmakers" (1993), p. A2.
42. Personal interview with Lillian Gallo, June 29, 1984, Beverly Hills, California.
43. Phillips (1987).

Chapter Seven

1. Wilson ([1917] 1966).
2. Leavitt and Lipman-Blumen (1995).
3. Johnson, Skon, and Johnson (1980); Skon, Johnson, and Johnson (1981); Johnson and others (1981).
4. These studies were conducted between 1924 and 1980.
5. Reviewing 122 North American studies of competitive, cooperative, and individualistic classrooms conducted between 1924 and 1980, the researchers determined that in 65 cases cooperation led to higher achievement than competition. In only 8 studies did they find the opposite result. In 36 studies, the researchers detected no significant difference in the achievement levels of students in competitive and cooperative classrooms (Johnson and others, 1981).
6. The researchers found that in 108 studies, cooperation, more than independent work, was more likely to be associated with higher achievement. In only 6 studies did working alone lead to higher achievement than did cooperation. In 42 studies there was no statistical difference in achievement between the two types of classroom environments (Johnson and others, 1981).
7. Qin, Johnson, and Johnson (1995).

8. Deutsch (1993).

9. Gray (1989), p. xviii.

10. This concept bears great similarity to Alexis de Tocqueville's notion of "self-interest rightly understood," in which each party to an enterprise consistently accomplishes the most for himself or herself, as well as for the group, by some minimal sacrifice of his or her overall needs. See particularly Chapter Eight, "How the Americans combat individualism by the principle of self-interest rightly understood," in de Tocqueville ([1853] 1959), Vol. II.

11. Gray (1989), p. 5.

12. In 1984, the management consulting firm Booz, Allen, and Hamilton studied fifty companies having an office of the chairman in 1974. By 1984, almost half had abandoned the committee arrangement. At the time of the Booz, Allen study, the birth and mortality rates of such committee arrangements were about the same (Kleinfield, 1984).

13. Deutsch (1993); Anderson and Morrow (1995).

14. Sherif and others (1954) designed carefully controlled experiments at a summer camp in Oklahoma, near Robber's Cave (a reputed hideaway for Jesse James and Belle Star). The researchers easily induced in-group cohesion and intergroup hostility among two groups of eleven- and twelve-year-old boys. Only a planned superordinate goal brought the two groups together after the experimentally induced hostility.

15. Tjosvold and Chia (1989).

16. Axelrod (1984).

17. Axelrod (1984).

18. Husar (1991).

19. Perhaps the ultimate in contributory relational behavior involves a new role: surrogate motherhood. Pat Anthony, forty-eight, of Johannesburg, South Africa, bore triplets for her daughter. "I did this because my daughter, not me, was desperate for children and unhappy because of it," the contributory Mrs. Anthony declared ("Grandma," 1987, p. 2).

20. Lash (1971). See also Cook (1992).

21. In one well-publicized situation, the *New York Times* disclosed that "a reporter for *Women's Wear Daily* was denied a place on the Latin-American trip after that paper, ignoring a call from Mrs. Carter's press office, reported how much money Mrs. Carter had spent in a day of clothes-shopping on Seventh Avenue in New York" (Charlton, 1977, p. A1).

22. Quinn (1979), p. B1.

23. Clifford (1987), p. A18.

24. Personal interview with Anita Roddick, November 23, 1993, Stanford, California.

25. Personal interview, November 23, 1993.

26. Cialdini and De Nicholas (1989).

27. Cialdini and others (1976).

28. Cialdini and others (1976).

29. Cialdini and De Nicholas (1989), p. 627.

30. Halberstam (1986).

31. Iacocca (1984).

32. Halberstam (1986), p. 90.

33. Halberstam (1986), p. 89.

34. Halberstam (1986), p. 89.

35. Geyelin and Felsenthal (1994), p. B6.

Chapter Eight

1. Telephone interview with Wendy Kopp, March 31, 1994.

2. Astin (1994).

3. Kissinger (1979).

4. Drogin (1994).

5. Collins and Lapierre (1975), pp. 94–95.

6. *Citizen Carter*, Discovery Channel, March 4, 1991.

7. D. Williams (1989).

8. Leavitt and Lipman-Blumen (1995).

9. Potts (1994), p. 20.

10. Whitman (1990).

11. Kraft (1994), pp. A1, A8.

12. Kraft (1994), p. A8.

13. Drogin (1994), p. A9.

14. Caro (1993).

15. Caro (1993).

16. Personal interview with Kermit Campbell, March 25, 1994, West Hollywood, California.

17. Personal interview, March 25, 1994.

18. Personal interview with Lillian Gallo, June 29, 1994, Beverly Hills, California.

   Jon Dana, motion picture entrepreneur, recently recounted a story about Lillian Gallo that reveals the long-term consistency of her social behavior. In 1979, when Dana was working for Samuel Goldwyn, Jr., as director of creative affairs, he received a phone call. A female voice on the other end of the line greeted him: "My name is Lillian Gallo. You don't know me, but I'm involved with film production. I always watch the people Sam Goldwyn hires, because he has such good judgment about people, but he never can keep them. The people he hires always go on to do great things. I wanted to introduce myself so that one day, when you are doing great things and I call you, you'll remember me." (Personal communication with Jon Dana, February 24, 1995)

19. Personal correspondence.

20. Personal correspondence.

21. Personal interview with Wendy Kopp, March 31, 1994.

22. Personal interview, March 31, 1994.

23. Personal interview, March 31, 1994.

24. Personal interview, March 31, 1994.

25. Personal interview, March 31, 1994.

26. Personal interview with Kermit Campbell, March 25, 1994.

27. Personal interview, March 25, 1994.

28. Personal interview, March 25, 1994.

29. Videotaped interview with "Peter Allen."

30. Videotaped interview with "Peter Allen."

31. Schiff (1995), p. 31.

32. Drucker (1974).

Chapter Nine

1. Personal interview with Anita Roddick, November 23, 1993, Stanford, California.
2. Max Weber described the notion of the "ideal type," which identifies the full complement of characteristics entailed in a phenomenon, even though real-life examples may not exhibit the entire range. In the Weberian tradition, I enumerate as best I can the full set of connective leadership characteristics. Not all connective leaders use every behavior described. Nonetheless, we count as connective leaders those individuals who consistently use a core of Stage 3 strategies (Weber, [1925] 1946).
3. Personal interview with Billy Shore, March 11, 1994.
4. Personal interview, March 11, 1994.
5. Cialdini (1984).
6. Axelrod (1984).
7. Personal interview with Morton Meyerson, August 6, 1994, Los Angeles, California.
8. Lipman-Blumen (1984). For a more recent and expanded treatment of the meaning and sources of power relationships, see Lipman-Blumen (1993).
9. Gardner (1990).
10. Personal interview with Robert Fisher, August 11, 1994, Los Angeles, California.
11. Personal interview with Morton Meyerson, August 6, 1994.
12. Personal interview, August 6, 1994.
13. Personal interview, August 6, 1994.
14. Personal interview with Anita Roddick, November 23, 1993, Stanford, California.
15. Maslow (1954).
16. In his autobiography, Iacocca wrote: "I began by reducing my own salary to one dollar a year. Leadership means setting an example. . . . I didn't take one dollar a year to be a martyr. I took it because I had to go into the pits. I took it so that when I went to Doug Fraser, the union president, I could look him in the eye and say: 'Here's what I want from you guys as your share,' and he couldn't come back to me and ask: 'You SOB, what sacrifice have *you* made?' That's why I did it, for good, cold, pragmatic reasons. I wanted our employees and suppliers to be thinking: 'I can follow a guy who sets that kind of example. . . .' I call this equality of sacrifice. When I started to sacrifice, I saw other people do whatever was necessary. That's how Chrysler pulled through" (Iacocca, 1984, p. 229).
17. Axelrod (1984).
18. Kaplan (1992), p. A20.
19. Dowd (1995), p. 7.

Chapter Ten

1. Bennis (1989), p 119.
2. Bennis and Slater (1968).
3. Knecht (1994).
4. Shrivastava (1985, 1987); Asia-Pacific People's Environment Network (1986). See also Fink (1986) and Perrow (1984).
5. Gardner (1990).
6. Pinchot (1986).

7. For an interesting example in the computer industry, see Kidder (1981). See also Leavitt and Lipman-Blumen (1995).

8. Drucker (1969).

9. Foster (1986).

10. Lipman-Blumen and Schram (1984).

11. Carson (1962).

12. Brown and others (1985).

13. National Research Council (1972).

14. Foster (1986).

15. E. C. Williams (1989).

16. See Lipman-Blumen (1991, 1987) for further information on the *L-BL Achieving Styles Inventory*.

17. The total number of subjects was 5,167.

18. Wilson (1955).

19. At the Peter F. Drucker Graduate Management Center, within the Achieving Styles Project, my graduate students and I have been conducting behavioral observations of individuals' achieving styles. Preliminary results confirm the validity of subjects' self-reports.

20. From an operational standpoint, we measure an organization's achieving styles using the *L-BL Organizational Achieving Styles Inventory,* a forty-five-item Likert scale based on the individual *L-BL Achieving Styles Inventory* (ASI). For a detailed description of these inventories, see Lipman-Blumen (1991, 1987).

21. Schein (1985); Martin (1992); Denison (1990).

22. Stokely (1986).

23. See Janis (1972).

Chapter Eleven

1. Bernard (1981).

2. Bass (1990).

3. Eskilson and Wiley (1976).

4. Aries (1976).

5. Adams and Yoder (1985).

6. Dobbins and Platz (1986).

7. Eagly (1991).

8. Smith (1986).

9. Seifert (1984).

10. Dobbins and Platz (1986).

11. Lipman-Blumen and others (in press).

12. Lipman-Blumen and others (in press).

13. Bass (1990).

14. Miller (1976).

15. de Beauvoir (1974).

16. Wool and Pearlman (1947).

17. Cochran (1954).

18. Tobias and Anderson (1973), p. M9–16. See also U.S. Department of Labor (1946).

19. Tobias and Anderson (1973), p. M9–18.

20. Tobias and Anderson (1973), p. M9–18. Emphasis in original. See also "Emil Mazey Collection" (n.d.), boxes 37 and 39.
21. U.S. Department of Labor (1948).
22. Friedan (1974).
23. U.S. Department of Labor (1990).
24. Ornstein, Mann, and Malbin (1990), pp. 700–702.
25. Schein, Mueller, and Jacobson (1989).
26. Grant (1988).
27. Bales (1953).
28. Bales and Slater (1955).
29. Parsons (1955).
30. Korabik (1990).
31. Komarovsky (1953).
32. Korabik (1990); Dobbins and Platz (1986); Baril, Elbert, Mahar-Potter, and Ready (1989); Powell and Butterfield (1989).
33. Baril, Elbert, Mahar-Potter, and Ready (1989).
34. Grant (1988).
35. Gregory (1990).
36. Astin and Leland (1991).
37. Astin and Leland (1991), p. 158.
38. This paragraph draws heavily on Lipman-Blumen and others (in press), pp. 68–69.
39. Kunstel (1995).
40. Kunstel (1995).
41. Thatcher (1993).
42. Tuohy (1993).
43. Thatcher (1993).
44. Thatcher (1993), p. 25.
45. Thatcher (1993), p. 22.
46. Thatcher (1993), p. 23.
47. Blaise (1992). See also Gupte (1992).
48. Wood (1993), pp. 1–2.
49. Wood (1993), pp. 1–2.
50. Personal correspondence from Elena Lagadinova, December 20, 1995.
51. Davis (1991).
52. Maremont (1988); Chatzky (1992); Elmer-Dewitt (1993); Zinn (1991); for another view, see Helgesen (1990). See also Owen (1993).
53. Roddick worked for the Department of Women's Rights in the International Labour Organization of the United Nations in Geneva, where she became fully acquainted with the problems of Third World countries.
54. Roddick (1991), p. 24.
55. Roddick (1991), p. 221.
56. Zinn (1991).
57. Roddick (1991), p. 19.
58. Personal interview with Anita Roddick, November 23, 1993, Stanford, California.
59. Personal interview, November 23, 1993.
60. Entine (1995); Birchall and others (1995), p. 526.

61. *Women in Entertainment* (1994).
62. Personal interview with Marcy Carsey, December 6, 1994, Studio City, California. Subsequent quotations of Carsey in this section are excerpts from the same interview.
63. Byrne (1990).
64. Personal interview with Frances Hesselbein, May 3, 1993, Claremont, California.
65. For a penetrating analysis of the Girl Scouts during the Hesselbein years, see Raskoff (1994).
66. Parsons and Bales (1955).
67. A sample of 154 full-time housewives gave vicarious relational a first-rank choice (Lipman-Blumen, Handley-Isaksen, and Leavitt, 1983).
68. Although the trend was the same for female middle managers, who reported they used entrusting strategies more than either male upper or middle managers, the differences were not great (that is, not statistically significant).
69. Lipman-Blumen and others (in press).
70. Beardsley, Stewart, and Wilmes (1987).
71. Varwig (1989).
72. Komives (1994, 1991a, 1991b).
73. Varwig (1989).
74. Komives used a specifically designed Student Leadership Practices Inventory (LPI), based on the Leadership Practices Inventory (LPI) of Kouzes and Posner (1987). The language cited was originally articulated by Kouzes and Posner and later used by Komives.
75. Komives (1991a).
76. *Transformational* is used here in the sense first described by Burns (1978), and later by others to suggest leadership practices that intellectually and emotionally inspire and motivate followers/constituents to perform beyond even their own expectations.
77. Even though her political constituency was composed of both males and females, Lagadinova's election within a one-party system makes it difficult to consider any meaningful implications about the attractiveness of connective leaders to voters in a democratic context.

Chapter Twelve

1. de Sénancour ([1804] 1901).
2. Becker (1973), p. 26.
3. Becker (1973), p. 26.
4. March (1995), pp. 2–3.
5. March (1995), p. 5.
6. March (1995), p. 3.
7. Zilboorg (1943).
8. Fromm (1941).
9. Becker (1973).
10. Most major religions revolve around a central myth of self-sacrifice, coupled with courageous confrontation with and sublime transcendence over death.
11. Csikszentmihalyi (1990), pp. 222, 240.
12. Csikszentmihalyi (1990), p. 221.
13. This and the following sections draw from Csikszentmihalyi (1990), pp. 221–223.

14. Levinson and others (1978).
15. Levinson and others (1978).
16. Csikszentmihalyi (1990), p. 222.
17. Csikszentmihalyi (1990), p. 222.
18. Csikszentmihalyi (1990), p. 223.
19. Wahl (1959), pp. 25–26.
20. Bailey (1988).
21. Lipman-Blumen (1973); Lipman-Blumen (1974).
22. Weber ([1925] 1968).
23. Geertz (1973); Geertz (1974).
24. Csikszentmihalyi (1990).
25. Hecht and Cockburn (1989b).
26. Robert M. Adams, translator of Machiavelli's *The Prince* (1977), says the word "*virtu*... can mean anything from 'strength,' 'courage,' 'manliness,' or 'ingenuity' to 'character,' 'wisdom,' or even (last resort) 'virtue'" (Machiavelli, [1513] 1977, p. xviii).

References

Adams, J., & Yoder, J. D. (1985). *Effective leadership for women and men.* Norwood: Ablex.

Anderson, C. A., & Morrow, M. (1995). "Competitive aggression without interaction: Effects of competitive versus cooperative instructions on aggressive behavior in video games." *Personality and Social Psychology Bulletin, 21*(10), 1020–1030.

Aries, C. (1976). "Interaction patterns and themes of male, female, and mixed groups." *Small Group Behavior, 7,* 7–18.

Asia-Pacific People's Environment Network (APPEN). (1986). *The Bhopal tragedy—one year after.* Penang, Malaysia: Sahabat Alam Malaysia (Friends of the Earth Malaysia).

Astin, A. (1994, October 26). *Higher education and the future of democracy.* Inaugural lecture, the Allen Murray Center. Los Angeles: University of California.

Astin, H. S., & Leland, C. (1991). *Women of influence, women of vision: A cross-generational study of leaders and social change.* San Francisco: Jossey-Bass.

Auden, W. H. (1947). *The age of anxiety.* New York: Random House.

Avolio, B. J., & Bass, B. M. (1988). "Transformational leadership, charisma, and beyond." In J. G. Hunt, B. R. Baliga, H. P. Dachler, & C. A. Schriesheim (Eds.), *Emerging leadership vistas* (pp. 29–49). Lexington, MA: Lexington Books.

Axelrod, R. (1984). *The evolution of cooperation.* New York: Basic Books.

Badaracco, J. L., Jr., & Ellsworth, R. R. (1989). *Leadership and the quest for integrity.* Boston: Harvard Business School Press.

Baez, J. (1987, June 14). "The backstage memoirs of Joan Baez: From Woodstock to Live Aid." *West,* pp. 6, 15ff.

Bailey, F. G. (1988). *Humbuggery and manipulation: The art of leadership.* Ithaca, NY: Cornell University Press.

Bales, R. F. (1953). "The equilibrium problem in small groups." In T. Parsons, R. F. Bales, & E. A. Shils (Eds.), *Working papers in the theory of action* (pp. 111–161). New York: Free Press.

Bales, R. F., & Slater, P. E. (1955). "Role differentiation in small decision making groups." In T. Parsons & R. F. Bales (Eds.), *Family, socialization, and interaction process* (pp. 259–306). New York: Free Press.

Banks, A. S., Muller, T. C., Phelan, S. M., Tallman, E., & Day, A. J. (Eds.). (1993). *Political handbook of the world: 1993.* Binghamton: CSA Publications, State University of New York.

Baril, G. L., Elbert, N., Mahar-Potter, S., & Ready, G. C. (1989). "Are androgynous managers really more effective?" *Group and Organization Studies, 14,* 234–249.

Barnard, C. I. (1938). *The functions of the executive.* Cambridge, MA: Harvard University Press.

Barthes, R. (1957). *Mythologies.* New York: Hill & Wang.

Bass, B. M. (1985). *Leadership and performance beyond expectations.* New York: Free Press.

Bass, B. M. (1990). *Bass & Stogdill's handbook of leadership: Theory, research, and managerial applications.* (3rd ed.). New York: Free Press.

Beardsley, K. P., Stewart, G. M., & Wilmes, M. B. (1987). "Achieving styles of students and student affairs professionals." *Journal of College Student Personnel, 28*(5), 412–419.

de Beauvoir, S. (1974). *The second sex* (H. M. Parshley, Ed. & Trans.). New York: Vintage Books.

Becker, E. (1973). *The denial of death.* New York: Free Press.

Bellah, R. N., Madsen, R., Sullivan, W. M., Swidler, A., & Tipton, S. M. (1985). *Habits of the heart: Individualism and commitment in American life.* Berkeley: University of California Press.

Benkelman, S., & Page, S. (1995, May 8). "Yeltsin's patriotic act: Russian seizes opportunity in war anniversary show." *Newsday,* p. AO4.

Bennis, W. G. (1989). *Why leaders can't lead: The unconscious conspiracy continues.* San Francisco: Jossey-Bass.

Bennis, W. G., & Nanus, B. (1985). *Leaders: The strategies for taking charge.* New York: HarperCollins.

Bennis, W. G., & Slater, P. E. (1968). *The temporary society.* New York: HarperCollins.

Bernard, J. (1981). *The female world.* New York: Free Press.

Birchall, R., Larenaudie, S. R., Born, P., Larson, S., et al. (1995, September 8). "The beauty top 50: A who's who of cosmetics." [Special Report: Holiday Fragrance.] *Women's Wear Daily,* p. 526.

Blaise, C. (1992, April 26). "India's Queen Lear." *Los Angeles Times,* book review, p. 1.

Bleakley, F. R. (1983, February). "The psychic rewards." *Venture,* pp. 72, 74ff.

Boorstin, D. J. (1973). *The Americans* (3 vols). New York: Random House.

Bradford, D. L., & Cohen, A. R. (1984a). *Managing for excellence.* New York: Wiley.

Bradford, D. L., & Cohen, A. R. (1984b). "The post-heroic leader." *Training and Development Journal, 38*(1), 40–49.

Brandt, R. (1994). "Bill Gates's vision." *BusinessWeek,* p. 57.

Braudel, F. (1981). *Civilization and capitalism, 15th–18th century. Vol. 1: The structures of everyday life.* New York: HarperCollins.

Braudy, L. (1986). *The frenzy of renown: Fame and its history.* Oxford: Oxford University Press.

Braverman, H. (1974). *Labor and monopoly capital.* New York: Monthly Review Press.

Bricker, C. (1978, December 5). "A nice guy who wants to keep finishing first." *San Jose Mercury News,* p. 1D.

Brooks, J. (1955). *Henry Ford: A great life in brief.* New York: Knopf.

Brown, L., Chandler, W. U., Flavin, C., Pollock, C., Postel, S., Starke, L., & Wolf, E. C. (Eds.). (1985). *State of the world 1985.* New York: W. W. Norton.

Bruck, C. (1988). *The predators' ball.* New York: Penguin Books.

Burns, J. M. (1978). *Leadership.* New York: HarperCollins.

Burrough, B., & Helyar, J. (1990). *Barbarians at the gate.* New York: HarperCollins.

Byrne, J. A. (1990, March 26). "Profiting from the nonprofits." *BusinessWeek,* p. 66.

Camus, A. (1960). *L'étranger* (The Stranger). New York: Knopf.

Caro, R. A. (1993). *The path to power: The years of Lyndon Johnson.* New York: Vintage.

Carroll, A. S. (1991). "The battle for the Amazon: Preserving Brazil's rain forests." *Radcliffe Quarterly, 77*(4), 27–29.

Carson, R. (1962). *Silent spring.* Boston: Houghton Mifflin.

"Catholic church in Austria faces new accusations." (1995, August 2). *International Herald Tribune* (Reuters), p. 5.

Charlton, L. (1977, November 6). "Rosalynn Carter: Balancing roles." *New York Times,* p. A1.

Chatzky, J. S. (1992). "Changing the world." *Forbes,* p. 83.

Chemers, M. M. (1993). "An integrative theory of leadership." In M. M. Chemers & R. Ayman (Eds.), *Leadership theory and research* (pp. 293–319). New York: Academic Press.

Cialdini, R. B. (1984). *Influence: How and why people agree to things.* New York: Quill.

Cialdini, R. B., Borden, R. J., Thorne, A., Walker, M. R., Freeman, S., & Sloan, L. R. (1976). "Basking in reflected glory: Three (football) field studies." *Journal of Personality and Social Psychology, 34,* 366–375.

Cialdini, R. B., & De Nicholas, M. E. (1989). "Self-presentation by association." *Journal of Personality and Social Psychology, 57*(4), 626–631.

Cialdini, R. B., Finch, J. F., & De Nicholas, M. E. (1990). "Strategic self-presentation: The indirect route." In M. J. Cody & M. L. McLaughlin (Eds.), *The psychology of tactical communication* (pp. 194–206). Clevedon, England: Multilingual Matters.

Clifford, F. (1987, October 27). "Elizabeth Dole becomes husband's southern strategy." *Los Angeles Times,* p. A18.

Cochran, J. (1954). *The stars at noon.* Boston, MA: Little, Brown.

Cochran, T. C., & Miller, W. (1961). *The age of enterprise.* New York: HarperCollins.

Cockburn, A. (1989, January 6). "The man who loved trees." *New Statesman and Society, 2*(31).

Collins, J. (1990, December). "On the edge." *Stanford Magazine, 18*(4), p. 43.

Collins, L., & Lapierre, D. (1975). *Freedom at midnight.* New York: Avon Books.

Conger, J. A. (1989). *The charismatic leader: Behind the mystique of exceptional leadership.* San Francisco: Jossey-Bass.

Conger, J. A., & Kanungo, R. N. (1987). "Towards a behavioral theory of charismatic leadership in organizational settings." *Academy of Management Review, 12*(4), 637–647.

Congressional Quarterly, Inc. (1991). *Congressional Quarterly's guide to Congress* (4th ed.). Washington, DC Congressional Quarterly, Inc.

Conrad, J. ([1902] 1994). *Heart of darkness.* New York: Penguin Books.

Cook, B. W. (1992). *Eleanor Roosevelt. Vol. 1: 1884–1933.* New York: Viking.

Cook, C. (1989). *The facts on file world political almanac* (vols. II and III). New York: Facts on File.

Copley, F. B. (1923). *Frederick W. Taylor: Father of scientific management.* (2 vols.). New York: HarperCollins.

Corbett, J. (1995, August 8). "Gingrich warns GOP on effort to end preferences." *Los Angeles Times,* pp. A1, A6.

Cox, H. (1995). *Fire from heaven.* Reading, MA: Addison-Wesley.

Csikszentmihalyi, M. (1990). *Flow: The psychology of optimal experience.* New York: Harper-Collins.

Dahlburg, J.-T. (1993, January 7). *Los Angeles Times,* p. A1.

Davis, D. (1991). *Katherine the Great: Katherine Graham and her Washington Post empire* (3rd ed.). New York: Sheridan Square Press.

De Pree, M. (1989). *Leadership is an art.* New York: Bantam Doubleday Dell.

Deck, L. P. (1968). "Buying brains by the inch." *Journal of the College and University Personnel Association, 19*(3), 33–37.

Denison, D. R. (1990). *Corporate culture and organizational effectiveness.* New York: Wiley.

Deutsch, M. (1993). "Educating for a peaceful world." *American Psychologist, 48*(5), 510–517.

Deveny, K., & Suein, L. H. (1994, January 18). "A defective strategy of heated acquisitions spoils Borden name." *Wall Street Journal,* pp. A1, A10.

Dobbins, G. H., & Platz, S. J. (1986). "Sex differences in leadership: How real are they?" *Academy of Management Review, 11*(1), 118–127.

Dowd, M. (1987, March 2). "McFarlane looks at what went wrong." *San Jose Mercury News*, pp. 1A, 10A.

Dowd, M. (1995, September 29). "Led by a president who is always learning." *International Herald Tribune*, p. 7.

Drogin, B. (1994, January 30). "'Freedom train' kicks off S. Africa campaign." *Los Angeles Times*, pp. A1, A10.

Drucker, P. F. (1969). *The age of discontinuity: Guidelines to our changing society*. London: Heinemann.

Drucker, P. F. (1974). *Management: Tasks, responsibilities, practices*. New York: HarperCollins.

Drucker, P. F. (1989, October 21). "Peter Drucker's 1990s." *Economist*, pp. 19–20ff.

Dublin, T. (1975). "Women, work, and the family: Female operatives in the Lowell mills, 1830–1860." *Feminist Studies, 3*, 30–39.

Duchêne, F. (1994). *Jean Monnet: The first statesman of interdependence*. New York: W. W. Norton.

Dunn, S., & Burns, J. M. (1995). "The lion, the fox, and the president." *Harvard Magazine, 97*(3), 41–44.

Eagly, A. H. (1991). *Gender and leadership*. Paper presented at annual meeting of American Psychological Association, San Francisco.

Elmer-Dewitt, P. (1993, January 25). "Anita the agitator." *Time*, pp. 52, 54.

"Emil Mazey Collection." (n.d.). In *Archives of Labor History and Urban Affairs*, Wayne State University.

Entine, J. (1995, October). "Rain-forest chic." *Report on Business Magazine*, pp. 41–52.

Eskilson, A., & Wiley, M. G. (1976). "Sex composition and leadership in small groups." *Sociometry, 39*, 183–194.

Feinberg, L. (1977, May 21). "Fairfax youth ranks second in U.S. mathematics test." *Washington Post*, Metro p. B1.

Fink, S. (1986). *Crisis management: Planning for the inevitable*. New York: AMACOM.

Foner, P. S. (1979). *Women and the American labor movement, from colonial times to the eve of World War I*. New York: Free Press.

Foster, R. N. (1986). *Innovation: The attacker's advantage*. New York: Summit Books.

Foucault, M. (1980). *Power/knowledge: Selected interviews and other writings, 1972–1977*. New York: Pantheon Books.

Foucault, M. (1983). "Afterword: the subject of power." In H. Dreyfus & P. Rabinow (Eds.), *Michel Foucault: Beyond structuralism and hermeneutics* (pp. 208–226). Chicago: University of Chicago Press.

Fox, R. L. (1980). *The search for Alexander*. Boston: Little, Brown.

Freeman, J. (1975). *The politics of women's liberation*. New York: David McKay.

Freud, S. (1935). *A general introduction to psychoanalysis: A course of twenty-eight lectures delivered at the University of Vienna* (J. Riviere, Trans.). New York: Liveright.

Friedan, B. (1974). *The feminine mystique*. New York: Dell.

Friedman, T. L. (1995, August 27). "The bomb and the boomerang: France meets an eco-superpower." *New York Times*, sect. 4, p. 15.

Frieze, I. H., Olson, J. E., & Good, D. C. (1990). "Perceived and actual discrimination in the salaries of male and female managers." *Journal of Applied Psychology, 20*(1), 46–67.

Frieze, I. H., Olson, J. E., & Russell, J. (1991). "Attractiveness and income for men and women in management." *Journal of Applied Social Psychology, 21*(3), 1039–1057.

Frieze, I. H., Parsons, J., Johnson, P., Ruble, D., & Zellman, G. (1978). *Women and sex roles: A socio-psychological perspective.* New York: W. W. Norton.

Fromm, E. (1941). *Escape from freedom.* New York: Discus Books/Avon.

Fuchsberg, G. (1994, January 7). "'Visioning' missions becomes its own mission." *Wall Street Journal,* pp. B1, B5.

Gallup, G., Jr. (1992). *The Gallup Poll.* Wilmington, DE: Scholarly Resources.

Gallup report no. 288. (1989, September). Princeton, NJ: Gallup Poll.

Gans, H. J. (1988). *Middle American individualism: The future of liberal democracy.* New York: Free Press.

Gardner, J. W. (1990). *On leadership.* New York: Free Press.

Garrow, D. J. (1986). *Bearing the cross: Martin Luther King, Jr., and the Southern Christian Leadership Conference.* New York: William Morrow.

Garrow, D. J. (Ed.). (1990). "Martin Luther King, Jr., and the spirit of leadership." In P. J. Albert & R. Hoffman (Eds.), *We shall overcome: Martin Luther King, Jr., and the black freedom struggle* (pp. 11–34). New York: Pantheon.

Geertz, C. (1973). *The interpretation of cultures.* New York: Basic Books.

Geertz, C. (Ed.). (1974). *Myth, symbol, and culture.* New York: W. W. Norton.

Gerard, J. (1990, October 28). "William S. Paley, who built CBS into a communications empire, dies at 89." *New York Times,* p. 22.

Geyelin, M., & Felsenthal, E. (1994, January 31). "Irreconcilable differences force Shea & Gould closure." *Wall Street Journal,* pp. B1, B6.

Giamatti, A. B. (1990). *Take time for paradise: Americans and their games.* New York: Summit Books.

Gibb, C. A. (1947). "The principles and traits of leadership." *Journal of Abnormal and Social Psychology, 42,* 267–284.

Gioia, D. (1992). *Hadley.* New York: Ticknor & Fields.

Gleick, J. (1987). *Chaos: Making a new science.* New York: Penguin Books.

Golden, C. S., & Ruttenberg, H. J. (1942). *The dynamics of industrial democracy.* New York: HarperCollins.

Goodwin, D. K. (1987). *The Fitzgeralds and the Kennedys.* New York: St. Martin's Press.

"Grandma, 48, pregnant—with daughter's triplets." (1987, April 7). Associated Press, Johannesburg, South Africa. *Los Angeles Times,* part 1, p. 2.

Grant, J. (1988). "Women as managers: What they can offer to organizations." *Organizational Dynamics, 16,* 56–63.

Gray, B. (1989). *Collaborating: Finding common ground for multiparty problems.* San Francisco: Jossey-Bass.

Greenleaf, R. K. (1970). *The servant leader.* Newton Centre, MA: Robert K. Greenleaf Center.

Greenleaf, R. K. (1977). *Servant leadership: A journey into the nature of legitimate power and greatness.* New York: Paulist Press.

Gregory, A. (1990). "Are women different and why are women thought to be different? Theoretical and methodological perspectives." *Journal of Business Ethics, 9,* 257–266.

Gupte, P. (1992). *Mother India.* New York: Robert Stewart/Charles Scribner's Sons.

Halberstam, D. (1986). *The reckoning.* New York: Avon Books.

Handy, C. (1992). "Balancing corporate power: A new federalist paper." *Harvard Business Review, 70*(6), 59–71.

Hanner, R. (1978, December 7). "'Elegant simplicity' is his guide." *Palo Alto Times,* sect. V, p. 1.

Havel, V. (1994, July 8). "The new measure of man." *New York Times,* July 8, 1994, Op-Ed page.

Hecht, S. B., & Cockburn, A. (1989a, June 23). "Defenders of the Amazon." *New Statesman and Society, 2*(55), 16–21.

Hecht, S. B., & Cockburn, A. (1989b). *The fate of the forest: Developers, destroyers, and defenders of the Amazon.* London: Verso.

Heclo, H. (1977). *A government of strangers: Executive politics in Washington.* Washington, DC: Brookings Institution.

Heidegger, M. ([1927] 1962). *Being and time* (J. Macquarrie & E. Robinson, Trans.). New York: HarperCollins.

Helgesen, S. (1990). *The female advantage.* New York: Double Day Currency.

Helmreich, R., Beane, W., Lucker, G. W., & Spence, J. T. (1978). "Achievement motivation and scientific attainment." *Personality and Social Bulletin, 4*(2), 222–226.

Hersh, S. M. (1983). *The price of power: Kissinger in the Nixon White House.* New York: Summit Books.

Hesse, H. ([1927] 1947). *Steppenwolf* (B. Creighton, Trans.). New York: Henry Holt.

"The high cost of a family business." (1993, June 21). *U.S. News & World Report.*

Hobsbawn, E. J. (1964). "Custom, wages, and work-load." In E. J. Hobsbawn (Ed.), *Laboring men: Studies in labor history.* New York: Basic Books.

Horner, M. (1968). *Sex differences in achievement motivation and performance in competitive and non-competitive situations.* Unpublished doctoral dissertation, University of Michigan, Ann Arbor.

Hounshell, D. (1984). *From the American system to mass production, 1800–1932.* Baltimore: Johns Hopkins University Press.

House, R. J., & Boas, S. (1993). "Toward the integration of transformational, charismatic, and visionary theories." In M. M. Chemers & R. Ayman (Eds.), *Leadership theory and research: Perspectives and directions* (pp. 81–107). San Diego: Academic Press.

Husar, J. (1991, December 8). "Paraplegic Wellman back on top by sheer force of will." *Chicago Tribune,* sec. 3, p. 15.

Iacocca, L. (1984). *Iacocca.* New York: Bantam Books.

Janis, I. L. (1972). *Victims of groupthink: A psychological study of foreign-policy decisions and fiascoes.* Boston: Houghton Mifflin.

Jenkins, J. A. (1986, October 12). "Mr. Power: Attorney general Meese is Reagan's man to head the conservative charge." *New York Times Magazine,* sec. 6, pp. 19, 89ff.

Johnson, D., Maruyama, G., Johnson, R., Nelson, D., & Skon, L. (1981). "Effects of cooperative, competitive, and individualistic goal structures on achievement: A meta-analysis." *Psychological Bulletin, 89*(1), 47–62.

Johnson, D., Skon, L., & Johnson, R. (1980). "Effects of cooperative, competitive and individualistic conditions on children's problem-solving performance." *American Educational Research Journal, 17*(1), 83–93.

Kafka, F. ([1930] 1943). *The castle.* New York: Knopf.

Kakar, S. (1970). *Frederick Taylor: A study in personality and innovation.* Cambridge: MIT Press.

Kaplan, R. D. (1992, May 5). "The Afghan who won the cold war." *Wall Street Journal,* p. A20.

Kidder, T. (1981). *Soul of a new machine.* New York: Avon Books.

Kierkegaard, S. ([1844] 1957). *The concept of dread* (W. Lowrie, Trans.). Princeton, NJ: Princeton University Press.

Kipling, R. ([1893] 1920). "Her majesty's servants." In *The second jungle book* (pp. 183–210). New York: Charles Scribner's Sons.

Kissinger, H. (1979). *White House years.* Boston: Little, Brown.

Kissinger, H. (1989). *Turning strategic vision into operational reality.* Speech at 1989 Top Management Forum, June 26–27 (Paris).

Kleinfield, N. R. (1984, October 28). "When many chiefs think as one." *New York Times,* sect. 3, p. 1.

Klemesrud, J. (1978, January 24). "The city's highest ranking woman takes it all in stride." *New York Times,* p. C37.

Knecht, B. G. (1994, February 17). "American Express embraces co-brands." *Wall Street Journal,* pp. B1, B9.

Kohn, A. (1992). *No contest: The case against competition.* Boston: Houghton Mifflin.

Komarovsky, M. (1953). *Women in the modern world: Their education and their dilemmas.* Boston: Little, Brown.

Komives, S. R. (1991a). "Gender differences in the relationship of hall directors' transformational and transactional leadership and achieving styles." *Journal of College Student Development, 32,* 155–165.

Komives, S. R. (1991b). "Getting things done: A gender comparison of resident assistant and hall director achieving styles." *Journal of College and University Student Housing, 22*(2), 30–38.

Komives, S. R. (1994). "Women student leaders: Self-perceptions of empowering leadership and achieving style." *National Association of Student Personnel Administrators Journal, 31*(2), 102–112.

Korabik, K. (1990). "Androgyny and leadership style." *Journal of Business Ethics, 9,* 283–292.

Kouzes, J. M., & Posner, B. Z. (1987). *The leadership challenge: How to get extraordinary things done in organizations.* San Francisco: Jossey-Bass.

Kraft, S. (1994, May 3). "Grace marks concession by de Klerk." *Los Angeles Times,* pp. A1, A8.

"Kremlin bets on good news." (1995, July 7). *Financial Times Limited* (Finance/Business Section).

Kunstel, M. (1995, September 5). "Women in Russia are seeking power to solve problems." *Palm Beach Post,* p. 1D.

Lash, J. P. (1971). *Eleanor and Franklin.* New York: W. W. Norton.

Leavitt, H. J. (1951). "Some effects of certain patterns of communication on group performance." *Journal of Abnormal and Social Psychology, 46*(1), 38–50.

Leavitt, H. J. (1986). *Corporate pathfinders.* New York: Viking Penguin.

Leavitt, H. J. (1992, June 14). *The business school and the doctorate.* Address presented to Centennial Seminar, University of Chicago.

Leavitt, H. J., & Lipman-Blumen, J. (1980, Summer). "A case for the relational manager." *Organizational Dynamics,* pp. 27–41.

Leavitt, H. J., & Lipman-Blumen, J. (1995). "Hot groups." *Harvard Business Review, 73*(4), 109–116.

Leavy, J. (1984, July 22). "The old school: Lessons in sustained excellence." *Washington Post Magazine,* pp. 46–47.

Levinson, D. J., Darrow, C. M., Klein, E. G., Levinson, M. H., & McKee, B. (1978). *The seasons of a man's life.* New York: Knopf.

Lewis, M. (1989). *Liar's poker: Rising through the wreckage on Wall Street.* New York: Penguin Books.

Lindholm, C. (1990). *Charisma.* Cambridge, MA: Basil Blackwell.

Lipman-Blumen, J. (1973). "Role de-differentiation as a system response to crisis: Occupational and political roles of women." *Sociological Inquiry, 43*(2), 105–129.

Lipman-Blumen, J. (1974). *Ideology, social structure, and crisis.* Unpublished paper presented at nineteenth annual meeting, American Sociological Association, August 25–29, Montreal.

Lipman-Blumen, J. (1984). *Gender roles and power.* Englewood Cliffs, NJ: Prentice-Hall.

Lipman-Blumen, J. (1988). *Individual and organizational achieving styles: A technical manual for researchers and human resource professionals.* Claremont, CA: Achieving Styles Institute.

Lipman-Blumen, J. (1991, 1987). *Individual and organizational achieving styles: A conceptual handbook for researchers and human resource professionals* (4th ed.). Claremont, CA: Achieving Styles Institute.

Lipman-Blumen, J. (1992a). "Connective leadership: Female leadership styles in the 21st-century workplace." *Sociological Perspectives, 35*(1), 183–203.

Lipman-Blumen, J. (1992b). *L-BL Achieving styles situational assessment inventory* (ASSAI). Claremont, CA: Achieving Styles Institute.

Lipman-Blumen, J. (1993). "The existential bases of power relationships: The gender role case." In H. L. Radtke & H. J. Stam (Eds.), *Power/gender: Social relations in theory and practice* (pp. 108–135). London: Sage.

Lipman-Blumen, J., Fryling, T., Henderson, M., Moore, C. W., & Vecchiotti, R. (in press). *New world, new leaders: Women in corporate roles.* Wellesley, MA: Wellesley College Center for Research on Women; commissioned by Business Leadership Council of Wellesley College.

Lipman-Blumen, J., Handley-Isaksen, A., & Leavitt, H. J. (1983). "Achieving styles in men and women: A model, an instrument, and some findings." In J. T. Spence (Ed.), *Achievement and achievement motives: Psychological and sociological approaches* (pp. 147–204). San Francisco: W. H. Freeman.

Lipman-Blumen, J., & Leavitt, H. J. (1976). "Vicarious and direct achievement patterns in adulthood." *Counseling Psychologist, 6*(1), 26–32.

Lipman-Blumen, J., & Leavitt, H. J. (1985a). *L-BL achieving styles inventory* (ASI). Claremont, CA: Achieving Styles Institute.

Lipman-Blumen, J., & Leavitt, H. J. (1985b). *Organizational achieving styles inventory* (OASI). Claremont, CA: Achieving Styles Institute.

Lipman-Blumen, J., Leavitt, H. J., Patterson, K. J., Bies, R. J., & Handley-Isaksen, A. (1980). "A model of direct and relational achieving styles." In L. J. Fyans, Jr. (Ed.), *Achievement motivation: Recent trends in theory and research* (pp. 135–168). New York: Plenum Press.

Lipman-Blumen, J., & Schram, S. (1984). *The paradox of success: The impact of priority setting in agricultural research and extension.* Washington, DC: U.S. Department of Agriculture.

Lipset, S. M., & Wolin, S. S. (1965). *The Berkeley student revolt: Facts and interpretations.* Garden City, NJ: Anchor Books.

Littler, C. R. (1978). "Understanding Taylorism." *British Journal of Sociology, 29,* 185–207.

Lublin, J. S. (1994, October 3). "It's shape-up time for performance reviews." *The Wall Street Journal,* pp. B1, B16.

McClelland, D. (1967). *The achieving society.* New York: Free Press.

McClelland, D. C., Atkinson, J. W., Clark, R. A., & Lowell, E. L. (1953). *The achievement motive.* New York: Appleton-Century-Crofts.

McGregor, D. (1957). "An uneasy look at performance appraisals." *Harvard Business Review, 35*(3), 94.

Machiavelli, N. ([1513] 1970). *The discourses on the first ten books of Titus Livius.* London: Penguin.

Machiavelli, N. ([1513] 1977). *The prince.* New York: W. W. Norton.

McKelvey, J. T. (1952). *AFL attitudes toward production: 1900–1932. Vol. 2.* Ithaca, NY: Cornell Studies in Industrial and Labor Relations.

Malinowski, B. (1955). *Magic, science, and religion.* Garden City, NJ: Doubleday Anchor.

Malinowski, B. (1992). *Malinowski and the work of myth.* Princeton, NJ: Princeton University Press.

Marburg, T. (1941). "Aspects of labor administration in the early nineteenth century." *Business History Review, 15*(1), 1–10.

March, J. (1995). "Information technology, decision making, and the human condition." Paper presented at twenty-fourth International Federation of Training and Development Organizations (IFTDO) World Conference on Personal Renewal, Helsinki, Finland.

Maremont, M. (1988, May 23). "A cosmetic company with a conscience." *BusinessWeek,* p. 136.

Marrow, A. J., Bowers, D. G., & Seashore, S. E. (1967). *Management by participation: creating a climate for organizational development.* New York: HarperCollins.

Martin, J. (1992). *Culture in organizations: Three perspectives.* New York: Oxford University Press.

Marty, M. E. (1985). "Muslims next door." In *1985 Britannica book of the year.* Chicago: Encyclopaedia Britannica.

Maslow, A. (1943). "A theory of human motivation." *Psychological Review, 50,* 370–396.

Maslow, A. (1954). *Motivation and personality.* New York: HarperCollins.

Mason, T., Mitchell, R., Hampton, W. J., & Frons, M. (1986, October 6). "Ross Perot's crusade: He's begun a one-man campaign to make GM competitive again." *BusinessWeek,* pp. 60–65.

Mauss, M. (1979). *Sociology and psychology: Essays* (B. Brewster, Trans.). London: Routledge & Kegan Paul.

May, R. (1950). *The meaning of anxiety.* New York: Ronald Press.

Mayo, E. (1933). *The human problems of an industrial civilization.* New York: Macmillan.

Meindl, J. R., Ehrlich, S. B., & Dukerich, J. M. (1985). "The romance of leadership." *Administrative Science Quarterly, 30,* 78–102.

Meyer, P. N. (1990, September 2). "The failure of traditional law schools." *New York Times,* sect. 3, p. 13.

Miller, J. B. (1976). *Toward a new psychology of women.* Boston: Beacon Press.

Mills, C. W. (1956). *The power elite.* New York: Oxford University Press.

Mitchell, R., & Oneal, M. (1994, August 1). "Managing by values." *BusinessWeek,* pp. 46–52.

Montgomery, D. (1979). *Workers' control in America: Studies in the history of work, technology, and labor struggles.* Cambridge, England: Cambridge University Press.

Morison, E. E. (1981). "The new liberal arts: Response I." In J. D. Koerner (Ed.), *The new liberal arts: An exchange of views.* New York: Alfred P. Sloan Foundation.

Murphy, K. (1993, April 6). "A new vision for Mohammed's faith." *Los Angeles Times. A World Report Special Edition: Islam Rising.*

Nakamura, J. (1995, July 26). "Economic forum: Poll results underwhelm business." *Daily Yomiuri,* p. 6.

Nanus, B. (1992). *Visionary leadership: Creating a compelling sense of direction for your organization.* San Francisco: Jossey-Bass.

National Research Council. (1972). *Report of the committee on research advisory to the U.S. Department of Agriculture (the Pound report).* Springfield, VA: National Technical Information Services.

Nelson, D. (1975). *Managers and workers: origins of the new factory system in the U.S., 1880–1920.* Madison: University of Wisconsin Press.

Nelson, D. (1980). *Frederick W. Taylor and the rise of scientific management.* Madison: University of Wisconsin Press.

Nevins, A., & Hill, F. E. (1954). *Ford. Vol. 1: The times, the man, and the company.* New York: Scribner's.

Nevins, A., & Hill, F. E. (1957). *Ford. Vol. 2: Expansion and challenge.* New York: Scribner's.

Nevins, A., & Hill, F. E. (1963). *Ford. Vol. 3: Decline and rebirth.* New York: Scribner's.

"Newsmakers: Say something nice or . . . " (1993, October 3). *Houston Chronicle,* p. A2.

Niebuhr, R. F. (1941–1943). *The nature and destiny of man.* London: Scribner's.

Ohmae, K. (1995). *The end of the nation state: The rise of regional economies.* New York: Free Press.

"Oliver North, businessman? Many bosses say that he's their kind of employee." (1987, July 14). *Wall Street Journal,* sec. 2, p. 35.

O'Reilly, B. (1994, January 24). "Reengineering the MBA." *Fortune,* pp. 38–47.

Ornstein, N. J., Mann, T. E., & Malbin, M. J. (1990). *Vital statistics on Congress, 1989–90.* Washington, DC: Congressional Quarterly, Inc.

Osnos, P. (1982, December 13). "In Stockholm, the prize is right." *Washington Post,* p. C15.

O'Toole, J., & Bennis, W. (1992). "Our federalist future: The leadership imperative." *California Management Review, 34*(4), 73–90.

O'Toole, K. (1994). "How well do we assess new technology? Social, economic impacts often misjudged." *Stanford University Campus Report,* pp. 6–7.

Ouchi, W. (1981). *Theory Z: How American business can meet the Japanese challenge.* New York: Avon Books.

Owen, D. A. (1993). "Anita Roddick: Founder, The Body Shop International PLC." Paper prepared for Executive Management Course 396, The Claremont Graduate School.

Owen, R. ([1857] 1967). *The life of Robert Owen.* London: Effingham Wilson; reissued 1967 by Augustus M. Kelley in 2 vols.

Park, J. (1989, April 5). "Wertmuller on love in the time of AIDS." *International Herald Tribune.*

Parrish, M. (1994, March 29). "Arco enters brave new era." *Los Angeles Times,* pp. D1, D6.

Parsons, T. (1955). "The American family: Its relations to personality and the social structure." In T. Parsons & R. F. Bales (Eds.), *Family, socialization, and interaction process* (pp. 3–33). New York: Free Press.

Parsons, T., & Bales, R. F. (Eds.). (1955). *Family, socialization, and interaction process.* New York: Free Press.

Pascale, R. T., & Athos, A. G. (1981). *The art of Japanese management.* New York: Warner Books.

Perrow, C. (1984). *Normal accidents: Living with high-risk technologies.* New York: Basic Books.

Pfeffer, J. (1981). *Power in organizations.* Boston: Pitman.

Pfeffer, J. (1992). *Managing with power: Politics and influence in organizations.* Boston: Harvard Business School Press.

Phillips, W. J. (1987). *In search of a leader.* (Occasional paper no. 2). Vancouver: Centre for Study of Church and Ministry.

Pinchot, G. (1986). *Intrapreneuring: Why you don't have to leave the corporation to become an entrepreneur* (2nd ed.). New York: HarperCollins.

Porter, L., & McKibbin, L. M. (1988). *Management education and development: Drift or thrust into the 21st century?* New York: McGraw-Hill.

Potts, M. (1994, January 31–February 6). "Some Johnny Appleseeds look back at their Mac." *Washington Post National Weekly Edition,* pp. 20–21.

Powell, G. N., & Butterfield, A. D. (1989). "The good manager: Did androgyny fare better in the 1980s?" *Group and Organization Studies, 14,* 216–233.

Qin, Z., Johnson, D. W., & Johnson, R. T. (1995). "Cooperative versus competitive efforts and problem solving." *Review of Educational Research, 65*(2), 129–143.

Quinn, S. (1979, July 25). "Rosalynn's journey: A whirlwind tour with one refrain: He's healthy, he's happy . . ." *Washington Post,* p. B1.

Raskoff, S. (1994). *Volunteering to "do gender": Adult volunteers in Girl Scouts.* Unpublished doctoral dissertation, University of Southern California, Los Angeles. (DAI 55–122A, p. 3996)

Reid, D. (1976). "The decline of St. Monday, 1766–1876." *Past and Present, 71,* 76–101.

Revkin, A. (1990). "The burning season: The murder of Chico Mendes and the fight for the Amazon rain forest." *Brown Alumni Monthly,* pp. 27–33.

Richardson, M. (1995, July 31). "ASEAN puts free trade on fast track." *International Herald Tribune,* p. 9.

Roddick, A. (1991). *Body and soul.* New York: Crown.

Rodgers, D. T. (1978). *The work ethic in industrial America, 1850–1920.* Chicago: University of Chicago Press.

Rodman, S. (Ed.). (1939). *A new anthology of modern poetry.* New York: Modern Library.

Roethlisberger, F. J., & Dickson, W. J. (1939). *Management and the worker.* Cambridge, MA: Harvard University Press.

Rose, R. L., Christian, N. M., & Nomani, A. Q. (1995, July 28). "Union merger sounds painless, but it won't be." *Wall Street Journal,* pp. B1, B12.

Roszell, P., Kennedy, D., & Grabb, E. (1989). "Physical attractiveness and income attainment among Canadians." *Journal of Psychology, 123*(6), 547–559.

Royko, M. (1971). *Boss: Richard J. Daley of Chicago.* New York: Signet Books.

Rubenstein, F. (1971). *A behavioral study of pollution: The role of perceived instrumentality in an externality situation.* Unpublished doctoral dissertation, Stanford University. (DAI 32–03B, p. 1505).

Russell, S. (1990, September 19). "Two East Bay firms may be candidates for biotech buyout." *San Francisco Chronicle,* p. C1.

Samuel, R. (1977). "The workshop of the world: Steam power and hand technology in mid-Victorian Britain." *History Workshop, 3,* 6–72.

Schein, E. (1985). *Organizational culture and leadership.* San Francisco: Jossey-Bass.

Schein, V. E., Mueller, R., & Jacobson, C. (1989). "The relationship between sex role stereotypes and requisite management characteristics among college students." *Sex Roles, 20,* 103–110.

Schiff, D. (1995, August 20). "An older, wiser, humbler wunderkind." *New York Times Magazine,* pp. 29–31.

Schlossberg, S. I. (1994). "Turning point for America: Resolving the crisis at the workplace." *Labor Law Journal, 45*(10), 603–617.

Schlossman, S., Sedlak, M., & Wechsler, H. (1987). *The "new look": The Ford Foundation and the revolution in business management.* Los Angeles: Graduate Management Admission Council.

Schudson, M. (1994). "Question authority: A history of the news interview in American journalism." *Media, Culture, and Society, 16*(4), 565–587.

Seifert, C. M. (1984). *Reactions to leaders: Effects of sex of leader, sex of subordinates, method of leader selection and task outcome.* Unpublished doctoral dissertation, Northern Illinois University. DAI *45*–12B, 3999.

Selz, M. (1994, October 12). "Small company goes global with diverse work force." *Wall Street Journal,* p. B2.

de Sénancour, É. P. ([1804] 1901). *Obermann: Selections from letters to a friend.* Cambridge, MA: Riverside Press.

Shaler, N. S. (1900). *The individual: A study of life and death.* East Norwalk, CN: Appelton & Lange.

Shaw, D. (1994, February 17). "Hunger for heroes, villains rooted in American psyche." *Los Angeles Times,* p. A18.

Sherif, M., Harvey, O. J., White, B. J., Hood, W. R., & Sherif, C. W. (1954). *Experimental study of positive and negative intergroup attitudes between experimentally produced groups. Robbers' Cave study.* Norman: University of Oklahoma. Multilithed.

Sherrill, M. (1994, February 5). "Wanting it . . . badly: To win, some people will do almost anything." *Washington Post,* pp. G1, G9ff.

Shirer, W. L. (1979). *Gandhi, a memoir.* New York: Washington Square Press.

Shrivastava, P. (1985). "Bhopal gas tragedy." *Social Scientist, 13*(1), 32–53.

Shrivastava, P. (1987). *Bhopal: Anatomy of a crisis.* Cambridge: Ballinger.

Simon, H. A. (1947). *Administrative behavior: A study of decision-making process in administrative organization.* New York: Macmillan.

Sinclair, U. (1911, June). *The American Magazine, 72*(2), 243.

Skon, L., Johnson, D., & Johnson, R. (1981). "Cooperative peer interaction versus individual competition and individualistic efforts: Effects of acquisition of cognitive reasoning strategies." *Journal of Educational Psychology, 73*(1), 83–92.

Slichter, S. H. (1941). *Union policies and industrial management.* Washington, DC: Brookings Institution.

Sloan, A. P., Jr. (1964). *My years with General Motors.* New York: Doubleday.

Smith, J. E. (1986). *Women in management (1979–1984): A review of the literature.* Paper presented at annual meeting of American Psychological Association, New York.

Smuts, R. W. (1960). "The female labor force: A case study in the interpretation of historical statistics." *Journal of the American Statistical Association, 55,* 71–79.

"'Something emerges: Very beautiful, very awesome.'" (1979, January). *Stanford Observer,* p. 1.

Spinoza, B. ([1677] 1910). *Ethics (and "De intellectus emendatione")* (A. Boyle, Trans.). London: Dent.

Stam, H. J. (1987). "The psychology of control: A textual critique." In H. J. Stam, T. B. Rogers, & K. J. Gergen (Eds.), *The analysis of psychological theory: Metapsychological perspectives* (pp. 131–156). Washington, DC: Hemisphere.

Stead, W. T. ([1902] 1972). *The Americanization of the world.* New York: Garland.

Stewart, T. A., Berlin, R. K., Graves, J. M., Martin, T. J., & Michels, A. (1993, January 11). "The king is dead." *Fortune,* pp. 34–41.

Stokely, L. (1986). *Organizational achieving styles in an undergraduate college.* Unpublished paper, The Claremont Graduate School.

Taylor, F. W. (1911a). "The principles of scientific management." *American Magazine,* 72(2), 244–245.

Taylor, F. W. (1911b). *Scientific management.* New York: HarperCollins.

Thatcher, M. (1993). *The Downing Street years.* New York: HarperCollins.

Thomas, R. R., Jr. (1992). "Managing diversity: A conceptual framework." In S. E. Jackson & Associates (Eds.), *Diversity in the workplace: Human resources initiatives.* New York: Guilford Press.

Thomas, W. I. (1951). *Social behavior and personality.* New York: Social Science Research Council.

Thompson, C. B. (Ed.). (1922). *Scientific management.* Cambridge: Harvard University Press.

"Thumbs up for Mandela, thumbs down for government: Poll." (1995, June 23). *Agence France Presse.*

Tichy, N. M., & Devanna, M. A. (1986). *The transformational leader.* New York: Wiley.

Tillett, A., Kempner, T., & Wills, G. (1970). *Management thinkers.* Middlesex, England: Penguin.

Tillich, P. (1944). "Existential philosophy." *Journal of the History of Ideas,* 5(1), 40–70.

Timnick, L. (1990, August 2). "Charges against Buckey dismissed." *Los Angeles Times,* sect. B, p. 1.

Tjosvold, D., & Chia, L. C. (1989). "Conflict between managers and workers: The role of cooperation and competition." *Journal of Social Psychology,* 129(2), 235–247.

Tobias, S., & Anderson, L. (1973). *What really happened to Rosie the riveter? Demobilization and the female labor force, 1944–1947.* New York: MSS Modular Publications.

de Tocqueville, A. (1959). *Democracy in America.* New York: Vintage.

Toffler, A. (1990). *Powershift: Knowledge, wealth, and violence at the edge of the 21st century.* New York: Bantam Books.

Tuohy, W. (1993, November 21). "She's ba-aack!" *Los Angeles Times Magazine,* pp. 26, 28ff.

Ulman, L. (1955). *The rise of the national trade union.* Cambridge, MA: Harvard University Press.

U.S. Bureau of the Census. (1943). *16th census of the United States, 1940. Population: Comparative occupational statistics for the United States, 1870–1940* (pp. 92–128). Washington, DC: Author.

U.S. Department of Labor. (1946). *Why women work.* New York: Author, Division of Industrial Relations.

U.S. Department of Labor. (1948). *Baltimore women war workers in the postwar period.* Suitland, MD (Washington National Records Center): Author, Women's Bureau.

U.S. Department of Labor. (1990, October). *Perspectives on working women: A databook* (Bulletin 2080, p. 10). Washington, DC: Author, Bureau of Labor Statistics.

U.S. Department of Labor. (1994). *1993 Handbook on women workers: Trends and issues.* Washington, DC: Author, Women's Bureau.

Varwig, J. E. (1989). *A comparison of male and female college student presidents on self-esteem, sex-role identity, achieving styles, and career aspirations by gender composition of student organization.* Unpublished doctoral dissertation, University of Maryland, College Park. (DAI 50–07A, p. 1965)

Vroom, V., & Yetton, P. (1973). *Leadership and decision making.* Pittsburgh: University of Pittsburgh Press.

Wahl, C. W. (1959). "The fear of death." In H. Feifel (Ed.), *The meaning of death* (pp. 25–26). New York: McGraw-Hill.

Walton, D. (1978, November 16). "Rockwell: Just a hick from Manhattan." *San Jose Mercury News*, pp. 1C, 3C.

Ware, N. (1959). *The industrial worker 1840–1860*. Gloucester, MA: Peter Smith.

Wartofsky, A. (1995, September 15). "Plunging into the darkness with Harvey Keitel." *International Herald Tribune*, p. 24.

Watson, J. D. (1968). *The double helix*. New York: Mentor Books.

Weber, M. ([1925] 1946). "The sociology of charismatic authority." In H. H. Gerth & C. W. Mills (Eds.), *From Max Weber: Essays in sociology* (pp. 245–252). New York: Oxford University Press.

Weber, M. (Ed.). (1947). *The theory of social and economic organization* (A. M. Henderson & T. Parsons, Trans.). New York: Oxford University Press.

Weber, M. ([1925] 1968). "The types of legitimate domination." In G. Roth & C. Wittich (Eds.), *Economy and society: An outline of interpretive sociology* (pp. 212–301). New York: Bedminster Press.

Whitman, D. (1990, July 16). "The unsettling power of a contentious zealot." (Obituary). *U.S. News & World Report, 109*(3), 10.

Whyte, W. H., Jr. (1956). *The organization man*. New York: Simon & Schuster.

Will, G. F. (1989). *Men at work: The craft of baseball*. New York: Macmillan.

Williams, D. (1989, February 26). "An emperor's funeral tests democracy in Japan." *Los Angeles Times*, part 5, p. 2.

Williams, E. C. (1989). *Leadership characteristics, management controls, and project characteristics: Their contribution to successful project management*. Unpublished doctoral dissertation, The Claremont Graduate School. (DAI 50–08A, p. 2570)

Wilson, S. (1955). *The man in the gray flannel suit*. New York: Simon & Schuster.

Wilson, W. ([1917] 1966). Senate address, January 22, 1917. In A. S. Link et al. (Eds.), *The papers of Woodrow Wilson* (Vol. 40, November 20, 1916, to January 23, 1917, p. 536). Princeton, NJ: Princeton University Press.

Wolff, K. H. (Ed. & Trans.). (1950). *The sociology of Georg Simmel: 1858–1918*. New York: Free Press.

Women in Entertainment. (1994). Vol. 14, Special Issue, p. S-13.

Wood, N. (1993, June 19). "Defiant president sees Sinn Fein chief." *Times*, pp. 1–2.

Wool, H., & Pearlman, L. M. (1947, August). "Recent occupational trends." *Monthly Labor Review, 65*, 139–147.

World almanac and book of facts. (1980). New York: Newspaper Enterprise Assoc.

World almanac and book of facts. (1993). New York: Pharos.

Wren, D. A. (1979). *The evolution of management thought* (2nd ed.). New York: Wiley.

Wright, R. (1993, January 19). "The leadership revolution." *Los Angeles Times*, pp. H1, H4.

Wycliff, D. (1990, July 25). "The short, unhappy life of academic presidents." *New York Times*, p. B7.

Zilboorg, G. (1943). "Fear of death." *Psychoanalytic Quarterly, 12*, 465–475.

Zinn, L. (1991, July 15). "Whales, human rights, rain forests, and the heady smell of profits." *BusinessWeek*, pp. 114–115.

Zuboff, S. (1984). *In the age of the smart machine: The future of work and power*. New York: Basic Books.

Name Index

A

Adams, G., 298
Adams, R. M., 364n.26
Akers, J., 11
Akihito, Emperor, 200
Alexander the Great, 40
Aquino, C., 13, 250, 294, 295
Arafat, Y., 197, 207, 252
Arias, O., 95
Astin, H. S., 293
Atkinson, J. W., 116–117
Auden, W. H., 348n.24
Avolio, B. J., 30
Axelrod, R., 174, 177

B

Baez, J., 154
Bailey, F. G., 30, 347n.2
Bakker, J., 88
Balanchine, J., 147
Bales, R. F., 291, 315
Barnard, C. I., 32
Barrett, T., 11
Barros, R., 105, 106, 336
Barrowman, M., 151, 152
Bass, B. M., 30
Becker, E., 39, 325–327, 328
Bell, A. G., 48
Bellow, S., 146
Bennis, W. G., 29, 257
Bernard, J., 286
Bhutan, King of, 246–247
Bhutto, B., 294
Bird, L., 147–148
Bonaparte, N., 156
Boone, D., 48
Botha, P. W., 205

Brandeis, L. D., 351n.25
Braudel, F., 77
Brown, M., 350n.13
Brown, W. M., 144
Burke, J., 235
Burns, J. M., 31–32
Bush, G., 125, 210, 235–236

C

Campbell, Kermit, 15–16, 210–211, 219–222, 237, 243, 341
Campbell, Kim, 13, 294
Camus, A., 348n.24
Carey, R., 147–148
Carnegie, A., 48, 142
Carsey, M., 232, 306–311, 323, 341
Carter, J., 200
Carter, R., 180, 200
Castro, F., 12, 197
Ceausescu, 80
Chirac, J., 355n.50
Churchill, W., 97, 156
Cialdini, R. B., 123, 185–186, 347n.36
Cillar, T., 294
Clinton, B., 52, 124–125, 181, 204, 231, 252–253
Clinton, H. R., 181–183
Collins, J., 143
Conger, J. A., 30
Conrad, J., 141, 142
Constance, T. E., 188
Corbett, M., 122, 178–179
Cresson, E., 13, 294
Crick, F., 153
Crockett, D., 48
Csikszentmihalyi, M., 329–330, 331, 334

Subject Index

191, 231; role of, in search for existential meaning, 242–245, 335–344; role of, in societal problems, 340–341; self-sacrifice of, 202–203, 247–248; sensitivity to situational cues of, 134–135; visions of, 338

Connective leadership, 3–4; accountability in, 18–19, 245–247, 248–249; in American organizations, 267–273; approaches of, to diversity, 16–21, 23–24, 239–240, 335–340; authenticity in, 18–19, 245–248, 252, 313; barriers to, 249–253; challenges of, 6–7, 11–16, 106–107; collaborative achieving style in, 176, 229–230, 237–238; and Connective Era, 8–11; constituency for, 249–251, 337–338; direct achieving styles in, 120, 230; and entrepreneurs, 263–264; entrusting achieving style in, 231–232; ethical instrumentalism in, 16–18, 27, 245–248; examples of, in unexpected places, 26–27; through expectation, 21–22; in high-tech companies, 266–267; and individualism, 23–24; instrumental achieving styles in, 194–195, 223; and interdependence, 16–24, 233–234, 235, 237–238; long-term perspective in, 21, 237–239; new priorities of, 14–16; in organizations, connective, 257–285; versus participative management, 23–24; peer groups versus hierarchies in, 237; politics of commonalities in, 19–20, 190–191, 335, 339–340; and power, 240–241; relational achieving styles in, 190–191, 230–231; relationship of achieving styles to, 118–119; role of, in search for existential meaning, 22–23, 99–100, 242–245, 325–326, 335–344; role of, in societal problems, 340–342; shifts to, 11–16; social achieving style in, 217; synergistic benefits of,

233–239; two-way connectiveness in, 234–236; vicarious achieving style in, 188–190; of women leaders, 297–314, 322–324

Connective Leadership Model: achieving styles in, 24–26, 113–115, 118–119, 226; action tools of, 25; diagrammatic representation of, 112; early development of, 118–119; uses of, 113–114, 226, 232–239; and women's leadership, 287–288. *See also* Achieving styles

Constitution, U.S., 51, 350*n*.5

Consumer movement, 67

Contacts, use of, in social style, 125, 209–211, 213–214. *See also* Networks; Social achieving style

Contributory achieving style: characteristics of, 183; examples of, 178–184, 358*n*.19; learning of, 128–129; among middle-level managers, 270; overview of, 122, 177–178; political spouses with, 179–184; sexual stereotyping of, 176–177; use of, by women versus men, 317–318

Control, illusion of, 38, 332, 349*n*.32

Controlling leadership style. *See* Power achieving style

Cooperation: in American leadership, 47–56; combined with individualism, 47–48, 51–52, 62, 71–72, 73–74; covert authoritarianism and, 24, 63, 66–69, 74–75, 175; optimal conditions for, 174–175; and participative management, 62–69. *See also* Collaboration; Participative management

Cooperative learning environments, 167–168

Corporate leaders: authoritarian, examples of, 56–60; collaboration among, 171–172; with collaborative achieving style, 171–172; with competitive achieving style, 152; connective, examples of, 227–228; with entrusting achieving style,